Urban and Regional Economics

Urban and Regional Economics

Philip McCann

OXFORD

UNIVERSITY PRESS

OXFORD

UNIVERSITY PRESS

Great Clarendon Street, Oxford OX2 6DP

Oxford University Press is a department of the University of Oxford.
It furthers the University's objective of excellence in research, scholarship,
and education by publishing worldwide in

Oxford New York

Athens Auckland Bangkok Bogotá Buenos Aires Cape Town
Chennai Dar es Salaam Delhi Florence Hong Kong Istanbul Karachi
Kolkata Kuala Lumpur Madrid Melbourne Mexico City Mumbai Nairobi
Paris São Paulo Shanghai Singapore Taipei Tokyo Toronto Warsaw

with associated companies in Berlin Ibadan

Published in the United States
by Oxford University Press Inc., New York

British Library Cataloguing in Publication Data

Data available

Library of Congress Cataloging in Publication Data

Data available

ISBN 0–19–877645–4

10 9 8 7 6 5 4 3 2 1

Typeset in Stone Serif and Argo
by RefineCatch Limited, Bungay, Suffolk
Printed in Great Britain by
The Bath Press
Bath

For my parents Kath and Joe,
and all my family and whanau

Acknowledgements

I would like to acknowledge the support of my colleagues in the Departments of Economics and Geography at the University of Reading, during the period in which this book took shape. In particular, I extend my thanks to Abi Swinburn for all of her help in the latter stages of compiling the manuscript. Half of the book was also written while I was at the Institute of Policy and Planning Sciences, University of Tsukuba, Japan. I am very grateful to Masayuki Doi and Noboru Sakashita for giving me the time and space to pursue my own writing. The book has benefited from the many discussions I have had with a wide range of people and I am grateful to each of them for their insights. I would like to thank the staff of Oxford University Press for their commitment to this book and their skilled assistance. Finally, I would like to thank my wife Clare without whose continuing encouragement, love, and support this book would not have been written.

P. McC

University of Reading
May 2001

Contents

List of Figures

xiv LIST OF FIGURES

List of Tables

Introduction

All economic phenomena take place within geographical space. Economic issues invariably involve either questions concerning the place specificity of particular activities, or alternatively questions relating to the overcoming of space and geographical distance. For example, all commodities are traded at various market locations. However, in order to reach the appropriate market locations, goods have to be transported and delivered across space. Similarly, service activities take place at particular locations, and the information required to carry out the activity must be transmitted or acquired across geographical space. In each case, the costs incurred in these spatial transactions will themselves partly determine the price and cost conditions at each market location. Yet, the reasons why particular markets are located at particular places are also economic questions, and as we will see in this book, the nature and behaviour of markets depends somewhat on their locations. Market performance therefore partly depends on geography. At the same time, the economic performance of a particular area also depends on the nature and performance of the various markets located within the area. Acknowledging that geography plays a role in determining economic behaviour, many discussions about the performance of particular local, urban, or regional economies are, in fact, fundamentally questions about the relationships between geography and the economy. Geography and economics are usually interrelated issues.

For many years, spatial questions have all too often been ignored by economists and economic policy makers. This is partly a problem of education. In most textbook discussions, the whole economic system is assumed to take place on a pinhead (Isard 1956). While for a long time there have been many urban economists, regional scientists, and economic geographers who have been explicitly concerned with spatial economic phenomena, for many years the majority of geographical issues were subsumed by Ricardian theories of comparative advantage and international trade. In the post-war Bretton-Woods world of relatively closed economies and currency convertibility restrictions, such assumptions may have appeared to many economists to be acceptable. However, in the modern era of free trade areas, new information and communications technologies, currency convertibility and increased capital and labour mobility, many of these traditional assumptions can no longer be justified. These recent developments have highlighted the fact that competition between individual regions of the same country is frequently both as important and as complex as competition between individual countries. Similarly, much international competition is actually dominated by competition between particular regions in different countries, rather than between whole countries. In each of these cases, the nature of the sub-national and super-national competitive relationships between various regions depends on the spatial distribution of industrial activities. Geography is an essential element of the economic system, and the economics of regional behaviour are just as important as that of national behaviour. The role of geography in the economy and the importance of the regional economic behaviour provide the motivation and justification for studying urban and regional economics.

Over the last decade there has been a significant increase in interest in spatial economic questions. In part, this has been because of the new institutional and technological developments mentioned above which have highlighted the need for explicit consider-ations of space in economic discussions. The writings of Paul Krugman (1991) and Michael Porter (1990) have also brought the importance of spatial economic issues to the attention of wider audiences within the international economics, business, and man-agement fields. The work of both of these authors has led to significant developments in our understanding of the relationships between space and the economy. However, there is a long and broad tradition of spatial economic analysis, the origins of which predate both of these authors. Building on the original seminal works of Weber (1909), Marshall (1920), Hotelling (1929), Palander (1935), Hoover (1948), Perroux (1950), Losch (1954), Moses (1958), Isard (1956), Chinitz (1961), Vernon (1960), Christaller (1966), Alonso (1964), Borts and Stein (1964), and Greenhut (1970), a huge number of authors have subsequently provided many fundamental insights into the complex nature of the relationships between geography and space. A consideration of these insights and the analytical techniques developed is essential in order to provide a comprehensive understanding of the nature and workings of the spatial economy.

Spatial economic analysis has broadly been split into two sub-fields, namely urban economics and regional economics. These are by no means mutually exclusive categories and many analyses will fall into both categories. The distinction between these two categories has really arisen as a result of asking slightly different questions. Urban eco-nomics, by definition, is generally concerned with asking questions about the nature and workings of the economy of the city. As such, the models and techniques developed within this field are primarily designed to analyse phenomena which are confined within the limits of a single city. Regional economics, on the other hand, tends to ask questions related to larger spatial areas than single cities, and the models and analytical techniques developed generally reflect this broader spatial perspective. However, as we will see in this book, there are many issues which can be analysed within either field, such as questions relating to the location of cities, the location of firms, or the migration behaviour of labour. In each urban or regional case, the choice of the appropriate analytical approach to adopt or the techniques to employ will in part be determined by the particular real-world context we are considering and the data which are available.

For the purposes of this book, an urban area is defined as a single continuous and contiguous area of urban development. The central questions of urban economics there-fore focus on the workings of the individual city. The definition of a region is rather more complex, because areas can be defined as individual regions in terms of their topography, climate, economy, culture, or administrative structure. For the purposes of this book we define regions in terms of spatial units. A region is defined here as a spatial area which is larger than a single urban area, but which is different from the spatial definition of a single nation. In general, we assume that regions are smaller than individual countries, and the central questions of regional economics therefore focus on the reasons why individual spatial parts of the same country behave differently to one another. Yet, the spatial classifications of urban and regional areas adopted here are by no means definitive. For example, some individual urban areas such as Los Angeles and Tokyo can be regarded as major regions in their own right. At the same time, some regional areas cut across national boundaries. For example, the economies of Detroit and Western Ontario are largely the same regional economy. Similarly, the economy of Seattle can be considered to be broadly part of the same regional economy as Vancouver, British Columbia. Meanwhile in Europe, the southern part of the Netherlands can be regarded as being largely part of the same regional economy as parts of eastern Belgium and the Nordrhein-Westfalen area of Germany. Furthermore, regions can also vary enormously either in geographical or population size. For example, the south-west region of the USA is the spatial size of the whole of western Europe, while the Tokyo regional population is larger than the whole population of Scandinavia. For analytical simplicity in this book we will therefore adopt the convention that regions are smaller than individual countries and larger than individual urban areas, with the additional assumption that a country is an area with a common currency and free internal capital and labour mobility.

Although many spatial economic topics can be analysed within either an urban or regional economics framework, this is not to say that the spatial unit of analysis, whether it is a single city or a multi-city region, is an arbitrary choice. Some economic phenomena primarily affect very localized individual urban areas, whereas the impacts of certain other economic phenomena are generally felt over much larger regional areas. The appropriate geographical area of analysis will therefore depend on the nature and spatial extent of the economic phenomena. At the same time, regions and cities are both valid areas for economic analysis also because economic policy is often implemented at these levels. Individual urban metropolitan governments have a role to play in determining transportation and land-use policies within the confines of the individual city, and some of the financing of such policies will be raised by local city taxation. The analysis of the impacts of such schemes must be made at the level of the individual urban area. Similarly, inter-urban transportation and land-use policies will have impacts on all of the cities within a region. As such the regions comprising the groups of cities become the appropriate areas of analysis, as the effects of such schemes may be rather different between the individual cities. As we will see in this book, the choice of the area of analysis will determine the models we employ and also how the results we generate are to be interpreted.

The object of this book is to provide an integrated approach to urban and regional economics, such that students are able to understand the broad range of relationships between economics and geography. By an appreciation of these relationships, students will come to understand the location-specific nature of many urban and regional economic issues. An understanding of the relationships between economics and geography will also better inform us of the long-run impacts of continuing economic integration across nations. This understanding will, in turn, hopefully encourage our future economic policy makers to make explicit consideration of the geographical aspects of economic policies, irrespective of whether they are government or corporate decision-makers. In the modern era of rapid communications technologies, decreasing trade barriers, increasing international labour mobility, and currency convergence, geography and economics must be discussed together. By adopting such an integrated approach, this book is somewhat different from many of the urban and regional economics undergraduate textbooks currently available. Urban economics books often tend to focus their discussions at the level of the individual urban area, with the object of their analysis being the urban land market. The explicitly spatial economic analysis generally takes place within the context of the individual urban area, and the analysis tends to be entirely microeconomic. The implications of the local urban economic phenomena for other cities and areas are often ignored. Regional economics texts, on the other hand, often tend to underplay the spatial aspects of economic behaviour, and instead adopt more of a macroeconomic approach to regional behaviour. Yet, this approach ignores both the spatial microeconomic foundations of regional behaviour, and also the effects of urban economic behaviour on the wider regional economies. The logic of this book is therefore to overcome many of the limitations of existing textbooks, by adopting both microeconomic and macroeconomic approaches to the discussions of both urban and regional economies, within an explicitly spatial framework.

This book is aimed specifically at intermediate level students, such as third- or fourth-year undergraduates or first-year postgraduates. The book is also written as a textbook which is accessible to a wide range of students from economics, business and management, urban planning, or geography. The only requirement for a student to follow this book without difficulty is that he or she should have taken introductory classes in micro- and macro-economics. All of the material in the book is explained with the aid of ninety-six diagrams and six tables, and each of the topics can be understood simply by reading the main text alone and following the diagrams carefully. For more advanced students, mathematical appendices to each chapter provide formal proofs of the key conclusions of each chapter. These appendices will be particularly appropriate for economics students or for postgraduate students of all disciplines studying urban and regional economics for the first time. The overall intention of this book is therefore to introduce the study of urban and regional economics to a wide range of students. Those students who continue on to postgraduate work will subsequently be equipped to read more advanced texts such as Isard *et al.* (1998) and Fujita (1989). Alternatively, those students who progress into employment positions which involve economic analysis and decision-making will be better able to understand the spatial impacts of their decisions.

The book comprises seven chapters. Each chapter takes a broad theme and discusses the various ways in which we are able to ask and answer questions related to the topic in question. The first three chapters adopt broadly a microeconomic approach to explicitly spatial economic questions. Chapter 1 discusses the various theoretical ways we can understand the location behaviour of individual firms. Chapter 2 extends these arguments to understanding the spatial behaviour of groups of firms and activities, and investigates the conditions under which individual spatial industrial behaviour gives rise to industrial clusters and urban areas. Once an urban area has arisen at a particular location, Chapter 3 then explains how the urban land market works and how local land allocations are determined. The three subsequent chapters then adopt a more aggregate approach to discussions of various regional economic issues which are generally understood primarily in macroeconomic terms. Chapter 4 discusses multiplier analysis and the ways in which the linkages between firms and activities in a local area affect the overall output of an area. Chapter 5 explains the response of spatial labour markets to local demand and supply changes, and discusses the particular problems associated with local labour-market adjustments and interregional migration flows. Chapter 6 then integrates the arguments in each of the previous chapters in order to discuss the various approaches we have to analyse regional growth behaviour. As with the first three chapters, however, the discussions in each of the three chapters which deal with these more macroeconomic issues are underpinned by explicitly spatial considerations. This allows us to identify the differences between analysis of economic phenomena at the urban or regional level and analysis at the national macroeconomic level. Finally, Chapter 7 discusses the nature of, and justification for, urban and regional economic policy. On the basis of the analyses in the previous six chapters, Chapter 7 explains how we can use urban and regional economic analysis to understand, predict, and target the impacts of various types of urban and regional policies. This will help us to achieve the desired spatial outcomes of public economic policy initiatives.

Chapter 1

Industrial Location: The Location of the Firm in Theory

1.1 Introduction to Classical and Neoclassical Models of Location

The level of output and activity of an area depends on the total quantities of factor inputs employed in the area, and the wealth of an area depends on the total payments received by those factors. Observation suggests that some regions exhibit dense concentrations of factors, with large numbers of people and investment located in the same area, whereas other regions exhibit sparse populations and low levels of investment. At the same time, observation also suggests that people are paid different wages in different areas, while land prices vary significantly between locations. Therefore, in order to understand the economic performance of a region it is necessary to understand why particular quantities of factors are employed in that area, and why the factors there earn the particular rewards that they do.

Production factor inputs are usually defined in terms of three broad types, namely capital, labour, and land, and the factor payments earned by these factors in the production process are profits, wages, and rents, respectively. In some analyses of the production process, additional factor inputs are also identified such as entrepreneurship and technology. However, in our initial discussion of the causes and reasons for particular types of industrial location behaviour, we will not initially distinguish these additional factors from the broad factor groups. We include entrepreneurship in our description of labour, and technology in our description of capital. Later in our discussion of the causes and reasons for particular types of industrial location behaviour, we will also investigate the additional issues associated with entrepreneurship and technology. In this chapter we will concentrate on the determinants of spatial variations in capital investment, and in later sections of the book we will focus on spatial variations in labour stocks, and variations in land prices.

We start our analysis by asking the question—what determines the level and type of capital invested in a particular region? When talking about capital, our most basic unit of microeconomic analysis is the capital embodied in the firm. In order to understand the level of capital investment in an area it is necessary to ask why particular firms are located there and why the particular levels and types of investment in the area are as they are. These are the questions addressed by industrial location theory. We begin by discussing three classical and neoclassical models of industrial location behaviour, namely the Weber model, the Moses model, and the Hotelling model. Each of these models provides us with different insights into the fundamental reasons for, and the consequences of, industrial location behaviour. After analysing each of these models in detail, we will discuss two alternative approaches to analysing industrial location behaviour, namely the behavioural approach and the evolutionary approach. A broad understanding of these various approaches to industrial location behaviour will then allow us to discuss the concept of agglomeration economies.

1.2 **The Weber Location-Production Model**

Our starting point is to adopt the approach to industrial locational analysis originally derived from the nineteenth-century German mathematician Laundhart (1885), but which was formalized and publicized beyond Germany by Alfred Weber (1909). For our analysis to proceed we assume that the firm is defined at a point in space; the firm is therefore viewed as a single establishment. We also adopt the standard microeconomic assumption that the firm aims to maximize its profits. Assuming the profit-maximizing rationale for the firm, the question of where a firm will locate therefore becomes the question of at which location a firm will maximize its profits. In order to answer this question we will begin by using the simplest two-dimensional spatial figure, namely a triangle. This very simple type of two-dimensional approach will subsequently be extended to more general spatial forms.

The model described by Figure 1.1 is often described as a Weber location-production triangle, in which case the firm consumes two inputs in order to produce a single output.

Notation for use with Figures 1.1 to 1.12:

m_1, m_2	weight (tonnes) of material of input goods 1 and 2 consumed by the firm
m_3	weight of output good 3 produced by the firm
p_1, p_2	prices per tonne of the input goods 1 and 2 at their points of production
p_3	price per tonne of the output good 3 at the market location
M_1, M_2	production locations of input goods 1 and 2
M_3	market location for the output good 3
t_1, t_2	transport rates per tonne-mile (or per ton-kilometre) for hauling input goods 1 and 2
t_3	transport rates per tonne-mile (or per tonne-kilometre) for hauling output goods 3
K	the location of the firm.

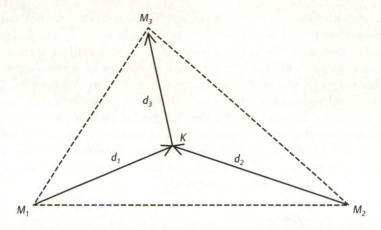

FIG. 1.1 Weber location-production triangle

We assume that the firm consumes material inputs 1 and 2, which are then combined by the firm in order to produce an output commodity 3. In the Weber location-production model, we assume that the coefficients of production are fixed, in that there is a fixed relationship between the quantities of each input required in order to produce a single unit of the output. Our production function therefore takes the general form:

$$m_3 = f(k_1 m_1, k_2 m_2). \tag{1.1}$$

In the very simplest case $k_1 = k_2 = 1$, in which case our production function becomes

$$m_3 = f(m_1, m_2). \tag{1.2}$$

This represents a situation where the quantity of the output good 3 produced is equal to the combined weight of the inputs 1 and 2. In other words for the purposes of our analysis here, we can rewrite (1.2) as

$$m_3 = m_1 + m_2. \tag{1.3}$$

The production locations of the input sources of 1 and 2, defined as M_1 and M_2, are given, as is the location of the output market M_3, at which output good 3 is sold. The prices per ton of the inputs 1 and 2 are given as p_1 and p_2, at the points of production M_1 and M_2, respectively. The price per tonne of the output good 3 at the market location M_3, is given as p_3. As such, the firm is a price taker. Moreover, we assume that the firm is able to sell unlimited quantities of output 3 at the given price p_3, as in perfect competition. The transport rates are given as t_1, t_2, and t_3, and these transport rates represent the costs of transporting 1 tonne of each commodity 1, 2, and 3, respectively, over 1 mile or 1 kilometre. Finally, the distances d_1, d_2, and d_3, represent the distances over which each of the goods 1, 2, and 3 are shipped.

We also assume that the input production factors of labour and capital are freely available everywhere at factor prices and qualities that do not change with location, and that land is homogeneous. In other words, the price and quality of labour is assumed to be equal everywhere, as is the cost and quality of capital, and the quality and rental price of land. However, there is no reason to suppose that the prices of labour, capital, and land are equal to each other. We simply assume that all locations exhibit the same attributes in terms of their production factor availability. Space is therefore assumed to be homogeneous.

If the firm is able to locate anywhere, then assuming the firm is rational, the firm will locate at whichever location it can earn maximum profits. Given that the prices of all the input and output goods are exogenously set, and the prices of production factors are invariant with respect to space, the only issue which will alter the relative profitability of different locations is the distance of any particular location from the input source and output market points. The reason for this is that different locations will incur different costs of transporting inputs from their production points to the location of the firm, and outputs from the location of the firm to the market point.

If the price per unit of output p_3 is fixed, the location that ensures maximum profits are earned by the firm is the location at which the total input plus output transport costs are minimized, *ceteris paribus*. This is known as the *Weber optimum location*. Finding the Weber optimum location involves comparing the relative total input plus output transport costs at each location. The Weber optimum location will be the particular location at which the sum *(TC)* of these costs is minimized. The cost condition that determines the Weber optimum location can be described as

$$TC = Min \sum_{i=1}^{3} m_i t_i d_i, \tag{1.4}$$

where the subscript i refers to the particular weights, transport rates, and distances over which goods are shipped to and from each location point K. With actual values corresponding to each of the spatial and non-spatial parameters, it is possible to calculate the total production plus transportation costs incurred by the firm associated with being at any arbitrary location K. Given our assumptions that the firm will behave so as to maximize its profits, the minimum cost location will be the actual chosen location of the firm.

In his original analysis Weber characterized the problem of the optimum location in terms of a mechanical analogy. He described a two-dimensional triangular system of pulleys with weights called a Varignon Frame. In this system, the locations of the pulleys reflect the locations of input source and output market points, and the weights attached to each string passing over each of the pulleys corresponds to the transport costs associated with each shipment. The point at which the strings are all knotted together represents the location of the firm. In some cases, the knot will settle at a location inside the triangle, whereas in other cases the knot will settle at one of the corners. This suggests that the optimum location will sometimes be inside the Weber triangle, whereas in other cases the optimum location will be at one of the corners. Nowadays, rather than using such mechanical devices, the optimum location can be calculated using computers. However, although it is always possible to calculate the optimum location of the firm in each particular case, of interest to us here is to understand how the location of the Weber optimum will itself be affected by the levels of, and changes in, any of the parameters described above. In order to explain this, we adopt a hypothetical example.

1.2.1 **The location effect of input transport costs**

Let us imagine that Figure 1.1 represents a firm that produces automobiles from inputs of steel and plastic. The output good 3 is defined as automobiles and these are sold at the market point M_3. We can assume that input 1 is steel and input 2 is plastic, and these are produced at locations M_1 and M_2, respectively. If the firm produces a car weighing 2 tonnes from 1 tonne of steel and 1 tonne of plastic, and the fixed transport rate for steel t_1 is half that for plastic t_2 (given that plastic is much less dense than steel, and transport rates are normally charged with respect to product bulk), the firm will locate relatively close to the source of the plastic production. In other words, the firm will locate close to M_2. The reason is that the firm will wish to reduce the higher total transport costs associated with shipping plastic inputs relative to steel inputs, *ceteris paribus*. The firm can do this by reducing the value of d_2 relative to d_1. On the other hand, if the firm had a different production function, such that it produces a car weighing 2 tons from 1.5 tonnes of steel and 0.5 tonnes of plastic, then even with the same values for the fixed transport rates t_1 and t_2 as in the previous case, the firm will now be incurring higher total transport costs associated with steel shipments, *ceteris paribus*. The reason for this is that although plastic is twice as expensive to ship per kilometre as steel, the total quantity of steel being shipped is three times that of plastic. The result is that the firm can reduce its total input transport costs by reducing the value of d_1 relative to d_2. The optimum location of the firm will now tend towards the location of production for the steel input M_1.

Within this Weber framework, we can compare the effects of different production function relationships on the location behaviour of the firm. For example, we can imagine that the two types of production function relationships described above—one which is relatively plastic intensive, and one which is relatively steel intensive—actually refer to the different production functions exhibited by two different competing automobile producers. Firm A exhibits the plastic-intensive production function, and firm B exhibits the steel-intensive production function. As we see in Figure 1.2, from the argument above we know that firm A will locate relatively close to M_2, the source of plastic,

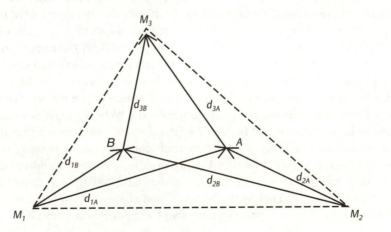

FIG. 1.2 Relative input transport costs and location

while firm B will locate relatively close to M_1, the source of steel. This is because, if we were to consider the case where steel and plastic inputs were shipped over identical distances, i.e. $d_{1A} = d_{2A}$, for firm A the total transport costs associated with plastic transportation would be greater than those associated with steel transportation. It therefore has an incentive to reduce the higher costs associated with plastic shipments by reducing d_{2A} and increasing d_{1B}. Alternatively, for firm B, for identical input shipment distances, i.e. $d_{1B} = d_{2B}$, the total transport costs associated with steel transportation would be greater than those associated with plastic transportation. It therefore has an incentive to reduce the higher transport costs associated with steel by reducing d_{1B} and increasing d_{2B}.

1.2.2 **The location effect of output transport costs**

Until now we have only considered the transport cost pull of the input sources on the location decision of the firm. However, the market itself will display a pull effect on the location behaviour of the firm. We can imagine the case of a power-generating plant which burns coal and coke, produced at M_1 and M_2, respectively, in order to produce electricity. We can regard the output of the plant as having zero weight or bulk. The output transportation costs of shipping electricity can be regarded as effectively zero, given that the only costs associated with distance will be the negligible costs of booster stations. In this case, the market point of the plant, whether it is a city or a region, will play no role in the decision of where to locate the plant. As such, the optimal location of the plant will be somewhere along the line joining M_1 and M_2. The optimal location problem therefore becomes a one-dimensional location problem. A discussion of this type of problem is given in Appendix 1.1.

In most situations, however, the output of the firm is costly to transport due to the weight and bulk of the output product. Different output weight and bulk will affect the optimum location of the firm relative to the location of the market and the inputs. Once again, we can illustrate this point by using our hypothetical example above of two automobile firms, A and B, each consuming inputs of steel and plastic. However, in this case we can imagine a situation where the input production functions of both firms were the same. In other words the relative input combinations for each firm, given as m_1/m_2, are the same. If both firms pay the same respective transport rates t_1 and t_2 for each input shipped, the relative locational pull of each input will be identical for each firm. However, in this situation we also assume that the firms differ in terms of their technical efficiency, in that firm A discards 70 per cent of the inputs during the production process, whereas firm B discards only 40 per cent of the inputs during the production process. Consequently, the total output weight m_3 of firm B is twice as great as that of firm A, for any total weight of inputs consumed. This greater output weight will encourage firm B to move closer towards the market point and further away from the input points than firm A. As see in Figure 1.3, firm B will therefore be more market-oriented than firm A in its location behaviour.

A more common situation in which similar firms exhibit different location behaviour with respect to the market is where the density of the product changes through the production process at different rates for each of the producers. For example, we can imagine our two automobile firms A and B, producing identical weights of output from

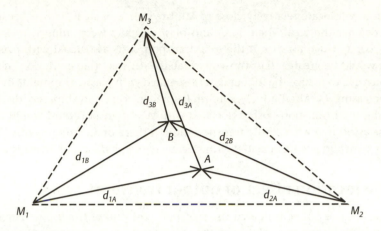

FIG. 1.3 Relative output transport costs and location

identical total weights of inputs. Here, the production functions of both firms are therefore the same. However, we can also assume that firm *A* specializes in the production of small vehicles suited to urban traffic, while firm *B* produces large four-wheel-drive vehicles suitable for rough terrain. As we have already seen, transport rates also depend on the bulk of the product, and products which have a high density will exhibit lower unit transport costs than products with a low density. In this situation firm *B* produces goods which are very bulky, whereas firm *A* produces goods which are relatively dense. Therefore, the output of firm *B* will be more expensive to transport than that of firm *A*, and this will encourage firm *B* to move closer to the market than firm *A*. Once again, as seen in Figure 1.3, firm *B* will be more market-oriented than firm *A*.

1.2.3 The location effect of varying factor prices

Our analysis so far has proceeded on the assumption that labour and land prices are identical across all locations, although in reality we know that factor prices vary significantly over space. The Weber approach also allows us to consider how factor price variations across space will affect the location behaviour of the firm. In order to understand this, it is necessary for us to identify the factor price conditions under which a firm will look for alternative locations.

We assume that the firm is still consuming inputs from M_1 and M_2 and producing an output for the market at M_3. Under these conditions, we know that the Weber optimum K^* is the minimum transport cost location of the firm, and that if all factor prices are equal across space this will be the location of the firm. Our starting point is therefore to consider the factor price variations relative to the Weber optimum K^* which will encourage a firm to move elsewhere. In order to do this, it is first necessary for us to construct a contour map on our Weber triangle, as described by Figure 1.3. These contours are known as *isodapanes*.

On a standard geographical map each contour links all of the locations with the same altitude. On the other hand, each isodapane contour here in a Weber map links all the locations which exhibit the same increase in total input plus output transport costs, per unit of output m_3 produced, relative to the Weber optimum location K^*. Increasing iso-dapanes therefore reflect increased total input plus output transport costs per unit of output m_3 produced, relative to the Weber optimum K^*. As the location of the firm moves away from the Weber optimum in any direction, the firm incurs increasing transport costs relative to the Weber optimum. In other words, the locations become less and less efficient, and the firm exhibits successively lower profits, *ceteris paribus*. We can also say that the firm incurs successively greater opportunity costs as it moves further away from the Weber optimum. If factor prices are equal across space, locations further away from the Weber optimum will become successively less desirable locations for invest-ment. Therefore, we need to ask by how much do *local* factor prices need to fall relative to the Weber optimum location K^* in order for the firm to move there?

If we take the case of location R, we can ask by how much do factor prices at R need to fall relative to the Weber optimum K^*, in order for the firm to move from K^* to R? As we

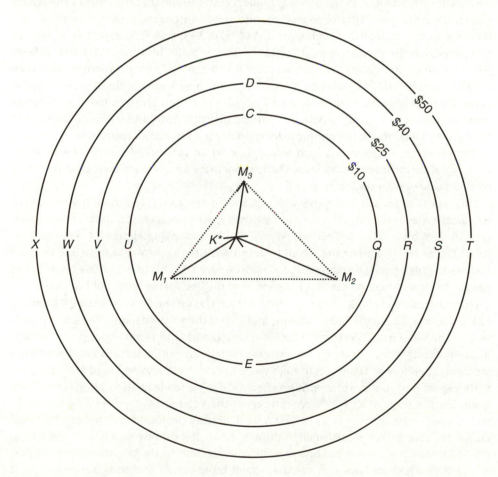

FIG. 1.4 Isodapane analysis

see from Figure 1.4, R is on the $25 isodapanes. If the costs of the labour and land factor inputs required to produce one unit of output m_3 at R are $20 less than at K^*, it will not be in the interests of the firm to move from K^* to R. The reason is that the fall in local factor input prices associated with a move from K^* to R will not be sufficient to compensate for the increased total transport costs as we move away from the Weber optimum. If the firm were to move from K^* to R in these circumstances, it would experience profits which were $5 unit of output m_3 less than at K^*. On the other hand if the local labour and land prices per unit of output as R were $30 less than at K^*, it would be in the interest of the firm to move. This is because the reduction in the local input factor costs associated with a move from K^* to R will now more than compensate for the increase in total transportation costs incurred by the move. If the firm were to move from K^* to R in these circumstances, it would experience profits which were $5 per unit of output m_3 greater than at K^*. This type of analysis can be applied to any alternative locations, such as Q, R, S, and T, in order to determine whether a firm should move and to which location.

For example, location Q is on the $10 isodapane, R is on the $25 isodapane, S is on the $40 isodapane, and T is on the $50 isodapane. Let us assume that the costs of the labour and land factor inputs required to produce one unit of output m_3, at Q, R, S, and T are less than the factor costs at K^* by amounts of $12, $20, $35, and $55, respectively. We can determine that the alternative locations Q and T are superior locations to K^*, in that both will provide greater profits than K^*, whereas R and S are inferior locations in that they exhibit reduced profits relative to K^*. However, of these superior alternatives, T is the better location because profits here are $5 per unit of output greater than at K^* whereas those at Q are only $2 greater. With this particular spatial distribution of local labour and land prices, location T is the optimum location of the firm. T is a superior location to the Weber optimum location at which total transport costs were minimized, because the lower local factor input prices more than compensate for the increased total transport costs associated with the location of T.

This type of approach also allows us to ask and answer a very important question: how will local wages and land prices have to vary over space in order for the firm's profits to be the same for all locations? This can be analysed by modifying Figure 1.4. We can construct Figure 1.5, by employing Figure 1.4, but then altering it by drawing a line from K^* eastwards which passes through Q, R, S, T, as in Figure 1.5. This line is defined in terms of geographical distance. We can then observe how the isodapanes intercept this line.

From the above example, we know that location Q is on the $10 isodapane, R is on the $25 isodapane, S is on the $40 isodapane, and T is on the $50 isodapane. The firm's profits will be the same in all locations if the local labour and land factor input prices at each location exactly compensate for the increased total transport costs associated with each location. Therefore in Figure 1.5 this allows us to plot the labour and land price gradient with respect to distance which ensures equal profits are made at all locations east of K^*, assuming the wage at K^* is w^*. We can repeat the exercise by drawing a line from K^* which passes west through U, V, W, and X, and plotting the local factor prices which will ensure the firm makes profits equal to those at K^* at all locations west of K^*. Combining this information allows us to construct the interregional factor price curve for our particular firm which ensures that it makes equal profits at all locations in the east–west direction. This is shown in Figure 1.6.

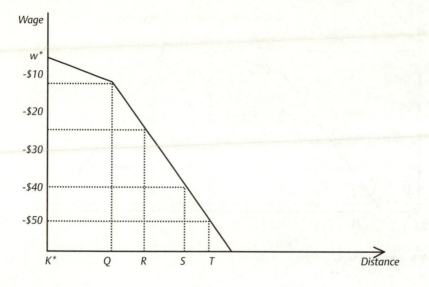

FIG. 1.5 Distance-isodapane equilibrium labour prices

This slope of the line is the interregional *equilibrium* factor price gradient for this particular firm along this particular axis. This equilibrium factor price gradient describes the variation in local factor prices, which ensures that the firm will be *indifferent* between locations. The firm is indifferent between locations along the east–west line, because the profits it can earn are the same everywhere along this line. As such, from the point of view of this firm, all locations along the east–west line are *perfect substitutes* for each other.

In principle, we can also construct similar factor price gradients for movements in any other direction away from K^*, such as movements passing through locations C, D, or E, in order to generate a two-dimensional equilibrium factor price map of the whole spatial economy.

The idea that locations can be perfect substitutes for each other, from the point of view of a firm's profitability, is important in terms of understanding the spatial patterns of industrial investment. For example, if a multinational manufacturing firm is looking for a new production site in order to develop its business in a new area, the likelihood of it going to any particular location will depend on the firm's estimate of the profits it can earn at that location. From the isodapane analysis of our Weber location-production model here, we know that the locations of key input sources such as M_1 and M_2 and market points such as M_3, will automatically mean that some locations are more profitable than others, with the Weber optimum being the most profitable location, *ceteris paribus*. Therefore, in order to make other locations attractive for investment, local factor prices have to fall relative to the Weber optimum. The attractiveness of any particular location as a new investment location for the firm will depend on the extent to which the local factor price falls can compensate for the increased transport (opportunity) costs associated with any suboptimal geographical location. If all local factor prices are interregional equilibrium prices, as described by Figure 1.6, the firm will be indifferent

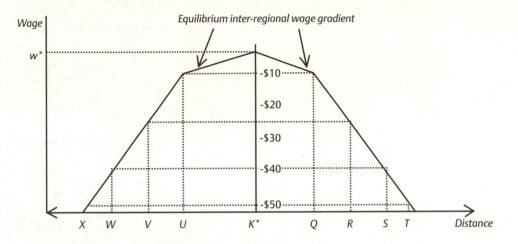

FIG. 1.6 Inter-regional equilibrium wage gradient

between locations. Under these circumstances, the firm will be equally likely to build its new production facility at any location. In other words, the probability of investment will be equal for all locations. Over large numbers of firms with similar input require-ments and similar output markets to this particular firm, the level of investment in any location should be the same as in all locations. On the other hand, if wages are not in equilibrium over space, certain areas will automatically appear more attractive as loca-tions for investment, thereby increasing the probability of investment there.

Geography confers different competitive advantages on different locations, which can only be compensated for by variations in local factor prices. However, in the above example, the equilibrium relationship between local factor prices and distance was only applicable to the particular firm in question here. This is because the interregional factor price gradient was calculated with respect to the Weber optimum of this particular firm. As we have seen, different firms will exhibit different Weber optimum locations, and this implies that different equilibrium interregional factor price gradients will exist for differ-ent types of firms exhibiting different transport costs, different production functions, and finally different input and output locations.

1.2.4 The locational effect of new input sources and new markets

Our analysis has so far discussed the locational effect of different transport costs, different production functions, and the resulting conditions under which a firm will be willing to move to alternative locations. We will now discuss the question of different input and output locations and the conditions under which a firm will search for alternatives. In the examples above, it was possible to use isodapane analysis to identify the factor price conditions under which a firm will move from one location to another. However, this process of movement itself may engender changes in the input sources employed and the output markets served.

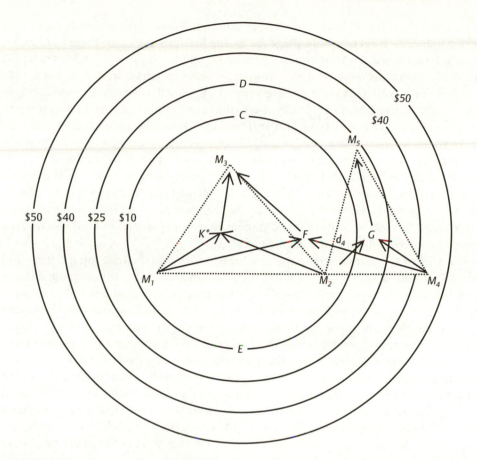

FIG. 1.7 New suppliers and new markets

In Figure 1.7 we can consider the situation where the firm relocates from K^* to F in response to the lower factor prices at F, which more than compensate for the additional input and output transport costs involving in consuming steel and plastic inputs from M_1 and M_2, and serving a market at M_3. Location F has therefore been determined as the new optimum location with respect to M_1, M_2, and M_3. However, in moving from K^* to F, it may be that alternative suppliers of identical inputs now become available. For example, the input supply location M_4 may be able to supply exactly the same steel input as M_1 but from a location whose distance from M_4 to F, which we denote as d_4, is now much closer to the firm than the distance d_1 from M_1 to F. Assuming the delivered price at location F of the steel input produced at M_4, is less than that of the input produced at M_1, i.e. $(p_4 + t_4 d_4) < (p_1 + t_1 d_1)$, the firm will substitute input supplier M_4 for M_1. This will produce a new Weber location-production problem, with the points M_4, M_2, and M_3 as the spatial reference points. This change in input suppliers will also imply that a new Weber optimum can be found, and that a new series of equilibrium local factor input prices could be calculated with respect to the new Weber optimum location.

With the points M_4, M_2, and M_3 as the spatial reference points, the new Weber optimum is G. At point G, it becomes advantageous for the firm to serve market point M_5, rather than M_3. This is because M_5 is nearer to G than M_3, and $(p_5 - t_5d_5) > (p_3 - t_3d_3)$. Therefore, the firm makes a greater profit from selling automobiles to market M_5 than to market M_3. The firm could switch markets completely from M_3 to M_5. Alternatively, it could decide to supply both markets M_3 to M_5. Under these conditions, it may be that a new optimum location of H arises, in which the firm at H buys from two supplier locations M_4 and M_2, and sells at two market locations, M_3 and M_5. More complex arrangements are possible. For example, in order to guarantee sufficient supplies of steel inputs for the newly expanded automobile market of $(M_3 + M_5)$, the firm may decide to continue to purchase steel from both M_1 and M_4, as well as purchasing plastic from M_2. Now we have a Weber location-production problem with M_1, M_2, M_3, M_4, and M_5 as spatial reference points. Once again, this will move the Weber optimum away from point H, and will also alter the inter-regional equilibrium wage gradient.

This type of geometrical arrangement, in which a firm has multiple input sources and multiple output market locations, is the norm for firms in reality. Although our analysis here has been developed primarily with only two input source locations and one output market location, the Weber location-production arguments and the associated isodapane analysis are perfectly applicable to the case of firms with multiple input and output locations. The reason for employing the triangular case of the two input locations and one output market location is that this particular spatial structure is simply the easiest two-dimensional model to explain. The model is designed to help us understand the advantages which geography confers on particular locations as sites for investment. A first key feature of the Weber model is therefore that it allows us to understand the factor price conditions under which other areas will become more attractive as locations for investment. Secondly, the model allows us to see location as an evolutionary process, in which changes in factor prices can engender changes in location behaviour, which themselves can change the supply linkages between suppliers, firms, and markets. Industrial location problems are inherently evolutionary in their nature as firms respond to new markets and products by changing their locations, and by changing the people they buy from and the people they sell to. All of these are spatial issues.

There is one final issue relating to the Weber model which needs to be addressed. In reality, firms are constantly changing their input suppliers and output markets in response to changes in input and output market prices. From our Weber analysis, these changes will also imply that the optimum location of the firm is continuously changing, and that in order to ensure the profitability of any particular location the equilibrium inter-regional factor price gradient must also be continuously changing. However, observation tells us that firms in reality do not move very frequently, and this raises the question of the extent to which the Weber model is a useful analytical tool to describe industrial location behaviour.

The reason why firms are not continuously moving is that the relocation process itself usually incurs very significant costs, such as the dismantling of equipment, the moving of people, and the hiring of new staff. Part of the transactions costs associated with relocation are also related to information and uncertainty, which are topics we will deal with later in the chapter. However, within the above framework we can easily incorporate these relocation costs, by including the annualized cost of these one-off relocation costs into our isodapane model. The existence of these additional costs simply implies that firms will move only when the factor cost advantages of alternative locations also compensate for these additional relocation costs as well as the increased transport costs. In other words, the equilibrium inter-regional wage gradient will be even steeper than under the situation where such costs are negligible. The Weber model therefore still allows us to identify the optimum location, and consequently the profit-maximizing behaviour of the firm in space, even in situations where relocation costs are significant. The observation that firms do not move frequently does not limit the applicability of the Weber model to real-world phenomena.

The one major location issue which the Weber model does not address, is that of the relationship between input substitution and location behaviour. In order to understand this relationship, we now turn to a discussion of the Moses location-production model.

1.3 The Moses Location-Production Model

The Weber model assumes that the quantities of each input consumed, m_1 and m_2, are fixed per unit of output m_3 produced. However, we know from standard microeconomic analysis that substitution is a characteristic feature of firm behaviour, and that efficiency conditions mean that firms will substitute in favour of relatively cheaper inputs, *ceteris paribus*. Substitution behaviour was first incorporated coherently into the Weber analysis by Moses (1958), and in order to see how substitution behaviour affects the location behaviour of the firm, we discuss here the main features and conclusions of the Moses approach.

In Figure 1.8, we construct an arc *IJ* in our triangle M_1, M_2, M_3, which is at a constant distance d_3 from the market point M_3. If we constrain our firm to locate along this arc, the distance from the location of the firm K to the market M_3 will no longer be a variable. Therefore, we can analyse the locational pull on the firm of changes only in the delivered prices of the inputs produced at M_1 and M_2.

For example, if the firm was located at *I*, the delivered price of input 1, given as $(p_1 + t_1d_1)$, will be a minimum, because the distance d_1 from M_1 to *I* will be a minimum. Similarly, the delivered price of input 2, given as $(p_2 + t_2d_2)$, will be a maximum, because the distance d_2 from M_2 to *I* will be a maximum. The delivered price ratio, given as $(p_1 + t_1d_1)/(p_2 + t_2d_2)$, will therefore be a minimum at location *I*. On the other hand, if the firm now moves to *J*, the delivered price of input 1 will be a maximum, because the distance d_1 from M_1 to *J* will be a maximum. At the same time, the delivered price of input 2 will be a minimum, because the distance d_2 from M_2 to *I* will be a minimum. Therefore, the delivered price ratio, $(p_1 + t_1d_1)/(p_2 + t_2d_2)$, will be a maximum at location *J*.

In standard microeconomic approaches to firm efficiency, the optimal input combination is determined by finding the point at which the highest isoquant attainable is tangent to the budget constraint. In this standard approach, the slope of the budget constraint is determined by the relative prices of the goods. From the above argument, we

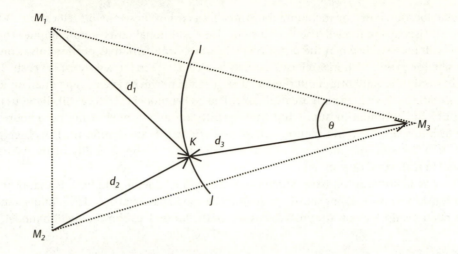

FIG. 1.8 Weber–Moses triangle

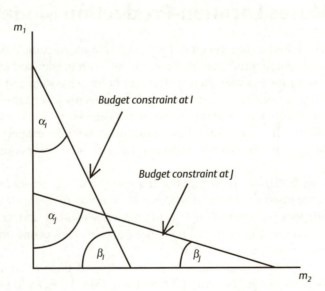

FIG. 1.9 Budget constraints at the end points I and J

can draw the budget constraints at locations I and J as shown in Figure 1.9, which represent equal total expenditure on inputs at each location. The delivered price ratios at locations I and J are given by the ratio of the tangents of the angles α_I/β_I and α_J/β_J, respectively.

Yet, this argument is also applicable to all locations along the arc IJ. If there are different delivered price ratios for different locations, this implies that for given source prices of the inputs p_1 and p_2, the slope of the budget constraints at each location along IJ must be different. As we move along the arc IJ from I to J, the delivered price ratio increases, and for every location along the arc *IJ* there is a unique delivered price ratio. This means that the usual approach to analysing microeconomic efficiency is not applicable to the firm in space, and must be adapted to incorporate the effects of location on the slope of the budget constraint. In order to do this we must construct the *envelope* budget constraint, which just contains all of the budget constraints associated with each of the locations along the arc *IJ*. This is done by drawing each of the budget constraints for each of the location points on the arc *IJ*, as in Figure 1.10, and the outer limits of this set of individual budget constraints will define the envelope budget constraint.

The Moses argument is that we can now apply standard efficiency conditions to this model, by finding the point at which the envelope budget constraint is tangent to the highest isoquant attainable. This is shown in Figure 1.11, where the point of maximum efficiency is at E^*.

At E^*, the optimum input combinations are given as m_1^* and m_2^*. However, E^* also represents an *optimum location* K^*. The reason is that the optimum input combination is found at a particular point on the envelope budget constraint. Yet, every point on the budget constraint also represents a unique location. Therefore, the optimum input mix and the optimum location of the firm are always jointly determined. One is never without the other. This is a profound insight. Where input substitution is possible, all location problems become production problems and all production problems become location problems.

We can illustrate the argument with an example. In our Weber–Moses triangle, we can imagine that a road-building programme takes place in the area around location M_1, the effect of which is generally to reduce the value of t_1 for all shipments of goods from this location, relative to all other locations. If all the other parameters remain constant, this will imply that the delivered price ratio $(p_1 + t_1 d_1)\,/(p_2 + t_2 d_2)$, at all locations along *IJ* will

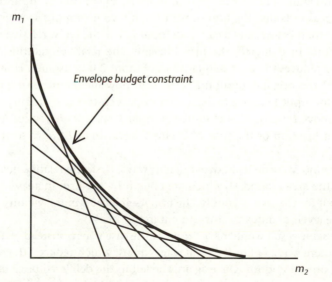

FIG. 1.10 The envelope budget constraint

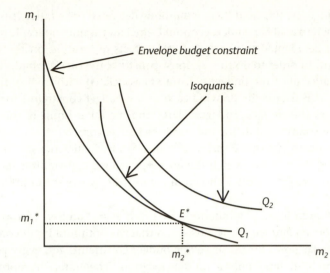

FIG. 1.11 Location-production optimum

fall. In other words, the slope of each budget constraint becomes steeper, *ceteris paribus*, and the envelope budget constraint also becomes steeper and shifts upwards to the left. Strictly speaking, in accordance with the income effect, the envelope will also shift outwards to the right, because the price of the input has fallen. However, in this discussion we focus only on the substitution effect of the change in slope of the envelope. For a given set of production isoquants, the optimum production combination will change from that represented by E^*.

As we see in Figure 1.12, at the new optimum E', the optimum input mix is now m_1' and m_2'. The reason is that the firm substitutes in favour of input 1, which is now relatively cheaper than before, and away from input 2, which is now relatively more expensive than before. In doing so, the firm increases the relative quantities of input 1 it consumes and reduces the relative quantities of input 2 it consumes. However, this also implies that at the original location K^*, the firm now incurs increasing total transport costs $(m_1t_1d_1)$ for input 1 relative to the total transport costs $(m_2t_2d_2)$ for input 2. Therefore, the firm will move towards M_1, the source of input 1, in order to reduce these costs. The new optimum location of the firm K' is closer to M_1 than E^*, and so the firm moves towards M_1.

The area around M_1 benefits in two different ways. First, the relative quantity of goods produced by the area around M_1 which are bought by the firm increases. This increases regional output for the area. Secondly, the firm itself locates in the vicinity of M_1, thereby increasing the levels of industrial investment in the area.

Exactly the same result would have arisen in the case where, instead of a road-building programme, there was a fall in the local wages at M_1, which reduced the source price p_1, relative to all other locations. Once again, the fall in the delivered price ratio at all locations leads to substitution in favour of the cheaper good and also relocation towards M_1.

We can contrast this Moses result with that of the Weber model. In the simple Weber

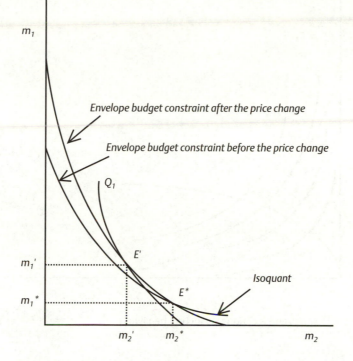

FIG. 1.12 A change in the location-production optimum

model, if the transport rate t_1 falls, *ceteris paribus*, the effect on the location of the firm is to move the locational optimum *away* from M_1. The reason is that input 2 now becomes relatively more expensive to transport, and because the coefficients of production are fixed, such that the relative quantities of m_1 and m_2 consumed remain the same, the firm will move towards the source of input 2 in order to reduce the total transport costs. The difference between the location-production results of the two models is that in the Weber model the fixed coefficients mean that no input substitution is possible, whereas in the Moses model of variable coefficients, input substitution is possible. In the latter case, the input substitution behaviour alters the relative total transport costs and consequently the optimum location behaviour of the firm. In reality, there is a continuum of possible location effects, dependent on the technical substitution possibilities. In situations where the elasticities of substitution are zero or very low, the results will tend to mimic those of the Weber model, whereas in situations where the elasticities of substitution are high, the results will tend towards those of the conclusions of the Moses model.

A second feature of the Moses model is that it allows us to examine the effect of returns to scale on the location-production behaviour of the firm. In particular, we can ask the question, how will the optimum location of the firm be affected by changes in the level of output of the firm? In order to answer this in Figure 1.13 we construct a series of envelope budget constraints, represented by the dotted lines, which correspond to different levels of total expenditure on inputs. Envelope budget constraints further to the right imply

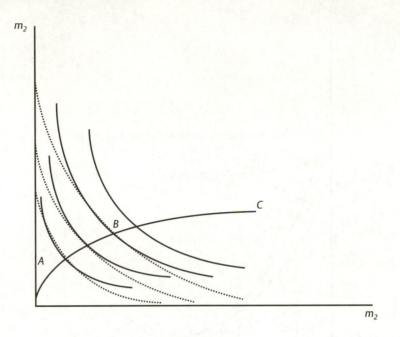

FIG. 1.13 Output changes and location-production behaviour

greater total expenditure levels on inputs. An isoquant map, represented by the solid curves, can now be combined with the envelope map. We can also apply the Moses argument, which states that the optimum point for each level of output and input expenditure is where each particular envelope is tangent to the highest isoquant, to the case of different output levels. By joining all the points of tangency we construct a line *ABC*, which is an output expansion path. Yet, this output expansion path is different from the usual form of an expansion path. Each point on the expansion path defines a particular optimum input combination. However, each point on the expansion path also defines an optimum location.

If the expansion path is curved downward, such as in the case of *ABC* in Figure 1.13, it implies that as the output of the firm increases, and the total quantity of inputs consumed increases, the optimum input mix changes relatively in favour of input 2. The optimum ratio of m_1/m_2 falls and the optimum location of the firm moves towards M_2. Alternatively, if the expansion path were to curve upwards, this would mean that as the output of the firm increases, the optimum input combination would change in favour of input 1. As the optimum ratio of m_1/m_2 increases, the optimum location of the firm would move towards the market.

This argument immediately leads to the conclusion that if the expansion path is a straight line from the origin, such as *FGH* in Figure 1.14, both the optimum input mix and also the optimum location of the firm will remain constant as output expands, *ceteris paribus*. The actual slope of the expansion path is not important, other than it implies a different optimum location. All that is required to ensure that once the firm has found its optimum location it will always remain at this optimum location as output changes, is

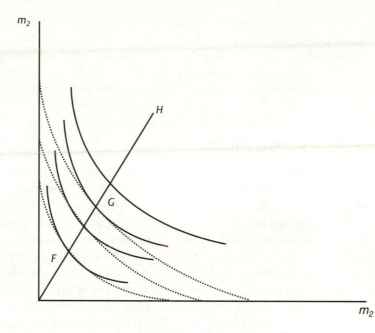

FIG. 1.14 The independent of output optimum location solution

that the production function of the firm exhibits a straight line expansion path from the origin. This is the basic Moses result.

This basic Moses result holds in the case where the firm is constrained to locate on the arc *IJ* at a fixed distance from the market. However, in the more general case where the distance from the market is also part of the location problem, the optimum location of the firm will be independent of the level of output, as long as both the production function of the firm and the transportation technology of the firm exhibit constant returns to scale. The Weber fixed-coefficients production function will satisfy the Moses requirement. However, there are other more general types of production functions allowing for input substitution, which also satisfy this requirement. These results are detailed in Appendix 1.2.

The Moses result can be viewed somewhat as the spatial equivalent of the firm in perfect competition. The firm is a price taker, and once it has determined its optimum production technique and optimum location, the firm will not change its behaviour, *ceteris paribus*. In other words, unless there are external changes in technology which alter the production function relationships, or changes in transportation technology which alter relative transport costs, or externally determined changes in the location of input goods sources and output market points, the firm will always remain at the same location employing the same input–output production techniques. It would be wrong, however, to view these spatial results as implying that the spatial economy is essentially static. From our discussion in section 1.2.4, we saw that the spatial economy exhibits evolutionary characteristics, with firms searching for new optimum locations in response to factor price changes, and subsequently searching for new input supplier and market output locations, in response to their relocation behaviour. The key insights, however, of the Weber and Moses models are that production behaviour and location behaviour are completely intertwined issues. Often this point is overlooked in textbook discussions of industrial economics and the theory of the firm. This is largely because location adds an extra dimension to the optimization problems, making the analysis somewhat more complex.

1.3.1 **The logistics-costs model**

There are a couple of possible limitations to the applicability of the Weber–Moses framework to real-world phenomena which need to be considered at this point. The first limitation is that the market price or revenue of the output good plays no role in the determination of the optimum location of the firm in either model. In the Weber model, the optimum location is determined solely by the transportation costs associated with the input and output goods, whereas in the Moses model, the input prices do play a role in the optimum location. In neither model does the market price have any effect on the determination of the optimum location. The second limitation of this framework is the emphasis on transport costs as a locational issue. In reality, transport costs tend to be only a very small percentage of total costs for most firms. However, both of these model weaknesses can be largely reconciled within a Weber–Moses framework by employing a broader description of distance-transport costs defined as 'total logistics costs', which includes all of the inventory purchasing and carrying costs associated with transportation (McCann 1993, 1997, 1998). Employing this logistics costs approach, it can be demonstrated both that the market price and market sales revenue do play a crucial role in determining the optimum location, and also that distance costs are very significant. In particular, as we see in Appendix 1.3, the higher value-adding activities will tend to be more market-oriented than lower value-adding activities, and will also tend to be less sensitive to inter-regional labour price changes. As such, market areas will tend to be surrounded by higher-value activities or activities further up the value-chain, whereas supply sources will tend to be surrounded more by lower value-adding activities or firms lower down the supply chain. At the same time, total logistics costs can also be shown to be very much more significant than transport costs alone, because each of the inventory purchasing and carrying cost components can be shown to be functions of distance. A final point here is that the total logistics costs approach can also be employed to account for the economies of distance and scale generally observed in transport pricing (McCann 2001) and discussed in Appendix 1.1.

1.4 **Market Area Analysis: Spatial Monopoly Power**

In our analysis so far we have assumed that the market location is simply a point in space. However, taking geography and space seriously in our models of firm behaviour also requires that we investigate the explicitly spatial nature of market areas. Market areas frequently differ over space, due to differences in spatial population densities, differences in income distributions across space, and differences in consumer demand across space according to regional variations in consumer tastes. However, even if there were no spatial variations in population densities, income distributions, and consumer demand patterns, space would still be an important competitive issue. The reason is that geography and space can confer *monopoly power* on firms, which encourages firms to engage in spatial competition in order to try to acquire monopoly power through location behaviour. In order to see this we can adopt the approach first used by Palander (1935).

In Figure 1.15, we have two firms A and B located at points A and B along a one-dimensional market area defined by OL. We assume that both firms are producing an identical product. The production costs p_a of firm A at location A can be represented by the vertical distance a, and the production costs p_b of firm B at location B can be represented by the vertical distance b. As we see, firm A is more efficient than firm B. The transport costs faced by each firm as we move away in any direction from the location of the firm are represented by the slopes of the transport rate functions. As we see here the transport rates for the two firms in this case are identical, i.e. $t_a = t_b$. For any location at a distance d_a away from firm A, the delivered price of the good is given as $(p_a + t_a d_a)$, and for any location at a distance d_b away from firm B, the delivered price of the good is given as $(p_b + t_b d_b)$.

If we assume that consumers are evenly distributed along the line OL, and we also assume that consumers, being rational, will buy from the firm which is able to supply at that particular location at the lowest delivered price, the total market area will be divided into two sectors OX and XL. The reason for this is that between O and X, the delivered price of firm A, given as $(p_a + t_a d_a)$, is always lower than that of firm B. On the other hand, at all locations between X and L the delivered price of firm B, given as $(p_b + t_b d_b)$, is always lower than that of firm A. Although firm A is more efficient than firm B, and although both firms produce an identical product, firm A does not gain all of the market. The reason is that location gives each firm some monopoly power over the area around itself. Firm A cannot capture all of firm B's market, even though it is more efficient than firm B, because the transport costs associated with shipping goods to market locations close to firm B increase the delivered price $(p_a + t_a d_a)$ to an uncompetitive level in market locations close to firm B. In terms of selling to consumers in the vicinity of firm B, firm A is unsuccessful simply because it is too far away. On the other hand, for sales in this area, firm B is successful simply because it is in the right location, even though it is less efficient in production.

This type of analysis can be extended to allow for differences in transport rates between

Price/Cost

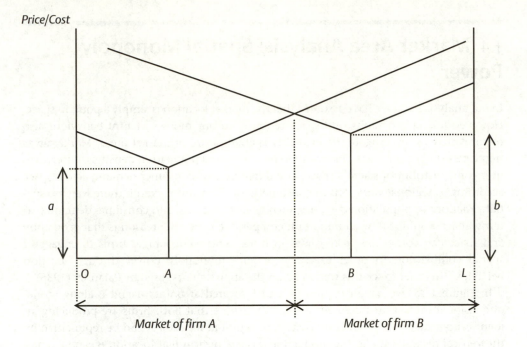

FIG. 1.15 Spatial market areas: a one-dimensional model with equal transport rates

firms as well as differences in production costs. In Figure 1.16a, b, we see that market areas can be divided up in a variety of ways in situations where the production costs and transport rates vary between the firm. Generally, the size of a firm's market area will be larger the lower are the production costs of the firm and the lower are the transport rates faced by the firm. However, only in the case where transport rates are zero is a lower production price sufficient to ensure a firm captures all of the market. The reason is that the existence of transport costs allows less efficient firms such as firm *B* to survive by providing each firm with some monopoly power over particular market areas. In general, the areas over which firms have some monopoly power are the areas in which the firms are located. For example, Figure 1.16b can be regarded as representing a case such as a local bakery, where firm *B* maintains a very small local market area in the face of competition from a national bakery, firm *A*, which produces at much lower unit production costs and transports in large low-cost shipments.

Monopoly power refers to the ability of the firm to increase the production price of the good p_a or p_b, and yet maintain some market share. In general, the greater is the monopoly power of the firm, the steeper is the firm's downward-sloping demand curve. In many textbook descriptions of monopoly or monopolistic power, the slope of the firm's downward-sloping demand curve is viewed as being dependent on brand loyalty, associated with advertising and marketing. However, location is also an important way in which many firms acquire monopoly power. The reason is that transport costs are a form of transactions costs, and from the theory of the firm, we know that the existence of transactions costs such as tariffs and taxes can provide protection for some inefficient

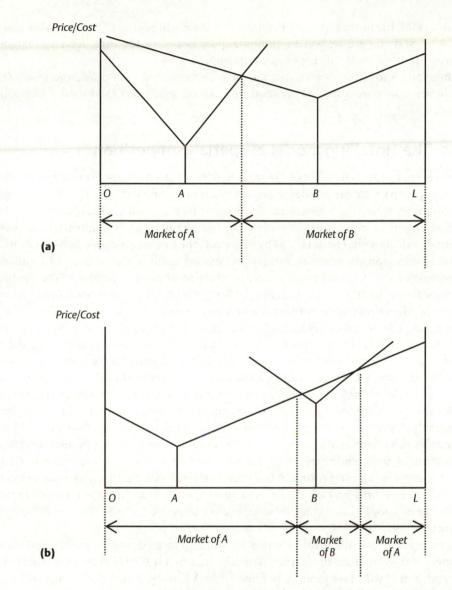

Price/Cost

O   *A*   *B*   *L*

Market of A   Market of B

(a)

Price/Cost

O   *A*   *B*   *L*

Market of A   Market
of B   Market
of A

(b)

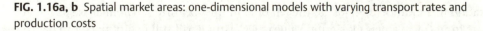

FIG. 1.16a, b Spatial market areas: one-dimensional models with varying transport rates and production costs

firms. Geography acts in a similar manner, because the costs of overcoming space in order to carry out market exchanges incur transport-transactions costs. In the context of Figures 1.15 and 1.16, there are two general rules governing the extent to which distance costs provide a firm with spatial monopoly power:

(i) First, the greater are the values of the transport rates t_a and t_b, the lower will be the fall in the market area of the firm, and the greater will be the monopoly power of the firm, for any marginal increase in the price of either p_a or p_b, *ceteris paribus*.

(ii) Second, the further apart are the firms, the lower will be the fall in the market area of the firm, and the greater will be the monopoly power of the firm, for any marginal increase in the price of either p_a or p_b, *ceteris paribus*.

Therefore, firms which are located at a great distance from each other, and which face significant transport costs, will consequently exhibit significant local spatial monopoly power.

1.4.1 The Hotelling model of spatial competition

The existence of spatial monopoly power provides an incentive for firms to use location as a competitive weapon in order to acquire greater monopoly power. This is particularly important in industries where firms do not compete primarily in terms of price, but instead engage in non-price competition, such a product quality competition. In competitive environments characterized by oligopoly, the interdependence between firms in the determination of output quantities and market share is also a result of locational considerations, as well as interdependence in terms of pricing decisions. The simplest demonstration of this is the Hotelling (1929) model, which describes firms' spatial interdependence within the context of a locational game.

In Figure 1.17 we adapt Figure 1.15 to the case where both the production costs and transport rates of firm A and firm B are identical. In other words, $p_a = p_b$ and $t_a = t_b$, and we assume that these prices do not change. As before, we assume that consumers are evenly distributed along OL and we also introduce the assumption that the demand of consumers is perfectly inelastic, such that all consumers consume a fixed quantity per time period irrespective of the price. In terms of firm strategy we assume that each firm makes a competitive decision on the basis of the assumption that its competitor firm will not change its behaviour. In the game theory literature this particular set of rules describing the nature of the competitive environment is known as 'Cournot conjectures'. Given that the firms are not competing in terms of their production prices, which are assumed to be fixed, each firm can only adjust its location in order to acquire greater market share. If the firms react to each other in sequential time periods, the location result can be predicted easily.

If we assume that the firms A and B are initially located at one-quarter and three-quarters of the way along the market, respectively, firm A will have monopoly power over OX and firm B will have monopoly power over XL. In this case, both firms will have identical market shares. In time period 1 firm A will therefore move from its original location to a location at C, just to the left of B. In this way firm A will increase its market share from OX to a new maximum value of OC. Firm B will still retain market share over BL, although its market share is now at a minimum.

Firm B will now assume that firm A will maintain its location at C, and so in time period 2, firm B will move just to the left of C. In time period 3, firm A will respond by moving to the left of firm B, and this process will continue until both firms are located at X, in the middle of the market. Once both firms are located at X, neither firm has any incentive to change its location behaviour, because any location change will involve a reduction in market share relative to their location at X. In game theory, any situation in which neither firm has any incentive to change its behaviour is known as a 'Nash equilibrium'.

Price/Cost

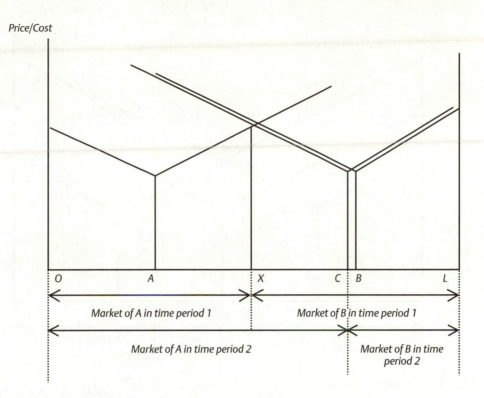

FIG. 1.17 The Hotelling location game

The locational result in which both firms are located at the centre of the market is the Nash equilibrium for this particular locational game. Consequently, once the firms reach this point they no longer continue to move. This is the Hotelling result. The details of this are given in Appendix 1.4.

At the conclusion of the Hotelling game we see that the market share of both firms located at X will be half of the market, exactly the same as at the start of the location game. However, from Figure 1.18 we see that the Hotelling result leads to a fall in consumer welfare relative to the original situation. Given that consumers all consume a fixed quantity per time period of the good produced by firms A and B, there is no substitution effect between the goods produced by firms A and B and other consumption goods. Therefore, the change in the delivered prices at the each location will accurately reflect the change in welfare of the consumers at each location. The net effect of these welfare gains and losses can be represented by the areas under the delivered price curves, which are arrived at by comparing the delivered prices at the respective locations at the start and the end of the Hotelling location game. The consumers who are located in the centre of the market benefit by generally reduced delivered prices, represented by *egjh* in Figure 1.18, whereas those located at the edges of the market lose by generally higher delivered prices, represented by (*defc*) + (*jklm*) in Figure 1.18. The gain in lower prices for the central consumers is outweighed by the

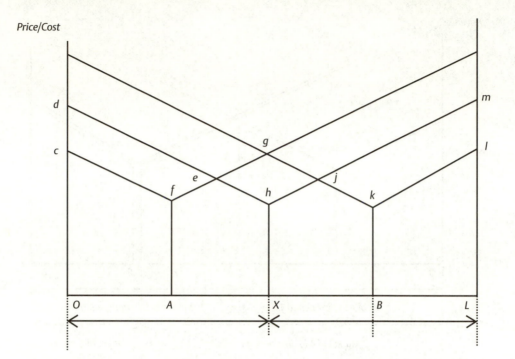

Price/Cost

FIG. 1.18 The welfare implications of the Hotelling result

increase in prices for the more peripheral consumers. The net effect is therefore a social welfare loss.

In one-dimensional space discussed here the Hotelling result holds for two firms. Meanwhile, in the two-dimensional case the Hotelling result holds for the case of three firms. However, beyond these numbers, there is no stable equilibrium result as firms keep changing their location. Moreover, even in the one-dimensional case, the Hotelling result only holds as long as the firms do not compete in terms of prices. If price competition is also a possibility, there is no Hotelling result (d'Aspremont *et al.* 1979). In Figure 1.19, we can consider the situation where firm *A* lowers its production price marginally in time period 1 when both firms are located at *X*. In time period 2 firm *A* gains all of the market. From our Cournot conjectures, firm *B* now assumes that firm *A* will maintain both its new lower price and its location at *X*. Therefore in time period 3 firm *B* also lowers its market price below that of firm *A*, and now gains all of the market. This process will continue and the long-run Nash equilibrium of this price war is that both firms will end up selling at zero profit while still being located at point *X*.

If the production costs are not zero, but rather are positive, the long-run result of this co-location competition will be to drive prices down to the marginal costs of production, which is the typical equilibrium result of a competitive market. However, the Hotelling model is implicitly about monopoly power, with firms able to use location as a means of generating monopoly power over a certain portion of their market. As we see in Chapter 2, the greater is their localized monopoly power, the greater will be the possibilities for

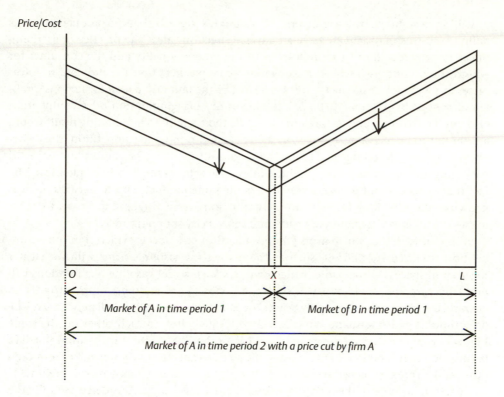

FIG. 1.19 The effect of price competition on the Hotelling result

the firm to raise additional revenues by employing monopoly practices such as price discrimination. Therefore, in order to generate localized monopoly power, as prices spiral downwards due to the Bertrand problem, each firm has some incentive to move away from its competitor in order to maintain monopoly power, and consequently positive profits, over some of the market area. However, neither firm has an incentive to move away first, because in doing so, the other firm will then be able to maintain its current prices at the centre of the market and dominate a larger market area than the firm which moved away from the centre. Therefore, unless there is some way in which the firms can mutually agree to move away from each other, a price war becomes inevitable with disastrous consequences for both firms. The relationship between the co-location of competing activities and the problem of a price war is known as the 'Bertrand problem'.

Competitor firms will consequently only locate next to each other in situations in which price competition is ruled out either by mutual agreement or by other forms of non-price competition. Yet, in these types of non-price competitive situations, the spatial clustering of competitor firms is a natural process. Many types of shops and showrooms, for example, such as those for clothing, electronics goods, automobiles, restaurants, and furniture, compete in industries dominated by non-price competition. In these industries prices are used to indicate product quality, and to indicate the types of consumers for whom the good is intended. As such, prices in these industries tend to be fixed. Firms are unwilling to compete by lowering prices because this suggests that the product quality is falling, and this may actually have an adverse effect on sales. The practice of ascribing prices to products in order to indicate both the product quality and the consumer for whom the product is intended is known as 'price placing', and the problem of lower prices implying lower product quality is related to the famous 'market for lemons' problem described by Akerlof (1970). At the same time, engaging in non-price competition also implies that the products are not identical, and therefore the Hotelling result would appear not to be relevant. However, in many cases of non-price competition, the differences between the products are largely superficial, involving primarily differences in packaging and appearance. The products in essence will essentially still be identical. The fact that firms attempt to make more or less the same products appear very different is known as the 'Hotelling Paradox'. In these situations, firms will tend to cluster together in space. This is exactly how retail parks and central city shopping areas arise.

On the other hand, where firms produce identical products in which non-price competition is extremely difficult, such as the market for gasoline, firms will not cluster together in space. Oil companies which own or franchise out gasoline retail stations will mutually agree not to locate their outlets too close to their competitors, in order to guarantee some market monopoly power for each station in its immediate vicinity. The only time in which gasoline stations will be located close to each other on the same highway is where they are separated from each other by a central reservation, median barrier, or major junction. In these cases, the stations are effectively separated from each other and customers denied the choice between the stations, because drivers are unable easily to switch sides of the road. Therefore, the stations can be considered as not being located together, but rather located away from each other.

The Hotelling result therefore provides us with two important sets of analytical conclusions. First, for competitor firms producing the same type of product and which also engage in non-price competition, the spatial competition for markets may encourage such firms to locate next to each other. In other words, spatial industrial clustering can arise naturally where price competition is not paramount. This is particularly important in many examples of retailing. Moreover, in this situation, the market will be split more or less equally between all of the firms in the spatial cluster. This ensures that no firm will be any worse off than its competitor due to an inferior location, a point we will discuss in section 1.5. On the other hand, for firms which produce more or less identical products for which non-price competition is very difficult to engage in, and in which there are no information problems, spatial competition will encourage such firms to move away from each other. The result of this process is industrial dispersion. Secondly, from a welfare point of view, consumers located close to a spatial cluster of firms will tend to experience a welfare gain relative to those located at a great distance away. The reason for this is that the costs of consuming the goods produced by the firms will tend to be much lower for those who are located close to the firms than for those who are located at a distance away. This is an important observation concerning agglomeration economies, a topic which we will discuss in the next chapter.

When applying these insights of the Hotelling framework to the real world, however, these two observations must be interpreted with caution, because there are some other situations in which price competition and spatial clustering are compatible. This is the case where prices are not predictable and are continually changing, such as in the case of many food markets or gambling activities. In these situations, although price competition is very keen, firms may gain from either short-term first mover advantages, or alternatively customer inertia in the face of rapid and frequent price changes. The co-location of retailing activities in this case is justified, as with the case of non-price retail competition, because this may encourage customers to buy more goods in general than they would otherwise if they were not presented with a broad range of consumption alternatives and the relevant price information about them. As such, all firms in the cluster are expected to gain, and co-location ensures that all firms benefit more or less equally. These arguments are related primarily to the questions of information, clustering, and externalities discussed initially in section 1.5 and at length in Chapter 2.

One final point concerning this Palander and Hotelling type of spatial market analysis is the criticism that in many real-world cases, individual firms charge the same delivered price for a given product at all locations. As such, spatial markets are not divided up according to delivered prices which vary with location. On the other hand, where delivered prices are invariant with respect to distance within a given market area, this implies that the marginal profitability of each delivery will be different according to the location of the customer. This is because the transport costs of outputs must be absorbed by the firm, thereby reducing the net marginal profits from sales as the delivery distance increases. In other words, the profits associated with deliveries to nearby customers will be much higher than those for deliveries to distant customers. As such, for any given spatial distribution of markets, the location of the firm will still determine the overall profitability of the firm. Moreover, as we see in Appendix 1.3 and Appendix 3.4, even for uniform delivered prices, firms are able to employ changes in the quality of service, such as changes in delivery frequencies, in order to mimic the spatial price effects of situations in which customers pay the transport charges in addition to the quoted source prices.

1.5 Behavioural Theories of Firm Location

The models discussed so far rely on the assumption that 'rational' firms will aim to use their location behaviour in order to maximize their profits. We have also assumed that the information available to the firms is sufficient for them to do this. However, in reality the information available to firms is often rather limited. Moreover, different firms will often have different information available to them. For this reason, some commentators have argued that firms cannot and do not make decisions in order to maximize their profits. Rather, they argue that firms make decisions in order to achieve alternative goals, other than simply profit maximization. Therefore, from the perspective of location theory, this critique might suggest that the underlying motivation of our models would need to be reconsidered. The critique has three themes, namely bounded rationality, conflicting goals, and relocation costs. The first two themes can be grouped under the general heading of *Behavioural Theories*, and were not originally directed at location models in particular. The third theme is essentially a spatial question.

The arguments concerning 'bounded rationality' are most closely associated with Simon (1952, 1959). This critique concerns the fact that firms in the real world face limited information, and this limited information itself limits firms' ability to be 'rational' in the sense assumed in microeconomics textbooks. These arguments are a more general critique of rationality within microeconomics as a whole. However, they have been argued to be particularly appropriate to the question of industrial location behaviour. The reason is that information concerning space and location is very limited, due to the inherent heterogeneity of land, real estate, and local economic environments. Therefore, when considering location issues, it would appear that the ability of the firm to be 'rational' is very much 'bounded' by the limited information available to it. In these circumstances, decisions guided by straightforward profit-maximization behaviour appear to be beyond the ability of the firm. Therefore, location models based on this assumption seem to oversimplify the location issue. Location behaviour may be determined primarily by other objectives than simply profit maximization.

Where firms face limited information, Baumol (1959) has argued that firms will focus on sales revenue maximization as the short-run objective of their decision-making. One reason for this is that sales revenue maximization implies the maximum market share for the firm in the short run. Where information is limited, current market share is deemed by many observers to be the best indicator of a firm's long-run performance, because it provides a measure of the monopoly power of the firm. The logic of this approach is that the greater is the market share of the firm, the greater is the current monopoly power of the firm, and the greater will be the firm's long-run ability to deter potential competitors through defensive tactics such as limit-pricing and cross-subsidizing. From the perspective of location models, this may imply that the firm will make location decisions primarily in order to ensure maximum sales revenues rather than maximum profits. In the Hotelling model above these two objectives coincide. However, if the costs of production or transportation faced by the firm were to vary with location along the line *OL*, as they do in the Weber and Moses-type models, the two objectives of sales maximization and profit maximization may not coincide at the same location point in the Hotelling model. The eventual location result will therefore depend on which particular performance measure the firm adopts and chooses to maximize.

The second critique of profit maximization as the decision-making goal of the firm is that of 'conflicting goals'. This critique is most closely associated with the work of Cyert and March (1963). The argument here is that in a world of imperfect information, the separation of ownership from decision-making in most major modern firms means that business objectives are frequently pursued which are different from simply profit maximization. Only shareholders have a desire for maximum profits in the short run. On the other hand, in modern multi-activity, multi-level, multi-plant, and multinational firm organizations, corporate decisions are the result of the many individual decisions made by a complex hierarchy of people, each with particular business objectives, and many of which are different from profit maximization. The reason is that the performance of different employees within a company is measured in different ways. For example, the directors' performance may be evaluated primarily by the firm's market share, whereas the sales manager's performance may be evaluated on sales growth. Similarly, the production manager's performance may be evaluated primarily by inventory throughput efficiency, whereas the personnel officer may be evaluated according to the number of days lost through industrial disputes. Given that each of these different decision-makers is evaluated on different criteria, the success, promotion, and consequently the wages earned by each of these workers will be evaluated differently. Therefore, the objectives pursued by different employees may be quite different from profit maximization. Under these conditions, the 'conflicting goals' critique suggests that firms will aim to 'satisfice'. In other words, the firm will aim to achieve a satisfactory level of performance across a range of measures. In particular, the firm will initially aim to achieve a level of profit sufficient both to avoid shareholder interference in directors' activities and also to avoid the threat of a takeover. Once this objective is achieved, the other various goals of the firm can be satisfied. For example, the firm may aim to achieve market share levels as high as possible without jeopardizing the efficiency cost gains associated with production and logistics operations. Equally, employees' pay may be increased in order to encourage firm loyalty. The point here is that the overall objective of the firm can be specified in various ways.

In Figure 1.20, the firm's total profit function $T\pi$ is constructed as the difference between the total revenue function TR and the total cost function TC. The firm may choose to produce at output levels Q_1, Q_2, and Q_3, which represent the minimum cost output, the maximum profit output, and the maximum revenue output levels, respectively. All of these levels of output produce a profit level sufficient to maintain a firm's independence π_s, but only one of these output levels Q_2 is the profit-maximization level of output.

From the point of view of location, if we have a set of spatial total cost and revenue curves, such as those described by Figure 1.20, the firm will make different location

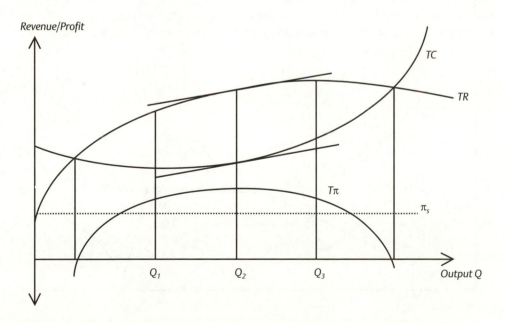

FIG. 1.20 Profit-maximizing, revenue-maximizing, and profit-satisficing

decisions, according to whether the firm is aiming to maximize profits in the short run or whether it is aiming to earn satisfactory profits in the short run along with achieving some other goals. For example, in Figure 1.21, if the firm is aiming to maximize profits in the short run it will locate at point P. On the other hand, if it is aiming to maximize sales it will locate at S, and if it is aiming to minimize production costs and to maximize production efficiency it will locate at C. If the firm had perfect information regarding these different spatial cost and revenue curves, we can argue that the firm will always move to point P. However, behavioural theories assume that information is imperfect. Given the limited information available and the conflicting goals within the organization, the actual location behaviour of the firm will depend on which is the particular dominant objective of the firm.

The third critique of the classical and neoclassical location models comes from the question of relocation costs. Relocation costs are the costs incurred every time a firm relocates. The models described above all assume that location is a costless exercise. However, relocation costs can be very significant, comprising the costs of the real-estate site search and acquisition, the dismantling, moving, and reconstruction of existing facilities, the construction of new facilities, and the hiring and training of the new labour employed. These significant transactions costs, along with imperfect information and conflicting goals, will mean that firms are unlikely to move in response to small variations in factor prices or market revenues. In Figure 1.21, the areas in which positive profits are made, i.e. where $TR > TC$, are known as 'spatial margins of profitability' (Rawstron 1958), and are represented by the areas between locations a and b, c and d, and e and f. The relationship between marginal location change and the profitability of the firm in these areas is given by $\delta(TR - TC)/\delta\delta$, and this is represented by the differences in the slopes of the spatial revenue and spatial cost functions as location changes. In the spatial margins of profitability in which the slopes of the spatial revenue and spatial cost functions are very shallow, the marginal benefit to the firm of relocation will be very

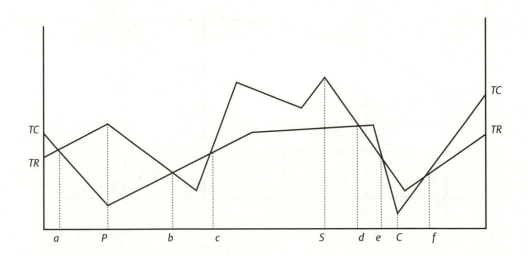

FIG. 1.21 Spatial cost and revenue curves

low. Therefore, in the presence of high relocation costs the firm will not move to a superior location even if the firm knows which alternative is superior. In conditions of imperfect information and bounded rationality, conflicting goals, and significant relocation costs, the behavioural approach would argue that once a firm has chosen a location, the firm will tend to maintain its location as long as profits are positive, and not use relocation as a competitive weapon. Rather, the firm will attempt to reorganize its factor allocations and activities between its current set of existing plants. At the same time, it will focus primarily on other price and non-price issues as competitive weapons, and the relocation of a plant, or the reorganization of multi-plant activities which involves either the closing or opening of a plant, will only be a last-resort strategy. On the other hand, where relocation costs are insignificant, the firm will be take advantage of spatial revenue and spatial cost differences and will be able to move to superior locations as a competitive strategy.

All of the behavioural critiques suffer from the weakness that, unlike the classical and neoclassical location models, the behavioural theories do not of themselves indicate why a firm chooses a particular location in the first place. In this sense the behavioural approach is not prescriptive. However, the classical models do need to be interpreted in the light of the behavioural critique of bounded rationality, imperfect information, conflicting goals, and relocation costs, as these are all features particularly characteristic of the spatial economy. This can be done by considering the evolutionary argument of Alchian (1950).

Alchian's argument is that the behaviour of firms in conditions of uncertainty can be understood by discussing the relationship between a firm and its environment, whereby a firm's environment is understood to encompass all the agents, information, and institutions competing and collaborating in the particular set of markets in which the firm operates. In Alchian's argument, we can characterize the uncertain economy by two broad types of environments. One is an 'adoptive' environment and the other is an 'adaptive' environment. These two classifications are not mutually exclusive, but serve as the two extreme stylized types, between which the real economy will exist.

In the 'adoptive' environment, all firms are more or less identical in that no firm has any particular or systematic information advantage over any other firms. The results of the competitive process will imply *ex post* that some firms will be successful while others will not, although *ex ante* no firms had any a priori knowledge that their products or techniques would be superior to those of their competitors. This characterization of the economy is Darwinian, in that the environment 'adopts' the firms which were better suited to the needs of the economy, even though the firms had no particular knowledge beforehand that this was the case. In statistical terms, in any given time period in the 'adoptive' environment, the probability of a particular single firm making a successful strategic decision is identical to that of all the other individual firms.

On the other hand, in the 'adaptive' environment, some individual firms are able to gather and analyse market information, simply by reason of their size. Large firms in general are able to utilize resources in order to acquire and process information relating to their market environment, and the purpose of these information-gathering activities by the firms is to subsequently use the information to their own advantage, relative to their competitors. In statistical terms, therefore, in any given time period in the 'adaptive' environment, the probability of a particular firm making a profitable strategic decision is increased by reason of its size.

In the real world of heterogeneous firms and imperfect information, smaller firms will tend to perceive themselves to be at an information disadvantage relative to larger firms. Therefore they will tend to make decisions which mimic or dovetail with those of the larger firms, in matters such as styles, protocols, formats, and technology. In part this is because they perceive the market leaders to be the best barometers of market conditions, and also because the behaviour of the market leaders itself often contributes significantly to the overall economic environment simply by reason of their size. By copying the behaviour of the larger firms the small firms therefore perceive that they will maximize the likelihood of their own success. The result is that large firms tend to overcome uncertainty by information-gathering and analysis, and small firms tend to overcome uncertainty by imitation.

This type of leader–follower behaviour is common in models of oligopoly and uncertainty. However, this behaviour is particularly pertinent to questions of location. In environments of uncertainty, larger firms will generally have the information and financial resources to make more considered location decisions than small firms. Major firms will be able to make location decisions more akin to those described by the Weber, Moses, and Hotelling models, given that they will generally have sufficient resources to evaluate the cost and revenue implications of their location choice. These large firms will attempt to make rational and optimal decisions, and the results of their location choices can be analysed by the types of classical and neoclassical models described above. On the other hand, small firms will generally be located where their founders were initially resident. There will have been no explicit initial location decision as such, when the firm began operating. Yet, over time, competition between firms will be partly a result of spatial differences in costs and revenues, and the relationship between profitability and location will eventually become a decision-making issue. In subsequent location decisions, many small firms will tend to choose locations close to the major market leaders for the reasons outlined by Alchian. Imitation therefore also takes place in terms of spatial behaviour. For firms which are risk-averse this is also a particularly good strategy, because as we see from the Hotelling model, locating close to competitor firms ensures that an individual firm's market share is no lower than that of an equivalent firm. Hotelling-type behaviour is therefore common for small firms clustering around major firms.

1.6 **Conclusions**

The foregoing discussions suggest that we can use classical and neoclassical models of location to consider the spatial behaviour of large firms, or firms in environments with good information and low relocation costs. At the same time, the discussion of the behavioural critique suggests that the leader–follower behaviour typical of many industries will tend to encourage small firms to cluster together in space close to larger firms. This process of industrial clustering, however, will lead to an increased demand for local land; consequently, local real-estate prices will tend to increase, as will local labour prices. These increases in the prices of local factor inputs will reduce profits, *ceteris paribus*, thereby reducing the attractiveness of the area as a location for the firms. This raises the question how long will the cluster of firms continue to exist profitably in the area? This question of industrial clustering is the topic of the next chapter, in which we discuss agglomeration economies, the growth of cities and urban hierarchies, and centre–periphery relationships.

Discussion questions

1 How does the location of input sources and output markets determine the location behaviour of the firm?

2 To what extent are firm-locational changes dependent on the substitution characteristics of the firm's production function?

3 In what ways can space confer monopoly power?

4 What role can location play in the competitive strategy of firms, and how are location and price strategies interrelated?

5 What role do logistics costs play in determining location behaviour?

6 What insights are provided for industrial location analysis by behavioural theories of firm behaviour?

Appendix 1.1 **The One-Dimension Location Problem**

Within the Weber framework, we can summarize the relative strength of the transportation 'pull' towards any particular input source point. If at any particular location, $\Delta(m_1 t_1 d_1) > - \Delta(m_2 t_2 d_2)$ as the firm moves away from input source 1 and towards input source 2 (where Δ represents a marginal change), the firm should move towards input source 1. This is because the marginal increase in the total transport costs for the shipment of input 1 is greater than the marginal fall in the total transport costs for the shipment of input 2. Alternatively, if $\Delta(m_1 t_1 d_1) < - \Delta(m_2 t_2 d_2)$, the firm will move closer towards input source 2. In the situation where $\Delta(m_1 t_1 d_1) = - \Delta(m_2 t_2 d_2)$, the firm can move in either direction, and will be indifferent between adjacent locations.

Within the Weber triangle, we can imagine a situation where the output good is weightless, such as in the case of the electricity generated by a power-station which consumes inputs of coal and coke from M_1 and M_2, respectively. In this case, the plant will be constrained to locate along the line joining M_1 and M_2. Here, the location problem becomes a one-dimensional problem. Initially we can analyse the situation where the transport rates are constant.

In this situation, any small change, denoted here by D, in the input shipment distance

d_1, will be associated with an equal and opposite change in the input shipment distance d_2. If $\Delta(m_1t_1d_1) > -\Delta(m_2t_2d_2)$, at any location along the line joining M_1 and M_2, as the firm moves away from input source 1, the firm will locate at M_1. Alternatively, if $\Delta(m_1t_1d_1) < -\Delta(m_2t_2d_2)$, at any location along the line joining M_1 and M_2, as the firm moves away from input source 1, the firm will locate at M_2. The reason for this is that if m_1, t_1, m_2, and t_2 are fixed, the only cause of change in the total transport costs for each input shipment is the change in the relative distances, which are always equal and opposite in this case. Therefore, the inequality which holds at any particular point on the line M_1M_2, will hold at all points on the line. This will encourage the firm to continue to move in the same direction. The optimum location behaviour of the firm is therefore to locate at the particular end-point M_1 or M_2 which has the lowest total transport costs. As we see in Figure A.1.1.1, in a one-dimensional space such as the line joining M_1 and M_2, where transport rates are constant, there is always an end-point optimal location solution, in this case at M_2. In microeconomics this is called a corner solution, because the optimum location will never be between, or interior to, the end points M_1 and M_2.

The situation becomes somewhat more complicated where the transport rates change with the distance of haulage. Transport rates per tonne-kilometre normally fall with increasing haulage distance, implying that the total input transport costs increase less than proportionately with the distance. On the other hand, in some circumstances transport rates per tonne-kilometre increase with distance, implying that total transport costs increase more than proportionately with distance. In these situations, we must also consider the effect of the change in transport rates with changes in distance, as the distance itself changes. As above, an optimal location for the firm will only be at an interior location, i.e. between the end points M_1 and M_2, where the marginal increase in the total transport costs for the shipment of input 1, as we move away from M_1, is equal to the marginal fall in the total transport costs for the shipment of input 2. If we denote the total transport costs associated with the input shipment of good 1 as $TC_1 = (m_1t_1d_1)$,

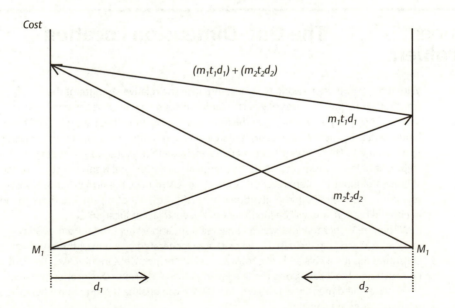

FIG. A.1.1.1 One-dimensional location problem with constant transport rates

and those associated with the input shipment of good 2 as $TC_2 = (m_2 t_2 d_2)$, the condition for an optimum location internal to M_1 and M_2, is where $\Delta TC_1 = - \Delta TC_2$, for a small location change. In order to identify such a situation it is necessary to use calculus to observe the first derivative of each of the relationships between total transport costs and distance in the situation where transport rates vary with haulage distance. By partial differentiation

$$\delta(TC_1)/\delta d_1 = m_1(t_1 + d_1(\delta t_1/\delta d_1))$$

and:

$$\delta(TC_2)/\delta d_2 = m_2(t_2 + d_2(\delta t_2/\delta d_2)).$$

An interior optimum location is possible where

$$m_1(t_1 + d_1(\delta t_1/\delta d_1)) = - m_2(t_2 + d_2(\delta t_2/\delta d_2)).$$

$$m_1 t_1 + m_2 t_2 = - (d_1(\delta t_1/\delta d_1) + d_2(\delta t_2/\delta d_2)).$$

Given that the left-hand side is positive, the right-hand side must also be positive for an interior optimum location. This implies that at least one of the terms $(\delta t_1/\delta d_1)$ or $(\delta t_2/\delta d_2)$ must be positive. In other words, the marginal change in transport costs for at least one of the input goods must be increasing with distance. The transport costs associated with at least one of the inputs must be increasing more than proportionately with distance, as distance increases, in order for there to be an optimum location between M_1 and M_2. We can see this in Figure A.1.1.2 where the interior optimum is at d^*.

On the other hand, if transport rates exhibit economies of distance, i.e. $(\Delta t_1/\Delta d_1)$ and $(\Delta t_2/\Delta d_2)$ are both negative, or fixed transport rates, i.e. $(\Delta t_1/\Delta d_1)$ and $(\Delta t_2/\Delta d_2)$ are zero, there is no interior solution. As we see in Figures A.1.1.3 and A.1.1.1, in these cases, which are the usual two situations, the optimal location will always be at an end-point such as M_1 and M_2. In A.1.1.3 the optimum location is at M_1 whereas in A.1.1.1 it is at M_2.

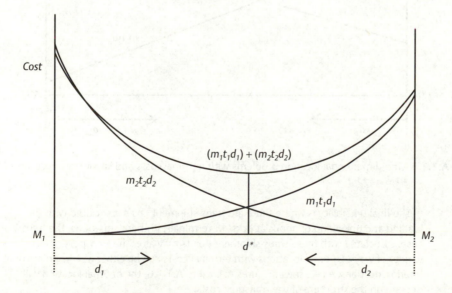

FIG. A.1.1.2 One-dimensional location problem with increasing transport rates

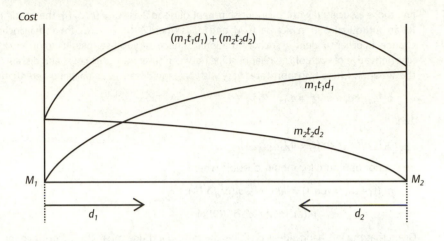

FIG. A.1.1.3 One-dimensional location problem with decreasing transport rates

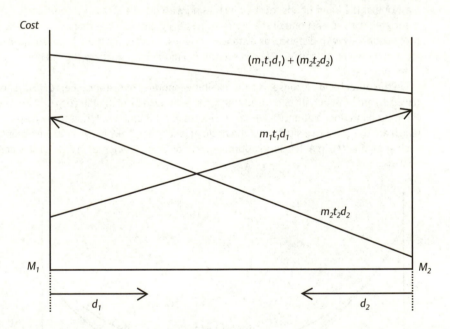

FIG. A.1.1.4 One-dimensional location problems with terminal costs and linear transport rates

The final possibility is where there are trans-shipment costs associated with the loading and unloading of goods at ports or terminals. In these situations, the 'terminal' costs associated with these trans-shipment points may alter the transport rates in a variety of ways. Optimal locations with terminal costs can be either at end-points or at interior locations. As we see in Figures A.1.1.4 to A.1.1.6, the optimal location will depend on the structure of the transport costs.

In Figure A.1.1.4. the transport rates are constant, although not equal to each other, and both transport cost functions exhibit terminal costs. In this case, the optimal location which minimizes total transport costs is at the end point M_2.

In Figure A.1.1.5, the transport rates are falling with distance, such that total transport costs are concave with distance, although they are not equal to each other. Both transport cost functions exhibit terminal costs. In this case, the optimal location which minimizes total transport costs is at the end point M_1.

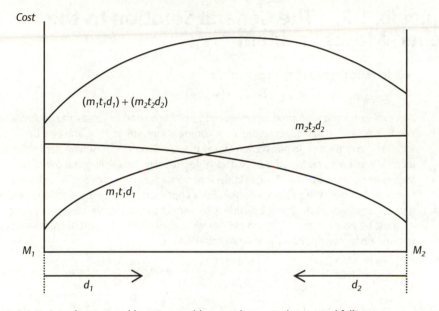

FIG. A.1.1.5 One-dimensional location problems with terminal costs and falling transport rates

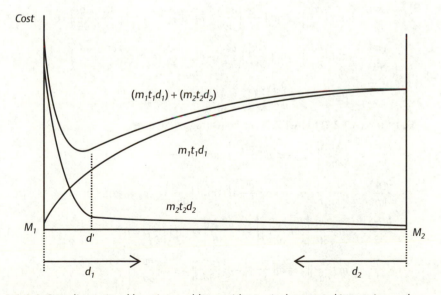

FIG. A.1.1.6 One-dimensional location problems with terminal costs and increasing and decreasing transport rates.

In Figure A.1.1.6, one of the transport rates is falling with distance, whereas the other is increasing with distance. Both transport cost functions exhibit terminal costs. In this case, the optimal location which minimizes total transport costs is at the interior location d'. The classic proof of the one-dimensional location problem is given by Sakashita (1968).

Appendix 1.2.   **The General Solution to the Weber–Moses Problem**

We can write the profit (π) function of the firm as

$$\pi = p_3 m_3 - (p_1 + t_1 d_1)m_1 - (p_2 + t_2 d_2)m_2 - t_3 d_3 m_3. \qquad \text{(A.1.2.1)}$$

Any profit maximization production-location point will need to satisfy the optimization conditions both with respect to the input combinations, m_1 and m_2, and also the locational coordinates. In our Weber–Moses triangle (Figure 1.8) we can define the locational coordinates in terms of two variables, namely the angle q and the output shipment distance d_3. Any changes in the input distances d_1 and d_2 can be defined in terms of changes in these two variables. For an optimum location-production result, the partial derivatives of the profit function with respect to the four variables m_1, m_2, θ, and d_3, must be equal to zero. Following Miller and Jensen (1978), by partial differentiation, the first-order conditions for profit maximization are

$$\frac{\partial(\pi)}{\partial m_1} = -(p_1 + t_1 d_1) - m_1 d_1 \left(\frac{\partial t_1}{\partial m_1}\right) - t_3 d_3 \left(\frac{\partial m_3}{\partial m_1}\right) - m_3 d_3 \left(\frac{\partial t_3}{\partial m_3}\right)\left(\frac{\partial m_3}{\partial m_1}\right) = 0. \qquad \text{(A.1.2.2)}$$

$$\frac{\partial(\pi)}{\partial m_2} = -(p_2 + t_2 d_2) - m_2 d_2 \left(\frac{\partial t_2}{\partial m_2}\right) - t_3 d_3 \left(\frac{\partial m_3}{\partial m_2}\right) - m_3 d_3 \left(\frac{\partial t_3}{\partial m_3}\right)\left(\frac{\partial m_3}{\partial m_2}\right) = 0. \qquad \text{(A.1.2.3)}$$

$$\frac{\partial(\pi)}{\partial \theta} = -m_1 t_1 \left(\frac{\partial d_1}{\partial \theta}\right) - m_1 d_1 \left(\frac{\partial t_1}{\partial d_1}\right)\left(\frac{\partial d_1}{\partial \theta}\right) - m_2 t_2 \left(\frac{\partial d_2}{\partial \theta}\right) - m_2 d_2 \left(\frac{\partial t_3}{\partial d_2}\right)\left(\frac{\partial d_2}{\partial \theta}\right) = 0. \qquad \text{(A.1.2.4)}$$

$$\frac{\partial(\pi)}{\partial d_3} = -m_1 t_1 \left(\frac{\partial d_1}{\partial d_3}\right) - m_1 d_1 \left(\frac{\partial t_1}{\partial d_1}\right)\left(\frac{\partial d_1}{\partial d_3}\right) - m_2 t_2 \left(\frac{\partial d_2}{\partial d_3}\right) - m_2 d_2 \left(\frac{\partial t_2}{\partial d_2}\right)\left(\frac{\partial d_2}{\partial d_3}\right)$$

$$- m_3 t_3 - m_3 d_3 \left(\frac{\partial t_3}{\partial d_3}\right) = 0. \qquad \text{(A.1.2.5)}$$

Equations (A.1.2.2) to (A.1.2.5) can be rearranged to give

$$\frac{\partial(\pi)}{\partial m_1} = -\left(\frac{\partial m_3}{\partial m_1}\right)\left[t_3 d_3 + m_3 d_3 \left(\frac{\partial t_3}{\partial m_3}\right)\right] - m_1 d_1 \left(\frac{\partial t_1}{\partial m_1}\right) - (p_1 + t_1 d_1) = 0. \qquad \text{(A.1.2.6)}$$

$$\frac{\partial(\pi)}{\partial m_2} = -\left(\frac{\partial m_3}{\partial m_2}\right)\left[t_3 d_3 + m_3 d_3 \left(\frac{\partial t_3}{\partial m_3}\right)\right] - m_2 d_2 \left(\frac{\partial t_2}{\partial m_2}\right) - (p_2 + t_2 d_2) = 0. \qquad \text{(A.1.2.7)}$$

$$\frac{\partial(\pi)}{\partial \theta} = -m_1 \left(\frac{\partial d_1}{\partial \theta}\right)\left[t_1 d_1 \left(\frac{\partial t_1}{\partial d_1}\right)\right] - m_2 \left(\frac{\partial d_2}{\partial \theta}\right)\left[t_2 + d_2 \left(\frac{\partial t_2}{\partial \theta}\right)\right] = 0. \qquad \text{(A.1.2.8)}$$

$$\frac{\partial(\pi)}{\partial d_3} = -m_1 \left(\frac{\partial d_1}{\partial d_3}\right)\left[t_1 + d_1 \left(\frac{\partial t_1}{\partial d_1}\right)\right] - m_2 \left(\frac{\partial d_2}{\partial d_3}\right)\left[t_2 + d_2 \left(\frac{\partial t_2}{\partial d_1}\right)\right]$$

$$- m_3 \left[t_3 + d_3 \left(\frac{\partial t_3}{\partial d_3}\right)\right] = 0. \qquad \text{(A.1.2.9)}$$

Equations (A.1.2.6) and (A.1.2.7) together define the production relationships at the optimum between each of the inputs and the output. Meanwhile equations (A.1.2.8) and (A.1.2.9) together define the location of the firm at the optimum. To understand the production function characteristics which will ensure that the optimum location of the firm is independent of the level of output, we need to observe the conditions under which the marginal rate of substitution between the inputs remains constant for all levels of output. For an optimum location which is independent of the level of output, equations (A.1.2.8) and (A.1.2.9) must be satisfied because the firm will not move. Therefore, we need only observe the production relationships. By rearranging equations (A.1.2.6) and (A.1.2.7) we arrive at

$$\frac{\partial m_3}{\partial m_1} = \frac{-m_1 d_1 \left(\frac{\partial t_1}{\partial m_1} \right) - (p_1 + t_1 d_1)}{\left[t_3 d_3 + m_3 d_3 \left(\frac{\partial t_3}{\partial m_3} \right) \right]}$$

(A.1.2.10)

and

$$\frac{\partial m_3}{\partial m_2} = \frac{-m_2 d_2 \left(\frac{\partial t_2}{\partial m_2} \right) - (p_2 + t_2 d_2)}{\left[t_3 d_3 + m_3 d_3 \left(\frac{\partial t_3}{\partial m_3} \right) \right]}.$$

(A.1.2.11)

The term $(\delta m_3/\delta m_1)$ is the marginal product of input 1 at the optimum, and the term $(\delta m_3/\delta m_2)$ is the marginal product of input 2 at the optimum. Dividing (A.1.2.11) by (A.1.2.10) gives us an expression for the marginal rate of substitution between the two inputs at the optimum, thus

$$\frac{\partial m_3/\partial m_2}{\partial m_3/\partial m_1} = \frac{-m_2 d_2 \left(\frac{\partial t_2}{\partial m_2} \right) - (p_2 + t_2 d_2)}{-m_1 d_1 \left(\frac{\partial t_1}{\partial m_1} \right) - (p_1 + t_1 d_1)}.$$

(A.1.2.12)

The expression (A.1.2.12) is constant, i.e. the marginal rate of substitution between the inputs is constant, in the case where there are no economies of scale in transportation. In this situation, the ratio $(\delta t_1/\delta m_1) = (\delta t_2/\delta m_2) = 0$, and the expression reduces to

$$\frac{\partial m_3/\partial m_1}{(p_1 + t_1 d_1)} = \frac{\partial m_3/\partial m_2}{(p_2 + t_2 d_2)}$$

(A.1.2.13)

In other words, the marginal product of input 1 divided by the *delivered* price of input 1 is equal to the marginal product of input 2 divided by the *delivered* price of input 2. These conditions are the spatial equivalent of standard microeconomic efficiency conditions, and this general Weber–Moses result has also been shown to hold in the case of multiple inputs and outputs (Eswaran *et al.* 1981). Note that economies of distance play no role in the result, because once the firm is located at the optimum location, the distance relationships are all unchanging. Production functions which satisfy the conditions here are functions which are linear or which are homogeneous of degree one. On the other hand, in situations where transport rates exhibit economies of scale, the results of the Weber–Moses problem become much more restrictive.

Appendix 1.3   The Logistics-Costs Location-Production Model

An alternative broader specification of the distance costs associated with moving goods can be provided by including all of the inventory costs associated with the shipment of goods. The justification for this is that moving goods over space takes time, and between individual shipments, firms must hold inventories of goods to maintain supplies. The holding of these inventories itself incurs costs, so the firm must consider the relationship between the costs of moving goods, and the costs of not moving, i.e. holding inventories. If we include all of the costs associated with the holding of inventories plus the shipment of input good i over space, we can define the total logistics costs of the input shipments per time period as:

$$TLC_i = \frac{m_i}{Q_i}S_i + \frac{IQ_i(p_i + t_id_i)}{2} + m_it_id_i, \tag{A.1.3.1}$$

where the parameters m, p, t, d are the same as in the above sections, and Qi is the weight of an individual input shipment, Si is procurement costs of inputs, and I holding cost coefficient of input inventories.

The first terms on the right-hand side of (A.1.3.1) represents the ordering and procurement costs which are incurred each time an input shipment is received, but which are independent of the shipment size. In manufacturing firms, these costs will also include machinery set-up costs, and can be shown to be very significant. As these costs are independent of the shipment size but are incurred each time an input shipment is received, these total ordering costs are a multiple of the shipment frequency, i.e. the number of shipments per time period. The second term on the right-hand side represents the inventory capital holding costs, which are a function of the average value of inventories held per time period. These costs are the capital interest plus insurance costs associated with holding inventories. Assuming we consume inventories at a constant rate, and that stocks are replenished in a timely manner such that our inventory levels stay constant, these costs can be seen to be a function of the delivered price of the goods. In other words, inventory costs are a function of transport costs. Finally, the third term on the right-hand side of (A.1.3.1) represents the familiar transport costs term used above.

Using a similar logic we can also define the logistics-costs associated with shipments of output goods, denoted with the subscript 'o', as

$$TLC_0 = \frac{m_0}{Q_0}S_0 + \frac{IQ_0(p_0 - t_0d_{0i})}{2} + m_0t_0d_0. \tag{A.1.3.2}$$

In this case, the capital costs associated with holding inventories are the opportunity costs of output revenue which are incurred by not shipping outputs in a continuous manner and selling them at the market price of p_o.

For both input and output goods, the aim of the firm is to determine the optimum shipment size Q^* which minimizes the sum of the total logistics costs for any given locational arrangement of input supply points and output markets. However, this is not as straightforward as it might initially appear, because it can be shown that while the optimal shipment size Q^* is a function of the transport rates, transport rates are also a function of the optimal shipment size. In order to circumvent these problems, the definition of transport rates must be respecified to allow for discrete shipments. While the details of this problem are beyond the scope of this book (McCann 1993, 1998, 2001), it can be demonstrated under very general conditions that the optimal shipment size (McCann 2001), and therefore the optimal average weight of inventories $Q^*/2$ to be held, is a positive function of the distance of the shipment, and the transport costs associated with the shipment. This also implies that the ordering costs, which are an inverse multiple of the size of Q, are also a function of the transport costs. The combined sum of all the interrelated components of total logistics costs can be shown to be a concave function of distance transport costs (McCann 1998), with distance cost curves similar in shape to those in Figure A.1.1.5.

By employing this broader logistics-costs description of the costs associated with transporting goods over geographical distances, we can now re-evaluate the Weber–Moses problem within a logistics-costs framework. Under very general conditions (McCann 1993, 1998), we can show that there is no solution to the independent of output optimum location problem. Moreover, as we see in Figure A.1.3.1, as the value added by a firm increases, the optimum location of the firm K^* moves towards the market.

As the value added by the firm increases, or the higher up the input–output value-chain is the firm, the steeper is the negatively sloping inter-regional equilibrium wage gradient, which would allow a firm to move away from a central market point (McCann 1997, 1998). We can see this in Figure A.1.3.2, in which the point M represents a location containing both markets and input source points.

The inter-regional equilibrium wage gradient associated with total logistics costs, rather than simply transport costs, becomes steeper, i.e. it changes form R_1 to R_2, as the value added by the firm increases, or as the firm moves up the value-adding chain. In other words, in order to encourage a firm to move away from a Weber optimum location at M where wages are w_M, inter-regional wage differences will need to be greater in order for a high value-adding firm to relocate. On the other hand, a low value-adding firm, or a

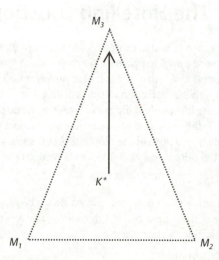

FIG. A.1.3.1 Logistics-costs optimum location and value added by the firm

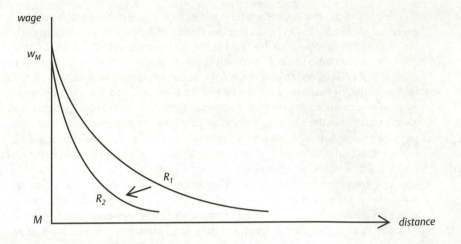

FIG. A.1.3.2 Inter-regional equilibrium wage gradient associated with logistics-costs

firm lower down the value-adding input–output chain, will be able to move in response to relatively minor inter-regional wage differences (McCann 1997, 1998). Moreover, in Appendix 3.4, knowing that the optimum shipment size Q^* is inversely related to the trip frequency f, we are able to show that the inter-regional equilibrium wage gradient must be convex with respect to distance, as in Figure A.1.3.2.

The overall location-production conclusions to come out of the logistics-costs approach to the Weber–Moses framework is therefore that high value-adding firms tend to be both more market-oriented, and much less responsive to regional wage differences, i.e. they are much less footloose, than low value-adding firms.

Appendix 1.4   **The Hotelling Location Game**

Before a Hotelling game of spatial competition takes place along a market OL, as we see in Figure A.1.4.1, we assume that we have two firms A and B, with A located to the left of B. The distance from O to A is denoted as a, and the distance from L to B is denoted as b. The distance from O to the market boundary is denoted as x', and the total distance OL is denoted as d. In order for this duopoly to exist there must be three conditions satisfied. The first condition is that a consumer located at point O must always buy from firm A. In other words, the delivered price of the output of A at O must always be less than the delivered price of the output of B at O. This can be written as

$$P_A + t_A a < P_B + t_B(d - b). \tag{A.1.4.1}$$

Secondly, a consumer located at point L must always buy from firm B. In other words, the delivered price of the output of B at L must always be less than the delivered price of the output of A at L. This can be written as

$$P_B + t_B b < P_B + t_A(d - a). \tag{A.1.4.2}$$

At the same time, thirdly, there must also be an indifferent consumer at a distance x'

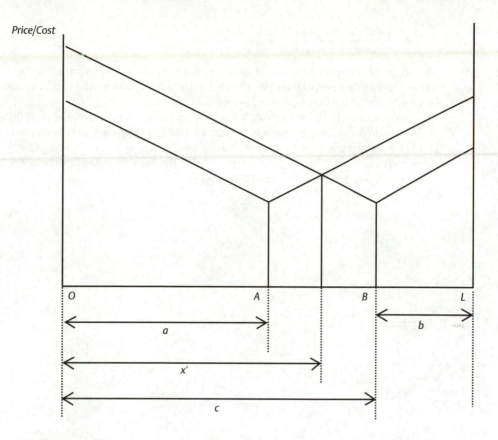

FIG. A.1.4.1 The Hotelling spatial framework

somewhere between A and B. For this indifferent consumer the delivered prices must be the same. In other words

$$P_A + t_A(x' - a) = P_B + t_B(d - b - x').$$

(A.1.4.3)

If we set $t_A = t_B$, then rearranging equation (A.1.4.3) gives

$$P_A - P_B + 2tx' - ta - td + tb = 0.$$

(A.1.4.4)

If the transport rates t_A and t_B for the two firms are the same, and the source prices, P_A and p_B, of the two firms are also the same, we have

$$x' = \frac{a + d - b}{2}.$$

(A. 1.4.5)

The value of x' given in equation (A.1.4.5) represents the size of the market captured by firm A, and the size of the market captured by firm B can thus be represented as

$$d - x' = d - \left(\frac{a + d - b}{2}\right) = \frac{b + d - a}{2}.$$

(A. 1.4.6)

Recalling from Figure A.1.4.1 that $c = (d - b)$, we can rewrite (A.1.4.5) as

$$x' = \frac{a + d - (d - c)}{2} = \frac{a + c}{2}$$

As such, if the transport rates are the same and also the product source prices are the same, the boundary between the two firms is exactly halfway between the two firms, and is independent of the transport rates, as we would expect.

For a given source production price P_A, known as a 'mill' price, the market revenue of firm A depends on maximizing the value of x'. From (A.1.4.5) and the arguments in section 1.4.1, we see that this is increased by increasing a and reducing b as much as possible, while still ensuring that firm A is to the left of firm B. This location change then triggers the leapfrogging behaviour described in section 1.4.1.

Chapter 2
The Spatial Distribution of Activities

2.1 Introduction

In the preceding chapter we discussed the theoretical issues which affect the location behaviour of the individual firm. Each of the models presented provides us with a way of analysing the particular microeconomic effects on firm location behaviour, of various influences such as transport costs, local factor prices, production and substitution possibilities, market structure, competition, and information. In our Weber and Moses location theory models, we saw that the optimum location of the firm can be either at an intermediate location, or alternatively at a location close to the market or the firm's suppliers, depending on the transport rates and the production relationships. The Hotelling model predicted that firms will cluster together in space for reasons of spatial competition only in situations where price competition is ruled out. Alternatively, behavioural models of uncertainty suggest that spatial clustering could be a rational response to spatial competition in conditions of uncertainty and information heterogeneity.

In reality the actual location behaviour of the firm is a result of a complex mix of each of these influences. Therefore, this still leaves us with the problem of determining which particular influences are actually the dominant influences in which situations. Unfortunately, without information on the individual firm and industry, however, the various microeconomic models above do not lead to any systematic conclusion as to whether firm optimal location behaviour is more likely to result in industrial clustering or industrial dispersion. Yet, in describing the general observable features of industrial location behaviour, two particular features stand out.

The first generally observed feature of industrial location behaviour is that most industrial activities tend to be clustered together in space. These clusters may take the form of industrial parks, small towns, or major cities, but the general observation appears to be true. Many productive and commercial activities do take place in the immediate vicinity of other such activities. This observation therefore raises the obvious question of why it is that activities are generally grouped together geographically. At the same time, as we have discussed in the previous chapter, not all activities take place in the same location. Some activities are generally dispersed over large areas, with goods being shipped generally over large distances. But the general observation still holds that activities are usually clustered together in space.

The second generally observed feature of industrial location behaviour is that there is a size distribution of spatial clusters, with different ranges of activities taking place in different clusters. In particular, within an individual country or market area, there will usually be a single largest city cluster which exhibits almost all types of activities, followed by larger numbers of other smaller clusters which increase in number as their individual size falls. The smaller clusters will tend to exhibit a smaller range of activities taking place within them than the larger clusters. These observations are collectively known as an 'urban hierarchy', and the particular reasons for the development of such a system of cities are an important topic.

In sections 2.2 to 2.5 of this chapter, we will discuss in detail the various arguments and explanations as to why industrial activities are often observed to be clustered geographically. In the following sections 2.6–2.6.2 and Appendix 2.1, we subsequently discuss the arguments for firm dispersal. Finally, in sections 2.7 to 2.8 and Appendix 2.3 we discuss models and techniques which we use to describe the aggregate structure of the urban system and the urban hierarchy.

2.2 Industrial Clustering: Returns to Scale and Geography

In attempting to explain the observation that activities are generally clustered together in space, it is necessary to employ the notion that economies of scale can be place-specific. To see this, we can consider the spatial outcomes of the alternative hypothetical case where all firms achieve constant returns to scale. If, for whatever reason, a large group of such firms in the same sector or a range of sectors ends up being located in the same place, the result of this clustering will be a large level of investment at that particular location. These firms will require land and space for their activities, and the high demand for land at the particular location will force up its price. If everything else is unchanged, and if the firms all achieve constant returns to scale, the increase in the price of land will reduce the profitability of all of the firms at that location. Similarly, the increase in the local land price will mean that the living costs of the labour employed will also go up. In order to maintain the local labour supply the firms will also have to increase wages. Once again, this will reduce the profitability of all the firms in the area. The reduced profits will mean that firms located here will be less competitive than their competitors located elsewhere and will struggle to survive in the market. Some firms will move away to alternative locations while others will simply go out of business. Eventually the cluster will disappear. This hypothetical example is, however, inconsistent with the general observation that most activity clusters do continue to exist.

On the other hand, let us imagine a situation where each of the firms in the same locality achieves significant economies of scale precisely because of the large number of firms located in the area. In this situation, the high level of investment in the local area will still imply high local land prices and high labour prices as before. However, the difference now is that these increased factor prices may be more than compensated for by the increased efficiency on the part of each firm. The result of this will be even higher profitability for all the local firms, even though the local factor prices may be higher than elsewhere. Other firms from other areas may now also consider moving into our area contributing to a further growth in the levels of local investment, factor prices, and firm profitability. This in-migration of new firms will lead to a cumulative process of local growth.

This hypothetical example is consistent with the observation that most activity clusters do continue to exist. However, in reality, the growth of local clusters tends not to be a process which is continuously cumulative as in the latter example. The reason for this is that this would imply that all activity would end up at one location! Therefore, in order to discuss the existence of spatial industrial clusters, it is necessary to employ the notion that place-specific economies of scale do exist, but also to acknowledge that there may be limits to such effects.

2.3 Agglomeration Economies

Location-specific economies of scale are generally known as agglomeration economies. The existence of agglomeration economies was acknowledged by classical authors such as Weber, but it was Alfred Marshall who first provided a detailed description of the sources of these economies. In Marshall's (1920) schema, these economies are generally under-stood to be external economies, which are independent of a single firm, but which accrue to all of the firms located in the same area. A good description of the Marshall approach is given by Krugman (1991a). However, as well as Marshall's description of the sources of agglomeration economies, there is also Hoover's (1937, 1948) classification of types of agglomeration economies. Hoover's description is a rather different characterization from that of Marshall, but given that both approaches are frequently adopted, it is necessary to be explicit about their differences.

2.3.1 The sources of agglomeration economies

Marshall (1920) observed that firms often continue to cluster successfully in the same locations. From our example above, this implies that increasing returns to scale must be achieved by the firms in the cluster. Marshall provided three reasons why such economies of scale might be achieved. In other words, he identified three possible sources or origins of such economies of scale. These are information spillovers, local non-traded inputs, and a local skilled labour pool.

(i) **Information spillovers**

If many firms in the same industry are grouped together in the same location, it implies that the employees of any one particular firm have relatively easy access to employees from other local firms. This easy access can be either through the facility to have frequent direct face-to-face contact in business meetings, or alternatively though frequent informal contacts such as lunch meetings, sports activities, or other such social occasions. The important point about such informal meetings is that they allow tacit information to be shared between the participants. Tacit information is information which is incomplete and which is shared on a non-market basis, and can relate to issues such as new products, personnel, technology, and market trends. The participants in such meetings will each give information which is partial in order to acquire other information which is also partial. This process of the mutual trading of information allows each of the market participants to build up a more coherent picture of the overall market environment, thereby improving their ability to compete in the market. The more such participants there are in the local area, the more complete a picture can be assembled by each participant. The advantage of spatial clustering in this case is therefore that proximity maximizes the mutual accessibility of all individuals within the cluster, thereby improving the information available to all local participants. In market environments characterized by rapidly changing information, such clustering affords the agglomerated firms an information advantage relative to all other firms, and the extent of this advantage depends directly on the number of such firms which are located in the same area.

A good example of this are the international financial markets, which are centred on highly concentrated areas such as Wall Street (New York), the City of London, and the Maronouchi district of Tokyo. In this sector, international financial market information is changing by the minute. Managers have to make important decisions on a daily basis, and these decisions often involve rapid negotiations with other participants within the banking syndicates of which each financial institution is a part. Immediate access to market participants is essential.

(ii) **Non-traded local inputs**

In situations where many firms in the same industry are grouped together in the same area, there will be possibilities for certain specialist inputs to be provided to the group, in a more efficient manner than would be the case if all of the firms were dispersed. These inputs are described as 'non-traded' in order to distinguish them from consumed inputs of the type described in the Weber and Moses models. For example, if we once again take the case of the financial markets, areas such as Wall Street and the City of London have many specialist legal firms and software firms, whose only role is to provide specialist services to the international financial sector. The provision of such specialist services is very expensive. However, where there are many firms within the industry which are located at the same place, the average cost of this service provision to each market participant will be low. The reason is that the costs of setting up such services will be spread over a large number of local customer firms. Similarly, in automotive engineering clusters in cities such as Detroit (Michigan), Birmingham (UK), and Turin (Italy), there are specialist testing firms. Their only role is to test the accuracy and safety of industrial components, using highly specialized and expensive equipment. The cost of employing such equipment would be prohibitive to most market participants, but the fact that a large number of firms within the same sector who require such testing services are also located at the same place allows the costs to be spread across the group. A second type of non-traded local input is that of specialist local infrastructure. In the City of London there is a specialist dedicated wide-band fibre-optic cable system which is designed to allow the maximum possible flows of data between the local financial institutions, while excluding the general public. Access to the system comes about only through location in the City. All the local market participants benefit from the specialist infrastructure, and the cost of it is spread across all of the beneficiaries. As above, the costs of the non-traded local inputs to each firm within the group will fall as more firms join the cluster.

(iii) Local skilled-labour pool

The third source of agglomeration economies is the existence of a specialized local labour pool. This allows firms to reduce their labour acquisition costs, and there are two aspects to this. The first is that firms require sufficient quantities of labour to respond to market conditions. Therefore, if market demand conditions improve rapidly, a firm will wish to expand its labour force quickly, and will need to undertake a search process to acquire the workers. Secondly, the firm will also need to ensure that the employees are able to carry out the tasks correctly. In many sectors the costs of training labour and skill-acquisition can be extremely high. This is because workers will need to be provided with specialist courses and instruction. Also, the opportunity costs involved with the time involved in these training activities can be extremely high. However, if a firm is located in an area which already has a large local pool of workers with the specialist skills required by the particular industry, the costs to the firm of expanding its workforce will be relatively low. This is because the firm will have to undertake few or no retraining activities. For industries in which skills-acquisition costs are high, or in which the opportunity costs of time are significant due to rapidly changing market conditions, a local pool of skilled workers will therefore be of great benefit. The labour acquisition costs on the part of the firms, which include both the search costs and the retraining costs, will be reduced relative to firms in dispersed locations.

Together, these three sources of agglomeration economies can allow firms within a cluster to experience economies of scale which are external to any single firm, but which are internal to the group. The key feature of each of these sources of agglomeration economies is that spatial clustering reduces information transactions costs. Clustering increases the likelihood that the appropriate information will be transmitted, that the specialist requisite services will be provided, and the appropriately skilled labour will be available, at that location, relative to other dispersed locations.

2.3.2 The types of agglomeration economies

The sources of agglomeration economies described above allow firms within the same industry which are clustered together in space to achieve localized external economies of scale. However, in many areas, groups of firms in different industries can be clustered together geographically. For example, major cities may contain hundreds of industrial clusters. The exact nature of the agglomeration economies may therefore be different in different locations. In order to describe the particular nature of agglomeration economies in any particular area, economists often adopt a classification which was first employed by Ohlin (1933) and Hoover (1937, 1948). This classification splits agglomeration economies into three types, namely internal returns to scale, localization economies, and urbanization economies.

(i) Internal returns to scale

Some firms achieve significant economies of scale in their production simply by reason of their size. These economies of scale are regarded as being internal to the firm, in that the efficiency gains are explicitly deemed to be a result of the size of the individual firm. As such, these internal economies do not concur with the Marshall description above of economies of agglomeration as being external. Yet, the notion of economies of scale here is explicitly spatial in that it is assumed that the internal economies of scale are generated because a large level of investment takes place at one particular location, rather than across a range of different locations. A large factory, such as the Fiat automobile plant in Turin, or the Boeing Everett hanger in Seattle, requires a large quantity of capital and a large labour force to be located at the same place. These internal production economies of scale are therefore associated with a high spatial concentration of both investment and people. As such, a large stock of factors are clustered together in space, although in this case they are within the definition of a single firm. However, the point is that the internal economies of scale are location specific.

(ii) Economies of localization

Localization economies are the agglomeration economies which accrue to a group of firms within the same industrial sector located at the same place. For example, in the case of Seattle, there are many firms that produce specialist aerospace components which are supplied directly to Boeing. Similarly, in automobile clusters such as in Detroit, Michigan and Birmingham, UK, there are many firms producing specialist supplies for the major automobile-producing firms. There are several ways in which the local supply firms can benefit from close proximity to their major customer firms, which are the firms achieving the internal returns to scale. According to Marshall's first source of agglomeration economies, the supply firms may benefit from frequent information exchanges with the customer firms, thereby increasing the mutual understanding and familiarity of these firms at different stages within the production process. Sometimes, this will also involve exchanges of personnel and consultants. These activities can facilitate product development in markets where the risks are high. Also, as with Marshall's two other sources of agglomeration economies described above, the firms in the same sector can benefit from specialist non-traded local services and a local skilled-labour pool. Each of Marshall's sources of agglomeration can therefore contribute to localization economies, the definition of which is therefore that they accrue within a particular industrial sector.

(iii) Economies of urbanization

Urbanization economies are those economies of agglomeration which accrue to firms across different sectors (Jacobs 1960). For example, in the case of the cities mentioned above, namely Seattle, Detroit, Birmingham, and Turin, the economy of each of these cities is centred around a single plant or a group of very large plants each of which exhibits internal returns to scale. Around these plants are many supplier firms and the group of customer and supplier firms together achieve localization economies. However, each of these cities is much larger than simply the single sector of aerospace in Seattle, and the automobile sector in Detroit, Birmingham, and Turin. In order for other activities to continue to be clustered in these cities, they must also experience economies of scale. For example, all of the people who live and work in the sectors achieving localization economies will require legal, real estate, retail, educational, health care, and leisure services. Similarly, the firms themselves may require services such as marketing, advertising, catering, packaging, transportation, real estate, and security, among others. These various activities, although not directly related to the sector experiencing internal returns to scale and localization economies, will still cluster in the local economy in order to provide services for the firms and employees of this sector. This clustering is in response to the large local market possibilities which exist. However, as before, these firms will experience increased local factor prices, which must be compensated by economies of scale if the clustering is to continue. The agglomeration economies experienced by these other sectors are termed urbanization economies.

In the Hoover typology, internal returns to scale are firm-specific economies of agglomeration, localization economies are industry-specific economies of agglomeration, and urbanization economies are city-specific economies of agglomeration. The difference here between the three classes of agglomeration economies therefore depends on the definition of the boundaries of the firms and the sectors.

For example, the difference between the location-specific internal returns to scale and localization economies depends only on the boundaries of the individual firm within an individual sector. To see this, we can consider a case where a group of separate firms within the same industry are clustered together and experience localization economies. If this group are subsequently all bought over by a single firm, any economies of scale they achieve due to spatial proximity will now be counted as internal to the individual firm. This scenario is illustrated by examples such as the localized growth of General Motors in Detroit and Rover Cars in Birmingham, UK. The change in the firm boundaries due to the change in the ownership structure, does not of itself alter the fact that location-specific economies of scale are operating at this particular place. On the other hand, we can consider the opposite case where a large location-specific activity is fragmented. For example, a chemicals complex at Teesside in the UK was formerly entirely owned by a single firm ICI. Subsequently, parts of the plant were sold off to other chemicals firms such as DuPont, although the various parts of the complex continued to produce for each other as before. What would previously be counted as internal returns to scale would now be classified as localization economies. As before, the change in the ownership structure will not fundamentally alter the fact that location-specific economies of scale are operating at this particular place.

We can employ a similar set of examples to consider the differences between localization economies and urbanization economies. For example, there is a large group of electronics plants in central Scotland belonging mainly to Japanese and US integrated electronics firms, which produce products such as silicon wafers, integrated circuits, computers, military hardware, and consumer electronics goods. This area is often known as 'Silicon Glen' and this group of plants are widely acknowledged as experiencing localization economies (Haug 1986; McCann and Fingleton 1996; McCann 1997). However, if some of the parent firms undergo restructuring and decide to sell off their subsidiary plants in Scotland, many of the plants will change industry sector. For example, firms producing silicon wafers will now be classed as chemicals firms, firms producing military electronics components will now be classed as military goods firms, and firms undertaking activities such as wire-harnessing will now be classed as electrical engineering firms. These ownership changes will mean that the plants will now be defined as representing a variety of industries, rather than a single industry. Any location-specific economies of scale which continue to exist will now be defined as urbanization economies rather than localization economies as before. Yet, these changes do not always simply reflect changes in firm boundaries. In some cases, the definition of agglomeration economies may also indicate more fundamental changes in the nature of the agglomeration economies than simply changes in firm ownership. We will deal with this issue in section 2.5. Before this, however, it is necessary to review a range of other descriptions of industrial clusters.

2.4 Other Descriptions of Industrial Clusters

As well as the classic Marshall and Hoover descriptions of agglomeration economies there are a range of other models which discuss particular aspects of industrial clustering. Each of these models is also regularly adopted by analysts to describe various types of clusters, so we will briefly discuss them here. They are the three long-established models known as the growth pole model, the incubator model, and the product cycle model, as well as two more recent models which are the Porter model (1990, 1998) and the new industrial areas model.

2.4.1 The growth pole model

The growth pole model was originally associated with the work of Perroux (1950), although it employed some of the ideas of Schumpeter (1934). Perroux described economic relationships in terms of monetary space, in which there are certain polarities regarding financial transactions. In other words, the decisions made by key large firms have major financial implications for other firms which are linked to the key firm through customer–supplier relationships. Perroux described these key large firms as 'growth poles', and the decisions they make which affect other firms relate primarily to issues such as innovation. The concept was translated into spatial planning terms primarily by Boudeville (1966), in which it was argued that the spatial behaviour of an area will be affected by the location behaviour of certain major firms or plants. For example, if large firm investments or public investment projects are implemented at a particular location, this location-specific investment can act as a focus for local growth. Other local firms may be able to use the advantage of proximity in order to increase their local sales to the new investment, thereby generating localized growth in the hinterland of the investment. These beneficial effects, however, will take time to develop. For example, as we saw in section 2.1 above, the immediate effect of a large location-specific investment may be an increase in local factor prices. This may reduce local efficiency in the short run and also lead to some localized crowding-out effects. In the growth pole literature these negative local effects are collectively known as 'backwash effects'. However, as the positive economic aspects of the growth pole begin to take effect, the beneficial 'spread effects' are assumed to dominate the negative backwash effects within the hinterland region, thereby engendering positive local growth over the long run. The major point raised by the growth pole model is that large innovative firms or investment activities will tend to have significant impacts on the local development of industrial clusters. Innovation alone may not be of such significance, nor will size alone, although a combination of the two may engender significant local growth effects. The weakness of the approach, however, is the lack of any coherent analysis of the costs and benefits of such investment schemes. Good reviews of this literature are provided by Richardson (1978) and Parr (1999a, b).

2.4.2 The incubator model

The incubator model is associated with the work of Chinitz (1961, 1964) and was derived from observations of the industrial structure of Pittsburgh and New York. The argument of Chinitz is that industrial clusters which are highly diversified, and which contain a range of different types of industries and firm sizes, will act as superior 'incubators' for the development and growth of new firms. The reason for this is that in such an environment, there will be a variety of local business services available to these small firms which will facilitate their growth. On the other hand, in industrial clusters dominated primarily by large firms, many of these requisite services will not be available, because the large firms will be able to supply such activities internally. This will consequently reduce the growth potential of the local industrial cluster. Chinitz's argument is important, because it suggests that the issues of firm ownership structure, as discussed in section 2.2.2, may also play an independent role in affecting the growth of the cluster. In particular, it suggests that the size distribution of firms within the cluster may be important for the growth of the cluster.

2.4.3 The product-cycle model

The product-cycle model is associated with the work of Vernon (1960, 1966) and is one of the approaches most frequently used to describe the qualitative aspects of spatial investment patterns. The most common use of the product-cycle model has been in discussions of international investment flows (Vernon 1966), although the origins of the theory are actually found in observations of city clusters (Vernon 1960). Vernon's argument is that firms will separate activities by location according to the stage in the life-cycle of the product, which in turn is reflected by the activities of the particular plant. For example, in high-level industrial clusters, such as in dominant central cities, firms will tend to locate information-intensive activities such as research and development and high-level decision-making, which together relate to the early stages of the life-cycle of the product. The reason is that these activities require large information inputs, and in particular, information which is generally non-standardized. The non-standardized nature of the product or process is precisely due to the newness of the product or technique. Following the Marshall argument above, these activities may therefore benefit from the informal information spillovers associated with localized clustering. Meanwhile, highly skilled employees will also be required to carry out such activities, and once again, from the Marshall argument, it may be consistently easier to find these workers in such clustered areas. On the other hand, once a product and the associated production process has been designed, tested, and developed, the firm will be able to issue a blueprint which documents all of the aspects of the product and its production. This information will now be available to other branches of the firm organization. The information regarding the product is thus standardized and, as production increases, the product becomes 'mature'; in other words, it is no longer so novel. Over time, the production techniques tend to become better understood and relatively easier to carry out. As this happens, the requirement for information inputs and highly skilled labour tends to fall, with the result that the firm can move the production process to other lower-cost and lower-skilled areas. The product-cycle argument therefore implies that more geographically peripheral areas, which tend to exhibit lower labour costs and lower labour skills, will also tend to have plants producing more mature, less novel, and more standardized products. The result is that there will tend to be a clear separation of activity types between central city-regions and more peripheral areas. The important observation of the product-cycle model is that there may therefore emerge a qualitative distinction between the types of activities which take place at the economic centre or at the periphery of any geographical area.

2.4.4 **The Porter model**

Within the business management community there has been much interest in the arguments of Porter (1990, 1998*a*, *b*). Porter argues that clustering may act as an alternative organizational form to the standard markets and hierarchies dichotomy associated with the work of Williamson (1975). He argues that clustering provides individual firms with another way of organizing their transactions in an environment of rapidly changing information and technology. This particular form of spatial industrial organization maximizes the transfer of technology and information flows between the firms, and is particularly important in the case of small firms which rely mainly on external sources of information and technology. However, the key point of Porter's argument is that proximity also engenders mutual visibility between competitors. In others words, firms are able to observe the competitive developments of each other, and this visibility itself acts as a spur to all firms to continue to improve their own individual competitiveness. The result of this process of localized competition is that the competitiveness of the cluster as a whole is increased.

2.4.5 **The new industrial areas model**

The new industrial areas, or new industrial spaces model, derives primarily from a series of observations within the field of urban planning and geography (Scott 1988). Certain industrial clusters, such as the electronics cluster in Silicon Valley (Saxenian 1994), the electronics and biotechnology cluster in Cambridge, UK (Keeble and Wilkinson 1999), and the small-firm manufacturing industry of the Emilia-Romagna region of Italy (Scott 1988) have shown themselves to be major centres of innovation. These observations have led to suggestions from many observers that industries which are made up of spatial clusters of small firms tend to be more highly innovative than industries comprised mainly of large firms (Saxenian 1994), because such environments provide the appropriate 'milieux' for such innovations to take place (Aydalot and Keeble 1988). In particular, as well as Marshall's classic sources of the agglomeration economies, it is also argued that networks of important business relationships operate between local decision-makers which allow for risk-taking. These relationships are perceived to depend on strong mutual trust between the participants, which is assumed to have developed partly due to geographical proximity. While there is still widespread disagreement among observers concerning these particular conclusions (Suarez-Villa and Walrod 1997; Simmie 1988; Arita and McCann 2000), the relationship between firm sizes, innovation, and industrial clustering has led to a great deal of interest among public policy planners. The primary motive for this is the belief that understanding this relationship may improve public policy initiatives to foster such developments elsewhere (Castells and Hall 1994). A problem with much of this literature, however, is deciding whether these observations are genuinely new, or rather simply new forms of an old phenomenon.

2.5 **Clusters, Firm Types, and the Nature of Transactions**

A problem with discussing the nature of, and reasons for, industrial clustering is that it is very difficult both empirically and theoretically to distinguish between each of the above reasons for and descriptions of industrial clustering. From an empirical point of view, distinguishing between urbanization economies and localization economies can be notoriously difficult (Glaeser *et al.* 1992; Henderson *et al.* 1995), because many industrial clusters such as cities will contain all types of clusters both within and across a range of sectors. From a theoretical perspective, the Marshall description is important in allowing us to understand the sources of agglomeration economies within an individual industry sector, while the Hoover approach is important from the point of view of identifying the particular firms and sectors which experience these agglomeration economies. However, it may appear that the distinction between the three Hoover classifications is rather arbitrary, given that mergers and acquisitions mean that firms are frequently changing ownership and sectors. Moreover, the relationship between the Marshall and Hoover classifications may be further complicated by each of the issues raised by the growth pole, the incubator, the product cycle, the Porter, and the new industrial area models. Yet, there are clear differences between the types of industrial clusters which exist in reality, according to the nature of relations between the firms within the individual clusters and the particular features they exhibit (Gordon and McCann 2000).

In order to understand these relations, it is necessary for us to focus on the characteristics of firms which exist in the cluster, and the transactions which take place within the cluster. Adopting this approach, we see that there are three broad typologies of spatial industrial clusters, as defined in terms of the features they exhibit (Gordon and McCann 2000). These are the *pure agglomeration*, the *industrial complex*, and the *social network*. The key feature which distinguishes each of these different ideal types of spatial industrial cluster is the nature of the relations between the firms within the cluster.

The characteristics of each of the cluster types are listed in Table 2.1, and as we see, the three ideal types of clusters are all quite different. In reality, all spatial clusters will contain characteristics of one or more of these ideal types, although one type will tend to be dominant in each cluster. Therefore, from an empirical point of view or from a public policy perspective which seeks to influence the behaviour of the cluster, it is necessary to determine which of these particular ideal types of industrial cluster most accurately reflects the characteristics and behaviour of any particular cluster.

In the model of pure agglomeration, interfirm relations are inherently transient. Firms are essentially atomistic, in the sense of having no market power, and they will continuously change their relations with other firms and customers in response to market arbitrage opportunities, thereby leading to intense local competition. As such, there is no loyalty between firms, nor are any particular relations long term. The external benefits of

Table 2.1 Industrial clusters

Characteristics	Pure agglomeration	Industrial complex	Social network
firm size	atomistic	some firms are large	variable
characteristics of relations	non-identifiable fragmented unstable	identifiable stable trading	trust loyalty joint lobbying joint ventures non-opportunistic
membership	open	closed	partially open
access to cluster	rental payments location necessary	internal investment location necessary	history experience location necessary but not sufficient
space outcomes	rent appreciation	no effect on rents	partial rental capitalization
notion of space	urban	local but not urban	local but not urban
example of cluster	competitive urban economy	steel or chemicals production complex	new industrial areas
analytical aproaches	models of pure agglomeration	location-production theory input–output analysis	social network theory (Granovetter)

clustering accrue to all local firms simply by reason of their local presence, the price of which is the local real estate market rent. There are no free-riders, access to the cluster is open, and consequently it is the growth in the local real estate rents which is the indicator of the cluster's performance. This idealized type is best represented by the Marshall model, and the localization and urbanization economies of Hoover, but also contains elements of both the Porter, Chinitz, and Vernon models. The notion of space in these models is essentially urban space in that this type of clustering only exists within individual cities.

The industrial complex is characterized primarily by long-term stable and predictable relations between the firms in the cluster. This type of cluster is most commonly observed in industries such as steel and chemicals, and is the type of spatial cluster typically discussed by classical (Weber 1909) and neoclassical (Moses 1958) location-production models, representing a fusion of locational analysis with input–output analysis (Isard and Kuenne 1953). Component firms within the spatial grouping undertake significant long-term investments, particularly in terms of physical capital and local real estate, in order to become part of the grouping. Access to the group is therefore severely restricted both by high entry and exit costs, and the rationale for spatial clustering in these types of industries is that proximity is required primarily in order to minimize interfirm transport transactions costs. Rental appreciation is not a feature of the cluster, because the land which has already been purchased by the firms is not for sale. This ideal type of cluster reflects the internal returns to scale argument of Hoover and aspects of the growth pole model of Perroux more closely than the other cluster types. The notion of space in the industrial complex is local, but not necessarily urban, in that these types of complex can exist either within or outside of an individual city.

The third type of spatial industrial cluster is the social network model. This is associated primarily with the work of Granovetter (1973, 1985, 1991, 1992), and is a response to the hierarchies model of Williamson (1975). The social network model argues that mutual trust relations between key decision-making agents in different organizations may be at least as important as decision-making hierarchies within individual organizations. These trust relations will be manifested by a variety of features, such as joint lobbying, joint ventures, informal alliances, and reciprocal arrangements regarding trading relationships. However, the key feature of such trust relations is an absence of opportunism, in that individual firms will not fear reprisals after any reorganization of interfirm relations. Interfirm cooperative relations may therefore differ significantly from the organizational boundaries associated with individual firms, and these relations may be continually reconstituted. All of these behavioural features rely on a common culture of mutual trust, the development of which depends largely on a shared history and experience of the decision-making agents. This social network model is essentially aspatial, but from the point of view of geography, it can be argued that spatial proximity will tend to foster such trust relations, thereby leading to a local business environment of confidence, risk-taking, and cooperation. Spatial proximity is necessary but not sufficient to acquire access to the network. As such, membership of the network is only partially open, in that local rental payments will not guarantee access, although they will improve the chances of access. The social network model therefore contains elements of both the Porter model (1990, 1998*a*, *b*) and the new industrial areas model (Scott 1988), and has been employed to describe the characteristics and performance of areas such as Silicon Valley and the Emilia-Romagna area of Italy. In this model space is once again local, but not necessarily urban.

As we have already noted, all industrial clusters will contain features of one or more of these ideal types. However, determining the major features of any particular cluster will require us to consider which of these particular types is dominant. The reason is that empirically each of these cluster types will have different manifestations. For example, in the pure model of agglomeration, the dominant feature will be an appreciation in local real estate values, with no particular purchasing or decision-making linkages being evident between local firms. Discussions of the strength of local-purchasing or decision-making linkages, or the types of local alliances undertaken by firms, will not indicate agglomeration behaviour. On the other hand, in the case of the industrial complex there will be no real estate effects, but the dominant feature will be a stability of both purchasing and decision-making linkages. However, measuring the scale of such linkages is less important than measuring the duration of the linkages. Finally, in the network model, although the market environment will be highly competitive, the dominant feature of the firm relations will be a willingness to undertake a variety of informal collective and cooperative activities which cut across organizational boundaries, such as joint lobbying or interfirm credit availability. Measuring real estate appreciation or the strength of local purchasing linkages will not tell us very much. Industrial clusters are therefore of a variety of types, the observation and measurement of which is also a complicated topic.

2.6 Industrial Dispersal

All of the arguments in sections 2.2 through to 2.5 have attempted to understand and classify why it is that firms are often clustered together in space. However, observation tells us that not all activities are located together. Activities in primary industries tend to be spatially dispersed. For example, quarrying and mining only take place in particular areas where the appropriate minerals can be extracted economically. The geological conditions may require that such activities can only take place in a dispersed spatial pattern of locations. Similarly, agricultural activities as a whole tend to be distributed rather evenly over space, simply because of the requirement of land as an input to the agricultural production process. At the same time, there are many commercial and industrial activities which also tend to be dispersed. As we saw in Chapter 1, oligopolistic environments in which price competition is a major feature will tend to encourage competitor firms to move away from each other. However, many markets exhibit alternative spatial pricing strategies, in which delivered prices may be either invariant with location and distance, or only partially dependent on distance. In these cases, some of the location considerations discussed so far may no longer be entirely appropriate. Therefore, in section 2.6.1 it is necessary to consider such alternative spatial pricing situations, and to understand how these issues may contribute to industrial dispersal. In sections 2.6.2 and

2.6.3, the additional issue we also address is the problem of determining how far away the firms will disperse.

2.6.1 Spatial pricing, price discrimination, and firm dispersal

In some markets, the delivered prices quoted by firms will be the same irrespective of location. In situations such as this, the types of spatial competition issues raised by the Hotelling model will no longer be relevant. Rather, in these situations it is more appropriate for us to employ a Weber type of approach in considering the location behaviour of the firm. The reason is that, even though the quoted delivered price is invariant with location, the firm will still use location as a means of maximizing its profits. The only difference between this approach and the simple Weber model outlined in Chapter 1 is that in this case the market is a continuous two-dimensional space rather than a single point. However, if we know the quantities of outputs shipped to each area of the spatial market, it is quite straightforward in principle to calculate the geographical centre of the market, weighted both by space and the quantity demanded at each location. The Weber analysis can then be applied in an orthodox manner. From our knowledge of this approach, it is clear that similar firms employing similar input supply sources and serving the same market will tend to locate in the same area, thereby contributing to industrial concentration, although such behaviour will not be evidence of agglomeration economies (McCann 1995). On the other hand, if there were a variety of firms producing different products from different input sources, we would expect there to be a variety of different firm locations. As such, firms will tend to be rather dispersed.

The argument that certain features of spatial pricing behaviour can encourage industrial dispersal, however, can be strengthened if we assume that quoted market prices are not identical at all locations, but that there exists a degree of spatial monopoly power in the market. In this case, the firm may use its monopoly power to engage in price discrimination, so as to extend its spatial market area outward from its own location. Allowing for the fact that demand in many cases is elastic, and that delivered spatial prices will be a function of the haulage distance, the firm may employ price discrimination in these situations in order to discriminate against local customers and in favour of distant customers. The logic of this is that the firm will already have monopoly power over the local customers. Therefore, it is able to raise the delivered prices it charges to these local customers in order to reduce the higher prices it charges to distant consumers. From section 1.3 of the previous chapter, it is clear that this type of spatial price discrimination will increase the spatial market areas of individual firms, increase the average distance over which goods are shipped, and thereby can also increase the tendency towards firm dispersion. This argument is most closely associated with the work of Greenhut (1970) and Greenhut and Ohta (1975) and is discussed in detail in Appendix 2.1.

2.6.2 Linkage analysis and product value/weight ratios

As we see in section 2.6.1 and Appendix 2.1, the reasons for individual industrial dispersal depend on the pricing features of the particular market. However, we can still ask if there are any broad observations which indicate the typical overall relationship between spatial industrial dispersal and the nature of the market. One way of discussing the question of industrial dispersal in general terms is to discuss the nature of industrial linkages. The spatial purchasing patterns of industrial or household consumers are comprised of a series of individual spatial linkages between the producers and the consumers. These spatial linkages represent the distance characteristics of the individual transactions undertaken by the purchasers, and as such, can be understood as the outcome of the individual location decisions described in Chapter 1. Aggregate linkage analysis attempts to determine whether there are particular patterns to such linkages by observing many individual linkages. One of the most common findings of aggregate linkage analysis is that there is a relationship between industrial linkages and the nature of the products being transported. In particular, the higher is the value–weight ratio of the product, the greater will be the average distance of shipment (Lever 1972, 1974; Hoare 1975; Marshall 1987). This is because the value weight/ratio of a product is the price of each unit of the product, however defined, defined in terms of the price per tonne of the product. This common linkage observation therefore states that products which are of higher value tend to be transported over greater distances.

A frequent justification for this observation is that high-value products can be transported over large distances because the high value of the product can absorb long-distance transportation costs. On the other hand, for low-value products, the transport costs will be very high relative to the value of the good even over short distances, thereby restricting the distance over which these goods can be shipped. For example, high value–weight Japanese electronics goods are shipped to markets all over the world, whereas many low-value–weight vegetables tend to be produced and sold locally. This argument, however, is rather weak. For example, it cannot explain why so many low-value agricultural and dairy products are shipped over enormous distances from New Zealand to the rest of the world. Nor can the argument explain why low-value clothing and toys are shipped over enormous distances from developing countries to industrialized nations. At the same time, it cannot explain why so many high-value products are shipped over short distances between various countries within a common market area, such as the European Union.

The major problem with this simple linkage argument is that it implicitly assumes that the quantities of all capital invested in any production process, and the quantity of all outputs produced by any production process, are approximately equal. We can see this if we consider that the revenue earned by the firm from the sales of its products is necessary to cover all the costs of its production. However, the performance of any particular production activity is defined not in terms of the total profits earned, but in terms of the rate of return, which is given as the total profits earned divided by the capital initially invested. The denominator term is the quantity of capital initially invested and not the weight of output produced. Only if the total weight of output produced is identical can the total profits earned be compared between any two production activities. Moreover, in terms of the rate of return, only if the quantities of capital initially invested are also identical can the rate of return be compared between any two activities. In order to understand the general patterns of linkage lengths it is therefore also necessary to consider the total quantities of output produced and the total quantities of capital invested. Simple value/weight ratios can be very misleading.

This particular linkage observation is probably best understood from another perspective. This alternative perspective is that the technology required in order to produce and market high-value non-standardized products means that such products tend to be produced in a smaller number of locations and by a smaller number of producers than low-value standard products. The result of this is that for the high-value products, the average distance of shipment will tend to increase, simply because the number of supply locations will tend to be fewer. On the other hand, the low-value goods will tend to be produced in many locations, thereby reducing the average shipment distance. Different types of production will thereby take place in different numbers of locations. Standard lower-technology production will take place in many locations, whereas newer- and higher-technology production activities will tend to take place in a smaller number of locations. The overall result is that the size of the individual market areas, and the average distance of shipment from supplier to customer, will be different for different products, with a general observation that higher-value products will tend to be shipped over larger market areas.

2.6.3 Reilly's Law of market areas

The arguments in the previous two sections have suggested that spatial market areas will be different for different firms. In part, these differences will be due to differences in the types of goods the firms produce, but also these differences will depend on the pricing behaviour of the firms. These different market areas in turn imply that the average distance of shipment for different goods will be different. As we have seen, the average distance of shipment may be related to the value weight ratio of the products. However, what we do not know as yet is whether there is anything predictable about the actual distances over which goods are shipped to consumers between adjacent producers. In other words, we need to consider whether there is anything predictable about the particular sizes of the individual market areas.

The first attempt at quantifying the market area and the distance of shipment of goods comes from the 'law' of market areas or retail gravitation, first discussed by Reilly (1929, 1931). This is not a law as such, but rather an empirical observation of the relationship between the size of the market or supply location, and the ability of the market or supply location to attract customers located at a distance away. Reilly's Law states that the ability of the market or supply location to attract customers is directly related to the size of the market or supply point, and indirectly related to square of the distance of shipment. The size of the market or supply point is defined here in terms of the number or variety of goods being produced or available at that point, and the distance of shipment of the goods is defined here in terms of the distance over which consumers must travel to the market in order to acquire the goods. In the situation where we have two competing market or supply locations, such as the retail centres of two cities, Reilly's Law provides us with a convenient method of calculating the market boundary between the two retail centres, along similar lines to the approach adopted in section 1.3 of the previous chapter.

If the distance between two retail centres A and B is given as x, and the distance from A of a consumer on the boundary of the market between A and B is given as a, Reilly's Law can be specified as

$$\frac{A}{a^2} = \frac{B}{(x-a)^2}.$$ (2.1)

If the relative sizes of the two retail centres is given as

$$\frac{A}{B} = r,$$ (2.2)

then we have

$$r = \frac{a^2}{(x-a)^2},$$ (2.3)

which, as we see in Appendix 2.2, rearranges to

$$a = \frac{x\sqrt{r}}{1+\sqrt{r}}.$$ (2.4)

The actual location of the market boundary between the two retail centres will be dependent on the relative 'pulls' of the markets and the factors inhibiting the overcoming distance.

The pull of the market is the relative attractiveness of the market as a location for purchasing, and in Reilly's approach, the attractiveness of the retail location, represented by the size of the retail centre, depends on the variety of goods which can be purchased at the same location. In other words, a larger centre implies that a greater variety of goods can be purchased on each trip to the centre. Implicit in Reilly's approach here is a notion of purchasing economies of scope, in that a single journey to a single centre will partially or completely substitute for many individual journeys to purchase a range of products. The greater is the variety of goods available at the retail centre, the greater will be the attractiveness of purchasing from there even from a significant distance. At the same time, Reilly's approach also assumes that the marginal costs of overcoming distance become successively greater as distance increases. This could be represented by, for example, an increasing marginal disutility of travel time. Obviously, if the retail centres are the same size the value of r will be 1, and $a = x/2$. As such, in this unique case the market boundary will be equidistant between the two markets. More generally, however, the different distances between retail centres and their market area boundaries will be determined by the interaction of the relative attractiveness of the centre in terms of the possible economies of scope, and the accessibility of the centre, which depends on distance.

Although Reilly's market area approach is a simple empirical rule of thumb, it does however provide us with a fundamental insight into the nature of market areas. Goods will be purchased over greater market areas, with the result that goods will also be shipped over greater geographical distances, from centres which produce a greater variety of goods, *ceteris paribus*. This observation therefore suggests that the greater urbanization economies associated with larger cities will also imply larger hinterland market areas, and larger shipment distances for the goods produced in the city. On the other hand, more local market areas with short-distance goods shipments, will tend to be dominated by purchases of a lower variety of goods.

If we now reconsider the linkage analysis argument of section 2.6.2, along with the agglomeration arguments discussed in sections 2.3 to 2.5, we can argue that higher-value goods will tend to be produced or marketed in a smaller range of locations than low-value goods, thereby increasing the market areas and the shipment distances of these goods. This conclusion can be made consistent with the Reilly observations, if the major retail locations of these high-value goods also tend to be in the larger urban centres. The agglomeration discussions of sections 2.3 to 2.5 would lend support to this argument, in that the greater information, skills, and technology inputs required in the production of high-value goods will tend to be more readily available in major urban centres. In other words, if the larger urban centres are generally the major production or retail locations of high-value goods rather than the smaller urban centres, which tend mainly to be the source of lower-value goods, the linkage observations will be broadly consistent with Reilly's approach. Note that these conditions still allow for the fact that the major centres are also sources of low-value goods as well as high-value goods. The point is that if large urban centres are the source locations of a high variety of goods, spanning across the range from low- to high-value goods, the market areas of these centres will tend to be much larger than those for the small centres, whose product ranges are much smaller. The result of this is that the average linkage distance length of high-value/weight ratio goods will tend to be higher than for the lower-value/weight ratio goods, many of which will simply be purchased locally. The production of high-value/weight ratio goods will there-fore tend to be very dispersed across a small number of locations, separated by significant geographical distances. Meanwhile, lower-value/weight ratio goods will tend to be pro-duced in a large number of locations, each with a smaller market area. As we saw in section 2.6.2 above, there are many individual exceptions to this argument. However, these general observations are still very important in that they provide the foundations for models which describe the evolution of the urban system. This is the major topic which will be discussed in the remainder of this chapter.

2.7 Urban Hierarchies and Central Place Theory

The above sections describe the many theoretical reasons behind both the spatial cluster-ing and spatial dispersion of industrial activities. However, in reality the mix of these simultaneous tendencies towards either clustering or dispersion does not appear to pro-duce a spatial pattern which is entirely random. Observations from many countries sug-gest that there is a certain regularity in the spatial patterns of activity, and this regularity has two aspects. First, the spatial distribution of cities exhibits certain typical features, and secondly, the numerical distribution of such cities also exhibits certain typical fea-tures. Nations tend to be dominated by one or two primal cities, generally located in the centre of the major populated regions of the country. These cities will tend to be the production locations of most of the outputs produced by the economy. Other more peripheral regions will tend to be focused around successively smaller cities which dom-inate less populated hinterland areas. These smaller cities will also tend to produce a smaller range of outputs than the primal cities. At the same time, as the size of the individual city falls, the number of such cities generally increases. The result is that both the size and spatial distribution of the urban centres exhibit something of a hierarchical pyramidal pattern, as depicted in Figure 2.1.

The dominant city, which has the largest population, is defined as the city with the highest rank-ordering. The next group of similar-sized cities are defined as the second level in the rank-ordering of city sizes, and the subsequent group of smaller similar-sized cities as comprising the third level in the rank-ordering of the urban hierarchy. Exactly why the national-regional economy should exhibit such a spatial hierarchical pattern is the subject of much debate, and traditionally has been the focus of an area of research known as 'central-place' theory. In the following sections we will discuss three different approaches to central-place theory. Initially we will discuss the two approaches set within a two-dimensional framework, namely those of Christaller (1933) and Losch (1944). Subsequently, in Appendix 2.3 we also introduce the more recent 'new economic geography' approach to such questions, which follows the work primarily of Krugman (1991*a*, *b*) and Fujita *et al.* (1999*a* and 1999*b*).

2.7.1 The Christaller approach to central places

The first general discussion of the urban system came from a German scholar, Walter Christaller (1933), whose work was based on observations of the spatial distributions of cities and towns in Southern Germany. The Christaller model of central places is consequently primarily inductive rather than deductive, in the sense that the model is based more on observation of reality rather than on the extrapolation of any schema constructed from first principles (Parr 2002).

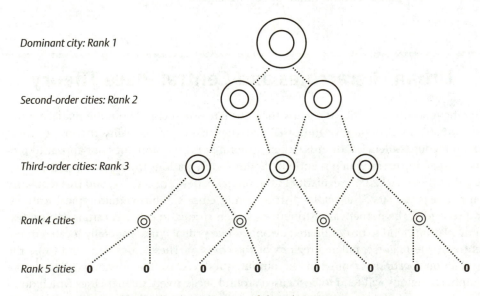

Dominant city: Rank 1

Second-order cities: Rank 2

Third-order cities: Rank 3

Rank 4 cities

Rank 5 cities

FIG. 2.1 The spatial and hierarchical organization of the urban system

The Christaller system assumes that there is a hierarchy of N different goods $g = (1, 2, \ldots N)$, a hierarchy of N different market area levels, $m = (1, 2, \ldots 724; N)$, and a hierarchy of N different-level urban centres, $u = (1, 2, \ldots N)$. Higher-order goods provide for larger spatial market areas, and it is assumed that there is a direct correspondence between the hierarchical position of each good and the size of its spatial market area. In other words, a good of level $g = 2$ will exhibit a spatial market of area $m = 2$, and a good of level $g = 3$ will exhibit a spatial market of area $m = 3$. Moreover, it is assumed that for an evenly distributed rural population, the relative size of the market area for a good of one level and a good of the level immediately below it, is always a constant, given as k. In other words, the ratio of the size of the market area of good $g = 3$, which we denote as $m = 3$, divided by the size of the market area of good $g = 2$, which we denote as $m = 2$, is given by k. This rate of increase of market area is assumed to hold for any successive move up through the hierarchical level of goods produced within the economy. Christaller also assumed that there was a direct correspondence between the hierarchical level of the urban centre and the range of goods it supplied. Any urban centre of level $u = (1, 2, \ldots N)$ is assumed to supply all of the goods $g = (1, 2, \ldots N)$ up to and including the corresponding level. Therefore a city of level $u = 3$ is assumed to supply goods $g = (1, 2, 3)$. The level of the urban centre thus corresponds to the range of goods produced in the city.

Given these assumptions, Christaller attempted to construct the particular spatial pattern which ensured that all locations were supplied with all goods from the minimum number of supply points (Beavon 1977, 22). As we see in Figure 2.2 which represents a spatial economy with three levels of urban centres, markets, and goods, the Christaller system arrived at a series of overlapping hexagonal market areas, in which the number of urban centres is inversely related to the variety of goods produced at each location. The justification for these particular spatial market patterns comes in part from observation, as has already been mentioned, but also from the principle that the maximum market coverage is provided for from the minimum number of production points. Allowing for the analytical limitations involved in the initial assumptions which motivate the system, the major contribution of Christaller's work is to show that a hierarchical urban system can exist automatically with a variety of different-sized spatial market areas.

2.7.2 The Losch approach to central places

The second major contribution to central-place theory also came from a German scholar, August Losch (1944, 1954). The Loschian approach, which is entirely deductive (Parr 2002), can be understood primarily as a microeconomic approach to understanding the urban system. In the situation where the economy is defined by a variety of firms producing a variety of goods, Losch's aim was to determine the 'ideal' economic landscape from first principles, where 'ideal' in this sense is understood to mean the most efficient spatial allocation of activity, and by assumption, the one which will thus arise naturally from a competitive economy. On the assumption that the real economy is competitive, the ideal landscape will therefore be the spatial pattern towards which the economy will tend to converge.

In order to discuss the Loschian framework we initially make assumptions similar to those of the Weber model, in that we assume that land is everywhere homogeneous with

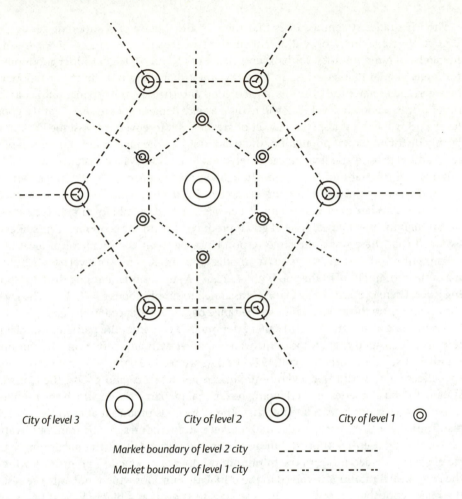

City of level 3   City of level 2   City of level 1

Market boundary of level 2 city   – – – – – – – – – –

Market boundary of level 1 city   – · – ·· – · – ·· – ·· – ··

FIG. 2.2 The Christaller model of the urban system

transportation possibilities equal in all directions. Within Losch's framework, we also assume that consumers are evenly located across space, and that the demand for the output of an individual firm exhibits some price elasticity. We can contrast this assumption with the Weber and Moses model assumptions, in which the firm's demand is infinitely elastic, and that of the Hotelling model in which the firm's demand exhibits zero elasticity. Assuming some price elasticity of demand for the output of an individual firm means that as the delivered price of the firm's output increases with shipment distance d, the quantity of output demanded Q_d at the delivery location at distance d falls.

In Figure 2.3, if the f.o.b. source price of the good produced by the firm at location K is given as p, the level of demand at locations immediately adjacent to K will be Q_K. However, as the delivered price of the output $p + td$ increases, where t is the transport rate per kilometre, the quantity demanded will fall. At some price $p + tD$, associated with a shipment distance of D, the quantity demanded will be zero.

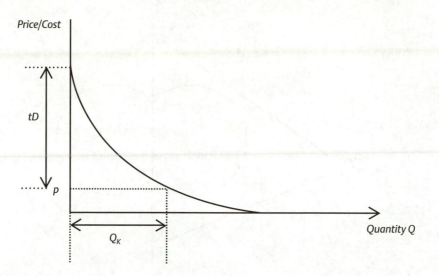

FIG. 2.3 The firm's demand schedule in the Loschian framework

As we see in Figure 2.4 which provides a three-dimensional perspective of the market area and location of the individual firm, if the firm is located at production point K, the distance D represents the radius of the limit of the firm's market area, and the market area is given as πD^2. This circle therefore defines the limit of the area within which the firm's demand is positive. A more complete specification of this two-dimensional demand function is given in Appendix 2.4.

If we now assume that spatial competition is possible on our two-dimensional plane we also have to decide how this will alter the circular market area of the individual firms. As

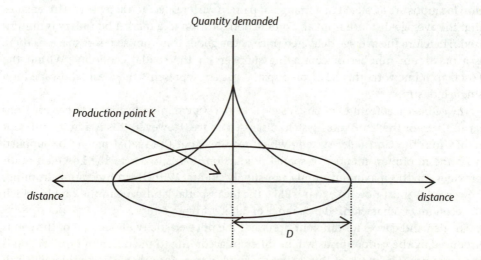

FIG. 2.4 The firm's market area in the Loschian framework

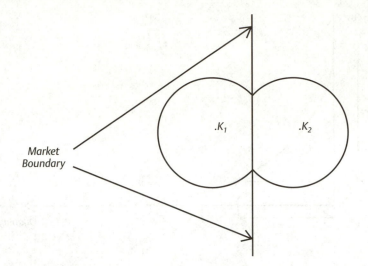

FIG. 2.5 The firm's market area with spatial competition

we see in Figure 2.5, if two identical firms producing identical goods are located close to each other at K_1 and K_2, the market will be split along the line which is equidistant between the two firms.

Therefore, if we now assume that competition ensures that all the land is to be occupied by identical firms, Losch's argument is that the spatial economy will exhibit a honeycomb pattern of hexagons, as described by Figure 2.6, in which the points K_1 to K_8 represent the actual locations of the individual firms at the centre of each of the individual market areas. Each hexagonal market area will contain an identical firm located at its centre. The argument here is that with hexagonal market areas, the individual production locations are arranged in a triangular pattern with respect to each other. This ensures that the average distance from any production location to a market boundary is minimized. Therefore the average delivered price of the goods is minimized over space, as there is a maximum number of competing suppliers in the spatial economy. Within the Loschian framework, this hexagonal spatial pattern represents the ideal landscape for a single industry.

The geometrical features of Losch's ideal spatial system initially appear to be very similar to those of the Christaller system discussed above. However, this is a quite different result from the Christaller system, which required that the spatial market be supplied from the minimum number of spatial production points, whereas the Loschian result provides for the maximum number of supply points. With this observation in mind, however, we must now ask what will be the ideal spatial landscape in the case in which the economy is characterized by a range of different types of firms?

The demand curves for different firms and the price elasticity of demand of the goods produced by the various firms will be different according to the different types of goods they produce. The result of this is that the market areas for different types of goods will also be different according to the characteristics of the individual demand curves. Allow-

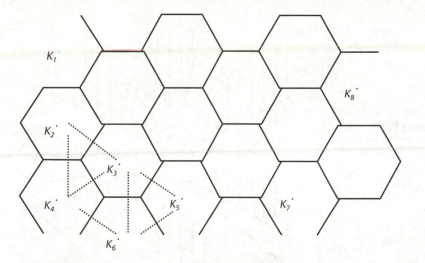

FIG. 2.6 The spatial distribution of the markets of identical firms

ing for the caveats discussed in section 2.6.2 above, we can assume that high-value products tend to be price-inelastic, due to product quality and product heterogeneity, whereas low-value products tend to be highly price-elastic due to product homogeneity. Therefore in general, firms producing goods whose demand curves are highly price-elastic will tend to exhibit small market areas. The reason is that the demand for the product will be very sensitive to the transport cost mark-up on the source price of the good, with demand falling sharply over even small delivery distances. On the other hand, goods whose demand curves are highly price-inelastic will be relatively insensitive to transport cost mark-ups. The result of this is that demand will fall only slowly with increasing delivery distance, thereby tending to increase the market area. At the same time, different firms producing different goods will also exhibit different supply cost curves, and it is the interrelationship between the demand curves and the supply curves which will determine the actual sizes of the individual hexagonal market areas. The ideal Loschian hexagonal spatial pattern will therefore be different for different types of firms. Firms producing highly price-elastic goods, such as many agricultural commodities, will tend to exhibit small hexagonal market areas and be located at many points, whereas firms producing low price-elastic goods will tend to exhibit larger hexagonal spatial areas and be located at fewer points.

In a situation such as this where the economy is made up of a variety of firms producing a variety of products, and where the spatial economy exhibits a variety of hexagonal market area patterns, the Loschian argument is that the most efficient economic landscape is one where the maximum number of firms are located at the same point. The logic of this argument is that the maximum number of firms located at the same point will allow agglomeration economies to take place within each of the sets of firms which are located at the same place.

The mathematics and geometry of the Loschian argument and results are beyond the scope of this book, although the general conclusions of Losch are quite straightforward.

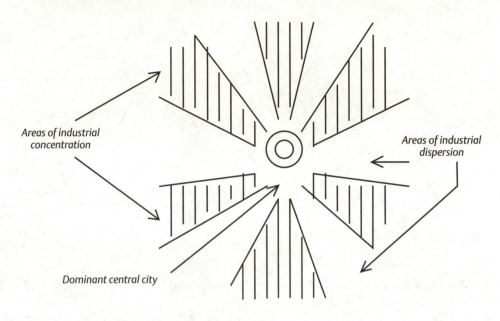

Areas of industrial concentration

Areas of industrial dispersion

Dominant central city

FIG. 2.7 The Loschian ideal landscape

As we see in Figure 2.7, Losch concludes that the economy of any spatial area will tend to be dominated by a central primal city, the hinterland of which will be characterized by smaller settlements and alternating areas of industrial concentration and dispersion. The rationale and justification for Losch's actual conclusions have been the source of much debate (Beavon 1977), but Parr (2002) concludes that the primary contribution of Losch's work is to show that industrial concentration and urbanization can arise independently of local peculiarity or particularity.

2.8 The Empirical Description of the Urban System: The Rank-Size Rule

In section 2.7 it was mentioned that observations from many countries suggest that there appears to be something of a regularity to the size distribution of the cities within a country. This apparent regularity is often discussed in terms of what is known as the rank-size rule.

As with any economic observations of distributions we can write a very general description of a distribution function as $f(x)$, whereby $f(x)$ shows the frequency with which a variable X takes a given value x in the sample or population. If X is continuous, the cumulative distribution which shows the number of observations not greater than x can be written as (Chiang 1984):

$$F(x) = \int_0^x f(x)dx. \tag{2.5}$$

In the case of cities, as we have already mentioned, most cities within a country will tend to be small, with successively larger cities being progressively fewer in number. The result of this is that a frequency distribution $F(x)$ of urban areas, ranked according to the size (x) of the individual urban area, will tend to be very skewed to the left. Yet, we know from our discussions in sections 2.1 to 2.5 that very large urban areas play a crucial role in the behaviour and performance of the overall economy, due primarily to the presence of agglomeration economies. The result of this is that urban and regional economics tends to place a greater emphasis on the behaviour and performance of these large urban clusters, which are relatively few in number. For this reason, city-size distributions are measured from the right-hand side of the distribution. In other words, if the total number of urban areas is given as T, the city-size distribution function $R(x)$ is defined as $R(x) = T[1 - F(x)]$. The city-size function $R(x)$ therefore describes the number of urban areas which are greater in size than x. As the actual city-size distribution is skewed we employ a non-linear function. Within urban and regional economics, the usual functional form of the city-size distribution is a modified version of the Pareto-income distribution function (Mills 1970; Mills and Hamilton 1994) given as

$$R(x) = Mx^{-a}, \tag{2.6}$$

where M is the population of the dominant metropolitan area. For any country, the size distribution of the urban areas can be estimated econometrically by taking a log transformation of this function. In other words we estimate the function

$$\log R(x) = \log M - a \log x. \tag{2.7}$$

On the basis of many empirical observations, however, a simple common assumption is that the value of a is close to 1. In other words our city-size distribution function is given as

$$R(x) = Mx^{-1}, \tag{2.8}$$

where x is the individual city size, and $R(x)$ is the rank order of the particular city within the urban hierarchy. The situation in which the value of a in equation (2.7) is assumed to be close to 1 is known as the simple rank-size rule or Zipf's (1949) Law. The simple rank-size rule can be rewritten as

$$xR(x) = M, \tag{2.9}$$

which states that the size of the individual city multiplied by its rank order is a constant M, where M is defined as the population of the largest urban centre in the country. For the largest metropolitan area, the population will be M and its rank order will be one. For the second-rank urban areas, the population will be approximately half that of the dominant city, and for the third-rank urban areas the populations will be approximately one-third that of the dominant city. Obviously, the rank-size rule is neither a rule nor a law, but it is a useful approximation in many countries.

Some countries correspond fairly closely to the rank-size rule. For example, in the UK, the largest urban area, defined as being a contiguous urban agglomeration, is London, which in 1998 had a population of 7.2 million (ONS 2000). The second-order urban centres in the UK, in terms of population, are Manchester and Birmingham, each with a population of 2.3 million and the Leeds–Bradford urban area, with a population of 2.1 million. The second-order urban centres give a combined population of 7 million. The urban distribution of these two ranks of cities therefore appears to conform quite reasonably to the simple rank-size rule. However, the third-order urban agglomerations in the UK are the Glasgow, Liverpool, Sheffield, and Newcastle economies, with populations of 1.4 million, 1.4 million, 1.3 million, and 1.2 million, respectively. The combined population of the third-order centres is 5.3 million, which is somewhat lower than would be predicted by the rank-size rule. However, we can still regard the rank-size rule as a useful approximation of the urban distribution of the UK.

In the case of Italy, the largest urban agglomeration in 1992 was that of Milan, with a population of 5.3 million (UN 1992), while the second-order centres were Naples and Rome, with populations of 3.6 million and 3.1 million, respectively. In the case of Italy, the relationship between the first- and second-rank cities appears to correspond quite closely to the simple rank-size rule. However, the third-rank Italian cities are those of Turin and Genoa, with populations of 1.5 million and 1.0 million, respectively. All other urban centres are significantly smaller than these two, which suggests that, as with the UK, the observations tend to diverge from the simple rank-size rule as we move down the urban hierarchy. Similarly, in the case of Germany, the largest urban agglomeration in 1992 was that of Essen-Ruhr, at 6.4 million, followed by those of Frankfurt and Berlin, with populations of 3.7 million and 3.5 million, respectively (UN 1992). However, as with both the UK and Italy, the third-rank cities in Germany do not appear to correspond quite so closely to the simple rank-size rule, given that the populations of Cologne, Düsseldorf, Hamburg, Stuttgart, and Munich are 2.9 million, 2.8 million, 2.6 million, 2.5 million, and 2.2 million, respectively (UN 1992).

On the other hand, many countries in the newly industrializing parts of the world exhibit an urban distribution which is very different from the rank-size distribution. For example, the Thai capital of Bangkok is somewhere between forty and seventy times larger than the second-order urban centres, depending on the spatial definition used (Kittiprapas and McCann 1999). Similarly, the 1992 population of Buenos Aires was 11.8 million, whereas that of the second largest city in Argentina, Rosario, was only 1.1 million (UN 1992). This difference between the urban distributions of the industrialized and newly industrializing economies may suggest that the highly skewed urban distributions within many newly industrializing economies are something of a transition phenomenon. In other words, as these newly industrializing economies continue to develop and grow, their spatial economies will tend to move towards the more even rank-size spatial distribution associated with industrialized economies.

The long-run simulation results of Fujita *et al.* (1999*a* and 1999*b*), discussed in Appendix 2.3, do suggest that the rank-size rule does indeed approximate to the long-run spatial distribution of a mature spatial system. Moreover, Gabaix (1999*a, b*) has argued that the rank-size rule is a natural result of a growth process which is independent of the size of the centre. However, caution needs to be exercised with such interpretations, because as we have already stated, the rank-size rule is neither a rule nor a law. Moreover, depending on the slope coefficients we employ in equation (2.7), there are a variety of rank-size relationships possible. Finally, there are many mature economies, such as Ireland, Denmark, France, and South Korea, which exhibit highly skewed urban distributions which do not approximate to any form of rank-size relationship.

2.9 Measuring Spatial Concentration and Regional Diversification

The extent to which industrial activities are spatially concentrated or dispersed across the various regions of an economy can be discussed from two broad perspectives. The first approach is to measure the extent to which a given national industry is evenly distributed spatially across the national urban system. The second approach is to take a given region and to consider the relative contribution of each industry to the regional industrial structure.

In the first approach, the most direct method of measuring the extent to which a given national industry is evenly distributed spatially across the national urban system comes from what is known as the Hirschmann–Herfindahl index (Ellison and Glaeser 1997). This is defined as

$$G_i = \sum_{r=1}^{m} (s_{ir} - x_r)^2,$$
(2.10)

where G is the Hirschmann–Herfindahl index, s_{ir} represents the share of industry sector i's national employment in each region r, and x_r represents the share of aggregate national employment in each region r.

Following Black and Henderson (1999), expression (2.10) can be rewritten as

$$G_i = \sum_{r=1}^{m} \left[\frac{E_{ir}}{E_{in}} - \frac{E_r}{E_n} \right]^2,$$
(2.11)

where E_{ir} is employment in sector i in region r, E_{in} is employment in sector i in country n, E_r is employment in region r, and E_n is employment in country n.

The Hirschmann–Herfindahl index of industrial spatial concentration is given by the sum over all regions of the squared deviations of each region's share of total national manufacturing. Where an industry is evenly distributed across the urban system, such that its spatial distribution exactly mirrors that of the urban hierarchy, the value of G will be zero. Alternatively, as the industry tends towards being more spatially concentrated, the Hirschmann–Herfindahl index tends towards a maximum value of 2. However, given that the deviations are squared, the index tends to be dominated by the two or three largest cities (Black and Henderson 1999). The Hirschmann–Herfindahl index of industrial spatial concentration captures the degree to which a particular industry's spatial distribution reflects that of the national urban hierarchy. In other words, the index can be used to measure the extent to which an industry tends to cluster in space. Higher values of the index indicate that the industry in question tends to cluster in a small number of locations. As such, from the arguments in sections 2.2 to 2.5, in cases where the Hirschmann–Herfindahl index is a high value, we would suggest that such an industry tends to benefit from agglomeration economies. Alternatively, where the index value approaches zero, we would expect that the industry tends not to benefit from clustering.

The second approach to considering the extent to which industries are clustered or dispersed across space is to take a given region and to consider the relative contribution of each industry to the regional industrial structure. This approach provides us with a range of measures of the specialization, or alternatively of the diversity, of individual regions rather than industries. Duranton and Puga (2000) suggest that the simplest method of capturing regional industrial diversity is simply to compute

$$RDI_r = \frac{1}{\sum_i |s_{ir} - s_{in}|},$$
(2.12)

where RDI_i is the relative diversity index of the region r, s_{ir} represents the share of industry i in region r, and s_{in} represents the share of industry i in the national economy n. For an individual region, equation (2.12) represents the inverse of the summed differences between each regional and national industrial share. Using the same notation as in equation (2.11), in terms of employment equation (2.12) can be rewritten as

$$RDI_r = \frac{1}{\sum_i \left| \frac{E_{ir}}{E_r} - \frac{E_{in}}{E_n} \right|}.$$
(2.13)

The value of the relative diversity index increases as the regional employment distribution approaches that of the national economy.

A very similar index of regional specialization comes from Blair (1995, 113). Once again, using the notation of equation (2.11) the index of regional specialization can be defined as

$$IRS_r = \sum_i a \left[\frac{E_{ir}}{E_r} - \frac{E_{in}}{E_n} \right].$$
(2.14)

where a takes the value of 1 if $E_{ir} \backslash E_r > E_{in} \backslash E_n$, and a takes the value of zero otherwise. The index of regional specialization is calculated as the sum of all of the positive differences between the regional industrial employment shares and the national industrial employment shares.

A final alternative index is proposed by Amiti (1998), in which the location quotients (see section 4.3 of Chapter 4 for a detailed discussion of location quotients) of each of a region's industries are ranked in descending order. The cumulative sum of the location quotient numerator terms is plotted against the cumulative sum of the denominator terms. The regional specialization Gini coefficient is then calculated as twice the area between the plotted line and the 45-degree line.

As we will see in section 4.3 and Appendix 4.2.1 of Chapter 4, there is a close affinity between each of these particular indices of spatial industrial concentration and regional diversity, and several other indices which are also employed in order to indirectly measure regional trade flows.

2.10 Conclusions

This chapter has discussed the various reasons why the spatial pattern of industrial activity exhibits both concentration and dispersion. Different industries will exhibit different spatial patterns, according to the extent to which they benefit from spatial proximity. There are a variety of potential benefits from spatial industrial clustering, the impacts of which will be different for different firms in different locations. However, at the same time, in other industrial sectors there will be a preference for the dispersal of firms. As we have seen, the underlying reasons why particular industries tend to benefit from spatial concentration or dispersion are many and varied, and at present there is no full consensus on these issues. Yet these various patterns of spatial industrial concentration and dispersion do tend to give rise to a hierarchical pattern of urban centres, the regularity of which can be captured by a range of empirical measures.

Discussion questions

1   Explain the role played by information acquisition costs in determining industrial location behaviour.

2   What are the sources of agglomeration economies and how can we classify the different types of agglomeration effects?

3   What other descriptions of industrial clusters do we have? What is the contribution of information, uncertainty, and trust to these other cluster descriptions?

4   What different approaches do we have to explain the structure of urban hierarchies?

5   In what ways do the 'new economic geography' models differ from traditional central-place models?

6   What is the relationship between urban size and urban diversity or specialization? How can we measure this relationship?

Appendix 2.1 Spatial Monopoly and Price Discrimination

In standard microeconomic arguments of third-degree price discrimination in which a firm sells the same good in different markets, it is always argued that a firm will price discriminate so as to equate the marginal revenue earned in each market. We can also apply the same logic to the case where market areas are differentiated by location explicitly as a function of the distance over which the goods are shipped. The total revenue TR can be defined as $TR = PQ$, where P is the price of the good and Q is the quantity produced. Therefore the marginal revenue can be defined as:

$$MR = \frac{\partial(TR)}{\partial Q} = P + \frac{\partial P}{\partial Q}Q, \tag{A.2.1.1}$$

which can be rewritten as

$$MR = \frac{\partial(TR)}{\partial Q} = P + \frac{\partial P}{\partial Q}Q\left(\frac{P}{P}\right), \tag{A.2.1.2}$$

which gives

$$MR = \frac{\partial(TR)}{\partial Q} = P + \left(\frac{\partial P}{P}\right)\left(\frac{Q}{\partial Q}\right)P, \tag{A.2.1.3}$$

Therefore, remembering that

$$-\frac{\partial Q/Q}{\partial P/P} = e, \tag{A.2.1.4}$$

where e is the price elasticity of demand, we have

$$MR = P\left(1 - \frac{1}{e}\right). \tag{A.2.1.5}$$

With this general aspatial expression for marginal revenue, we can now consider the distance costs which will eat into any revenue earned at any location. Following Greenhut (1970) and Greenhut and Ohta (1975), if we define distance costs as td, where d is the distance and t is the transport rate, the theory of third-degree price discrimination suggests that the marginal revenue net of transport costs gained at all locations should be the same. In other words, the value of $(MR - td)$ for all locations should be the same. If we set the net marginal revenue at any given value k, such that $(MR - td) = k$, this implies that k is invariant with respect to d. Therefore

$$MR - td = P\left(1 - \frac{1}{e}\right) - td = k \tag{A.2.1.6}$$

holds for all locations. If we set $t = 1$ for simplicity, this can be rewritten as

$$k = P - P_e^{-1} - d, \tag{A.2.1.7}$$

which, by differentiating with respect to d, with the knowledge that k is invariant with respect to d, allows us observe the behaviour of delivered prices as distance changes, under a regime of price discrimination thus:

$$\frac{\partial k}{\partial d} = \frac{\partial P}{\partial d} - \left(\frac{\partial P}{\partial d}\right)\frac{1}{e} + P\frac{1}{e}\left(\frac{\partial e}{\partial P}\right)\left(\frac{\partial P}{\partial d}\right) - 1 = 0.$$

(A.2.1.8)

This can be rewritten as

$$\frac{\partial k}{\partial d} = \frac{\partial P}{\partial d}\left[1 - \frac{1}{e} + \frac{a}{e}\right] - 1 = 0,$$

(A.2.1.9)

where

$$a = \frac{\partial e/e}{\partial P/P},$$

(A.2.1.10)

which represents the proportionate change in the price elasticity of demand relative to the proportionate change in price. Our above expression can be rearranged to give

$$\frac{\partial P}{\partial d}\left[\frac{e - 1 + a}{e}\right] - 1 = 0.$$

(A.2.1.11)

Therefore

$$\frac{\partial P}{\partial d}\left[\frac{a - (1 - e)}{e}\right] = 1$$

(A.2.1.12)

and

$$\frac{\partial P}{\partial d} = \frac{e}{a - (1 - e)}.$$

(A.2.1.13)

The change in delivered prices with respect to delivery distance therefore depends on the value of a. If $a = 1$ there will be no price discrimination in favour of distant customers. The value of $\delta P/\delta d$ will be equal to one, which means that prices will increase linearly with distance. On the other hand, if $a > 1$, the value of $\delta P/\delta d$ will be less than one, which means that prices will increase less than linearly with distance. In this case, the firm is discriminating delivered prices in favour of distant customers and against local customers, over whom the firm already has a monopoly. If $a < 1$ the value of $\delta P/\delta d$ will be less than 1, which means that the firm will discriminate against distant customers by increasing transport mark-ups beyond the actual cost of the freight. However, given that a rational firm will always attempt to maximize its market area, *ceteris paribus*, this theoretical possibility makes no sense. Moreover, as Greenhut and Ohta (1975) point out, as long as demand falls to zero at some price level, then a cannot be less than unity. Therefore we can rule this latter observation out.

From the point of view of market areas, this price discrimination argument implies that market areas can be extended under conditions where firms have some level of spatial monopoly power. The larger is the firm and the greater is the consequent level of firm monopoly power, the greater will be the market area of the firm and the greater will be its ability to employ price discrimination. Therefore, the larger is the firm and the greater its level of monopoly power, the greater will be the average distance over which goods are shipped and the greater will be the possibilities for firms to be spatially dispersed.

Appendix 2.2   The Derivation of Reilly's Law

Reilly's Law states that

$$\frac{A}{a^2} = \frac{B}{(x-a)^2}. \tag{A.2.2.1}$$

Therefore, if $r = A/B$, we have

$$r = \frac{a^2}{(x-a)^2}. \tag{A.2.2.2}$$

This implies that

$$\sqrt{r} = \frac{a}{x-a} \tag{A.2.2.3}$$

and

$$x - a = \frac{a}{\sqrt{r}}. \tag{A.2.2.4}$$

This can be rewritten as

$$x\sqrt{r} - a\sqrt{r} = a, \tag{A.2.2.5}$$

which gives

$$x\sqrt{r} = a(1 + \sqrt{r}). \tag{A.2.2.6}$$

Therefore we have

$$a = \frac{x\sqrt{r}}{1 + \sqrt{r}}, \tag{A.2.2.7}$$

which gives the distance of the market boundary a from retail location A (Richardson 1978). More complete two-dimensional descriptions of Reilly's Law can be found in Hoover and Giarratani (1985) and Parr (1997).

Appendix 2.3   The Krugman–Fujita Model

The two central-place approaches discussed in section 2.7 are set explicitly within a two-dimensional spatial framework. However, there is a sense in which these two approaches are rather static, in that the historical evolution of these ideal spatial urban systems is ignored. In both of the above models it is implicitly assumed that the spatial outcomes of the competitive market process will automatically converge towards something close to the ideal landscapes. Yet, until recently, these assumptions have not been tested. Some new insights have been provided by the recent area of research commonly known as 'new economic geography' which follows the work primarily of Krugman (1991*a*, *b*; 1993), Fujita and Krugman (1995), and Fujita *et al.* (1999*a*, *b*). The models developed within this particular research programme have attempted to generate and simulate Christaller-type general equilibrium results within a monopolistic competition framework. The analyses are set in one-dimensional space, and the models are based on a set of simple assumptions regarding the costs of distance, the utility of consumers, and the productivity of manufacturing and agriculture. While a detailed analysis of this particular research field is well beyond the scope of this book, following Krugman (1991a, b) and Fujita et al. (1999b) the basic tenets of these models are outlined here. There are three basic assumptions upon which these complex new economic geography models are built. These assumptions relate to the welfare effects associated with product variety, the productivity of manufacturing, and finally the costs of transporting goods.

In terms of welfare effects, the Krugman–Fujita models assume that the economy is split into two sectors, namely agriculture and manufacturing. Manufacturing industry is assumed to produce a variety of outputs under monopolistically competitive conditions, whereas agriculture is assumed to produce a homogeneous product under conditions of perfect competition. All consumers are assumed to have the same tastes, defined by the simple Cobb–Douglas utility function

$$U = M^{\mu}A^{1-\mu}, \tag{A.2.3.1}$$

where M is the composite index of consumption of manufactured goods, A is the consumption of agricultural goods, and μ is the expenditure share of manufactured goods.

However, embedded within this utility function is a sub-utility function which describes the aggregate demand for the variety of manufactured products. This function is based on the monopolistic functional form first employed by Dixit and Stiglitz (1977), and is given as

$$M = \left[\sum_{i=1}^{n} (m_i)^{\rho} \right]^{1/\rho}, \tag{A.2.3.2}$$

where m_i represents the consumption of each individual variety of manufactured good, and ρ is a parameter with a range between zero and one, representing the strength of the consumer preference for product variety among n manufactured goods. If ρ is close to one, the different goods are almost perfect substitutes for each other, and the demand curve for each firm tends towards being horizontal. On the other hand, the closer ρ is to zero, the greater is the consumer preference for product variety, and the more price-inelastic is the demand curve for any individual firm. If we set $\sigma = 1/(1 - \rho)$, and assume that there is a continuum of n varieties of manufactured goods, we can write the demand function for manufactured goods as a CES (constant elasticity of substitution) function as

$$M = \left[\int_0^n m_i^{(\sigma-1/\sigma)} di \right]^{\frac{\sigma}{\sigma-1}}, \tag{A.2.3.3}$$

where σ represents the elasticity of substitution between any two varieties of manufactured good, varying between infinity for perfect substitutes and unity for highly differentiated products. Fujita et al. (1999, 46–8) show that if the prices of the individual manufactured goods m_i are defined as p_i, the general cost of living index, which defines the minimum costs of purchasing a single unit of the composite manufactured good M, can be defined as

$$C_m = \left[\int_0^n p_i^{(1-\sigma)} di \right]^{\frac{1}{1-\sigma}},$$ (A.2.3.4)

If the number of product varieties available increases, the fact that consumers value product variety means that the cost of attaining any given level of utility falls. Therefore, the cost of living falls. We can see this because if all manufactured goods are sold at the same price P_m, equation (A.2.3.4) reduces to

$$C_m = P_m n^{1/(1-\sigma)},$$ (A.2.3.5)

In other words, as the number of varieties n of manufactured products increases, the fall in the cost of living is greater for lower values of the elasticity of substitution σ. Similarly, for a given elasticity of substitution σ, the cost of living is inversely proportional to the number of product varieties.

In terms of the productivity of firms, it is assumed that agriculture exhibits constant returns to scale and is a perfectly competitive economy. On the other hand, manufacturing is assumed to exhibit increasing returns to scale of the form

$$L_m = a + b X_m,$$ (A.2.3.6)

where L_m represents the labour employed by each manufacturing firm, and X_m represents the manufactured output of the firm. This simple specification of increasing returns to scale implies that for each firm, the labour required to produce any level of output exhibits both a fixed overhead component, independent of the level of output, and a variable component directly related to the level of output. The existence of increasing returns to scale, along with consumers' preference for product variety, means that each firm will produce a single unique good. In this monopolistically competitive environment, the number of firms therefore will be the same as the number of products produced.

From the perspective of the monopolistic producers, the perceived elasticity of demand for their own product is σ. Therefore the output price mark-up on their marginal cost can be expressed as

$$P_i(1 - 1/\sigma) = bw_m = MC,$$ (A.2.3.7)

where w_m is the wage for manufacturing labour and p_i is the output price. This gives

$$P_i = \left(\frac{\sigma}{\sigma - 1} \right) bw_m.$$ (A.2.3.8)

With zero profits, we know that price equals marginal cost. Therefore, the ratio of $\sigma/(\sigma - 1)$ acts also as an index of economies of scale, as well as being a parameter of consumer preference for variety. Assuming freedom of entry within the monopolistically competitive environment leads to zero profits, then revenue must equal costs. In other words

$$P_i^* X_m = w_m(a + bX_m),$$ (A.2.3.9)

where p_i^* is the equilibrium output price. Combining (A.2.3.8) with (A.2.3.9) we have

$$X_m^* = \frac{a(\sigma - 1)}{b},$$ (A.2.3.10)

where X_m^* is the profit-maximizing equilibrium level of output of the firm, and the equilibrium labour demand L_m^* for the firm is thus:

$$L^*_m = a + \frac{a(\sigma - 1)}{b} = a\sigma. \tag{A.2.3.11}$$

If there are L_M workers in a region, the number of manufactured goods produced in the region will therefore be

$$n = \frac{L_M}{L^*_m} = \frac{L_M}{a + bX^*_m} = \frac{L_M}{a\sigma}. \tag{A.2.3.12}$$

As such, in this particular formulation, the number of varieties of outputs produced in a region, and consequently the number of firms in the region producing the outputs, can all be expressed simply in terms of the variety of goods available.

The third central element of the Krugman–Fujita approach is the particular way in which distance costs are modelled. Distance costs are defined in terms of 'iceberg' transport costs, an approach previously employed by Samuelson (1952) and Mundell (1957). The iceberg analogy comes from the idea that the transport costs involved in towing an iceberg can be understood as causing an iceberg to melt away during the journey. The costs of overcoming distance are therefore regarded as 'eating into' the quantity of the good being shipped, and the consequent decay or shrinking of the good thereby ensures that only a fraction of the good actually arrives at any particular location. In the Krugman–Fujita approach, the iceberg specification of distance costs is applied more generally to all goods shipments. Assuming a constant the rate of decay for each unit of distance travelled, given as τ, where $0 < \tau < 1$, iceberg transport costs can be described generally as

$$P_{id} = P_i e^{-\tau d}, \tag{A.2.3.13}$$

where P_i is the source f.o.b price per tonne of the good, τ is the constant rate of decay of the good with respect to the distance d, and P_{id} is the delivered price of the quantity of good actually delivered at the distance d. This description of distance costs implies that the costs of distance are a function of the value of the good produced, because the level of decay is proportional to the source price of the good. At the same time, we see that the greater is the haulage distance, the greater will be the level of decay, and consequently the smaller will be the quantity of goods actually delivered. Therefore, in order to ensure that a given quantity of goods is actually delivered at any particular location, the total quantity of goods purchased at the source location must increase as the delivery distance increases, in order to offset the process of goods-decay. In other words, for any given source value of the good, the total level of goods expenditure increases with haulage distance at a rate proportional to $e^{\tau d}$. The iceberg transport costs associated with delivering a given weight of product at any given distance can therefore be understood to increase exponentially with distance as described by Figure A.2.3.1.

If we compare Figure A.2.3.1 with the distance-transport cost functions discussed in the appendices to Chapter 1, we see that the behaviour of iceberg transport costs with respect to distance is rather different from the types of transport cost functions typically employed in location theory models. As we have seen, the general form of transport cost functions employed in location theory models are either linear or concave with distance. These reflect the usual empirical observations of the relationship between transport costs and haulage distance (McCann 2001).

The Krugman–Fujita models integrate these three issues, namely product variety competition, economies of scale, and transport costs within place-specific

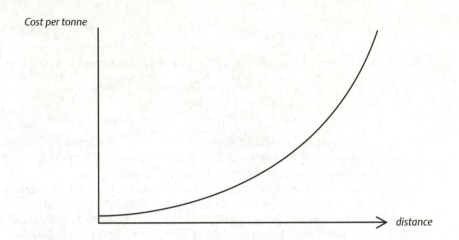

FIG. A.2.3.1 Iceberg transport costs and haulage distance

considerations, within a framework of labour mobility. Labour moves between locations according to real wages, which as usual, are defined as nominal wages deflated by the local cost of living index. The nominal wages paid to workers are higher the better is the access of (i.e. the closer is) a firm to a market, the greater is the local market income, and the lower is the level of local product competition. Conversely, the cost of living increases according to the geographic distance, and the lack of local product competition. Large cities with a wide range of manufacturing activities producing a high variety of products will be relatively inexpensive to live in, in real terms, because the high variety of goods locally available will allow any given level of utility to be achieved at lower real cost. At the same time, these areas will also produce goods at relatively low cost because of the intense local competition, thereby allowing large market areas to be captured. However, the point about the exponential form of the iceberg transport cost function is that the market area tends towards being finite, subject to the source prices of the goods. Therefore some small cities, or cities which are geographically peripheral with low product competition and high source prices, will still be able to capture small local-market areas. The role of distance-transport costs is therefore to act as a counterbalance to the effect of localized increasing returns to scale in the major cities. Within this integrated framework, the Krugman–Fujita models show how cities can naturally grow and decline as national and international market areas expand. In particular, these models suggest how Christaller-type urban hierarchies, approximating to the rank-size rule, can be a natural response to economic development over time.

Many variants of these 'new economic geography' models have already been developed. In particular, Holmes (1999) has argued that the growth of the city will result not only in an increase in the variety of goods produced, but also in an increase in the quantity of locally produced goods. This is a departure from the standard Dixit–Stiglitz model, whereby the equilibrium output of any particular locally produced differentiated good is independent of the local population.

Appendix 2.4   **The Loschian Demand Function**

If we consider Figure 2.3, in which the market demand of the firm is defined in one-dimensional terms, we see that the quantity demanded Q is a function of the delivered price of the good. As such, we can write in very general terms that

$$Q = f(p + td), \tag{A.2.4.1}$$

where p is the source price of the good, t is the transport rate per kilometre, and d is the haulage distance. The total market sales of the firm are therefore given by the sum of all the individual demands at each location. This can be written as

$$Q = \int_{0}^{D} f(p + td)dd, \tag{A.2.4.2}$$

where D is the distance to the edge of the market.

Equation (A.2.4.2) is the integral of each of the individual demands along the one-dimensional spatial plane moving away from the firm's production point in one direction only. However, in order to consider the firm's demand in a two-dimensional spatial plane, it is necessary for us to consider the demand defined by equation (A.2.4.2) for movements in any direction away from the firm's production location.

From Figure 2.4 we see how the Loschian spatial market area for the firm without adjacent competitors is defined. If we modify Figure 2.4 to give Figure A.2.4.1 we can see how the two-dimensional spatial market can be conceived of as being comprised of segments. The total area of the spatial market is defined by that particular portion of the total circular market which the firm has. In Figure A.2.4.1, the market segment is defined by the angle θ. If the firm only has a one-dimensional market along the east–west line, the angle θ will be zero degrees. Alternatively, if the firm has half of the circular spatial

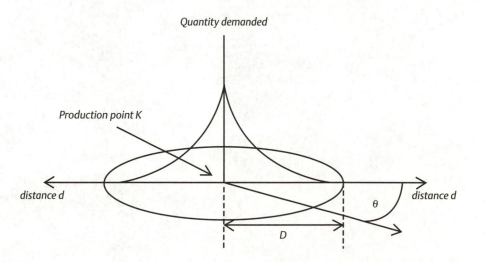

FIG. A.2.4.1 The firm's market area in the Loschian framework

market, the angle θ will be 180 degrees, or π radians. In the case of the Loschian spatial market where there are no adjacent competitors, the firm has all of the circular spatial market, such that the angle of π will be 360 degrees or 2π radians.

In order to find the total market revenue for the firm it is therefore also necessary to calculate the firm's market demand function, given by equation (A.2.4.2), as a function of the two-dimensional spatial market area. To do this we integrate equation (A.2.4.2) as a function of the two-dimensional spatial area:

$$Q = \int_0^{2\pi} \left\{ \int_0^D f(p + td)dd \right\} d\theta. \qquad (A.2.4.3)$$

Equation (A.2.4.3) defines the total sales of the firm as being the volume of the cone in Figures 2.4 and A.2.4.1.

Chapter 3
The Spatial Structure of the Urban Economy

3.1 Introduction

In the two previous chapters we discussed the reasons for the variations in the spatial patterns of industrial investment and activity. As we have seen, firms will locate in different areas for different reasons, and where this behaviour leads to the co-location of firms we observe spatial concentrations of investment. In some cases, the various advantages which are sometimes associated with spatial concentrations of such activity, give rise to the growth of both cities and also hierarchical systems of cities. As we know, individual cities can grow to be very large, and in some cases as large as some individual small countries. There will, however, be a variety of different people living within such spatial concentrations, and also there will be a variety of activities taking place within the city. This consequently brings us to the question of how such people and activities are distributed within the individual urban economy.

In discussing how people and activities are distributed within the urban economy we focus on the question of urban land use. In other words, we try to explain why certain groups of people, or certain industrial activities, occupy land at particular locations within the city economy. Observation of the behaviour of urban economies suggests that there are two key features common to all urban areas. These features are that, in general, land prices tend to fall with increasing distance from the city centre at a diminishing rate, and that the average land area occupied by each household or business activity tends to increase with increasing distance away from the city centre. Given that there is a market for land in which land is allocated according to users, in order to understand the allocation of land within the city and the relationship between location and land prices, we must therefore ask the question of how much people or firms are willing to pay in order to occupy land at any particular location. In sections 3.2 to 3.4 of this chapter we will construct a set of models, namely a von Thunen model and a bid-rent model, which are most commonly used to explain such phenomena. In the subsequent sections, these models will be contrasted with alternative explanations of the structure of urban land use and land prices.

We begin by constructing a one-dimensional model of the relationship between location and land-rent, based on the analysis of von Thunen (1826). The von Thunen model is the simplest model describing the relationship between location and land use, and will act as the building block upon which our subsequent models are developed. This approach allows us to understand how much land is employed in productive activities, and how land can be allocated between competing uses. This fixed-coefficients von Thunen model will then be extended to a more general variable-coefficients model, known as a 'bid-rent' model. The bid-rent model, which allows for substitution behaviour between land and other production or consumption factors, is the orthodox model of the urban economy. We will see that applying conventional production and consumption theory to the bid-rent model, this provides us with a range of conclusions regarding the distribution of urban land, the location of urban activities and people, and the land prices charged at each location.

3.2 The von Thunen Model

In order to construct a von Thunen model, we assume that there is a specific market point located at M, at which all agricultural goods are traded, and we assume that all land is owned by absentee landlords. We assume that all farmers producing the same agricultural good, exhibit the same production technology and the same fixed production coefficients. We assume that land is of identical quality at all locations and also that there is freedom of entry into the agricultural market. Therefore, any production locations which can be shown to be profitable will result in the agricultural land at that particular location being used for production.

For example, let us assume that a farmer growing wheat can produce one tonne of wheat from one hectare of land, by combining one hectare of land with one unit of non-land inputs. Non-land inputs will be a combination of any of the factor inputs employed except land, such as human labour, animal labour, or human-produced capital inputs such as agricultural machinery. As long as these factor relationships are fixed, it becomes quite straightforward for us to consider how much rent the wheat farmer will be willing to pay for a hectare of land, depending on its location.

In order to see this, we can assume that the price of a tonne of wheat at the market location M is $100, and that the transport cost t of bringing wheat to the market is $1 per tonne-mile or per tonne-kilometre. As we see from Figure 3.1, if the farmer was located immediately adjacent to M, the haulage distance d from the production location to the market M would be zero. As such, the farmer will incur no transport costs, and all $100 sales revenue can be spent on payments to the land and non-land production factor inputs. If the non-land inputs require payments of $50, the maximum rent the farmer can pay for a hectare of land immediately adjacent to M will be $50. At a distance of 20 kilometres, the maximum the farmer will be able to pay for a hectare of land is $30, while at a distance of 50 kilometres, the maximum the farmer will be able to pay for a hectare of land will be zero. Beyond 50 kilometres, there will be no wheat produced and sold at M. The reason is that the market price of the wheat will not cover the costs of producing plus transporting the wheat to the market from beyond this distance. As such, the von

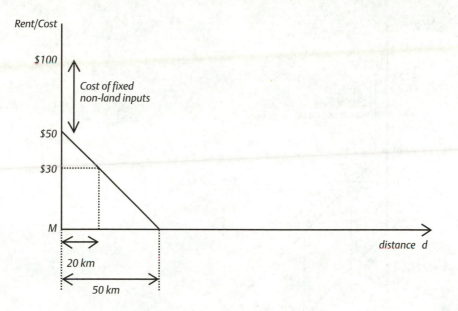

Fig. 3.1 Von Thunen land-rent gradient

Thunen model predicts that there will be a negative land-rent gradient, in which land prices will fall directly with haulage distance in order to exactly compensate for higher distance transport costs. At the same time, the von Thunen model also predicts that there will be a finite limit to the spatial extent over which wheat will be produced for sale at the market M, beyond which no production will take place.

This basic argument can now be extended to allow for changes in the price of the good, or changes in the rewards to the factors. For example, in Figure 3.2 if we imagine that the market price of wheat increases from $100 to $150 per tonne, this now implies that the maximum the farmer will be willing to pay for a hectare of land immediately adjacent to M is $100. The intercept of the land-rent gradient therefore moves upwards from $50 to $100. At a distance of 20 kilometres from M, the farmer will be willing to pay $80 rent for the hectare of land, and at 50 kilometres from M the farmer will now be willing to pay $50 rent per hectare. Moreover, the maximum land-rent will now be equal to zero at a distance of 100 kilometres, rather than at 50 kilometres as was previously the case. As such the distance limit of the land cultivated for wheat production and sale at M will have increased by 50 kilometres from 50 kilometres to 100 kilometres. Within this limit, the maximum possible rents payable to land at all locations have increased. An increase in the market price therefore brings forth an increase in the quantity of land brought under cultivation and a consequent increase in the quantity of output produced and sold, just as we would expect from basic demand and supply theory.

Exactly the same result as above will also arise if the required payments for the non-land inputs falls from $50 to zero, with a fixed market output value of $100. In this case, the fall in the payments to non-land inputs will all be exactly compensated for by greater payments to the land inputs.

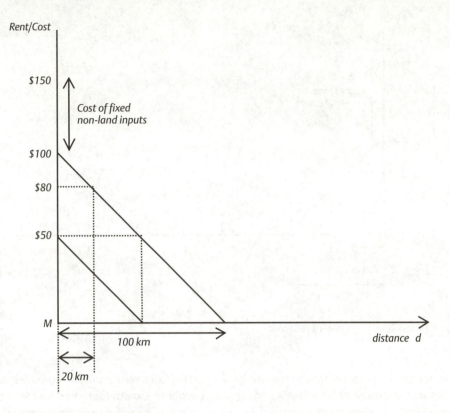

Fig. 3.2 The effect of increased market prices on the von Thunen land-rent gradient

The effect of changes in the transport rates is slightly different from changes in the output market prices or changes in the non-land factor payments. This can be explained with the help of Figure 3.3. For a market price of $100, and non-land input payments of $50, the maximum the farmer will be able to pay for land immediately adjacent to M will be $50, irrespective of the transport rate. The reason for this is that the total transport costs incurred by the farmer at a distance $d = 0$ from M are always zero. As such, the intercept of the land-rent gradient will remain at $50, irrespective of the transport rate. If, however, the transport rate t falls from $1 per tonne-kilometre to $0.5 per tonne-kilometre, the maximum rent the farmer will now be able to pay at a distance of 20 kilometres from M will be $40. Meanwhile, at a distance of 60 kilometres the farmer will be able to pay a maximum of $20, and the maximum land-rent will now be equal to zero at a distance of 100 kilometres. Once again, the distance limit of the land which is brought under cultivation to produce wheat for sale at M has increased from 50 kilometres to 100 kilometres. At the same time, within this limit, the maximum possible rents payable to land at all locations have increased, except for the land which is immediately adjacent to the market. The relationship between rental values and the quantity of land employed is therefore slightly different between the case of changes in transport rates and the case of changes in either the output market prices or the non-land factor payments. Each of the potential changes in the quantity of land used and the maximum

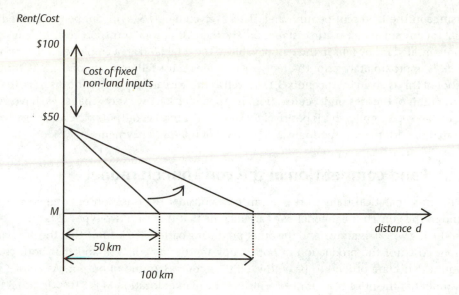

Fig. 3.3 The effect of reduced transport rates on the von Thunen land-rent gradient

rents payable described above will obviously be reversed for equal and opposite changes in the respective cost parameters.

In the von Thunen model, we treat land as simply a factor input in the production process, just like any other production factor, except for the fact that land payments are viewed as being residual. This assumption is based on the approach of Ricardo (1921) and means that rental payments to land are distributed only after all other non-land factors and transport costs gave been paid. The maximum rents per hectare generated by the von Thunen model can therefore be described thus

> Land rent = Output revenue − Non-land payments − Transport costs
> per hectare   per hectare   per hectare   per hectare

In the models above, for simplicity we have assumed that a single hectare of land is employed in the production of wheat. However, if we relax this assumption and allow for different quantities of land to be employed, with non-land inputs being employed in the equivalent fixed proportion levels, a more general description of the von Thunen land rent payable is

> Land-rent per unit area × land area = Output revenue − Non-land payments − transport costs

Land rent per unit area, such as per square metre or per hectare, multiplied by the land area is simply the residual from the total output revenue after all transport costs and non-land inputs have been paid. Therefore, the land-rent per unit area is the residual from the total output revenue after all transport costs and non-land inputs have been paid, divided by the land area employed S.

The slope of the negative land-price gradient with respect to distance is given by the change in the land rent per unit area. This is given by $-t/S$. This can be understood in that for any small increase in distance Δd, the increase in total transport costs $t\Delta d$ must be compensated for by falls in the rent payable to the total land area employed S. Therefore, if Δd is approximately zero, the rent per unit area must fall at a rate of $-t/S$. A formal proof of this is given in Appendix 3.1. As well as this we can also derive the distance to the outer limit of the area under cultivation. In Appendix 3.1.1 we show that as we have seen in the above example, this is positively related to the market output price, and negatively related to both the transport rate and the level of non-land payments.

3.2.1 Land competition in the von Thunen model

With this analytical framework, we can now consider the question of competition for land in the von Thunen model. We can imagine that there are two types of farmers, one producing wheat as above, and the other producing barley. We assume that the non-land input costs for the production of both crops are the same at $50 and that both crops require 1 hectare of land to be cultivated to produce 1 tonne of output. As before, we assume that the price of a tonne of wheat at the market location M is $100, and that the transport cost t of bringing wheat to the market is $1 per tonne-mile or per tonne-kilometre. The maximum rental values for the land producing wheat fall from a value of $50 per hectare immediately adjacent to M, to a value of zero at a distance of 50 kilo-metres. At the same time, we can assume that the market price of 1 tonne of barley at M is $150 and the transport cost t of bringing wheat to the market is $2.5 per tonne-mile or per tonne-kilometre. Under these conditions, the maximum rental values for the land producing barley fall from $100, at locations immediately adjacent to M, down to zero at a distance of 40 kilometres. If there is competition for land, we can assume that the land will be allocated according to whichever usage is able to pay the highest rents at any particular location. This assumption is also based on the approach of Ricardo (1821).

As we see from Figure 3.4, the land close to the market will be employed in the produc-tion of barley, and the land further away from the market will be employed in the pro-duction of wheat. The outer limit of the area under cultivation will be 50 kilometres. As we see in Appendix 3.1.2, we are able to calculate the distance at which the land use changes is 25 km, simply by calculating the distance at which the rental price for the two crops is equal.

If the transport rate on barley falls to $1 per tonne-kilometre, the area of land employed in the production of barley will now extend to 100 kilometres from M. In other words, all of the land around the market M will be employed in the production of barley. As such, the production of wheat will no longer be competitive in the vicinity of M, and all the land will be transferred over to a single use. A similar result will arise if given the original transport rates, the market price of wheat simply rises to $150. In this case, all of the land within a distance of 100 kilometres of M will be transferred over to the production of wheat.

If we consider the results of the one-dimensional model in terms of a two-dimensional plane, it is clear that the von Thunen model predicts that the land will be allocated between competing uses in terms of concentric rings around the market point M. In the above example, the result will be two concentric rings, with barley production close to

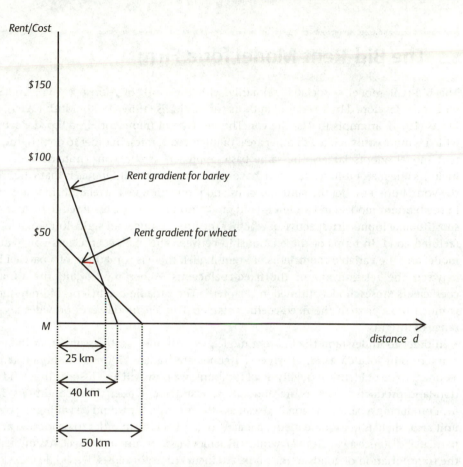

Fig. 3.4 Competing land uses in the von Thunen model

the market, and wheat production in a ring of land outside of the barley-producing area. We can obviously extend this type of argument to more than two competing land uses, in which case the land will be divided up into a series of three or more concentric zones.

Implicit in these types of argument are three Ricardian assumptions, two of which have already been mentioned. The first is that land-rent is treated as a residual, and the second is that land is allocated according to its most profitable use, or alternatively to the highest bidder, at that location. The third assumption is that the supply of land at any location is a fixed quantity. In other words, we assume land supply is perfectly inelastic. This questions of land supply and also land ownership are questions we will deal with later in the chapter. For the moment, however, we will accept the second and third Ricardian assumptions, but develop the von Thunen-type approach into a broader, more orthodox type of model in which land payments are not viewed simply as a residual. Rather, in this broader type of model, known as a 'bid-rent' model, we assume that land and non-land production factors can be treated as mutually substitutable inputs. This allows us to discuss land use within a mainstream microeconomic framework.

3.3 **The Bid-Rent Model for a Firm**

The bid-rent model, associated primarily with the work of Alonso (1964), and subsequently developed by a series of authors such as Mills (1969, 1970), Muth (1969), and Evans (1973), attempts to cast the von Thunen type of framework in a broader setting, which is more easily related to other areas of microeconomics. In order to do this, the bid-rent model adopts largely the same basic approach as the von Thunen model, but includes one major difference. As we have just indicated, the difference is that whereas in the von Thunen model the land and non-land production factor relationships are fixed, in the bid-rent model land and non-land production factors are assumed to be mutually substitutable inputs, irrespective of whether the firm produces an agricultural or a manufactured good. In terms of the relationship between the fixed coefficients von Thunen model and the variable coefficients bid-rent model, there is something of a parallel here between the relationship of the fixed-coefficients Weber model and the variable-coefficients Moses model outlined in Chapter 1. The variable-coefficients bid-rent model is much broader than the fixed-coefficients von Thunen model, and provides a wider range of insights.

In order to understand the bid-rent model, we will once again assume that there is a market point located at M, at which all goods are traded. However, although land is assumed to be of identical quality at all locations, we now will also assume that land and non-land production factors are mutually substitutable. Under these conditions, for a firm producing a particular good, we can ask the firm what it would be willing to pay per unit area, such as per square metre, per acre, or per hectare, in order to be located at any particular distance away from M, while still achieving a certain profit level. Assuming that the transportation of goods to the market M incurs transport costs, we would expect the rents payable by the firm to fall with increasing distance. As we saw above, for a fixed transport rate per tonne-kilometre, in the von Thunen model the rent gradient is a negatively sloped straight line. However, in the case of a bid-rent curve, the rents payable by the firm will fall with distance, but at a decreasing rate. In other words, as we see in Figure 3.5, the bid-rent gradient describes a rental slope which is both negative and convex to the origin M.

In order to understand the reasons for this observation, we need to reconsider the question of factor substitution. In standard microeconomic production theory, in the case where a firm employs two production factor inputs, such as capital and labour, a firm will equate the slope of the budget constraint with the slope of the maximum attainable isoquant. If the price of one of the production factors falls, thereby making it relatively cheap in comparison to the other factor, the firm will rearrange its consumption of factors by substituting in favour of the relatively cheap factor and away from the relatively expensive factor. The firm will continue to substitute its factors until once again the slope of the budget line is equal to the slope of the highest attainable isoquant.

In the case of a bid-rent curve we construct the rents payable by the firm which will allow the firm to produce at the same level of profitability, irrespective of the distance from M. However, we know from our von Thunen model that as we move further away

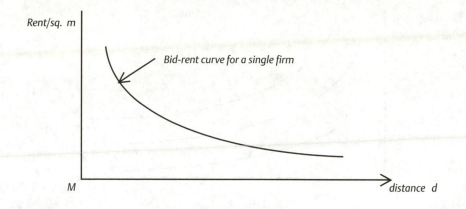

Fig. 3.5 Bid-rent curve for an individual firm

from M, the price of land must fall. Assuming that the price of non-land inputs stays constant irrespective of distance, this means that the price of land must fall relative to the price of non-land inputs as the distance away from M increases. Production theory suggests the firm will substitute in favour of land and away from non-land inputs as the firm moves away from M. Moreover, as the distance away from M increases, the firm should continue progressively to substitute in favour of land. Alternatively, given that the price of land increases as we move towards the market point M, the firm should progressively substitute away from land and in favour of non-land inputs as the firm moves closer to the market M. This means that if the firm consumes the optimum consumption of factor inputs for each location, given the particular relative prices of land and non-land factor inputs at each location, the firm will consume both different relative and absolute quantities of land and non-land inputs at each location. Close to the market the firm will consume small parcels of land and large quantities of non-land inputs, whereas far away from the market, the firm will consume large areas of land and small quantities of non-land inputs. Therefore, as the firm moves away from the market, the non-land/land consumption ratio will fall, whereas as the firm moves closer to the market, the non-land/land consumption ratio will rise.

As with the von Thunen model, the negative slope of the bid-rent curve with respect to distance is given by the change in the land-rent payable per unit area. The slope of the bid-rent curve is given by $-t/S$. Although this initially appears the same result as the von Thunen model, it is fundamentally different in the sense that in the case of the bid-rent curve, the land area S is not fixed, but rather increases with increasing distance. If the transport rate t is constant, the negative slope of the bid-rent curve must become shallower with distance, because the value of S will be increasing. The result of this substitution behaviour is that the bid-rent curve for the firm with substitutable factor inputs is convex to the origin, as we see in Figure 3.5. The reason for this is simply that the slopes of the production isoquants, along which the factor substitution takes place, are also convex. A proof of this is given in Appendix 3.2.

A second feature of bid-rent analysis is that the higher is the position of the bid-rent curve, the lower is the profitability of the individual firm. In other words, in Figure 3.6,

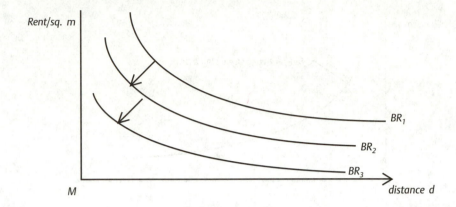

Fig. 3.6 Bid-rent curves for an individual firm

the firm profitability π associated with bid-rent curve BR_1, which we can write as $\pi(BR_1)$, is less than that associated with bid-rent curve BR_2, which in turn is less than that associated with BR_3. In Figure 3.6, therefore, $\pi(BR_1) < \pi(BR_2) < \pi(BR_3)$. The reason for this is that given a firm's budget constraint, the lower are the prices of the land consumed for any given sales revenue, the greater is the profitability of the firm. In general, however, we adopt the convention that firms will pay rents to ensure that net utility is zero. This is because our assumptions of freedom of entry into the land market would suggest that if some sectors are systematically making profits in excess of other sectors, investment flows will move into the most profitable sectors and away from the less profitable sectors, thereby tending to equate profit rates across sectors to those of normal or zero profits. The result of this is that the bid-rent curves of firms and industries will tend to reflect the normal or zero profit conditions.

If there are competing producers, some of whom exhibit fixed coefficients of production in which factor substitution is not possible, as in the von Thunen model, and others for whom land and non-land inputs are mutually substitutable according to the bid-rent argument, land will always be allocated to the flexible producer. We can see this in Figure 3.7 if we compare two producers producing the same output quantity which sells at the same price per tonne at the market M. We can imagine a point at a distance D from M at which a rent per square metre R_D payable by both firms is just sufficient for both firms to earn zero profits. At this point, if the land and non-land inputs employed by both firms are identical, the rent curve for both firms will coincide. However, as we move towards the market point M, the rents payable by the flexible firm will increase at a faster rate than those payable by the inflexible firm. The reason is that the flexible firm will progressively substitute non-land inputs for land as it moves closer to the market M, thereby reducing the total quantity of land consumed, while increasing the rent per unit area. If there are sufficient numbers of competing producers of each type of firm, the flexible firms will occupy all of the land around the market. Reversing the argument, a similar conclusion can be arrived at by assuming that the rent curves for the two types of firms coincide at the intercept M with the same production coefficients. In this case, as we move away from M, the bid-rent curve of the flexible firms will be shallower than that of the fixed-

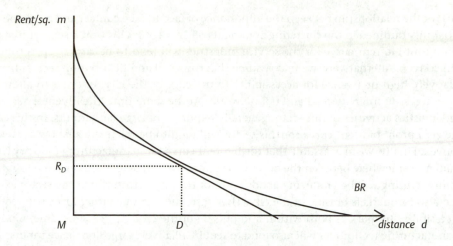

Fig. 3.7 Rents payable for fixed- and variable-coefficients firms

coefficients firms, thereby once again ensuring that the flexible firms will be able to pay higher land-rents at all locations. The result of this argument is that where fixed and flexible production techniques are competing for land, in general the land will be allocated to the flexible production techniques, which allow for the mutual substitution of land and non-land inputs.

3.3.1 Land competition in the industry bid-rent model

In order to understand land competition within the bid-rent framework we adopt a similar approach to that employed in the von Thunen model. We assume that the supply of land at each location is fixed, that all land is owned by absentee landlords, and that land will be allocated according to the activity or persons able to pay the highest rent. We can assume that in the diagrams above the major market point M represents the centre of economic activity, to which all activities in the area relate. From the arguments outlined in Chapter 1 and Chapter 2 relating to the clustering of industrial activities, M can simply be defined as the economic centre of the city or metropolitan area. In other words, M represents the central business district, or *CBD* for short.

  Within any city there will be a large variety of activities competing for land. In other words, these various activities will be competing for locations within the city according to their ability to pay land-rents. However, for simplicity we can imagine that within the city there are only three types of activities, namely the service industry, manufacturing industry, and retailing and distribution industry. We can assume that the production technology is different for each of these three sectors. However, if we assume that within each of these three sectors, all the firms are homogeneous in terms of their production technology and the quantity and value of their outputs, we can analyse the urban economy simply in terms of three different types of firms.

  For example, we may assume that service sector firms have a very high preference for market accessibility, relative to all other sectors. We can defend this assumption on the basis of the relationship between the importance of face-to-face contact and geographical proximity outlined in the clustering arguments of Chapter 2. This would suggest that the zero profit bid-rent curve for the service industries will tend to be very steep, although still convex. Alternatively, we may assume that the retail and distribution sectors have a relatively high preference for accessibility to the edge of the city, in order to allow for good access to intercity road and rail networks. At the same time, the inventory storage and logistics activities of this sector generally require very large land inputs. In this case, the zero profit bid-rent curve for this sector will tend to be relatively shallow as well as convex. Finally, we may assume that the bid-rent curve for manufacturing industry has a gradient somewhere between the other two sectors. We can defend this argument in that manufacturing will be producing goods both for the city within which the sector exists, and also for markets outside of the city. Therefore, the manufacturing firms will require accessibility to markets both within and outside of the city. At the same time, modern manufacturing techniques will also tend to require relatively large floorspace inputs. The result of this is that the bid-rent curve for manufacturing will be steeper than that of the retail and distribution sector but shallower than the services sector. With these assumptions, and also assuming the freedom of market entry ensures equilibrium profits are zero for all sectors, we can describe the land allocation and rents payable within the urban economy by Figure 3.8.

In Figure 3.8, with the particular set of assumptions we have made above regarding the production technologies of each of the three sectors, we see that the service sector dominates the downtown area between the central business district, M, and the outer fringe of the service sector at a distance d_s from M. The manufacturing activities dominate the area surrounding the city centre between d_s and their outer fringe at d_m, and the retailing and distribution sectors dominate the suburban areas between d_m and their outer fringe at a distance d_r from M. The actual urban land-rental gradient with respect to distance will be given by the *envelope* of the three bid-rent curves, described by the curve $WXYZ$. In other words, the actual rental gradient is given by the rental curve which just includes the highest rent payable by any of the three sectors at any given location, given their individual bid-rent curves. As we see, the urban land-rent gradient is convex to the point M, which implies that rents fall at a slower rate as we move further away from the city centre.

As we see in Figure 3.8, the actual urban rent gradient is different from the individual bid-rent curves. The only hypothetical case in which the rent gradient and the bid-rent curves could be the same would be where there is only one type of production activity, in which case the bid-rent curves for all individual firms will be identical. In all other cases, in which there is competition for land between different activities, the rent gradient will be the envelope of the individual bid-rent curves.

In this type of model, the distance to the edge of the city is determined by the point at which it is profitable to convert agricultural land to urban land usage. In other words, the distance to the edge of the city is determined by the point at which the rents payable by urban activities are just greater than those payable by the agricultural sector r_A. Assuming the profitability of agricultural land is given, irrespective of the distance to the particular city centre, the agricultural bid-rent curve will be horizontal, as given in Figure 3.7. However, even if the profitability of the agricultural land is dependent on location from the city centre, as in the von Thunen framework, we can assume that the agricultural bid-

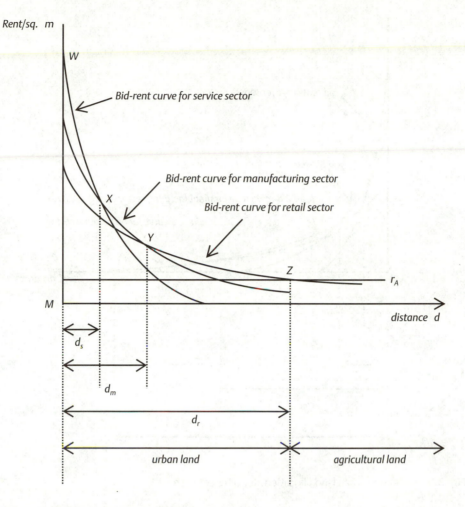

Fig. 3.8 Urban land allocation for different sectors

rent curve will be very shallow relative to the other sectors, whose performance is very much more dependent on accessibility to the particular city centre. As such, within a competitive environment, the distance to the edge of the city will still be determined by the point at which it is profitable to convert agricultural land to urban land usage. In Figures 3.9 to 3.15 we assume for analytical and diagrammatic simplicity that r_A is given as zero, and therefore we concentrate only on the urban rent and urban land area.

The actual land allocation results outlined in Figure 3.8 depend both on our assumptions of the relative preference for accessibility to the centre or edge of the city, on the part of the different types of activities, and also on the particular way we have categorized the different activities. For example, in Figure 3.9 we can split up the retail and distribution sector in principle into two distinct groups, namely retail and distribution. In this case, we may hypothesize that retail activities will exhibit a relative preference for accessibility to central city locations in order to take advantage of any retail agglomeration

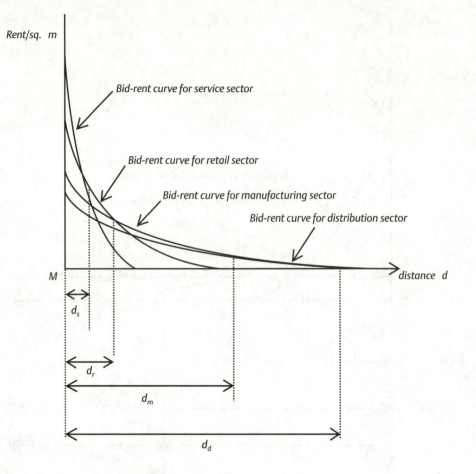

Fig. 3.9 Alternative urban land allocations for different sectors

effects. On the other hand, the distribution sector may have a relative preference for accessibility to the edge of the city for the reasons outlined above. As we see in Figure 3.9, under the assumptions the urban land will be allocated in an alternative manner, in which the service sector still dominates the city centre with its outer fringe at d_s, but with retailing activities located immediately adjacent to the service activities, with their outer fringe at d_r. Outside of these central areas, the manufacturing industry will tend to dominate the land in immediate proximity to the retailing sector with an outer fringe at d_m, and finally the distribution sector will once again be on the edge of the city with its outer fringe at a distance d_d on the city limit.

In principle, we can take this argument even further. For example, we can split up the retail sector into two groups, namely the traditional type of small- to medium-sized retail stores in which shops are relatively specialized in certain product ranges, and the large multiproduct sales outlets which favour large-floorspace sales areas. In this case, we may argue that the former type of retail outlet will exhibit a higher preference for accessibility to the city centre, whereas the latter type will exhibit a higher preference for edge of the city locations, in order to facilitate market access to the hinterland of the city. In this case, we would have the edge of the city areas dominated both by large floorspace shopping malls along with distribution activities, while central areas will exhibit smaller more specialized shops. Alternatively, we could split up the service sector into international business services and personal household services, or we can split the manufacturing sector into large-scale engineering or small-scale workshop activities. In each of these cases, the location preferences of the disaggregated sectors will tend to be different from the aggregate sectors discussed above. Therefore, what we see is that our analytical description of a city in part depends on how we classify the different types of activities which are competing for land in the urban economy. However, although a city is comprised of many activities, there will be certain similarities in the preferences and behaviour of large groups of activities. Therefore, we can simplify our analysis by treating groups of different activities as though they are part of a homogeneous individual group. The justification for this grouping may depend in part on observation and empirical evidence, and our assumptions may therefore be different for different cities in different countries. Different cities will exhibit different characteristics according to different preferences on the part of the firms in the city. There is therefore no ideal type of city structure, although the city structure exhibited by Figure 3.8 is frequently assumed to represent the simplest description of the most common type of urban land allocation.

3.4 The Bid-Rent Model for a Residential Household

Within economics, the question of the allocation of urban land between residential households is discussed in more or less the same manner as the allocation of urban land between firms and activities. The assumptions regarding the nature of land and the land market are the same for the household as for the firm. In other words, we assume that all land is homogeneous, land supply is fixed, all land is owned by absentee landlords, and that land is allocated to the person willing to pay the highest rent. We assume that the object of the rational individual person is to maximize utility given the choices and constraints facing the person. For the individual person or household we also assume that the individual person gains utility from the consumption of both land and non-land human-produced inputs, and that these are mutually substitutable.

In order to construct a bid-rent curve for an individual person with these assumptions, we must once again assume that there is a geographical point M, represented by the central business district of a city, which is the point towards which all household employment activity is focused. In other words, we assume that all employment takes place at a single point, and that workers have to commute from their place of residence to the central business district in order to acquire work. Under these conditions, we can ask an individual person earning a given wage at the central business district M, what they would be willing to pay per unit area, such as per square metre or per hectare, in order to be located at any particular distance away from M, while still achieving a certain utility level. Assuming that the cost of commuting to the central business district M incurs transport costs, we would expect that land-rents will fall with increasing distance, thereby altering the relative prices of land and non-land inputs at all locations. The individual person will attempt to consume land and non-land inputs in exactly the proportion which maximizes the individual's utility, given the relative costs of the land and non-land inputs at each location. As with the individual firm above, the bid-rent curve of the individual person can be shown to be convex to the origin.

Assuming the individual person's cost of commuting is given as t per kilometre, the slope of the bid-rent curve of the individual person can be shown to be given by $-t/S$, as with the case of the individual firm. Once again, the land area S is not fixed, but rather increases with increasing distance as individuals substitute in favour of land and away from capital as land prices fall, thereby reducing the non-land/land consumption ratio. Alternatively, as the household location moves towards the city centre, the individual will substitute non-land inputs in favour of land, thereby increasing the non-land/land consumption ratio. Therefore, if the transport rate t is constant, the negative slope of the bid-rent curve must become shallower with distance, because the value of S will increase with distance. The result of this substitution behaviour is that the bid-rent curve for the individual person, who gains utility from the consumption of mutually substitutable land and non-land inputs, is convex to the origin, as we see in Figure 3.10. The reason for this is simply that the slopes of the indifference curves, along which the factor substitution takes place, are also convex. A proof of this is given in Appendix 3.2.

When we are discussing the question of the utility gained from the consumption of land and non-land inputs, and the rents payable by an individual for a unit area of land, one important point to note is that the higher is the position of the bid-rent curve, the lower is the utility of the individual. In other words, in Figure 3.10, the personal or household utility U associated with bid-rent curve BR_1, which we can write as $U(BR_1)$, is less than that associated with bid-rent curve BR_2, which in turn is less than that associated with BR_3. In Figure 3.9, therefore, $U(BR_1) < U(BR_2) < U(BR_3)$. The reason for this is that

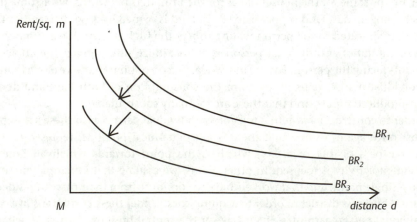

Fig. 3.10 Bid-rent curves for an individual person

given a person's budget constraint, depending on their employment income, the lower is the price of the land consumed, the greater is the utility of the consumer. As such, utility can be understood in these terms as the residual welfare, net of the payments for the consumption of land inputs.

In general, however, we usually adopt the convention that households will pay rents such as to ensure that net utility is zero. In other words, all income is spent on land, non-land inputs, and commuting to the city centre, such that there is no surplus. The reason for this is that we also assume that there is competition for land between homogeneous individuals within any given income or social group, as well as between different income or social groups. This will be sufficient to ensure that households' net utility is zero, and the result of this is that the bid-rent curves of individuals will tend to reflect the zero net utility conditions.

3.4.1 Land competition in the household bid-rent model

If all households are homogeneous, in terms of both the wage-income earned and their consumption preferences, the bid-rent curve of the individual person will be the same as the residential rent gradient for the city. However, in reality, the incomes of people tend to differ markedly according to the different types of employment activities in which people are engaged. The employment wages earned by individuals determine the overall income, and therefore the overall budget-constraint faced by the individual person. If we accept that these income differences reflect in part personal differences in skills and educational opportunities, we can assume that these income differences will not be competed away quickly. Moreover, if such income differences are also partly transmitted between generations because of inheritances, the result of this will be the development of a society made up of different groups of people, who are primarily distinguished in terms of their income levels.

Models of household urban land allocation generally assume that society is indeed comprised of distinct income groups, whose locational preferences differ primarily according to the income category within which an individual household falls. The simplest description of this is given in Figure 3.11, in which we assume that society is comprised of three broad income groups, namely low income, middle income, and high income. If the slopes of the bid-rent curves for all three income groups were the same, this would imply that all of the urban land would be occupied by the high-income group, simply because the high-income group could outbid both of the lower-income groups at all locations. Therefore, in order for all income groups to occupy land in a city at the same time, we must assume that the slopes of the bid-rent curves for each of the income groups is rather different. In Figure 3.11, which represents the urban land allocation of many cities particularly in North America, the land occupied by the low-income group is between M and d_L, the land occupied by the middle-income group extends from d_L to d_m, and the land occupied by the high-income group extends from d_m to d_h. As before, the urban land-rent gradient is given by the envelope $NOPQ$ of the individual income group bid-rent curves, and is convex to the city centre M. The edge of the city is given as the point at which the rent from residential land is just greater than that from agricultural activities. The absolute area of land occupied by each individual household will be

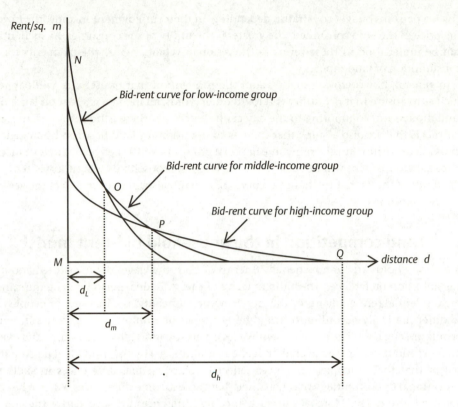

Fig. 3.11 Residential urban land allocation for different income groups

different according to their distance from M and also according to their income, with higher-income groups occupying larger areas of land at all locations. Moreover, as before, the non-land/land consumption ratios will tend to fall with increasing distance.

The land allocation results given in Figure 3.11 are based on strong assumptions relating to the behaviour and preferences of the different income groups. Low-income people are assumed to be constrained in terms of their location possibilities, because their low wage incomes, and therefore their limited budgets, limit their ability to incur the transport costs associated with anything other than short-distance commuting. The bid-rent curve of the low-income group is therefore very steep, because the transport costs associated with increasing commuting distance quickly reduce the money they have available to spend on land and non-land inputs. We assume that both the middle- and high-income groups earn sufficiently high wage incomes to allow them to incur significant commuting costs if they so choose. However, in order for these two groups to coexist in a city the slopes of the bid-rent curves of these two income groups must be different from each other, and also different from that of the low-income group. As we see in Figure 3.11, the slope of the bid-rent curve of the high-income group is generally assumed to be shallower than that of the middle-income group, which in turn is shallower than that of the low-income group. The implications of this assumption are quite important, in that it implies that we also assume that as incomes increase, individuals have an increasing preference for land consumption, which is stronger than any preference for increased accessibility to the city centre.

In order to see this, we can assume that people who earn high wage incomes have a high opportunity cost of time, in that the opportunity cost to these people of non-wage activity is high. As wages increase, the increased opportunity costs of time will increase the desire for proximity to the work location in order to reduce commuting time, the opportunity cost of which will have risen. On the other hand, however, as incomes increase we assume that people have a greater preference for space. If we observe that higher-income groups generally live in the suburban areas of a city, within a bid-rent model, this implies that the negative slope of the bid-rent curve falls as income increases. Therefore, in this bid-rent framework we must assume that the income elasticity of demand for space is higher than the income elasticity of the demand for reduced travel time. A proof of this is given in Appendix 3.2.1.

As before, our description of the allocation of urban land in part depends on our description of the different income groups. For example, we may be able to split up the high-income group into two quite distinct categories. For example, there may be a high-income group which is comprised of relatively older people in senior management positions, who have dependent children and young families. These individuals may exhibit a high preference for space in order to accommodate a family unit with more than one or two individuals. As such, their bid-rent curve will tend to be very shallow. On the other hand, many high wage-earners will also be young single people working in dynamic city-centre industries such as corporate finance. Many of these younger people will not have dependants, and will live in family units primarily of only one or two income-earning people. This latter group of high earners may exhibit a relatively low preference for space, instead preferring good accessibility to the work location. Their bid-rent curves will thus be very steep. If we split up these two groups, we see that the urban land allocation will be as described by Figure 3.12. This type of residential pattern broadly represents the urban land allocation in cities with large international financial activities, such as London, New York, Paris, and Tokyo.

In this case, as we see in Figure 3.12, the land will be occupied by high-income young people between the centre of the city at M and the outer fringe of residence of the young high earners at a distance d_y from M. The land which is immediately adjacent between d_y and d_L will be occupied by the low-income group, the land occupied by the middle-income group will extend from d_L to d_m, and the land occupied by the high-income group will extend from d_m to d_h. As we see, the area of land occupied by the low-income group in Figure 3.12 will have fallen relative to the area of land occupied by this group in Figure 3.11. Specifically, the width of this area of land will have fallen from d_L to $(d_L - d_y)$. This implies that for a given bid-rent curve, the low-income people will be occupying a smaller total area. In other words, if the population of this group remains the same, the average area occupied by individual households within this group will have fallen and the residential density will have increased. Given that individual utility is in part a function of the quantity of land consumed, the utility of the low-income group must therefore be reduced by the presence of the young high-income earners.

Apart from the way in which we categorize different groups, another possible way in which our model results may change is that our assumptions regarding the relative

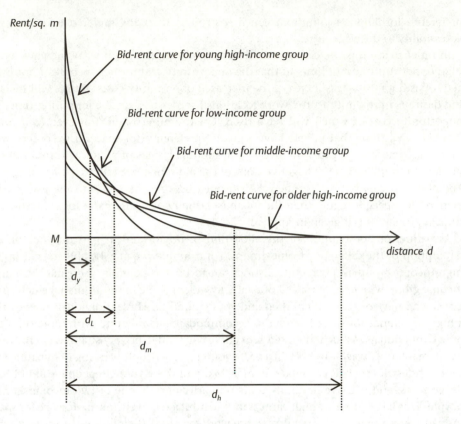

Fig. 3.12 Residential urban land allocation with two different high-income groups

preferences for space and accessibility may not always be justified. For example, in some situations it may be that the income elasticity of demand for accessibility is generally greater than the income elasticity of demand for space. In this case, as we see in Figure 3.13, the urban land allocation will be reversed from that which is given in Figure 3.11, in that high-income earners will live in the city centre, with middle-income earners in immediately adjacent areas, and low-income groups located on the edge of the city. In Figure 3.13, the high-income earners will live between the city centre M and the outer fringe of their residence at a distance d_h from the city centre M. The middle-income earners will live immediately adjacent to the high-income earners between d_h and the outer fringe of their residence at a distance d_m from M. Finally, the low-income earners will occupy the land at the edge of the city between d_m and the urban fringe at a distance d_L from the city centre M. In this case, the city will tend to be very small in area, relative to the city described by Figure 3.11, and the residential density will be very high. This is because the outer fringe of the city will be defined with respect to the limited commuting transport costs payable by the lower-income groups. Cities which exhibit urban land allocations of this type are cities such as Bangkok and Manila, in which heavy traffic congestion due to insufficient infrastructure, limits the ability of people to commute over

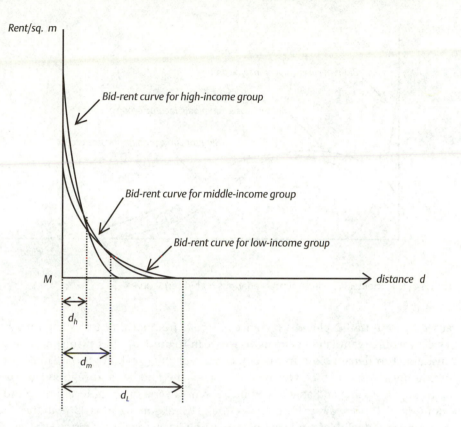

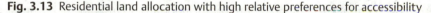

Fig. 3.13 Residential land allocation with high relative preferences for accessibility

anything other than short distances. The opportunity costs of travel time become very high for all wage-earners, but particularly for higher-income groups, which respond by purchasing land in the city centre.

3.4.2 The treatment of environment in the household bid-rent model

So far in our bid-rent analysis we have assumed that land at all locations is homogeneous, and differs only according to location. However, land at different locations will inevitably be associated with qualitatively different environments. When firms or individuals consume land at a particular location, they also consume the environmental amenities which are provided at that particular location. These amenities are often location-specific, in that the quality of the environment can change as the location changes. This will be reflected in the rent payable at each location by individuals, because implicitly they will be purchasing different bundles of environmental goods at different locations.

   In order to see this, we can consider the example of the pollution generated by city-centre activities. In Figure 3.14 we can assume for simplicity that the city centre is the major source of urban environmental pollution, due to the generation of exhaust gases

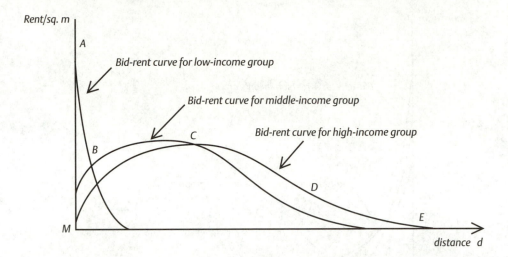

Fig. 3.14 The effects of environmental variations on bid-rent curves

caused by local traffic, plus the presence of smoke from local factories and fumes from city-centre office ventilation systems. As we see in Figure 3.14, the low-income groups are constrained to remain close to the city because of their inability to pay long-distance commuting transport costs. On the other hand, the middle- and high-income house-holds may be willing and able to pay higher rents over a range of locations in order to acquire land further away from the centre. The reason for this is that the natural environmental quality of land will increase with distance from the city centre, as it will suffer less from the harmful effects of pollution. For the middle- and high-income groups, the bid-rent curves will therefore be upward-sloping over a large distance, because they will be willing to pay higher rents in order to avoid the pollution damage to their environment. However, beyond a certain distance the localized effects of the city-centre pollution will be negligible, and the behaviour of rents with respect to distance will be as predicted by the simple bid-rent model. The shape of the rent gradient *ABCDE* in Figure 3.14, which at first rises with distance and subsequently falls with distance, can be described as being concave with distance between *B* and *D*, but convex between *A* and *B* and between *D* and *E*.

  In reality, however, the relationship between environmental quality and the urban rental gradient may be much more complex than simply the generally concave rent gradient of Figure 3.14. The reason is that defining exactly what constitutes 'environment' is itself rather difficult. Urban environmental amenities may be considered to include leisure and entertainment facilities. If these are predominantly located in the city centre, this will tend to increase city-centre rents relative to those at more distant locations. Alternatively, increasing distance from the city centre may imply that the level of greenery and foliage increases, thereby improving the local environmental amenities. This will tend to reduce the negative slope of the rent gradient with distance. Environment may also be considered from the point of view of social amenities. For example, low-income areas in city centres may be associated with certain social problems such as

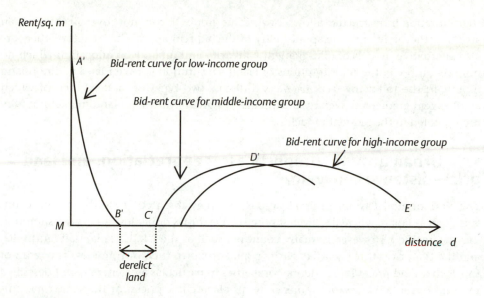

Fig. 3.15 Derelict urban land

crime. In this case, as we see in Figure 3.15, it may be that the rent gradient $A'B'C'D'E'$ falls
to zero in certain areas between B' and C', as higher-income groups prefer to pay a rent
premium in order to isolate themselves from lower-income groups. The result of this is
that there will be a band of derelict space which remains largely unoccupied by households. Similarly, in such cases, the poor security implications of locating in these areas
may imply that firms will not wish to invest. The result will be an inner-city 'no man's
land', which is a phenomenon often observed in urban areas. Once again we can argue
that this result is due to the relationship between the location of land and the qualitative
characteristics of the local environment.

The point about all of these observations is that the relationship between the rental
gradient and the nature of the environment is not at all clear-cut. If there are environmental changes associated with location, the urban land-rent gradient may increase, fall,
or even change sign, as the distance from the city centre increases. See Appendix 3.2.2 for
a formal discussion.

3.5 Alternative Explanations of the Convex Relationship between Land Prices and Distance

The bid-rent model is the dominant model of land price–distance convexity in terms of
its popularity as an analytical approach. However, in reality the problems associated with
isolating bid-rent functions from the effects of environmental variations, the weakness
of the assumption of absentee landlords, and the fact that in most urban areas public

transportation infrastructure allows low-income groups to commute over all of the urban area, together may limit the applicability of the bid-rent approach. Therefore, there are also alternative models of rent-gradient convexity and urban land allocation which do not rely on the bid-rent assumptions of factor substitution between land and non-land inputs. In the following sections we will discuss two types of models, each of which ascribes rent gradient convexity to particular features of the urban land market not fully incorporated in the bid-rent model.

3.5.1 Urban growth, property asset appreciation, and land price–distance convexity

The bid-rent model assumes that all land is owned by absentee landlords. In some countries such as Japan, where the level of home ownership is rather low, such an assumption may be justified. However, in many countries, such as the UK, Canada, Italy, Australia, and the USA, over three-quarters of the population own their own homes. The result of this is that land prices for residential properties in particular are generally not described in terms of rental values, but rather in terms of purchase prices. At the same time, this level of home ownership introduces another aspect into the behaviour of the urban property market which is the ability to gain from the appreciation in the value of land, and this feature itself can alter the distance–rent gradient. Land exhibits the peculiar feature that it can be regarded either as a consumption good with utility-bearing qualities as assumed in the bid-rent model, or as a capital asset investment good. People will therefore purchase land according to whether they perceive land to be primarily a consumption or investment good. From a macroeconomic perspective, at different times in the business cycle the dominant characteristic of land purchases may change, with the investment aspect of land tending to dominate during a period of rapid growth, and the consumption aspect of land dominating during a period of price stability or declining prices.

Over a long-run period of urban growth, however, the relationship between the price of land and the urban location is also in part determined by the relationship between the consumption and investment values of land. The reason for this as we will see shortly is that the rate of rental growth is location-dependent. Therefore, if we consider the asset value of landed property from the perspective of investing in property in order to generate rental income growth, the present value of the property, and consequently its current market price, will also depend on location. The argument in this section is therefore that the relationship between the distance from the city centre and the price of property can be convex due to the partially compensating effect of positive rental growth on the negative distance–rent relationship. In order to see this in this section we follow the arguments of Capozza and Helsey (1989) and DiPasquale and Wheaton (1996).

In the von Thunen model described by Figure 3.1, in which land is consumed in fixed individual quantities such that the density of land usage is constant, and in which transport costs per kilometre are assumed to be fixed, the rental price payable at any particular location increases linearly as we move closer to the market point M. The reason that a higher rent is payable as we move closer to the market is because the rent is a compensation for reduced transport costs to the market, relative to more distant locations. Under these conditions, if the land-rent at the edge of the city is zero, for a unit area of land, the rent $r(d)$ can therefore be described as

$$r(d) = t(D - d), \tag{3.1}$$

where D is the distance to the edge of the city, t is the transport rate per kilometre, and d is the distance of the location of the land from the market or central business district point M. If for some reason the land price at the edge of the city r_D is greater than zero, due to the level of agricultural rents for example, the land-rent per unit area would be given as

$$r(d) = t(D - d) + r_D, \tag{3.2}$$

Following a similar argument, if the land is also developed with housing infrastructure, the rent per unit area of the developed property $R(d)$ will be given as

$$R(d) = t(D - d) + r_D + k, \tag{3.3}$$

where k represents the annualized mortgage costs of constructing the housing infrastructure. Figure 3.16 is constructed by applying the logic of Figure 3.2 to equations (3.1)–(3.3), in the case where the land-rent on the edge of the city r_D is greater than zero, and where the annualized costs of house building per square metre k are also included in the property rental value.

With this information, we can now consider the case where the rental gradient given in Figure 3.1 moves upwards and outwards according to a rise in the income earned at the market point M, as in Figure 3.2. If the wage-income earned at the city centre M increases, the rent payable per unit area at M by a representative resident will increase from R_{M1} to R_{M2}. If this increase in city-centre wages attracts more people to the city, the area of a city

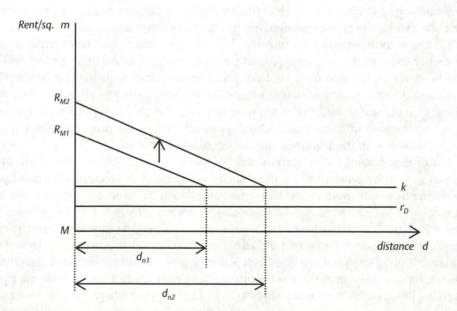

Fig. 3.16 Income growth and city growth

will increase. As the population of the city increases from n_1 to n_2, the urban boundary will move outwards from d_{n1} to d_{n2} as in Figure 3.16. In other words, the distance from the edge of the city to the central business district M, denoted as D in equation (3.1), increases. In an environment of growth, where the city expands over a long period, we can observe the behaviour of the property rental growth at any location by differentiating (3.3) with respect to D thus

$$\frac{\partial R(d)}{\partial D} = t, \tag{3.4}$$

which multiplying both sides by $\delta D/R(d)$ gives:

$$\frac{\partial R(d)}{R(d)} = \frac{t}{R(d)} \partial D. \tag{3.5}$$

We can rearrange this expression in terms of growth rates by multiplying the right-hand side by D/D thus:

$$\frac{\partial R(d)}{R(d)} = \frac{tD}{R(d)} \left(\frac{\partial D}{D}\right). \tag{3.6}$$

Equation (3.6) tells us that at a given point in time, for a given rate of growth of the radius of the city ($\delta D/D$), the rate of growth of the property rental earnings will be higher where the property rent is the lowest. In other words, the rate of rental growth will be highest at the edge of the city, and will fall as we move towards the city centre and away from the urban boundary.

Equation (3.6) is specified in terms of the rent $R(d)$ of the property. However, in markets where land is purchased as an asset, the difference in rental growth across locations, described by equation (3.6), provides the possibility for differences in property purchase prices across locations due to differences in asset value appreciation, rather than simply according to transport costs. In Appendix 3.3.1 we show that as the rate of rental growth is higher the further away the property is from the city centre, the greater will be the long-run capital gain from land purchases further away from the city centre. This increased capital gain associated with distance will partially offset the negative effect of increased distance on the property price. The property price–rent ratio will therefore increase with distance, and the result will be that the property-price gradient will be convex with the distance from the central business district.

A similar argument can be employed in a situation where a city is constrained in its spatial growth by geographical features such as mountains or lakes, or alternatively by severe land-use planning 'green belt' constraints, such as those employed in the UK, South Korea, and the Netherlands. This situation described by Figure 3.17 represents the case where the central business district wage-incomes grow over time such that the city-centre wages payable increase from R_{M1} to R_{M2}, but the city is unable to expand beyond the distance limit d_P set by either a green-belt planning policy or simply by the geography. As we see, for any given increase in wage-incomes earned at the city centre, if the transport costs are linear with distance, the rental growth will be higher where rents are lower, and will consequently be the highest at the edge of the city. These differences in rental growth across locations once again provide for different capital gains associated with rental

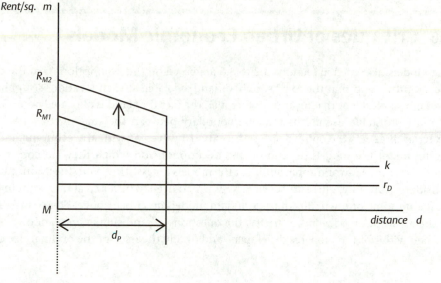

Fig. 3.17 Income growth and city growth with spatial land constraints

growth at different locations. As we see in Appendix 3.3.2, the result of this is that, as in the case above, the increased property price–rent ratio will increase with distance, and the property-price gradient will be convex with the distance from the central business district.

3.5.2 Trip frequency

A second approach to understanding the convex relationship between rental prices and the distance from the city centre is that of the issue of trip frequency. All of the models discussed so far assume that the frequency of trips from any location to the city centre is constant. Implicitly, we usually assume that all the people commute to the city centre each day. However, for many people employed in a wide variety of activities such as sales, retail, and distribution, the number of trips to a central business district may not be fixed. In these cases, the trip frequency itself may become a decision variable, and the rent payable at any location will therefore depend on the costs dependent on the frequency of trips. In such circumstances, the optimum trip frequency will depend on the balance between the costs of making a trip and the opportunity costs of not making a trip. As we see in Appendix 3.4, where trip frequency is also a decision variable, for a wide variety of cost relationships the rent–distance gradient can be shown to be convex, even when input factors exhibit fixed relationships (McCann 1995).

3.6 **Critiques of Urban Economic Models**

The models discussed in sections 3.2 to 3.5 are based on the assumptions that the city is monocentric, and that the fixed supply of land available at each location is supplied to the highest bidder at that location. Moreover, the fact that land is allocated according to its most profitable use means that the boundary between the edge of the city and its hinterland reflects the optimal size of the city. However, as with any economic models, the results of the models depend on the assumptions on which they are constructed. Therefore, the real-world applicability of the models for assisting policy decisions must be considered carefully. There are several issues which need to be raised at this point in order to qualify some of the results of the standard models described above. These issues relate to the assumption of monocentricity, the questions of land supply and landownership, the behaviour of the property developers, and finally the issue of the optimal size of the city.

3.6.1 **Monocentricity**

The simple models assume that the city is monocentric. In other words, these models assume that there is a single dominant spatial reference point, with respect to which all location and land price decisions are made. In reality, however, large cities have many sub-centres, which act as local focal points for business and commercial activity. These sub-centres can often be viewed as local small-scale agglomerations, and the reasons for the existence of such sub-centres can be attributed to any of the issues discussed in Chapter 2. In cases such as this, as we see in Figure 3.18, the local rental prices may

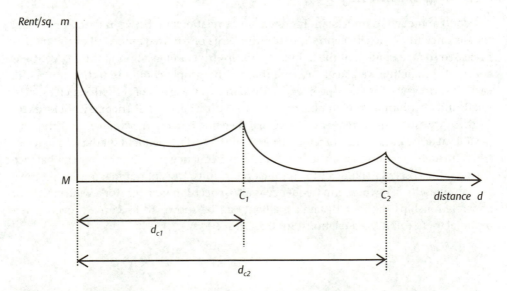

Fig. 3.18 A multicentric city

increase in the immediate vicinity of these sub-centres, such as C_1 and C_2 at a distance d_{c1} and d_{c2} from M, thereby complicating the simple downward-sloping distance-land price gradient described above. However, the existence of such sub-centres does not pose a major problem for our models. The reason is that we can consider the overall urban-rent gradient as simply the envelope of two types of bid-rent gradients, namely those which are determined with respect to the major urban centre, and those which are determined primarily with respect to the urban sub-centre. The former are the bid-rent curves discussed above. The latter are the bid-rent curves of the firms or households whose activities serve specifically local customers, such as retail, food, and clothing establishments. In addition, if the existence of such sub-centres is associated with environmental variations, the issues discussed in section 3.4.2 will also become pertinent.

However, while the calculation of land prices and location will become more complex the greater the number of such urban sub-centres, the arguments outlined above do generally hold. The reason is that all cities have a dominant central business district with respect to which all urban land prices are at least partially determined. As we see in Figure 3.18, only the land prices immediately within the vicinity of the sub-centre will be determined primarily by demand for access to the sub-centre. Land prices at all other locations will be determined by the general urban bid-rent curves with respect to the city centre.

3.6.2 Land supply and land ownership

One of the issues which complicates economic models of urban land allocation is the question of land supply. As we have seen, most models adopt the Ricardian assumption that a fixed supply of land at each location is allocated to the highest bidder as soon as an alternative use becomes more profitable. In other words, land supply is assumed to be perfectly elastic at each location. However, the pattern of ownership of land may affect the nature of the supply of land, and there are two aspects to this: the first is the quantity of land held by each individual landowner, and the second is the time period of the tenure of the landowner.

In microeconomic analysis, we typically assume that a monopoly supplier which controls a high proportion of the market output will use his monopoly power to mark up the price of the goods above the marginal cost of supply. From the point of view of land supply, it is often argued that a similar phenomenon exists. In other words, a landowner who owns a high proportion of the land in a particular area will be able to force up the price of the land above the competitive market rate, thereby restricting development. This is the standard monopoly-pricing argument applied to land markets. However, it is also possible to argue that the opposite may occur. In order to see this it is necessary to consider how the costs of land supply are determined. For a landowner, the costs of landholding are the opportunity costs of lost profits from land sales. This is the argument which underlies our assumptions until now. In other words, for a landowner with agricultural land, as soon as the opportunity cost of an alternative use is greater than the return on the current use of the land, the landowner will sell the land and its use will change. It may be, however, that the marginal cost of land supply is also a function of the quantity of land held and time period over which the land is held. The argument here is that owners may ascribe subjective marginal 'attachment' value to the land (Dynarski 1986), which depends on both the quantity of land held and the time period of tenure. Attachment value here refers to any subjective utility ascribed to the ownership of the land, and as such the true opportunity cost of landholding will be the opportunity cost of the alternative profits, minus the attachment value. On the basis of the law of diminishing marginal utility, Evans (1983) argues that large landowners attribute either zero or low attachment value to any marginal parcel of land, because they already have extensive landholdings. The result of this is that any such marginal parcel of land will be sold at the market price determined by the opportunity cost of land. On the other hand, according to the law of diminishing marginal utility, small landowners will tend to ascribe large attachment values to their land, because any marginal land sale will entirely or substantially deplete their current landholding stocks. From the perspective of the landowners, this argument suggests that the opportunity cost of land sales in a given area will therefore tend to be inversely related to the size of the individual landholdings in that area. The result of this is that the more fragmented is the landownership in any given area, the higher will tend to be the market prices (Dynarski 1986). In an area with heterogeneous owners in terms of their landholdings, the price of land may differ between adjacent properties due to different attachment values on the part of landowners. The result of this is that land market development will tend to be piecemeal.

A similar argument may be applied to the question of the length of tenure. Landholders who have owned a property for a long period may tend to have developed a larger attachment value to the property than landholders who have only owned the property for a short period. This inflated opportunity cost may inflate land prices above simply the best use value. Once again, in an area with heterogeneous owners in terms of the length of their current ownership tenure, the price of land may differ between adjacent properties due to different attachment values on the part of landowners. As before, the result of this is that land market development will tend to be piecemeal.

Piecemeal urban development, particularly on the urban fringe, can also be explained in terms of information and pecuniary asymmetries between land buyers and sellers, and the existence of transaction costs. However, the point about all the arguments in this section is that the simple assumption that land supply is fixed in any location, and that land is simply supplied to the highest use value, is not always realistic. Other institutional issues surrounding landholding and land tenure must also be explored. These institutional issues will in addition include questions relating to the behaviour of property development firms. Such firms engage in land speculation, buying land in advance and often through intermediaries, in order to build up landholdings. These firms often make no attempt to supply land on the basis of the current market price, instead hoping to make greater profits on future development. The rationale for such behaviour can be understood on the one hand from the perspective to acquire a monopoly supply position in a local market. This may allow the firm to force up the subsequent future sale price in an orthodox monopoly argument, as described above. On the other hand, in the case of land the determination and definition of a monopoly position is as much a question of location as it is a question of land area. Small landholdings in strategically crucial locations can provide monopoly power. In the case where a seller perceives a large buyer wishes to buy a large area of local land in order to undertake a major development, the small seller may attempt to force up the market price in order to extract as much consumer surplus as possible from the buyer. However, where the potential buyers are all small, the seller will have little opportunity for such price mark-ups. The result of all these different types of interactions is that the market prices for land at any location may vary simply because of issues relating to industrial organization. For discussions of the behaviour of the property market see Evans (1985) and Ball *et al.* (1998).

3.6.3 **The optimal size of a city**

The arguments outlined in Chapter 2 imply that there is no optimal size for a city, but rather that there may be an optimal city size distribution and urban spatial hierarchy. There is, however, an argument which suggests that the actual size of a city may systematically be greater than its optimum size (Alonso 1971). This argument is an adaptation of the theory of the firm and can be understood from Figure 3.19 in which the population of the city is drawn along the horizontal axis, and the costs and benefits of the city are measured along the vertical axis.

In this argument it is assumed that the costs of city dwelling, which include both private and public costs, exhibit economies of scale over a certain range of city size. For example, such cost efficiencies may include urban agglomeration economies, plus economies of scale in the provision of public and social infrastructure. Beyond a certain size, however, it may be that a city begins to experience diseconomies of scale, associated with increased congestion and pollution. If the benefits of urban dwelling increase with city size, due to a greater variety of local employment and consumption opportunities, simple efficiency theory would suggest that the optimal size of the city should be at the point Q^* where marginal costs equal marginal benefits and the net average benefits are maximized. However, the argument here is that the city will grow to a size of Q', at which total costs equal total benefits, and average costs AC equal average benefits AB. The reason for this is that if city growth is unregulated, the marginal migrant to the city will perceive the

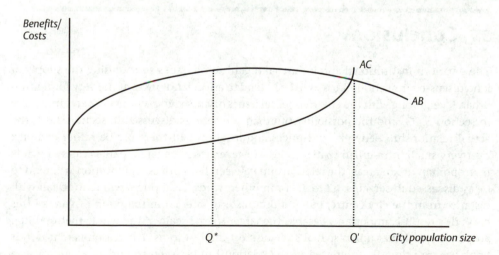

Fig. 3.19 The optimum size of a city

potential net benefits to migration to be positive at all city sizes below Q', and will ignore his own marginal contribution to the change in urban dwelling costs. Given that all migrants will ignore their own contribution to the change in urban costs, the resulting externality problem associated with large numbers of marginally erroneous individual calculations will mean that the city grows to Q' rather than Q^*.

The main problem with this argument, which is similar in logic to the arguments underlying the overcongestion of roads (Button 1993), is that it ignores the role of inter-urban migration. From Chapter 2 we know that there may be an optimal distribution of city sizes. Therefore, if certain cities grow too large, the implication of this is that the profitability of locating in these cities will be less than in other cities. In principle, this will encourage out-migration from these cities to other urban areas which are at less than their optimal size. This process will continue until all urban areas are close to their optimum sizes.

The market failure argument outlined by Figure 3.19 can probably be best understood in terms of the nature of physical urban growth. When a city is expanding, a lack of regulation will tend to mean that the city grows too large. The city growth will be manifested in terms of an increasing area of land being transferred from agricultural to urban usage and an associated increase in the infrastructure of the urban-built environment. As the effects of the excessive urban growth begin to manifest themselves over time, in terms of reduced urban profitability, efficiency, and welfare, the out-migration of activities and people creates the problem of urban dereliction. Physical building infrastructure cannot be demolished and redeveloped costlessly and quickly, and this process of growth and decline can lead to the types of environmental problems discussed in section 3.4.2. As such, this market failure argument is probably more applicable to discussions of the effects of growth and decline on the urban infrastructure, and the associated effects on local land prices, rather than to questions of the size of the individual urban economy, which are more properly questions of urban size distributions.

3.7 Conclusions

These various institutional and industrial organization issues surrounding the supply of land discussed in sections 3.6 to 3.6.2 will tend to affect land prices at the very local intra-urban level. Along with the environmental issues discussed in section 3.4.2 and indirectly in section 3.6.3, and the possibility of urban sub-centres discussed in section 3.6.1, the actual relationship between land prices and location will therefore be rather complex over very small intra-urban spatial scales. However, over the large spatial scales of whole metropolitan urban areas, the relationship between land prices and location will tend to be as discussed in sections 3.2 to 3.5.3. In other words, land prices will tend to fall with distance from the city centre, but at a diminishing rate. From the point of view of this book this result is important, because the larger spatial scale of the whole metropolitan area is the particular urban spatial scale of most interest to us. The reason is that in this book we are primarily interested in the relationship between the urban economy as a whole and the regional and inter-regional economy as a whole.

Discussion questions

1 What are bid-rent curves? How can an analysis of bid-rent curves help us to understand the shape of urban land price gradients?

2 How is urban land allocated between different competing income groups?

3 How are urban land allocations different between different types of cities in different countries?

4 What is the effect of environmental changes on bid-rent curves and urban rental gradients?

5 Apart from bid-rent analysis, what other ways are there of explaining the shape of urban land-price gradients?

6 Under what conditions will the actual size of the individual city differ from its optimum size?

Appendix 3.1   **The Slope of the Rent Gradient in the Von Thunen Model**

In the von Thunen framework we can define the total profit accruing to the farmer as

$$\pi(d) = pm - iK - rS - mtd, \tag{A.3.1.1}$$

where π is price per tonne of output at the market M, d is haulage distance from the market M, i is price per unit of non-land production inputs, K is composite capital good of non-land production inputs, r is rental price per unit area of land, m is total quantity of output produced per time period, t is transport rate per tonne-kilometre, p is price per tonne of the good at the market, and S is land area employed.

The profit per unit of output is thus given as

$$\frac{\pi(d)}{m} = p - i\frac{K}{m} - r\frac{S}{m} - td, \tag{A.3.1.2}$$

If we let $K_m = K/m$ and $S_m = S/m$, whereby K_m, and S_m, represent the quantities of composite capital and land inputs required to produce one tonne of output, and we also denote $\pi_m = \pi(d)/m$, where π_m is the profit per unit of output, we have:

$$\pi_m = p - iK_m - rS_m - td, \tag{A.3.1.3}$$

which can be rewritten as:

$$\pi_m = (p - td) - iK_m - rS_m, \tag{A.3.1.4}$$

In other words, the profit per unit of output is the source price of the good at the point of production, given as the market price minus the transport costs, minus the total production factor payments. The maximum rent payable per unit area of land can be calculated by setting $\pi_m = 0$ thus:

$$\pi_m = (p - td) - iK_m - rS_m = 0,$$ (A.3.1.5)

which can be rearranged to give

$$r = \frac{(p - td) - iK_m}{S_m}.$$ (A.3.1.6)

Equation (A.3.1.6) describes the maximum rent payable per unit area of land, as being the rent payable, after all other factors and transport costs have been paid, which ensures that total profits are zero. The relationship between rents and distance can be found by differentiating (A.3.1.6) with respect to distance d thus:

$$\frac{\partial r}{\partial d} = -\frac{1}{S_m}\left[t + \frac{\partial t}{\partial d}d\right].$$ (A.3.1.7)

If transport rates are constant, i.e. if $\delta d / \delta t = 0$, then the rent-distance gradient is given by

$$\frac{\partial r}{\partial d} = -\frac{t}{S_m}$$ (A.3.1.8)

exactly as discussed in section 3.2.

Appendix 3.1.1   Distance to the Edge of the Von Thunen Area of Cultivation

In order to calculate the distance to the edge of the area of cultivation, we simply set $r = 0$, thus

$$0 = \frac{(p - td) - iK_m}{S_m},$$ (A.3.1.9)

which rearranges to

$$d = \frac{p - iK_m}{t}.$$ (A.3.1.10)

The conclusions reached in section 3.2 can all be verified from this equation. By observing that the cross partial derivative ($\delta d / \delta p$) of equation (A.3.1.10) is positive, we see that the distance limit of cultivation increases as the market output price increases. Similarly, the cross partial derivative ($\delta d / \delta t$) is negative. Therefore, as transport rates increase, the distance limit of cultivation falls. Finally, the cross partial derivatives ($\delta d / \delta i$) and ($\delta d / \delta K_m$) are also negative, which implies that as the payments to non-land production inputs increase, the distance limit of cultivation falls.

Appendix 3.1.2   Distance to a Change of Land Use in the Von Thunen Model

In the case of competing land usage, in order to calculate the distance at which the land use changes we simply set the rental prices in each production to be equal. From equation (A.3.1.6) the land-rent in wheat production is given by

$$r = \frac{(100 - 1d) - 50}{1},$$ (A.3.1.11)

and the land-rent in barley production is given by

$$r = \frac{(150 - 2.5d) - 50}{1}.$$ (A.3.1.12)

Therefore, if the rents are equal between the two uses we have

$$\frac{(100 - 1d) - 50}{1} = \frac{(150 - 2.5d) - 50}{1},$$

which gives $d = 25$, as we see in Figure 3.4.

Appendix 3.2 **The Slope of the Bid-Rent Curve**

The bid-rent curve assumes that the household or firm consumes land and non-land inputs in the optimum quantities for any location, given the particular price of land at each location. Moreover, we assume that the quantities and prices paid for the inputs ensures that the net utility of the individual is zero, and the net profitability of the firm is zero. The analysis of the two cases proceeds in more or less the same manner, with the only difference being that the household land consumption decision is modelled using a utility function, whereas the firm land consumption decision is modelled using a profit function. Therefore, here we will focus only on the case of the individual household residential location decision and the utility gained by such a decision. Within a bid-rent framework, we can write the utility function of an individual household as

$$U = U(K(d), S(d)),$$ (A.3.2.1)

where K is composite capital good representing non-land inputs and S is land area. The quantities of both land and non-land inputs consumed are assumed to be functions of distance d from the central business district.

The objective of the household is to maximize net utility subject to a given income budget constraint. This can be written as

$$MaxU = U(K(d), S(d))$$

subject to the budget constraint

$$Y - iK - rS - T \geq 0,$$ (A.3.2.2)

where: Y is budget constraint determined by the wage income, i is price of non-land inputs, r is rent per unit area of land, and T is transport costs.

In a bid-rent model the price of land at each location must fall with distance, because of the transport-distance costs incurred in commuting to the urban centre. Therefore, in terms of efficiency analysis, at each location the household must consume land and non-land inputs in the particular quantities so as to equate the ratio of the marginal utilities from their consumption with their price ratio. The price ratio of non-land and land inputs is given by $-i/r$, and the ratio of the marginal utilities of non-land and land inputs is given by MU_K/MU_S. However, MU_K/MU_S is also equal to the marginal rate of substitution of land

and non-land inputs, given as $\Delta S / \Delta K$, where Δ represents any marginal change in quantity of the inputs consumed. Therefore we have

$$-\frac{i}{r} = \frac{\Delta S}{\Delta K}. \tag{A.3.2.3}$$

For any marginal change in inputs consumed associated with a change in the distance, we can write

$$-\frac{i}{r} = \frac{\Delta S}{\Delta K}\frac{\Delta d}{\Delta d}, \tag{A.3.2.4}$$

which can be rearranged to give

$$i\frac{\Delta K}{\Delta d} + r\frac{\Delta S}{\Delta d} = 0. \tag{A.3.2.5}$$

However, equation (A.3.2.5) cannot be a complete description of the efficiency conditions a bid-rent function must fulfil, because the effect of distance changes on the costs of land and non-land inputs is not symmetrical. For a small change in distance Δd, the price of land r will fall by a small amount Δr. On the other hand, we assume that the price of non-land inputs i is independent of location. It is therefore necessary to specify each of these relationships as

K is a function of distance	$K = K(d)$
S is a function of distance and rent	$S = S(d, r)$
r is a function of distance	$r = r(d)$
i is independent of distance	
T is a function of distance	$T = td$, where T are total transport costs and t is the transport rate per kilometre.

With the particular specifications we can now rewrite (A.3.2.2) as

$$Y - iK(d) - r(d)S(d, r) - td \geq 0, \tag{A.3.2.6}$$

which if we set net utility to equal to zero gives

$$Y = iK(d) + r(d)S(d, r) + td. \tag{A.3.2.7}$$

Following Mills (1970), totally differentiating (A.3.2.7) with respect to distance such that net utility is constant gives

$$\frac{\partial Y}{\partial d} = i\left(\frac{\partial K}{\partial d}\right) + \left(\frac{\partial r}{\partial d}\right)S(d) + r(d)\left(\frac{\partial S}{\partial d}\right) + \left(\frac{\partial S}{\partial r}\frac{\partial r}{\partial d}\right) + \left(t + \frac{\partial t}{\partial d}\right) = 0. \tag{A.3.2.8}$$

From (A.3.2.5) we know that

$$i\frac{\partial K}{\partial d} + r\frac{\partial S}{\partial d} = 0.$$

Therefore,

$$\left(\frac{\partial r}{\partial d}\right)S(d) + \left(\frac{\partial S}{\partial r}\frac{\partial r}{\partial d}\right) + \left(t + \frac{\partial t}{\partial d}d\right) = 0. \tag{A.3.2.9}$$

which rearranges to:

$$\frac{\partial r}{\partial d} = -\frac{\left(t + \frac{\partial t}{\partial d}d\right)}{\left(S(d) + \frac{\partial S}{\partial r}\right)}.$$

(A.3.2.10)

If total transport costs are a function of distance the numerator term will always be positive. However, even if transport costs are constant with distance, such that $\delta t/\delta d$ is zero, and the numerator term reduces simply to t, we still cannot yet determine the sign of (A.3.2.10) because $\delta S/\delta r$ is negative.

In order to unequivocally establish the sign of (A.3.2.10) it is necessary to employ the Envelope Theorem (Takayama 1993). This theorem is used in situations where we assume that all variable inputs are employed at their optimal quantities, given the budget constraint and the prevailing prices. To employ the Envelope Theorem, it is necessary for us to distinguish between the variables which are direct and indirect functions of the distance.

The fall in the price of land will obviously alter the relative prices of the two inputs for a marginal increase in distance. This will cause a small increase ΔS in the optimum quantity of land to be purchased, and, for a given budget constraint, will consequently also reduce by a small amount ΔK the optimum quantity of land to be consumed for any marginal increase in distance. What we see is that for any budget constraint, the quantity of land consumed is an indirect function of the distance, because the quantity of land consumed is a direct function of the price of land, which itself is a direct function of the distance. At the same time, given the budget constraint, the quantity of non-land inputs consumed at any distance is an indirect function of the distance, because the quantity of non-land inputs consumed is a function of the quantity of land consumed at that distance, which itself is a function of the distance. This means we can rearrange and rewrite equation (A.3.2.7) as

$$r(d) = \frac{Y - iK^*(S,Y,d) - td}{S^*(Y,d,r)}$$

(A.3.2.11)

whereby S^* is the optimized quantity of land consumed, given the budget constraint, the distance, and the price of land, and K^* is the optimized value of non-land composite capital inputs, given the budget constraint, the distance, and the quantity of land employed. Applying the Envelope Theorem to (A.3.2.11), we assume that the values of the inputs S and K are always at their optimized values, S^* and K^*, for any given distance. This allows us to differentiate with respect to only those variables which are directly a function of distance. From (A.3.2.11) we see that the only such variable is the transport cost. Therefore

$$\frac{\partial r(d)}{\partial d} = -\frac{\left(t + \frac{\partial t}{\partial d}d\right)}{S^*},$$

(A.3.2.12)

which, if transport rates are constant, and the land is always consumed in optimum quantities gives

$$\frac{\partial r}{\partial d} = -\frac{t}{S}.$$

(A.3.2.13)

In other words, the Envelope Theorem tells us that for a marginal change in distance, the value of the indirect effect of $\delta S/\delta r$ in equation (A.3.2.10) is approximately zero, and only the direct effect of distance determines the bid-rent slope. The signs of equations (A.3.2.10) and (A.3.2.13) are unambiguously negative, and the value of the bid-rent slope is given by $-t/S$.

Appendix 3.2.1   The Relative Income Elasticities of the Demand for Land and Accessibility in the Bid-Rent Model

We can assume that the total expenditure on both transport costs and land is a function of the income of the household. If transport rates are a constant function of distance, from (A.3.2.13) the equation of the bid-rent curve is given by

$$\frac{\partial r}{\partial d} = -\frac{t}{S}. \tag{A.3.2.1.1}$$

To observe the effect of income changes on the bid-rent gradient we take the cross-partial derivatives of (A.3.2.1.1) with respect to income thus:

$$\frac{\partial\left(\frac{\partial r}{\partial d}\right)}{\partial Y} = -\frac{1}{S}\left(\frac{\partial t}{\partial d}\right) + \frac{t}{S^2}\left(\frac{\partial S}{\partial Y}\right). \tag{A.3.2.1.2}$$

If (A.3.2.1.2) is positive, the bid-rent curve becomes shallower for higher-income groups, as described by Figure 3.11. For the bid-rent curve to become shallower, therefore,

$$\frac{t}{S^2}\left(\frac{\partial S}{\partial Y}\right) > \frac{1}{S}\left(\frac{\partial t}{\partial Y}\right), \tag{A.3.2.1.3}$$

which can be rewritten as

$$\left(\frac{1}{\partial Y}\right)\left(\frac{\partial S}{S}\right) > \left(\frac{1}{\partial Y}\right)\left(\frac{\partial t}{t}\right). \tag{A.3.2.1.4}$$

Therefore, multiplying both sides by Y gives

$$\left(\frac{Y}{\partial Y}\right)\left(\frac{\partial S}{S}\right) > \left(\frac{Y}{\partial Y}\right)\left(\frac{\partial t}{t}\right), \tag{A.3.2.1.5}$$

which rearranges to

$$\frac{\left(\frac{\partial S}{S}\right)}{\left(\frac{Y}{\partial Y}\right)} > \frac{\left(\frac{\partial t}{t}\right)}{\left(\frac{Y}{\partial Y}\right)} \tag{A.3.2.1.6}$$

Therefore, from (A.3.2.1.6) the slope of the bid-rent curve will become shallower if the income elasticity of the demand for space is greater than the income elasticity of demand for reduced travel costs. Alternatively, reversing the inequality (A.3.2.1.6) such that the income elasticity of the demand for space is less than the income elasticity of demand for reduced travel costs, implies that the bid-rent curve becomes steeper with increasing income, as in Figure 3.13.

Appendix 3.2.2   **Environmental Changes and Bid-Rent Analysis**

If environmental damage is caused by city-centre pollution, such that the quality of the environment increases with distance away from the city centre, we can write $E = f_e(d)$, whereby E represents environmental quality, and $f_e(d)$ describes the functional relationship between environmental quality and distance from the city centre. We assume that environmental quality is a location-specific public good, and that E is independent of the quantity of land consumed at a location. We can regard the effect of improved environment as increasing the utility of the household, for any given level of expenditure on land and non-land inputs. Therefore, we can incorporate environmental quality within our utility function in general terms as

$$U = U(K(d), S(d), E(d)).$$ (A.3.2.2.1)

Following the argument in equation (A.3.2.11) above, we can therefore write

$$r(d) = \frac{Y - iK^*(S,Y,d) - td + Ed}{S^*(Y,d,r)},$$ (A.3.2.2.2)

which, once again differentiating with respect to d using the Envelope Theorem, gives

$$\frac{\partial r}{\partial d} = -\frac{\left(t + \frac{\partial r}{\partial d}d\right)}{S} + \frac{\frac{\partial E}{\partial d}}{S}$$ (A.3.2.2.3)

which gives

$$\frac{\partial r}{\partial d} = \frac{1}{S}\left[\frac{\partial E}{\partial d} - \left(t + \frac{\partial t}{\partial d}d\right)\right].$$ (A.3.2.2.4)

If the bracketed term in (A.3.2.2.4) is positive, the bid-rent curve will be upward-sloping. In other words, if the monetary value of the improvement in the environment with respect to distance is greater than the increase in total transport costs with respect to distance, the bid-rent curve will be upward-sloping. From the point of view of costs, the monetary value of the improvement in the environment can be understood in terms of the money that would be required in order to improve the current environment at the particular location to the required level. On the other hand, if the environmental improvements with respect to distance are less significant than the transport costs of distance, the slope of the bid-rent curve will still be negative, although shallower than would be the case with no environmental variations.

Appendix 3.3   **Land Purchase Price-Distance Convexity**

There is a class of models which derive a convex land-price distance relationship, without having to assume that there is a composite capital good which is substitutable with land. These models are motivated by the different potential capital gains in house prices associated with different locations.

Appendix 3.3.1   **Property Asset Appreciation and Land-Price Distance Convexity: the Role of Urban Spatial Growth**

The argument here follows that of DiPasquale and Wheaton (1996). For any land-based asset held in perpetuity earning an annual rent of $R(t)$, discounted at a rate of i, the present value of the property is given as

$$PV = \int_0^\infty R(t)e^{-t}dt,$$
(A.3.3.1.1)

which is an improper integral (Chiang 1984: ch. 13). If the rent payable at each time period is fixed, i.e. $R(t) = R$, equation (A.3.3.1) can be transformed by taking the limit of a proper integral thus

$$PV = \int_0^\infty Re^{-it}dt = \lim_{y\to\infty}\int_0^y Re^{-it}dt = \lim_{y\to\infty}\frac{R}{i}(1 - e^{-iy}) = \frac{R}{i}.$$
(A.3.3.1.2)

From equation (3.3) we have an expression for the rent payable for a unit size of property distributed at an even density around the central business district, given as

$$R(d) = t(D - d) + r_D + k.$$
(3.3)

Therefore, from (A.3.3.1.2), the present value of this property asset held in perpetuity paying the same rent as the current rent defined by equation (3.3) is given as

$$PV = \frac{t(D - d) + r_D + k}{i} = \left(\frac{tD}{i} - \frac{td}{i}\right) + \left(\frac{r_D}{i} + \frac{k}{i}\right).$$
(A.3.3.1.3)

The first bracketed term on the right-hand side reflects the current location value of the property in terms of the transport cost savings to the edge of the city, and the second bracketed term reflects the agricultural land plus construction value of the property, which we assume is independent of the location. In the case where a city grows in terms of the wage-incomes payable at the city centre, the urban population, and the city radius, we know from equation (3.6) that the growth in rents is greater for locations further away from the central business district. If we assume the growth rate of the urban radius $\delta D/d$ in the long-run takes a constant value of h, the first term in the first bracket on the right-hand side of equation (A.3.3.3) can be rewritten as $(tD/i - h)$. This is because as the city radius grows, the location value of any location interior to the city grows as the distance to the edge of the city increases. Therefore, assuming that $i>h$, the continually increasing transport cost saving from any location to the edge of the city partially compensates for the depreciating effect of the discounting on the future value of the location. Therefore we have

$$PV = \left(\frac{tD}{i - h} - \frac{td}{i}\right) + \left(\frac{r_D}{i} + \frac{k}{i}\right),$$
(A.3.3.1.4)

which can be rewritten as

$$PV = \left(\frac{r_D}{i} + \frac{k}{i}\right) + \left(\frac{tD}{i} - \frac{td}{i}\right) + \left(\frac{tDh}{i(i - h)}\right),$$
(A.3.3.1.5)

where

$$\left(\frac{tDh}{i(i-h)}\right) = \frac{tD}{i-h} - \frac{tD}{i}. \tag{A.3.3.1.6}$$

In other words, as we see from equation (A.3.3.1.5), in a situation of urban growth, the present value of the property is equal to the discounted value of the property given its current location relative to the edge of the city, plus the future growth in its location value.

Given that the present value of a property is its current market price, in order to understand the relationship between the price of the property P and the rent R of the property we can divide equation (A.3.3.5) by equation (3.3) thus:

$$\frac{P}{R} = \frac{\left(\frac{r_D}{i} + \frac{k}{i}\right) + \left(\frac{tD}{i} - \frac{td}{i}\right) + \left(\frac{tDh}{i(i-h)}\right)}{t(D-d) + rD + k}, \tag{A.3.3.1.7}$$

which can be rearranged to give

$$\frac{P}{R} = \frac{(i-h)r_D + (i-h)k + (i-h)t(D-d) + tDh}{i(i-h)} \Bigg/ t(D-d) + r_D + k, \tag{A.3.3.1.8}$$

which from equation (3.3) simplifies to

$$\frac{P}{R} = \frac{(i-h)R + tDh}{I(i-h)R} = \frac{1}{i} + \frac{tDh}{i(i-h)R}. \tag{A.3.3.1.9}$$

From equation (A.3.3.1.9) we see that the price/rent ratio increases as the rent falls. In other words, the further is the location of the property away from the central business district, the greater will be the price/rent ratio. Following the argument of equation (3.6), the reason for this is that more peripheral locations experience greater rental gains as a city grows, relative to central locations. On the other hand, if the city spatial growth h is zero, the price/rent ratio is given by $1/i$, and is therefore independent of location. Where cities do grow, the result of equation (A.3.3.1.9) is that even if transport costs are linear, and rents fall linearly with distance, the market price of properties will fall less than linearly with distance. More specifically, if the price/rent ratio increases with distance, property prices will be convex with distance.

Appendix 3.3.2   **Property Asset Appreciation and Land–Price Distance Convexity: the Role of Income Growth in a Spatially Constrained City**

In the situation where a city is constrained in its spatial growth either by physical geographical restrictions or by land-use planning restrictions, the radius of the city can be viewed as being held constant. In this case, once the city has expanded to occupy all of the available land, the agricultural rent will no longer be a determining factor in the urban rents. Therefore, all rental values must be calculated with respect to the wage-income Y earned at the city centre. Adopting the notation employed in section 3.5.1 and Appendix 3.3.1, and adapting equation (A.3.1.1.6) such that all measurements relate to a unit area size, i.e. $S = 1$, we can write an expression for urban property rents in a city of uniform density as:

$$R(d) = Y - td - k. \tag{A.3.3.2.1}$$

Differentiating with respect to income Y gives $\delta R/\delta Y = 1$, and therefore, $\delta R = \delta Y$. Dividing both sides by R, and multiplying δY by Y/Y, we have:

$$\frac{\partial R}{R} = \left(\frac{\partial Y}{Y}\right)\left(\frac{Y}{R}\right). \tag{A.3.3.2.2}$$

From equation (A.3.3.2.2) we see that the rate of rental growth is inversely related to the share of income accounted for by rent R/Y. In other words, as we move away from the city centre, the rate of rental growth increases.

These different possibilities for rental appreciation will imply different relationships between property prices and property rents at each location. Following the approach of Appendix 3.3.1, we can write the present value of a property at any location as

$$PV = \frac{Y}{i-g} - \frac{td}{i} - \frac{k}{i}, \tag{A.3.3.2.3}$$

where g here represents the constant long-run rate of growth of centre-city wage-incomes $\delta Y/Y$. The argument here is that, assuming $i>g$, the growth in incomes partially offsets the value-depreciating effects on future income of discounting. Equation (A.3.3.2.3) can be rearranged to give

$$PV = \frac{Yi - td(i-g) - k(i-g)}{i(i-g)}. \tag{A.3.3.2.4}$$

Given that the property market price P will be given by present value, we can therefore construct a price/rent ratio thus

$$\frac{P}{R} = \frac{Yi - td(i-g) - k(i-g)}{i - (i-g)} \Big/ Y - td - k, \tag{A.3.3.2.5}$$

which rearranges to

$$\frac{P}{R} = \frac{Yi + (i-g)(-td-k)}{i(i-g)(Y-td-k)}. \tag{A.3.3.2.6}$$

Equation (A.3.3.2.6) can be rewritten as

$$\frac{P}{R} = \frac{Yi + (i-g)(R-Y)}{I(i-g)R}, \tag{A.3.3.2.7}$$

which can be rearranged to give

$$\frac{P}{R} = \frac{Yi}{i(i-gR)} + \frac{1}{i} - \frac{Y}{iR}. \tag{A.3.3.2.8}$$

Therefore, we have

$$\frac{P}{R} = \frac{1}{I} + \frac{Yg}{i(i-g)R}. \tag{A.3.3.2.9}$$

From equation (A.3.3.2.9) we see that in the case of a city of uniform density which is spatially constrained, but which experiences incomes growth, the price/rent ratio of property increases for locations with lower rents. In other words, the price/rent ratio of a property increases with respect to the distance from the city centre, and the price–

distance gradient is therefore convex. On the other hand, as with equation (A.3.3.1.9), if there is no income growth the price/rent ratio reduces to equation $1/i$, and is therefore independent of location.

Appendix 3.4 Optimum Trip Frequency and Rent-Gradient Convexity

Following McCann (1995), we can set up a trip frequency optimization problem, in which a firm faces the cost minimization problem

$$C = \varphi d^\rho f^n + \theta f^{-m} + rS, \tag{A.3.4.1}$$

where d is distance to the city centre, f is frequency of journey, r is rent per unit area, S is land area, and C is total cost per time period.

m, n, θ, ρ, φ, are positive constants, such that φd^ρ is the total distance costs per journey, and θ is the opportunity cost of less than continuous (i.e. f is less than infinite) face-to-face contact.

The first term in equation (A.3.4.1) reflects the fact that total transport costs per time period are a function of the trip frequency, while the second term indicates that the opportunity cost of the lost market revenues of a firm may be negatively related to the trip frequency. In other words, as the trip frequency increases the firm will increase its market share up to a maximum when continuous face-to-face contact is maintained.

In a situation such as this, the firm must decide its optimum trip frequency. In order to calculate this, we differentiate with respect to f and set equal to zero thus

$$\frac{\partial C}{\partial f} = n\varphi d^\rho f^{n-1} - m\theta f^{-m-1} = 0. \tag{A.3.4.2}$$

The second-order condition can be shown to be positive such that this is the expression for minimum costs (McCann 1995). Rearranging (A.3.4.2) gives

$$\frac{m\theta}{f^{m+1}} = n\varphi d^\rho f^{n-1} \tag{A.3.4.3}$$

and thus

$$f^{n+m} = \frac{m\theta}{n\varphi d^\rho}. \tag{A.3.4.4}$$

Therefore, the optimum trip frequency per time period F can be written as

$$F = \left(\frac{m\theta}{n\varphi d^\rho}\right)^{\frac{1}{n+m}}. \tag{A.3.4.5}$$

Consequently, what we see is that the optimum number of journeys per time period is inversely related to the distance of the firm from the city centre. In order to calculate the rent payable at each location, assuming that all trips are undertaken at the optimum frequency $f = \Phi$, for each particular location, we can rewrite equation (A.3.4.1) thus

$$C = \varphi d^\rho F^n + \theta F^{-m} + rS, \tag{A.3.4.6}$$

where $c = X$ when $f = \Phi$. Setting to zero and applying the Envelope Theorem (Takayama 1993: 137–41) gives

$$\frac{\partial C}{\partial d} = \rho\varphi d^{\rho-1}F^n + \frac{\partial r}{\partial d}S = 0 \tag{A.3.4.7}$$

such that

$$\frac{\partial r}{\partial d} = \frac{-\rho\varphi d^{\rho-1}F^n}{S}. \tag{A.3.4.8}$$

From (A.3.4.5) we can write

$$F^n = \left(\frac{m\theta}{n\varphi d^\rho}\right)^{\frac{n}{n+m}}. \tag{A.3.4.9}$$

Therefore (A.3.4.8) can be rewritten as

$$\frac{\partial r}{\partial d} = -d^{\left(\frac{m\rho}{n+m}\right)}\left[\frac{\rho\varphi}{S}\left(\frac{m\theta}{n\varphi}\right)^{\frac{n}{n+m}}\right].$$

This is always convex in d as long as r is less than or equal to one. In other words, as long as total transport costs are less than linear (concave) or linear with distance, even where the land area of the firm or household is fixed, the rent gradient will still be convex with distance. The standard bid-rent result is achieved here even without substitution between land and non-land inputs. The point is that where trip frequency is itself a decision variable, as in the case of all transport, distribution, retail, and consumer shopping activities, plus all activities where the level of face-to-face contact affects the market share, the rent-gradient convexity is determined by the optimized trip frequency. This general argument can subsequently be applied to a range of different real-world examples (McCann 1995, 1998) with various alternative specifications of costs and factor quantities.

Chapter 4

Regional Specialization, Trade, and Multiplier Analysis

4.1 Introduction

In the first chapter we discussed the question of the location behaviour of the individual firm. As we saw, the reasons for the spatial behaviour of firms depend both on the characteristics of the firm and also on the characteristics of the various regions in which the firm could locate. Understanding industrial location behaviour then allowed us in Chapter 2 to explain the economic motivation for the growth of cities and industrial clusters. Our analysis focused on the issues which determine industrial clustering and industrial dispersion, and in particular on the various types of spillovers and links which take place between firms in the same area. In Chapter 3, the localized growth of an industrial cluster was then used as the basis of our comparative analysis of urban land prices and urban land distribution.

One of the issues raised by these arguments which has not yet been dealt with, is the local impact of any local industry changes, such as industry expansion or contraction, or alternatively of the local impact of any local microeconomic changes, such as firm relocation, firm expansion, or firm closure. Following the arguments in Chapters 1 and 2, any firm relocation, firm expansion, or firm closure within a local economy, must have consequences specific to the rest of local economy, as well as those consequences for the economy in general. The reason for this is that such changes will alter the demand for locally supplied factor inputs, and these demand changes will also engender further changes locally along the lines discussed in Chapter 3. As we will see in this chapter, the transmission of these effects will be mediated by the interfirm linkages which exist in the local economy, plus the linkages which exist between the local firms and the suppliers of local factor inputs. In general we would expect the strength of these impacts broadly to be associated with the size of the change involved. In particular, where the individual firm involved is very large, any changes in the firm size or organization will have potentially major impacts on the local economy.

This type of argument can also be extended to the aggregate level where firm relocations, expansions, or contractions take place at the level of a local industry as a whole. Following the arguments in Chapters 2, 3, and 4, changes in the output and performance of an individual local industrial sector will have implications for other sectors in the local economy. However, from the arguments of Chapter 2, we would expect that the strength of these effects will depend on the extent to which the region is specialized in the activities of the sector in question. If a region is highly specialized in a particular industrial sector, the aggregate effect on the local economy of any changes in the performance of this sector would be expected to be relatively large. On the other hand, where a region is highly diversified, in the sense that it contains a wide variety of local industrial activities, we would expect that changes in the performance of an individual local sector would have a relatively smaller effect on the local economy. The local impacts of these changes can be analysed in terms of the aggregate effects of the individual microeconomic changes. This allows us to understand the relationship between a local region and a local industrial sector. The fortunes of an industrial sector and a local region therefore become interdependent.

The analysis of the impacts of industrial change on a host economy, through an assessment of the various linkages between firms and factor inputs, is known as *multiplier analysis*. This involves consideration of the regional trade patterns which exist both within and between regions. However, unlike countries, by definition, regions do not have the facility to collect continuous data on the level and patterns of their trade flows with other regions. Therefore, in the absence of regional trade data, it is necessary for us to employ measures which indirectly impute trade patterns to a region. The process of indirectly estimating regional trade patterns is done on the basis of observations of the regional industrial structure. Under various conditions, these observations allow us to impute regional trade patterns. With these imputed regional trade data we are then able to consider the regional effects of the expansion or contraction of a local regional industrial sector.

In this chapter we will initially deal with three different approaches to regional multiplier analysis. These approaches are economic base models, Keynesian regional income multipliers, and input–output analysis. While the models are somewhat different from each other, they each throw light on to different aspects of the nature of the local impacts associated with industrial changes, and also on to different aspects of the process by which such impacts are transmitted.

Each of these three model techniques is based on the two fundamental assumptions that first, local factor prices are fixed, and secondly, there are no local factor supply constraints. The first assumption implies that the marginal costs associated with a local output or employment expansion are constant. In other words, marginal costs and average costs are both equal to each other and fixed. At the same time, the second assumption implies that local output and employment can expand without facing any local capacity constraints. Taken together, these two assumptions imply that regional output or employment can increase indefinitely in a linear manner, in which average costs stay constant. Although these assumptions may appear unrealistic at first, they are useful for analytical purposes here in order to indicate the trade-linkage relationships between different industrial sectors within the same regional economy. The issues raised by changes in the local availability of factor inputs, or by changes in the local supply prices of factor inputs, will be discussed in Chapter 5. Moreover, as we will see in Chapter 7, in conditions of local unemployment, there are many cases in which these assumptions, and the models constructed on them, can be defended as a basis for regional policy.

We will begin by discussing the economic base model, the most general of the three approaches. The economic base model will then be contrasted with the Keynesian regional income multiplier model. As we will see, the Keynesian regional multiplier is rather different from the Keynesian multiplier employed in national income models, but can be made compatible with the regional economic base model. Thirdly, we will introduce the input–output approach to regional modelling. Although this is analytically the most sophisticated of the three multiplier techniques, in that it deals with inter-regional trade in a more comprehensive manner, this approach also benefits from the motivation and insights of the other two approaches. One final point we have not yet mentioned is that the process of indirectly estimating regional trade patterns, on the basis of observations of the regional industrial structure, is itself problematic. However, various measures of regional industrial diversity and specialization can be employed in order to facilitate this process. Therefore, we will conclude the chapter by considering the difficulties associated with some of the techniques which are available for estimating regional trade patterns on the basis of observations of regional industrial structures. These issues will also be discussed in detail in the appendices.

4.2 The Economic Base Model

The economic base model is conceived at the city-region level of aggregate analysis. Rather than analysing the impacts of industrial changes at a microeconomic level, the economic base model focuses on the links between aggregate sectors by characterizing a region as comprising two broad but distinct industrial sector-groupings. These two sector-groupings are knows as a *basic* sector, and a *non-basic* sector. The definition of these two groupings is that the basic sector is the sector whose performance depends primarily on economic conditions external to the local economy, while the non-basic sector is made up of the sectors whose performance depends primarily on the economic conditions internal to the local economy. The definition of external and internal dependence here relates to the location of the markets for the outputs of the sectors. Industries whose markets are national or global will tend to sell almost all of their output outside of the local city-region in which the industry is based. As such, the market demand for the output from this type of industry will be almost entirely dependent on market demand conditions outside of the local economy. These industries are classified as *basic* industries, or sometimes as *export-base* industries. On the other hand, there are many sectors whose output tends to be accounted for almost entirely by local consumers. This is very typical in industries such as retailing, hospitality and leisure, and activities such as legal services, real estate and consumer banking, education, health, and equipment maintenance, all of which tend to cater for households and small businesses. These industries comprise the *non-basic* sector, and within economic base terminology are also known as the *service* sector, although service here relates to the local orientation of demand, and is not to be confused with the definition of the tertiary sector.

In situations where regions are dominated by particular major industrial sectors, such as the automobile industries in Turin and Detroit, the aerospace industries in Everett-Seattle and Toulouse, and the international financial services industries in London and Frankfurt, the classification of the basic and non-basic sectors is a relatively easy matter, at least in principle. The basic sector will comprise the dominant exporting industry in the city-region, and the non-basic service sector will comprise all other sectors in the local area. On the other hand, as we will see shortly, for many cities or regions the distinction between the basic and non-basic sector is not so straightforward. Note here that we are defining exports in terms of selling outside of the city or region in which the industry is located. In other words, the definition of regional exports therefore includes both sales to customers in other parts of the same country as well as sales to customers in other countries.

In order to understand the economic base model let us imagine we are dealing with an area where we can easily specify which local industries are basic and non-basic. The most common form of economic base models treats employment as a proxy for the level of output. In this case, the employment structure in the local economy can be defined by

$$T = B + N,$$ (4.1)

where T is Total regional employment, B is Basic employment, and N is Non-basic employment.

Equation (4.1) simply says that total employment in an area is the sum of the employment in the basic industry and the employment in the non-basic sectors. In the economic base approach, we assume that the output of the non-basic sector is determined by the performance of the local economy as a whole, whereas the performance of the basic sector is determined by factors exogenous to the local economy. As such, we can write $N = nT$, where n is a coefficient between zero and 1 representing the sensitivity of employment generation in the non-basic sector to the total level of employment generated in the region. Rewriting equation (4.1) gives

$$T = B + nT,$$ (4.2)

which rearranges to

$$\frac{T}{B} = \frac{1}{1-n}.$$ (4.3)

The ratio T/B is called the economic base multiplier, and indicates the relationship between employment in the basic sector and employment in the total economy. The higher is the ratio T/B, the greater is the economic base multiplier. The economic base multiplier allows us to discuss the overall employment impacts associated with a change in the basic sector thus

$$\Delta T = \frac{1}{1-n}\Delta B.$$ (4.4)

Therefore, for any change ΔB in the employment levels in the basic sector, total regional employment will increase by ΔT.

Implicit in this argument is the assumption that the total employment of the region is a function of the employment generated by the basic sector. The strength of this link between total regional employment and basic sector employment is indicated by $1/(1-n)$, where n represents the strength or sensitivity of the linkage between the local economy and the locally oriented activities. That this is so can be understood in terms of our assumption that the performance of the local economy as a whole depends in part on the performance of the basic sector. At the same time, the employment generated by the basic sector will require inputs to be provided by the non-basic sector, which itself will generate further employment. The coefficient n can therefore be perceived as an expenditure-linkage parameter, reflecting the strength of demand by the basic sector for local non-basic inputs. The higher is the value of n, the smaller is the value of $(1-n)$ and the greater is the economic base multiplier $T/B = 1/(1-n)$.

In areas in which local interfirm linkages are very strong, the demand linkages between firms located in the same area will tend to be very high. In some of the industrial clustering situations described in Chapter 2, and in the cases mentioned above such as Turin, Detroit, Toulouse, and Frankfurt, the employment growth in a dominant firm or industry associated with an output expansion will create enormous additional growth possibilities for local supplier firms in other sectors. These growth possibilities arise from the increased provision of inputs both to the basic firms themselves and also to the increased number of employees of those firms. In circumstances such as these, the value of n will tend to be high, and consequently the value of the economic base multiplier will also be high. On the other hand, there will be some areas in which the relationship between the basic and non-basic industries will be rather weak. For example, in many areas dominated by agricultural industries, the falling demand for labour associated with the increasing use of agricultural mechanization may mean that local increases in agricultural output will have relatively small impacts on local employment growth in other sectors. In this case, both the value of n and the value of the economic base multiplier will tend to be very low. The use of economic base models therefore tends to be associated primarily with city-regions dominated by urban concentrations of both population and production.

Obviously, the economic base relationship may be somewhat more complex than the simple description given in equation (4.3). The non-basic sector may not behave in an entirely linear manner in relation to the basic sector, in that a certain level of non-basic activity may be somewhat independent of the basic sector. In this case, our economic base model may look something like

$$T = B + (N_o + n_1 T),$$ (4.5)

where N_o represents the level of non-basic employment activity which is autonomous of the basic sector. This rearranges to

$$T = \frac{N_o}{1 - n_1} + \frac{B}{1 - n_1},$$ (4.6)

in which case we once again have

$$\Delta T = \frac{1}{1 - n_1} \Delta B.$$ (4.7)

The result in equation (4.7) is the same as in equation (4.4). This implies that even if the non-basic sector is partly autonomous of the basic sector, in the situation where the marginal growth of the non-basic sector is constant with respect to the basic sector, the value of the economic base multiplier will be unaltered.

For practical purposes, models of the form described by equations (4.1) to (4.7) are useful for empirical purposes. The reason is that they are amenable to simple econometric estimation (Weiss and Gooding 1968) of the form

$$T = a + \beta B + e,$$ (4.8)

where the estimated values of a and β give us values for $N_o/(1-n)$ and $1/(1-n)$ respectively, in equation (4.6). In the simplest case outlined by equations (4.1) to (4.4), the value of $N_o/(1-n)$ will be zero and $1/(1-n)$ will be positive, whereas in the case where the non-basic sector is partly autonomous of the basic sector the situation will best be described by equations (4.5) to (4.7).

It is also possible to conceive of situations in which the marginal relationship between the total employment change in the basic and non-basic sectors is not constant. For example, some of the agglomeration arguments discussed in Chapter 2 imply that the sensitivity coefficient n, which defines the strength of the linkage between the local basic and non-basic sectors, may itself be a function of the size of the local basic sector. In these circumstances, it may be possible to describe the linkage between the sectors as something like

$$n = n_o + n_1 B.$$ (4.9)

In this situation, we have

$$T = B + (n_o + n_1 B)T,$$ (4.10)

which rearranges to

$$T = B \left(\frac{1 + n_1 T}{1 - n_o} \right)$$ (4.11)

and

$$\Delta T = \Delta B \left(\frac{1 + n_1 T}{1 - n_o} \right).$$ (4.12)

As we see in this case, the value of the economic base multiplier will increase with the size of the total level of employment in the region. The implication of this is that regional growth will become progressively more sensitive to growth in the basic sector as the size of the city-region increases. This scenario imposes much greater problems of empirical estimation than the previous models. Moreover, there is no reason to suppose it is indicative of generally continuing behaviour, as the limits to this explosive growth process will also depend on the arguments concerning the existence of diseconomies of agglomeration, as discussed in Chapter 2.

4.3 Identifying the Basic and Non-Basic Sectors

The argument in section 4.2 is based on the assumption that it is a relatively straight-forward matter for us to decide which industrial activities comprise the regional basic sector, and which industrial activities comprise the regional non-basic sector. In other words, we assume it is easy for us to determine which local industrial sectors are primarily regional exporting sectors, and which local sectors are primarily non-exporting sectors. As we mentioned above, in some city-regions which are highly specialized in particular activities, such as Detroit, Turin, and Toulouse, it is quite easy in principle to identify the major local basic exporting industries simply from observation. However, even in urban regions like these it may be that there are many other industries which are basic in nature, but which are not easily identifiable as being so, without additional information on the individual industries. Similarly, many regions appear not to be dominated by any par-ticular single industry or group of industries. Areas such as these tend to be very highly diversified in terms of the industrial activities which are represented locally. Therefore, determining which are the basic and non-basic sectors in these regions is not straight-forward. Consequently, without prior knowledge, in the case of many regions, determin-ing whether an industry is basic or non-basic is a rather inexact science.

There are three broad approaches to determining which local industrial sectors are the regional exporting sectors, namely the assumptions methods, the location quotient method, and the minimum requirements method. In the following sections we will deal with each of these three approaches in turn.

4.3.1 The assumptions method

The simplest approach to determining which local industrial sectors are basic and non-basic is to assume that all primary and secondary industries, which include all the extrac-tion, agricultural, and manufacturing sectors, are basic in nature, and that all tertiary sectors are non-basic. This is known as the 'Assumptions Method'. This approach, how-ever, must necessarily be inaccurate, because many tertiary activities, such as financial services, are frequently nationally and internationally traded activities. As such, they will be non-basic in nature. Similarly, many agricultural activities, and also extraction activ-ities such as quarrying, will tend to produce primarily for local markets, due to their relatively high transport costs. As such, many of these activities will be non-basic in nature. The simple basic and non-basic classification according to the assumptions method will therefore be subject to a large margin of error.

At the same time, there are many city-regions in which classification judgements based on experience and observation cannot easily identify basic and non-basic sectors. For example, in major cities such as New York, Paris, or London, the sheer number and variety of sectors means that identifying the basic and non-basic industries is almost impossible.

4.3.2 **Location quotients**

In situations such as these, where regional employment data is available the most commonly used technique of basic and non-basic classification is to employ what are known as regional 'Location Quotients' (*LQs*). The location quotient *LQ* describes the employment share of any sector in any region, relative to the national share of employment in the sector. A regional location quotient LQ_{ir} is defined as the ratio of the regional proportion of employment E in a given sector i in a given region r, relative to the national n proportion of employment in the same given sector. A regional location quotient is given as

$$LQ_{ir} = \frac{E_{ir}}{E_r} \bigg/ \frac{E_{in}}{E_n}, \tag{4.13}$$

where E_{ir} is Regional employment in sector I, E_r is Total employment in region r, E_{in} is National employment in sector I, and E_n is Total national employment.

In terms of economic base analysis, the logic behind the *LQ* argument is that if a region has an employment share in any given sector greater than the national average, the region must be relatively specialized in the production of the output of that particular sector. In this case, the $LQ_{ir} > 1$. If we assume for simplicity that for any given industry sector, all regions have the same linear production functions, and we also assume that all regional household consumption functions are identical, then a location quotient which is greater than 1 will imply that the region must be a net exporter of the output of the particular sector. Conversely, a location quotient of less than 1 implies that a region is a net importer of the good in question. A location quotient of unity implies zero net regional trade flows.

On the basis of this argument, we would expect that the location quotients for the automotive sectors in cities such as Detroit and Turin will be greater than 1, as these areas are relatively specialized in the automotive sector. At the same time, these areas are net exporters of automobiles, simply because the local economies of Detroit and Turin are small relative to the total markets of the local automotive sectors. Therefore, in these particular cases, the level of industrial specialization in these areas is taken as an indirect indicator of the level of their regional exports. Similarly, if the location quotient of a regional sector is less than the national average, the region must be a net importer of the goods produced by the sector. As an example, the level of employment in the whisky industry in England is almost zero, as almost all such UK employment is in Scotland. The location quotient for the whisky industry in all of the regions of England will be close to zero, although whisky is consumed in large quantities in all regions of England. As such, the English regions are all net importers of whisky. On the other hand, the location quotient for the whisky industry in Scotland will be very much greater than 1, because almost all of the UK output is produced in Scotland; Scotland is thus a net exporter of whisky.

This general location quotient argument can be applied to cities and regions in order to build up a picture of the regional importing and exporting patterns. Table 4.1 indicates the 1998 location quotient values for the aggregate industrial groupings within each of the three major UK agglomerations. These urban agglomerations are London, Birmingham, and Manchester.

Table 4.1 City location quotient distributions

	London	Birmingham	Manchester
Manufacturing	0.446	1.534	1.114
Construction	0.696	0.870	1.022
Wholesale and retail industries	0.936	0.918	1.082
Hotels and restaurants	1.206	0.776	0.914
Transport, storage, and communication	1.328	0.931	1.069
Financial intermediation	2.048	0.905	0.833
Real estate and general business services	1.625	0.896	0.965
Public administration	1.034	0.814	0.966
Education	0.803	1.053	1.026
Health and social work	0.779	0.856	1.000

Source: NOMIS

As we see in Table 4.1 these three major UK urban agglomerations of London, Birmingham, and Manchester exhibit rather different industrial structures. Both Birmingham and Manchester exhibit location quotient values of markedly greater than 1 for manufacturing industries. This suggests that both of these cities are relatively specialized in manufacturing activities, and consequently are net exporters of manufactured goods. Moreover, in both of these cities, manufacturing is the single largest industrial sector, which suggests that the manufacturing sector contains the largest number of people employed in regional exporting activities. On the other hand, in the case of London, although the absolute size of the manufacturing sector here is only marginally smaller than that of Birmingham and somewhat larger than that of Manchester, the location quotient value for manufacturing in London is very low. This suggests that London is a net importer of manufactured goods. However, if we consider the service sector activities of financial intermediation, and real estate and general business services in London, we see that London is very highly specialized in these sectors, whereas both Birmingham and Manchester are relatively unspecialized in these sectors. This implies that London is a net exporter of these service sector activities, whereas both Birmingham and Manchester rely on regional imports of these activities. Moreover, taken together, these service sector industries account for by far the largest employment share in the London economy. This implies that these sectors also account for the largest absolute number of people employed in regional exporting activities. The service sector activities of financial intermediation, real estate, and general business services can be considered to be a major basic sector of London. The other sectors in which London is also obviously a major net regional exporter are the hotel and restaurant activities associated with tourism, and also the transport and distribution activities associated primarily with the strategic location of London as a key access point for the UK and the European Union.

Given the information provided in Table 4.1, a measure of the extent to which each regional industrial structure is specialized, in the sense of the extent to which it differs from that of the national economy, can be provided by using any of the indices employed by Duranton and Puga (2000), Blair (1995), and Amiti (1998), as described in section 2.9 of Chapter 2.

The location quotient argument presented here can now be applied directly to the problem of the economic base. For any city or region we can simply group together all those industrial sectors whose location quotients are greater than 1, and categorize them as basic, and all sectors whose location quotients are less than or equal to 1 can be classified as non-basic. This is an exercise which was first carried out by Lichtenberg for the city of New York in 1954, a year in which the population of New York represented one-tenth of the total US population (Lichtenberg 1960; Hoover and Giarratani 1985). In order to understand the Lichtenberg approach, equation (4.13) above can be rearranged to give

$$LQ_{ir} = \left(\frac{E_{ir}}{E_r}\right)\left(\frac{E_n}{E_{in}}\right)$$

$$= \left(\frac{E_{ir}}{E_{in}}\right)\left(\frac{E_n}{E_r}\right),$$

$$LQ_{ir} = \left(\frac{E_{ir}}{E_{in}}\right) \Big/ \left(\frac{E_r}{E_n}\right). \tag{4.14}$$

Equation (4.14) redefines the location quotient in terms of the ratio of the proportion of national sectoral employment in a region relative to the proportionate size of the region. In the case of New York, the city represented 10 per cent of the 1954 population. Therefore, all New York industrial sectors which were found to account for more than 10 per cent of US national sectoral employment were assumed to be sectors which export goods and services to other parts of the national and international economy.

If we now apply the Lichtenberg logic to the case of the three UK cities described in Table 4.1, we can say that manufacturing industry can be considered to be the basic sector of both the Birmingham and Manchester economies. On the other hand, the combination of the service sector activities of financial intermediation, real estate, and general business services, along with the hotels, restaurants, transport, and distribution, can all be considered as a group to be the basic sector of the London economy.

A weakness of these approaches, however, is that the results generated do depend on the level of industrial aggregation (Karaska 1968). Given that the description of the regional economy in terms of a simple dichotomy between basic and non-basic activities is a rather broad definitional approach, for large population regions location quotient estimates used for these purposes are only really meaningful at rather large levels of industrial aggregation, as in Table 4.1. Alternatively, the approach can work in small spatial areas in which the region is specialized in a relatively small number of activities.

4.3.3 Minimum requirements approach

The two major analytical weaknesses of the location quotient approach, even allowing for the issues of sufficient data availability and the problems of aggregation described above, are the assumptions of a common production function for each individual sector across all regions, and the assumption of a common household consumption function for all regions. As we see from Chapters 1 and 2, variations in spatial industrial patterns can arise due to geographical differences in demand conditions. This implies that there may be spatial differences in consumption patterns. Similarly, from Chapters 1 and 3, industrial location behaviour can be associated with factor substitution, which itself will alter the relative quantities of individual factor inputs per unit of output produced. Each of these issues therefore calls into question the extent to which location quotients can really indicate the extent to which a regional sector is an exporting sector.

In response to these problems, a variation on the simple location quotient technique known as the minimum requirements technique was proposed by Ullman and Dacey (1960). This alternative approach is based on the argument that because regional economies are much more open than national economies, there is no theoretical reason why the national economy should the most appropriate benchmark for assessing whether a regional sector is basic or non-basic. In order to take account of this, the minimum requirements method employs an index which compares the regional sectoral employment structure within a particular region with that of similar-sized regions, rather than with that of the country as a whole. For regions of similar sizes, the smallest share of sectoral employment in any single region within the appropriate size band is taken to represent the local sectoral consumption requirement for regions of that size. All regional sectoral employment shares greater than this are assumed to represent employment in regional exporting industries. On this argument, the minimum requirements location quotient $MRLQ$ can be represented by

$$MRLQ_{ir} = \frac{E_{ir}}{E_r} \bigg/ \frac{E_{im}}{E_m},$$ (4.15)

where the subscript m represents the region with the minimum sectoral employment share. In principle, this method looks similar to the location quotient approach described by equation (4.13). As we see in Appendix 4.2, from the point of view of economic base studies, the attractiveness of the minimum requirements technique is that the basic/non-basic employment ratio is constant for all regions when summed across all sectors, although it is different for individual regional sectors. However, even apart from the problem of identifying the appropriate comparison regions, the analytical weakness of this approach is that it is not possible for a region to be a net importer of the output of any particular sector. The reason is that the $MRLQ$ value for any sector cannot be less than unity, because if a region's sectoral share is less than any alternative region of a similar size, the region in question will be taken as the minimum requirements benchmark region. All regions are therefore either net exporters or exhibit no net trade. This is obviously problematic. At the same time, in order to employ an economic base model of the form described by equations (4.1) to (4.8), it is not necessary for us to assume that all regions exhibit the same basic/non-basic employment ratio. All that is required is for the ratio to be fixed for the individual region in question.

4.3.4 **Choosing between the alternative economic base approaches**

In economic base models, the choice of technique adopted for determining the relative sizes of the basic and non-basic sectors will depend in part on the data which are available to us. The assumptions method is the most basic approach and relies on the least detailed sectoral employment information. The location quotient approach relies only on data for the region in question and national data, whereas the minimum requirements approach requires data on all regions. Unfortunately, these three techniques can give vastly different results. Therefore, because of the analytical problems with the minimum requirements technique discussed above and also in Appendix 4.2, the location quotient method is generally the most commonly used approach to determining the size of the regional basic and non-basic sectors.

Even if we are able to overcome the data problems discussed and to successfully identify the regional basic and non-basic sectors with a reasonable level of accuracy, a second issue which we have not yet discussed is the question of determining the value of the coefficient n in equation (4.2), where n represents the strength or sensitivity of the linkage between the size of the locally oriented sectors and the externally oriented activities within the local economy. From our discussions in Chapters 1 and 2, it is clear that these linkages could arise, first, due to direct expenditure on local factor inputs by the externally oriented sectors. The Weber–Moses arguments of Chapter 1 indicate that firm location behaviour may sometimes be associated with strong local input purchasing linkages. This will be the case where the optimal location is a corner solution at an end-point location. If the firms in question are primarily export-oriented firms with wide market areas, the result will be that a firm with a wide market area will exhibit strong local input purchasing. This will imply that the economic base linkage between the basic and non-basic sectors will be strong. At the same time, the agglomeration arguments of Chapter 2 suggest that there will be a second potential source of linkages between the basic and non-basic sectors. Additional linkages may arise due to information spillovers, whereby industrial clustering may lead to the improved flow of information between local firms. The implication here is that such improved information flows will improve the ability of locally oriented firms to respond to the input market needs of the local export-oriented firms, relative to more distant firms. This would suggest that the locally oriented firms will maximize their share of the market for inputs supplied to the local basic sector by being better able to customize their outputs to best suit the needs of the basic sector. This will be done in part by investing in the most appropriate technology at the most appropriate time. The argument is therefore that this process of appropriate investing, in response to the improved local information flows associated with proximity, will itself strengthen the linkages between the basic and non-basic sectors.

These arguments provide us with two sources of linkages between the basic and non-basic sectors, namely the direct expenditure on factor inputs and intermediate goods by basic firms, and the additional investment linkages possibly associated with agglomeration arguments. Both of these linkages are monetary linkages. However, distinguishing between these two sources of linkages between the basic and non-basic sectors can be difficult. Therefore, evaluating the impact of growth in the basic sector on the local economy, while taking into account both of these effects, can also be difficult. One way of discussing these different effects is by constructing an expenditure multiplier in which these monetary linkages are explicitly distinguished at the local regional level. The easiest way of doing this is to construct a Keynesian regional multiplier.

4.4 **Keynesian Regional Multiplier**

A model which is similar in nature to the economic base multiplier, and which can be made largely compatible with it, is that of the Keynesian regional multiplier. The Keynesian regional multiplier is adapted from the standard Keynesian national income-expenditure multiplier model familiar in introductory and intermediate macroeconomic textbooks. Assuming that marginal and average input costs remain constant, and assuming that there are no capacity constraints within the economy, the standard Keynesian national income-expenditure multiplier model can be described by Figure 4.1. In Figure 4.1, the change in income ΔY associated with any change in aggregate demand ΔAD can be described as $\Delta Y = k(\Delta AD)$, where k is the value of the multiplier. The multiplier therefore is given by the value of the ratio of the horizontal shift from Y_1 to Y_2, divided by the vertical shift from AD_1 to AD_2. In Figure 4.1, the successive rounds of expenditure are indicated by the converging income-expenditure path abc.

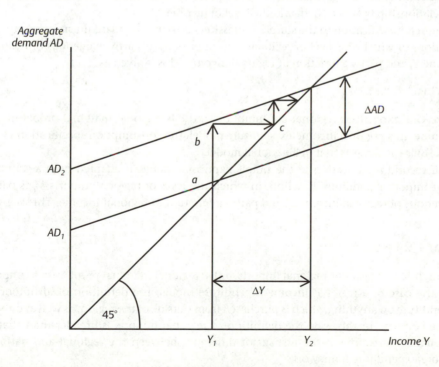

Fig. 4.1 Keynesian income-expenditure multiplier model

For a change in any of the individual components of aggregate demand, we can therefore multiply the individual change by the value of the multiplier to provide us with the overall income change, after all of the successive rounds of expenditure have taken place. This income-expenditure process may be dynamic in the sense that successive rounds of expenditure may take place over several time periods. However, as we see in Appendix 4.1, it is quite straightforward to reconcile the simple static Keynesian income-expenditure model with a dynamic model incorporating time into the model, such that the conclusions here hold in either case.

We can now apply this broad logic to the case of a region. However, from the discussions in the previous sections, there are particular features of the local regional economy which are somewhat different from those exhibited by the national economy. The result is that the Keynesian regional multiplier is also somewhat different from the standard national Keynesian multiplier. In order to see this we can set up a simple set of expressions out of which we will construct our multiplier model.

The standard Keynesian income-aggregate demand expression can be applied to a region as

$$Y_r = C_r + I_r + G_r + X_r - M_r, \tag{4.16}$$

where Y_r represents regional income, C_r represents regional consumption, I_r is regional investment, G_r is regional government expenditure, X_r are regional exports and M_r are imports. Each of the terms on the right-hand side of equation (4.16) represents an individual component of aggregate regional demand. These terms can be modified to show the relationship between them and the level of income.

Our first modification to the simple expression above is a standard linear consumption function, in which the level of regional consumption C_r is partly exogenous of regional income Y_r and partly a function of regional income. This is given as

$$C_r = \bar{C} + cY_r, \tag{4.17}$$

where $\bar{C}$ is exogenous regional consumption and c is regional marginal propensity to consume. In a regional income-expenditure model, the consumption specification given in (4.16) is the same as that in a national model.

Our second modification to the simple expression above is adapted from a standard linear import-expenditure function, in which the level of regional imports M_r is partly exogenous of regional income Y_r and partly a function of regional income. This is given as

$$M_r = \bar{M} + mY_r \tag{4.18}$$

in which $\bar{M}$ is exogenous regional imports and m regional marginal propensity to import.

In the case of a regional income-expenditure model, the definition of an import is expenditure on anything which is purchased from outside of the region, as well as outside of the country. In this way, the definition of regional imports is broader than that of national imports. This is the first major difference between the regional and national income-expenditure frameworks.

The income term Y_r in equations (4.17) and (4.18) is usually treated as the disposable income after tax. We can incorporate total regional taxation leakages T_r in a simple manner as

$$T_r = tY_r,\tag{4.19}$$

where t is the average regional tax rate, such that disposable income after tax is given as $Y_r(1-t)$.

With equations (4.16) to (4.19) we are now able to provide an income-aggregate demand expression for regional income. Assuming for the moment, as many national income-expenditure models do, that regional private sector investment I_r, government regional expenditure G_r and regional exports X_r are exogenous, we can substitute the information in equations (4.17) to (4.19) in equation (4.16) to give

$$Y_r = \bar{C} + cY_r(1-t) + I_r + G_r + X_r - \bar{M} - mY_r(1-t).\tag{4.20}$$

This can be rewritten as

$$Y_r - cY_r(1-t) + mY_r(1-t) = \bar{C} + I_r + G_r + X_r - \bar{M},\tag{4.21}$$

which rearranges to

$$Y_r = \frac{\bar{C} + I_r + G_r + X_r - \bar{M}}{1 - (c-m)(1-t)}.\tag{4.22}$$

The regional income Y_r is thus given as the sum of the exogenous components of aggregate demand multiplied by a regional multiplier k_r thus

$$Y_r = k_r(\bar{C} + I_r + G_r + X_r - \bar{M}),\tag{4.23}$$

where

$$k_r = \frac{1}{1 - (c-m)(1-t)}.\tag{4.24}$$

The value of the regional multiplier k_r is seen to depend crucially on the value of the bracketed term $(c-m)$, which represents the difference between the marginal propensity to consume and the marginal propensity to import from outside of the region. The term $(c-m)$ therefore represents the marginal propensity to consume locally produced goods. As the value of $(c-m)$ increases, the value of the regional multiplier increases, and as the value of $(c-m)$ falls, the value of the regional multiplier falls.

If we consider the effect of an increase in any one of the components of aggregate demand within the multiplier framework we can write

$$\Delta Y_r = \frac{\Delta(\bar{C} + I_r + G_r + X_r - \bar{M})}{1 - (c-m)(1-t)}.\tag{4.25}$$

This suggests that the greater is the regional value of the marginal propensity to consume locally produced goods, the greater is the value of the regional multiplier, and the greater is the increase in regional income. This observation fits well with the discussions in Chapters 1 and 2, in that regions with a strong supply of production factor and intermediate inputs will benefit greatly from any output increases on the part of the individual components of demand. The reason for this is that more of the income will be maintained within the region through successive rounds of expenditure between firms and local suppliers. On the other hand, regions characterized by firms which have very few local suppliers will tend to exhibit a high propensity to import m. The result will be that the marginal propensity to consume locally produced goods will tend to be very low, as will the value of the regional multiplier. The geography of interfirm linkages therefore largely determines the value of the regional multiplier.

The regional multiplier expression given in (4.25) is not substantially different from simple national multiplier models, except for the geographical definition of imports. However, there is a second major difference between regional and national income multiplier frameworks, and this focuses on the question of investment. In standard national models investment is treated as being exogenous, as it is regarded as being dependent primarily on issues such as inflation, interest rates, and expectations. As such, the level of investment is not regarded as being primarily dependent on the level of national income. However, within a regional framework the marginal propensity to invest in the local economy may be a function of local regional income. The reason for this is that local business confidence, and also the willingness of banks to provide loans to local businesses, may be dependent on the existing strength of the local economy, irrespective of national inflation expectations or interest rates (Dow 1982, 1987, 1997). The justification for this type of argument comes from the discussions of location and clustering in Chapters 1 and 2, in which clustering and proximity may improve flows of information between firms and between firms and consumers, and also may improve the efficiency of the local labour market, thereby increasing local income via agglomeration externalities. In situations such as this we can assume that local investment levels are partly exogenous in that they are dependent on national economic conditions, and also partly dependent on the level of local regional income. We can therefore write regional investment income as

$$I_r = \bar{I} + iY_r(1 - t),\tag{4.26}$$

where i is the local regional marginal propensity to invest in the local economy.

The third way in which regional income-expenditure flows are different from national flows is in terms of government expenditure. In national income-expenditure models government expenditure G is assumed to be exogenous of income, being dependent primarily on political issues. However, in the case of regions this is not so. Government expenditure in regions is in part dependent on the level of regional income. In particular, it can be argued that flows of government expenditure tend to be inversely related to the level of local regional income. For example, low-income areas often suffer from relatively high unemployment. In such cases, large flows of welfare benefits will tend to be directed into the regional economy. Similarly, low-income areas often are eligible for public subsidies from regional policy funds or urban policy schemes. On the other hand, high-income areas will receive relatively fewer public expenditure flows of the types just mentioned, because there will be less need for such flows. Government expenditure therefore acts as a partial stabilizer, countering changes in regional income. Therefore, in terms of regional income-expenditure models, the argument here suggests that public expenditure is in part an inverse function of local regional income. We can thus rewrite our government regional income-expenditure function as:

$$G_r = \bar{G} - gY_r(1-t), \tag{4.27}$$

where minus g represents the marginal propensity of government expenditure to be withdrawn from the local economy as regional income increases.

Now, if we substitute equations (4.17), (4.18), (4.19), (4.26), and (4.27) into equation (4.16) we have

$$Y_r = \bar{C} + cY_r(1-t) + (\bar{I} + iY_r) + (\bar{G} - gY_r) + X_r - \bar{M} - mY_r(1-t), \tag{4.28}$$

which rearranging in a similar manner to equations (4.20) to (4.22) gives us

$$Y_r = \frac{\bar{C} + \bar{I} + \bar{G} + X_r - \bar{M}}{1 - [(c-m) + (i-g)](1-t)} \tag{4.29}$$

and

$$Y_r = k_r(\bar{C} + \bar{I} + \bar{G} + X_r - \bar{M}), \tag{4.30}$$

where

$$k_r = \frac{1}{1 - [(c-m) + (i-g)](1-t)}. \tag{4.31}$$

This expression is essentially the same as equation (4.22), except for the fact that the denominator term in equation (4.29) is broader than that in (4.22). In equation (4.29) the denominator term in square brackets contains an additional term $(i-g)$, as well as the term $(c-m)$ which is the marginal propensity to consume locally produced goods, and $(1-t)$. This additional term $(i-g)$, which we can call the regional marginal (public plus private) propensity to invest in the local economy, reflects the total private local investment flows associated with local income levels, net of the public expenditure withdrawals associated with increasing regional income (Black 1981; Sinclair and Sutcliffe 1983). We assume that $i>g$, such that regional income growth is positively associated with overall public plus private sector investment growth. The type of multiplier model given by equation (4.31), which includes both the local customer–supplier expenditure linkages $(c-m)$ and the local investment linkages $(i-g)$, is sometimes known as a 'super' multiplier (McCombie and Thirlwall 1994).

As before, the justification for this type of model comes from the discussions in Chapter 2, in that business clustering in many cases is associated with increased regional income due to improved local information flows between customers, suppliers, and factor inputs. One of the features of areas characterized by such agglomeration economies is that there may be an associated increase in the entrepreneurial environment. In part this could be because of a greater general awareness of potential business investment opportunities, due to geographical proximity between market agents. At the same time, as we have seen, this could also imply that credit becomes more readily available for investment opportunities in already buoyant economies. For all of these reasons we can assume that the marginal propensity to invest in the local economy will be positively related to the level of local regional income.

One final point we must consider concerns the regional propensity for government investment to be withdrawn from the region as regional income increases, as described by equation (4.27). As a region grows, the absolute levels of government expenditure in the region will tend to increase as greater levels of investment are required to provide and maintain local public infrastructure such as roads, schools, and hospitals. This would suggest that the marginal propensity for government investment is a positive function of regional income. However, we can consider this effect as primarily a scale effect on public infrastructure investment in response to a growth in the local population. On the other hand, the effect described by equation (4.27) can be related to the income growth of either a stable or growing population, and relates both to the increasing out-transfer of welfare payment income, and to public infrastructure investment. In principle equation (4.27) can be modified to take both of these effects into account thus:

$$G_r = \bar{G} + (g' - g'')Y_r(1 - t), \tag{4.32}$$

where g' represents the marginal propensity to increase government investment on local regional public infrastructure as regional income increases in line with regional population growth, and g'' represents the marginal propensity to withdraw government expenditure as regional income increases for any given level of regional population. In principle, equations (4.28) to (4.31) can be adjusted to take account of this modification. However, in countries with welfare systems and some element of regional policy, we can assume that $(g' - g'')$ is generally negative. Otherwise we would see that government expenditure serves to systematically increase regional income disparities rather than reduce them. Given that such a situation cannot be sustainable in the long run, we can assume that $(g' - g'')$ is negative. Therefore we can write $g = (g' - g'')$, where g represents the net marginal propensity of government expenditure to be withdrawn from the local economy as regional income increases. As such, our multiplier model equations (4.27) to (4.31) do not need to be altered.

4.5 Comparing the Economic Base and Keynesian Regional Multipliers

As was mentioned above, although the economic base multiplier model and the Keynesian multiplier model are rather different conceptually from each other, they can be made more or less compatible with each other. In order to see this, we can convert our income-expenditure multiplier expression (4.29) into an export base multiplier model, which is analogous to the economic base models discussed in section 4.2. To do this we simply separate the export income component of aggregate regional demand from the other domestic regional income components thus

$$Y_r = \frac{X_r}{1 - [(c - m) + (i - g)](1 - t)} + \frac{\bar{C} + \bar{I} + \bar{G} - \bar{M}}{1 - [(c - m) + (i - g)](1 - t)}. \tag{4.33}$$

The first term on the right-hand side of (4.33), which is our export base multiplier, reflects the economic base multiplier described in terms of income flows rather than employment numbers. The second term on the right-hand side of (4.33) describes the income-expenditure multiplier associated with specifically local activities. If we consider a change in regional exports ΔX_r, the corresponding change in regional income Y_r can be represented as

$$\Delta Y_r = \frac{\Delta X_r}{1 - [(c - m) + (i - g)](1 - t)}. \tag{4.34}$$

Immediately we can see that equation (4.34) is the income-expenditure equivalent of our economic base equation (4.4) which was given as

$$\Delta T = \frac{1}{1 - n} \Delta B. \tag{4.4}$$

The increase in export income ΔX_r in equation (4.34) is the equivalent of the employment increase in the basic sector ΔB in equation (4.4). Similarly, the basic–non-basic linkage coefficient n in equation (4.4) is the employment equivalent of the income-expenditure expression $[(c - m) + (i - g)](1 - t)$ in equation (4.34). The same argument can be extended to the relationship between the income-expenditure multiplier equation (4.33) and the economic base equation (4.6), which was given as

$$T = \frac{N_o}{1 - n_1} + \frac{B}{1 - n_1}. \tag{4.6}$$

The second numerator term on the right-hand side of equation (4.33) is given as

$$(\bar{C} + \bar{I} + \bar{G} - \bar{M}).$$

This term represents the exogenous levels of regional income which are independent of regional exports. By comparing (4.33) with (4.6) we can see that the second numerator term on the right-hand side of equation (4.33) is the income-expenditure equivalent of N_o, which in the economic base model represents the level of regional employment autonomous of exports. These comparisons therefore allow us to see that the employment linkages between the basic and non-basic sectors are mediated through the local expenditure linkages generated by the transactions between the two sectors. These expenditure linkages can be of the form of direct expenditure on locally produced intermediate inputs and local factor supplies, the strength of which is given by the marginal propensity to consume locally produced goods $(c - m)$. Additional induced expenditure can also be generated by increases in local investment, which are represented by the regional (public plus private) propensity to invest $(i - g)$.

4.6 **Impact Analysis**

At the aggregate regional level, the impacts of an increase in regional export activity, associated with a growth of the basic sector in general, can be analysed in a straightforward manner by observation of equation (4.34). Similarly, using the same approach, we can also observe the regional multiplier effects of a change in any of the regional domestic components of demand given in equation (4.30), simply by multiplying the change in the particular component of aggregate demand by the regional multiplier, as described in equation (4.31). At the micro-level, however, the situation may be rather more complex.

We can imagine a situation where a firm, which serves a wide geographical market area, moves into a particular region. If the market area of the firm is much wider than the host region, it becomes immediately obvious that the exports of the region will increase due to the local presence of the immigrant firm. In the above expressions this implies that ΔX_r is positive. However, following the location theory arguments outlined in Chapter 1, a new firm may initially only have very weak links with the local economy in which it has located. This is because it may take time for a firm to develop strong linkages with the local economy. The manifestation of this will be that the firm's marginal propensity to consume locally produced goods may be much lower than the prevailing average regional marginal propensity to consume locally produced goods (Sinclair and Sutcliffe 1978, 1983). In a situation such as this, equation (4.33) will need to be adjusted to allow for two different expenditure effects.

The first effect comes from the direct expenditure by the new immigrant firm on locally produced goods and services. The additional regional income accounted for by the new immigrant firm is represented by ΔX_r. We can think of this as the first-round income injection. The second-round income injection can be considered to be the additional expenditure in the local economy by the new firm, which can be represented by $\Delta X_r(c_F - m_F)(1 - t_F)$, where c_F represents the firm's marginal propensity to consume, m_F represents the firm's marginal propensity to import, and t_F represents the firm's corporate tax rate. This second-round expenditure injection into the local economy represented by $\Delta X_r(c_F - m_F)(1 - t_F)$ will itself then be subject to the regional multiplier represented by equation (4.31). These will be the third and subsequent rounds of income injections. These different stages can be described as

$$\Delta Y_r = \Delta X_r + \frac{\Delta X_r(c_F - m_F)(1 - t_F)}{1 - [(c - m) + (i - g)](1 - t)}. \tag{4.35}$$

If we let

$$e_1 = (c_F - m_F)(1 - t_F)$$
$$e_2 = [(c - m) + (i - g)](1 - t),$$

we can write equation (4.35) as

$$\Delta Y_r = \Delta X_r \left(1 + \frac{e_1}{1 - e_2}\right),$$ (4.36)

which rearranges to (Wilson 1977)

$$\Delta Y_r = \Delta X_r \left(\frac{1 + e_1 - e_2}{1 - e_2}\right).$$ (4.37)

The type of model described by equation (4.37) is frequently employed in 'impact' analyses, in which we attempt to evaluate the regional development effects of individual structural changes to a region, such as the immigration of a new firm into a region, or the construction of a new infrastructure project within the region. Relative to standard multiplier models described by equations (4.16) to (4.31), equation (4.37) provides us with a more rigorous way of estimating the regional multiplier in cases such as this, by distinguishing the expenditure linkages directly associated with the firm or project in question and those which are due to general regional expenditure patterns. These impact analysis approaches are useful in providing reasonably quick estimates to such regional structural changes.

Linkage expenditure patterns can be defined both in terms of geography and also in terms of time. The geography of linkage patterns, as discussed in Chapters 1 and 2, will determine the value of the regional expenditure coefficients. However, this information will not tell us anything about the speed of such effects. In order to understand the temporal aspects of regional impact multipliers, all of the models described by equations (4.16) to (4.37) can be made more sophisticated by splitting up the various rounds of the income-expenditure process into discrete time periods. This allows us to integrate export base models with accelerator-type models (Hartman and Seckler 1967). There are, however, analytical weaknesses inherent in all of these types of Keynesian income-expenditure multiplier models, which we must consider. The problems concern the relationship between the values of the parameters contained in the coefficients e_1 and e_2, as a structural change of this sort takes place.

If a firm moves into an area, we know from our Weber analysis in Chapter 1 that the supply linkages of the firm are likely to be very different from the host region as a whole. In particular, the new firm's supply linkages will tend to be less localized than those of the firms or industries which have been located in the host region for a significant time period. Over time, the firm's local supply linkages, defined by e_1, may converge towards the regional average values, defined by e_2, as the firm seeks to employ more local suppliers. On the other hand, this may not be the case, either if firms are unable to find suitable local suppliers, or if corporate organizational concerns militate against the employment of local suppliers, instead requiring the firm to employ corporation-wide suppliers from other locations. If either of these latter situations occurs, the firm's regional linkage expenditure patterns, reflected in its marginal expenditure coefficients, may remain quite different from the regional linkage expenditure values. Over time therefore the immigration of the new firm may itself change the regional linkage values, and consequently the regional marginal expenditure values, averaged across all sectors. If the immigrant firm is very large relative to the size of the local economy, such as in the case of a newly opened automobile production plant, the regional expenditure coefficients may change very quickly. In some cases these changes may occur before all of the successive rounds of expenditure have had time to take place, in which case the value of the regional multiplier will itself have been changed by the immigration of the new firm.

The immigration of different types of firms into a region will therefore change the regional multiplier in different ways according to the particular linkage patterns of the firms in question. The reason for this is that firms of different types will exhibit different demand requirements for intermediate inputs and production factors. The demand requirements across the various sectors within the region will differ according to the expenditure patterns of the particular firm or sector we are observing. To address these problems coherently, it is therefore necessary for us to isolate each of the individual expenditure linkages between each of the sectors within the region, and between the region sectors and all other regions. Only then will we be able to distinguish between, and accurately estimate, the regional multiplier impacts of any particular regional structural change. In order to do this, we must undertake what is known as regional input–output analysis.

4.7 Regional Input–Output Analysis

The basic principle behind regional input–output analysis is to identify and disaggregate all of the absolute flows of expenditure between different industries, between consumers and industries, and between industries and factor supplies, in order to reveal the underlying trading structure of the regional economy. These individual expenditure linkages are then defined in proportionate terms, and the aggregate pattern of these proportionate relationships is used to construct detailed regional multipliers. It therefore becomes possible to identify how the regional economy in general, and also how each of the individual regional sectors, are affected by a change in the level of demand of one or more of the individual regional industrial sectors. As such, regional input–output analysis can avoid many of the analytical problems described in the section above as long as sufficient updated input–output data are available, which is a point we will return to at the end of this section.

The first stage of a regional input–output analysis is to construct a regional trade flow table. In order to understand the logic of this we will use a numerical example employed by Thorne (1969), in which region R is comprised of three industrial sectors X, Y, and Z. Table 4.2 indicates the absolute values of the current output and expenditure on inputs by each of the three sectors X, Y, and Z, plus the expenditure by final consumers in the region on finished goods. As we see in Table 4.2, at the current levels of regional output, local industry X spends $20 million on inputs from each of the other local industrial sectors Y and Z, $20 million on regional imports, and $40 million on local regional inputs. The respective expenditure flows of each of the sectors Y and Z can also be seen by reading down the column values in Table 4.2. Similarly, local household consumers are

Table 4.2 Regional expenditure flows

| Sales of ($m.) | Purchases of ($m.): | | | | |
	Industry X	Industry Y	Industry Z	Final consumers	Total output
Industry X	—	—	70	30	100
Industry Y	20	—	80	100	200
Industry Z	20	80	—	200	300
Regional factor inputs	40	110	140	—	290
Regional imports	20	10	10	30	70
Total input	100	200	300	360	960

seen to purchase $30 million worth of finished goods and services from local industry X, $100 million from local industry Y, $200 million from local industry Z, plus £30 million worth of finished goods and services produced outside of the region. At the same time, we can interpret the pattern of sales by each sector across each of the other sectors and household consumers by reading across the columns from left to right. For example, local industry Z sells $20 million worth of outputs to local industry X, $80 million to local industry Y, and $200 million to local consumers. Meanwhile, local factor inputs supply factor services worth £40 million, $110 million, and $140 million to each of the local industries X, Y, and Z, respectively. These values represent the combined total wages, rent, and interest earned by the local labour, land, and capital suppliers employed in the activities of each of the local industries X, Y, and Z. The final column on the right-hand side provides the total output sales for each sector.

The second stage in the input–output analysis involves defining the disaggregated expenditure flows for each of the three industries and the final consumers as described in Table 4.2 in terms of their proportionate size. In order to do this we simply divide the expenditure value in each of the cells of Table 4.2 by the respective column total at the foot of each of the columns. For example, in Table 4.2 we see that local industry Y currently purchases $80 million worth of inputs from local industry Z. By dividing 80 by the respective column total of 200, we see that the expenditure by industry Y on inputs from industry Z accounts for 0.4, i.e. 40 per cent, of the total input expenditure of industry Y. The value of 0.4 is defined as the regional expenditure coefficient of local industry Y's purchases of the output of local industry Z. By repeating this procedure for each of the cells in Table 4.2 we arrive at Table 4.3, which gives each of the individual regional expenditure coefficients for purchases by industries X, Y, and Z, as well as final household purchases. Table 4.3 can be considered a matrix of regional expenditure coefficients.

With Table 4.3 we can now consider the impact on the regional economy of an increase in the output demand of one of the local industrial sectors. For example, we can consider the situation where final consumers increase their consumption of the goods produced by local industry Z to $1000 million. In order to supply $1000 million worth of goods and services to final consumers, from Table 4.3 we know that local industry Z must also

Table 4.3 Regional expenditure coefficients

	Purchase coefficients of:			
	Industry X	Industry Y	Industry Z	Final consumers
Industry X	—	—	0.23	0.08
Industry Y	0.2	—	0.27	0.28
Industry Z	0.2	0.4	—	0.56
Regional factor inputs	0.4	0.55	0.47	—
Regional imports	0.2	0.5	0.03	0.08
Total inputs	1.0	1.0	1.0	1.0

purchase 23 per cent of its inputs from local industry X (i.e. 0.23x1000 = $230 million), 27 per cent of its inputs from local industry Y (i.e. 0.27x1000 = $270 million), 47 per cent of its inputs (i.e. 0.47x1000 = $470 million) from local factor suppliers, and 3 per cent of its inputs (i.e. 0.03x230 = $6.9 million) as regional imports. Industry X in turn will then spend 20 per cent of its income on additional inputs from local industry Y (i.e. 0.2x230 = $46 million), 20 per cent of its income on additional inputs from local industry Z (i.e. 0.2x230 = $46 million), 40 per cent of its income on additional local factor supplies (i.e. 0.4x230 = $92 million), and 20 per cent (i.e. 0.2x230 = $46 million) on regional imports. Meanwhile, industry Y will spend 40 per cent of its income on additional inputs from local industry Z (i.e. 0.4x270 = $108 million), 55 per cent of its income on additional local factor supplies (i.e. 0.55x270 = $148.5 million), and 3 per cent of its income (i.e. 0.03x270 = $8.1 million) on regional imports. Each of the three sectors in turn will continue to purchase additional inputs through the successive rounds of expenditure along the lines described in Appendix 4.1. Assuming that the expenditure coefficients remain constant through the successive rounds of expenditure, it is possible to calculate the total value of regional output and expenditure associated with local industry Z producing $1000 million worth of goods and services for local consumers.

Following Thorne (1969) the absolute output and expenditure values are given in Table 4.4. A final consumer demand of $1000 million for the output of local industry Z, results in a total regional output of $2868 million, because of the successive rounds of expenditure between each of the local industrial sectors. The value of the regional multiplier in this particular case is therefore total regional output divided by the particular output demand in question. In other words, the regional multiplier is given by 2868/1000 = 2.87.

From Table 4.3 we see that each industry has a different pattern of regional expenditure, as reflected by the different values of the regional expenditure coefficients. However, once the initial demand stimulus has been transmitted to the supplying sectors, the pattern of purchasing through the successive rounds of expenditure remains constant. Yet, what we immediately see from this example is that for any given level of final output, the actual value of the regional multiplier depends on the source of the initial output demand stimulus. For a fixed pattern of regional sectoral purchase coefficients, given in Table 4.3, the absolute value of the regional multiplier will depend crucially on the pat-

Table 4.4 Regional output and expenditure flows for consumner purchases of $1000 million from Industry Z

Sales of ($m.)	Purchases of ($m.):				
	Industry X	Industry Y	Industry Z	Final consumers	Total output
Industry X	—	—	282	—	282
Industry Y	56	—	322	—	378
Industry Z	56	152	—	1000	1208
Regional factor inputs	113	207	564	—	884
Regional imports	57	19	40	—	116
Total input	282	378	1208	1000	2868

tern of the first-round local purchases by the sector in which the initial demand stimulus arose. In the above case, if the output demand originated in local sector X, the value of the overall regional multiplier would have been much less, because sector X has a much higher propensity to import than either sector Y or sector Z. Therefore, the first-round expenditure injection into the regional industrial system would have been much lower than in the above case.

On first inspection, the individual regional expenditure coefficients in each of the cells of Table 4.3 may appear to be the input–output equivalent of n in the economic base model (equation 4.3), and $(c - m)$ in the Keynesian multiplier model (equation 4.24). However, in the input–output case the individual regional expenditure coefficients of Table 4.3 refer only to a single expenditure linkage between one individual purchasing sector and one individual supply sector. On the other hand, the values of n in the economic base model and $(c - m)$ in the Keynesian multiplier model represent aggregate average regional expenditure values across all regional purchasing linkages. As we see in Appendix 4.3, the actual input–output equivalent of the economic base or Keynesian multiplier models is determined by calculating the inverse of the matrix of all of the coefficients given in Table 4.3. It is this technique that allows us to calculate the values given in Table 4.4.

4.7.1 Additional comments on regional input–output analysis

The input–output multiplier is equivalent to, but much more precise and flexible than either the economic base multiplier (T/B in equation 4.3) or the Keynesian regional multiplier (k_r in equation 4.24). One reason is that the input–output multiplier automatically incorporates all of the issues raised by impact analysis, as discussed in section 4.6 above, concerning the fact that the first-round impact coefficient values (given as e_1 in equation 4.36) will depend on the source of the demand stimulus, and will be different from the regional expenditure coefficients of the successive rounds of local expenditure (given as e_2 in equation 4.36).

Secondly, the basic input–output model described here can be further modified to be made more directly comparable with the economic base (Billings 1969) and Keynesian regional multiplier models by splitting up final consumer demand into a local and a non-local component. In other words, by isolating whether the source of a demand stimulus originates primarily from outside of the region or within the region, we can consider the extent to which the region behaves as an export base, along the lines described in sections 4.5 and 4.6. In the example above, we can consider the situation where the region very much exhibits an export base type of structure by imagining that almost all of the final consumer demand is external to the region. In this case, the input–output structure described by Tables 4.2 to 4.4 will represent an economic base model. To a large extent it will also represent a Keynesian regional multiplier, except for the induced investment expenditure effects. As well as allowing us to consider the local effects of a regional export stimulus, we can also use this technique to investigate the regional multiplier effects of the immigration of a new firm into a region, by considering the first and subsequent rounds of expenditure directly and indirectly generated by the new firm.

Thirdly, the technique can be extended to construct a system of inter-regional input–output tables, in which trade flows between all sectors and across all regions are explicitly distinguished from trade flows between all sectors within individual regions. This allows inter-regional trade feedback effects to be analysed (Miller 1998), in which mutual trading relationships between the regions mean that a demand stimulus in one region generates an increased demand impact in a second region, which itself leads to an increased demand on the first region. Moreover, such models can be made dynamic in the sense that demand changes over time can be simulated.

Although the principle behind the regional input–output model is quite straightforward, in practice, however, the use of such techniques is much more complicated because the construction of regional input–output tables is itself a very difficult task. The reason is that without borders or a customs administration system, regions are not able to collect detailed trade statistics of flows of goods and services to and from other regions. Nor are they able to collect detailed internal trade statistics between sectors within the domestic economy. Therefore, we have little or no direct information as to the input–output coefficients which will enter each cell in a regional input–output table such as Table 4.3. In a very few cases such as Scotland and Wales regional input–output data are constructed fairly frequently from extremely large and detailed surveys carried out by government agencies. However, in most other cases such surveys are not possible. In these more usual situations where updated surveys are not available, the construction of regional input–output tables is therefore carried out in an indirect manner. In order to do this, there are two standard practices. The first approach is employed where no updated national input–output table exists. In this approach regional trade flows are estimated on the basis of regional sectoral employment distributions, which are calculated using location quotient techniques. In the second approach, where updated national input–output tables do exist, regional trade estimates are produced by adjusting the national input–output coefficients. The details of the techniques employed are discussed in Appendix 4.2. In situations where it is possible to test the accuracy of regional input–output tables constructed on the basis of these indirect approaches with actual regional trade survey data, the results suggest that there is often a high degree of error in the indirect methods. In particular, as we see in Appendix 4.2.2, regional trade estimates arrived at on the basis of location quotients generally tend to overestimate local multiplier values.

A final analytical issue relating to input–output analysis, but which also relates to the economic base and Keynesian regional multiplier models, concerns the realism of the assumption of the stability of the input–output coefficients through the successive rounds of expenditure. All three models are based on the assumption that the regional expenditure coefficients remain stable throughout the successive rounds of local expenditure. In other words, we assume that the marginal and average costs of production remain equal and constant as output expands. Furthermore, we also assume that all production functions are linear, in the sense that all input expenditure coefficients remain fixed, and that the relationship between inputs and outputs exhibits constant returns to scale. (Such production functions are referred to as linear input–output functions, or alternatively as Leontief functions, after the founder of input–output analysis Wassily Leontief (1953).) Taken together, these assumptions amount to saying that the prices of any factor inputs which are specifically local, such as labour and land prices, are invariant with the level of output.

In situations in which there are unemployed resources, and in particular in situations in which there is a pool of unemployed local labour at the prevailing regional wage rate, the input–output assumptions concerning constant marginal and average costs would appear to be good approximations of the real world. In these situations, the regional input–output model can be made compatible with, and provide extensions to, the Keynesian regional multiplier model (Hewings *et al.* 1999). Moreover, demographic changes in the composition of the local labour supply can also be made compatible with such assumptions (Batey and Madden 1981; Batey *et al.* 2001). On the other hand, where supply constraints become evident, the prices of the various local inputs will begin to rise. This may lead to some factor substitution effects, thereby contravening our multiplier assumptions. The extent to which the accuracy of our multiplier model is affected will therefore depend on the extent to which our linearity assumptions are violated across all regional sectors.

4.8 Conclusions

The question of regional industrial specialization, which was first introduced in Chapter 2, has implications for the pattern of trade which a region engages in. In particular, spatial industrial clustering implies that a region is relatively specialized in the production of the outputs of the locally clustered sector. The result is that the industrial sectors which are clustered in certain regions tend to provide the major exports for the regions in which they are located. Conversely, the majority of a region's imports will tend to come from the sectors which have a relatively low level of employment in the region. As we have seen in this chapter, the regional trade patterns which result from these patterns of regional industrial specialization, have implications for the relationship between the externally oriented regional export sectors and the locally oriented regional industrial sectors. These relationships are manifested in terms of employment and expenditure linkages, the structure of which can be understood in terms of regional multipliers. The basic observation to come out of these multiplier models is that a demand increase in one regional export sector will have even greater impacts for overall regional demand.

We have discussed the three broad approaches to identifying regional multipliers, namely the economic base model, the Keynesian regional multiplier model, and regional input–output analysis. These three approaches to regional multiplier analysis allow us to analyse the contribution of regional exports to the successive rounds of income and expenditure which remain in the local economy. Of the three techniques, the economic base model is seen to be analytically the simplest approach, in which estimates of the basic and non-basic sectors are most commonly made on the basis of regional industrial employment distributions. The Keynesian regional multiplier model adopts a different perspective in that it focuses on the issues which determine the nature of the monetary flows involved in each of the successive rounds of income and expenditure. As we have seen, however, the economic base model and the Keynesian regional multiplier model can be made more or less compatible, at least in analytical terms, in that local sectoral employment linkages will be mediated through local money expenditure linkages. Meanwhile, the input–output approach is much more comprehensive than the other two approaches, and avoids many of the analytical problems associated with the two techniques.

On the other hand, all three of the approaches suffer from the same two basic problems. The first problem is the issue of data availability, and the limitations of the various techniques for overcoming data availability problems. The second problem is the question of the assumption of constant regional average and marginal costs with excess regional capacity. As we have seen, in situations where there is excess labour supply, such assumptions can be justified. In particular, these approaches can be very useful in analysing the impacts of the policies adopted for rejuvenating underperforming regions. These issues will be dealt with in detail as part of our regional policy discussions in Chapter 7. At the same time, as we will see in the next chapter, these models can also throw some light on the downward adjustment mechanisms of regions which experience adverse demand shocks. On the other hand, where labour supply prices are changing, such as in situations in which there are local labour supply constraints, or alternatively where inter-regional labour migration is a major feature, regional multiplier models may exhibit rather greater limitations. These various issues surrounding the regional demand and supply of local labour are the central topics discussed in Chapter 5.

Discussion questions

1 What types of urban and regional economies are most suited to an economic-base type of analysis?

2 What empirical measures can we adopt for estimating basic and non-basic industries?

3 Within a Keynesian regional multiplier framework, examine the role played by the marginal propensity to consume locally produced goods in determining regional income.

4   How can a Keynesian regional multiplier framework be made consistent with an economic base model?

5   How is the structure of the regional multiplier affected by the types of firms which locate in a region?

6   What are the advantages of input–output techniques over other regional multiplier approaches?

Appendix 4.1   **The Simple Static and Dynamic Keynesian Multiplier Models**

We can construct a simple static Keynesian income-expenditure model thus

$$Y = AE \tag{A.4.1.1}$$

and

$$AE = C + I, \tag{A.4.1.2}$$

where Y is income, AE is aggregate expenditure, C is consumption, and I is exogenous investment.

We define consumption C as

$$C = \bar{C} + cY, \tag{A.4.1.3}$$

where $\bar{C}$ represents the exogenous component of income. From (A.4.1.3) we can therefore rewrite (A.4.1.2) as

$$AE = \bar{C} + cY + I = Y, \tag{A.4.1.4}$$

which rearranges to

$$Y = \frac{\bar{C} + I}{1 - c} = \frac{AE}{1 - c}, \tag{A.4.1.5}$$

where the numerator term represents the exogenous components of income. Now, if for example exogenous investment increases by ΔI, the multiplier effect can be described as $\Delta Y = k(\Delta AE) = k(\Delta I)$ where the value of the multiplier k is given by

$$k = \frac{1}{1 - c}. \tag{A.4.1.6}$$

This simple static version of the Keynesian income-expenditure multiplier can also be defined in simple dynamic terms by assuming that current consumption is a function of the income in the previous time period thus:

$$C_t = \bar{C} + cY_{t-1}. \tag{A.4.1.7}$$

If we also assume that the intertemporal equilibrium is defined by $Y_t = Y_{t-1}$ we can write:

$$C_t = \bar{C} + cY_t. \tag{A.4.1.8}$$

Following Levacic and Rebmann (1982. 23) the successive rounds of the income-expenditure process can now be described with the help of Table A.4.1. The total change

Table A.4.1 Successive time period rounds of expenditure

	Change in I	Change in C	Change in Y
First-period round of expenditure	ΔI	0	
Second-period round of expenditure	0	$c\Delta I$	$c\Delta I$
Third-period round of expenditure	0	$c^2\Delta I$	$c^2\Delta I$
nth-period round of expenditure	0	$c^{n-1}\Delta I$	$c^{n-1}\Delta I$

in income over each of the successive time periods and rounds of expenditure can thus be given as

$$\Delta Y = \Delta I + c\Delta I + c^2\Delta I + \ldots c^{n-1}\Delta I = \Delta I(1 + c + c^2 + \ldots c^{n-1}),$$ (A.4.1.9)

which multiplying both sides by $(1 - c)$ gives

$$\Delta Y(1 - c) = \Delta I(1 - c^n).$$ (A.4.1.10)

As $n \rightarrow \infty$, $c^n \rightarrow 0$. Therefore, as above, we can write $\Delta Y = k(\Delta AE) = k(\Delta I)$ where the value of the multiplier k is given by

$$k = \frac{1}{1 - c}.$$ (A.4.1.6)

The successive rounds of the income-expenditure process therefore take place through time, but the overall effect on income of a change in any of the components of demand can be described as in Figure 4.1.

Appendix 4.2   The Relationship between the Alternative Forms and Uses of Location Quotients in the Construction of Regional Input–Output Tables

There are two approaches to using employment data in the construction of regional input–output tables. The first approach used is where no updated national input–output tables exist, and the second approach is where such tables do exist.

Appendix 4.2.1   Estimating Regional Trade Using Location Quotients where an Updated National Input–Output Table is not Available

In cases where updated national input–output tables are not available, the absence of regional trade data means that the construction of subnational regional input–output tables is typically based on indirect methods of estimating regional trade flows. Once the trade flows between sectors have been calculated, it is quite straightforward to calculate the regional input–output expenditure coefficients. The most common method is based on the observation of regional employment patterns. Comparing regional sectoral employment shares with those of the national economy allows us to construct an index of net regional sectoral trade, under various assumptions. As we saw in section 4.3.2 this index is known as a location quotient (LQ) and from equation (4.13) its simplest form can be represented as

$$LQ_{ir} = \frac{E_{ir}/E_r}{E_{in}/E_n} = \frac{E_{ir}}{E_{in}} \div \frac{E_r}{E_n},$$

(A.4.2.1)

where E_{ir} and E_{in}, represent the total employment levels accounted for by sector i in region r and in the nation n, and E_r and E_n represent the total employment levels of the region and nation, respectively. In general terms, this approach posits that

(a) the greater is the LQ above unity, the larger will be the region's net sectoral exports;

(b) the greater is the LQ below unity, the larger will be the region's net sectoral imports; and

(c) for an LQ of unity, the region is neither a net exporter nor a net importer.

However, four assumptions are required for this index to give an accurate measure of net regional sectoral trade (Norcliffe 1983). These are that

(i) per capita sectoral productivity levels are invariant with respect to location;

(ii) per capita consumption levels and patterns are invariant with respect to location;

(iii) the national economy exhibits no net exports or imports for any sector; and

(iv) there is no inter-regional cross-hauling for any sector, such that for any regional sector which is an exporter, all local consumption of the output of that sector is accounted for by the local industry.

Where these conditions are met, for a region which is a net exporter of the output of sector i, the actual relationship between the LQ_{ir} and the level of regional sectoral export X_{ir} employment can be written as (Isserman 1977a, 1980):

$$X_{ir} = (1 - 1/LQ_{ir})E_{ir} = \left(\frac{E_{ir}}{E_{in}} - \frac{E_r}{E_n}\right)E_{in} \quad \forall LQ_{ir} > 1,$$

(A.4.2.2)

which can be converted to give net regional sectoral export values by substituting national sectoral output P_{in} for national sectoral employment E_{in} (Norcliffe 1983) thus:

$$X_{ir} = (1 - 1/LQ_{ir})P_{ir} = \left(\frac{E_{ir}}{E_{in}} - \frac{E_r}{E_n}\right)P_{in} \quad \forall LQ_{ir} > 1,$$

(A.4.2.3)

In the case where a region is a net importer of the output of sector i, assumptions (i)–(iv) allow us to describe the level of regional sectoral employment generated in all other regions in order to produce imports M_{ir} for our region as

$$M_{ir} = (1 - 1/LQ_{ir})E_{ir} = \left(\frac{E_r}{E_n} - \frac{E_{ir}}{E_{in}}\right)E_{in} \quad \forall LQ_{ir} > 1,$$

(A.4.2.4)

which once again can be converted to give net regional sectoral import values for our region as

$$M_{ir} = (1 - 1/LQ_{ir})P_{ir} = \left(\frac{E_r}{E_n} - \frac{E_{ir}}{E_{in}}\right)P_{in} \quad \forall LQ_{ir} > 1.$$

(A.4.2.5)

Given our assumptions (i)–(iv) the principle behind the simple LQ method is that the total level of regional production in any particular sector can be described as being proportionate to the relative contribution of regional to national sectoral employment. At the same time, the total regional consumption of the output of any particular sector is defined as being in proportion to the size of the region. The net regional sectoral trade flows are assumed to be defined by the differences in these values. If a region is calculated as having an *LQ* which is greater than or equal to unity, within a regional input–output framework, the input expenditure coefficient for that particular activity is assumed to be 1. On the other hand, for regional *LQ* values of less than 1, the region will be assumed to be a net importer of the goods. In these cases, the regional input–output expenditure coefficients are assumed to be proportional to the regional *LQ* values of less than 1.

In the simple *LQ* approach the regional consumption of the output of sector *i* is assumed to be a function of the regional population expenditure, defined by the total regional level of employment. However, even allowing for appropriate regional consumption adjustments, it is arguable that in many sectors there is no reason why the size of a region *per se* should have any bearing on regional consumption levels. This is true in the case of many intra-industry transactions not involving final household demand. In these cases, regional sectoral demand is more likely to be related to the local level of activity of the various industrial purchasing sectors within the region rather than to population levels as a whole. In order to account for the inter-regional spatial variation in intra-industry sectoral demand we can construct a cross-industry location quotient (*CILQ*) which is calculated as the ratio of the *LQ* of the supplying sector *i* over that of the purchasing sector *j*. Substituting the *CILQ* for the simple *LQ* in the equations (A.4.2.2) and (A.4.2.3) gives us

$$X_{ir} = \left(\frac{E_{ir}}{E_{in}} - \frac{E_{jr}}{E_{jn}} \right) E_{in} \quad \forall CILQ > 1, \tag{A.4.2.6}$$

and

$$M_{ir} = \left(\frac{E_{jr}}{E_{jn}} - \frac{E_{ir}}{E_{in}} \right) E_{in} \quad \forall CILQ > 1. \tag{A.4.2.7}$$

In the case where the purchasing sector *j* is defined as the household consumption sector, then (A.4.2.6) and (A.4.2.7) will coincide with equations (A.4.2.2) and (A.4.2.4).

There are also several other suggested location quotient formulations which combine the features of the *LQ* and *CILQ* models in a variety of ways (Round 1978; Flegg *et al.* 1995), but the general principles underlying all of the location quotient formulas are the same.

Both the location quotient approaches described here are based on a comparison of the regional and national employment structures. However, the minimum requirements approach (Ullman and Dacey 1960) discussed in section 4.3.3 suggests there is no theoretical economic reason to assume that the national economic structure is the most appropriate benchmark against which regional trade predictions can be generated. For regions of similar sizes, the smallest share of sectoral employment in any single region within the appropriate size band is taken to represent the local sectoral consumption requirement for regions of that size, and all relative regional sectoral employment shares greater than this represent regional export employment. The *MR* method can thus be represented as

$$X_{ir} = \left(\frac{E_{ir}}{E_r} - \frac{E_{im}}{E_m} \right) E_r, \tag{A.4.2.8}$$

where m is the region with the minimum sectoral employment share, and $(E_{im}/E_m)\,E_e$ is local regional consumption of the output of sector i.

Following Isserman (1980) it is possible to compare this approach with that of the LQ by noting that equation (A.4.2.2) can be rearranged to give

$$X_{ir} = \left(\frac{E_{ir}}{E_r} - \frac{E_{in}}{E_n} \right) E_r. \tag{A.4.2.9}$$

Similarly, we can compare the MR approach with that of the $CILQ$ by rearranging equation (A.4.2.6) to give

$$X_{ir} = \left(\frac{E_{ir}}{E_r} - \left(\frac{E_{jr}}{E_r} \right) \left(\frac{E_{in}}{E_{jn}} \right) \right) E_r. \tag{A.4.2.10}$$

The key difference between the MR approach and the LQ approaches to determining regional trade patterns is the question of the appropriate benchmark against which regional sectoral employment patterns are compared in order to arrive at a measure of regional sectoral consumption. This is reflected in the differing constructions of the second bracketed term in each model. The MR approach adopts the sectoral employment structure of similar size areas as the benchmark, whereas the LQ approaches both adopt the sectoral employment structure of the national economy as the appropriate benchmark.

The debate as to the accuracy of employment-based regional trade estimates is not a new one. Assumptions (i) and (ii) above are clearly very difficult to sustain, although, using regional consumption and output indices, it is possible for the LQ method to be adapted to some extent to take account of any regional variations in productivity and consumption due to technical differences in factor allocations, tastes, or transfer payments (Isserman 1977b; Norcliffe 1983). Similarly, where assumption (iii) is not tenable, these types of models can be somewhat adjusted to take account of national sectoral trade balances which are non-zero. Where a regional LQ is greater than unity, Isserman (1977b, 1980) suggests that we can estimate regional export employment as

$$X_{ir} = \left(P_r \frac{E_{ir}}{E_{in}} - c_r \frac{E_r}{E_n} (1 - e_{in}) \right) \frac{E_{in}}{P_r} \quad \forall LQ > 1, \tag{A.4.2.11}$$

where P_r is the labour productivity ratio between the region r and the nation n, c_r is the equivalent consumption ratio, and e_{in} is the ratio of national net exports to national output of sector i. This can be converted to estimate actual export values as before in by substituting P_{in} for E_{in} in equation (A.4.2.11). By similar reasoning, where the LQ value is less than unity we can write the regional import function as

$$M_{ir} = \left(c_r \frac{E_r}{E_n} - P_r \frac{E_{ir}}{E_{in}} \right) \frac{P_{in}}{P_r} \quad \forall LQ_{ir} < 1 \tag{A.4.2.12}$$

in the case where the national economy is not a net importer. Where the national economy is net importer of the output of sector i, the appropriate adjustment of the LQ model gives

$$M_{ir} = \left(c_r \frac{E_r}{E_n} - P_r \frac{E_{ir}}{E_{in}} \right) \frac{P_{in}}{P_r} + c_r \left(\frac{E_r}{E_n} \right) M_{in}, \tag{A.4.2.13}$$

where M_{in} is the national level of net imports of sector i, and this can be rearranged to give

$$M_{ir} = c_r \frac{E_r}{E_n}\left(\frac{P_{in}}{P_r} + M_{in}\right) - P_r \frac{E_{ir}}{E_{in}} P_{in}. \tag{A.4.2.14}$$

This specification allows us to take account of imports into a region from other regions as well as from other countries. The most difficult remaining problem, however, arises with assumption (iv), namely that of the absence of cross-hauling (Harris and Liu 1998). In reality, many products move repeatedly forwards and backwards across the same regional boundaries during the various stages of the production process. Similarly, the monopolistic competition model (Fujita *et al.* 1999b) discussed in Chapter 2 predicts that many of the products produced by the same industry will be moved in opposite directions between regions and locations.

Appendix 4.2.2   Constructing Regional Input–Output Tables by Adjusting National Tables

The use of the national employment structure as the appropriate benchmark comparison against which regional consumption indices are developed is the most common employment-based method used for estimating regional trade flows. The major reason for this is that detailed and updated input–output data often exist at the national level. Therefore, national inter-sectoral expenditure coefficients are available which may be used as a benchmark in the construction of inter-regional coefficient estimates. The usual approach to constructing regional expenditure coefficients from national expenditure coefficients is by multiplying each national coefficient by the appropriate *LQ* value in the cases where the *LQ* values are less than unity, and adjusting the national coefficient downwards accordingly to give the regional equivalent. Where the *CILQ* approach is used, the off-diagonals are adjusted in this manner, while the principal diagonals are still adjusted using the *LQ* approach (Smith and Morrison 1974). For regional *LQ* or *CILQ* values which are greater than or equal to unity, the national coefficient is left unchanged. This means that the adjustments made according to the quotients are asymmetric in that the strength of export orientation plays no part in the determination of the trading coefficients (Round 1978).

In order to understand the rationale behind this method of estimating regional input–output coefficients, in which adjustments are made to national input–output coefficients by multiplying them by the appropriate *LQ*s, we need to reconsider the simple adjustments which can be made to the *LQ* approach in order to take account to some extent of the unreality of assumptions (i), (ii), and (iii) in section A.4.2.2. If we assume for simplicity that there are no regional consumption or productivity variations per capital, from equation (14) we have

$$M_{ir} = \frac{E_r}{E_n}(P_{in} + M_{in}) - \frac{E_{ir}}{E_{in}}P_{in} \tag{A.4.2.15}$$

and thus

$$\frac{M_{ir}}{M_{ir} + P_{ir}} = \frac{\frac{E_r}{E_n}(P_{in} + M_{in}) - \frac{E_{ir}}{E_{in}}P_{in}}{\frac{E_r}{E_n}(P_{in} + M_{in})}, \tag{A.4.2.16}$$

which can be rearranged to give

$$\frac{M_{ir}}{M_{ir} + P_{ir}} = 1 - LQ_{ir}\left(\frac{P_{in}}{M_{in} + P_{in}}\right). \qquad (A.4.2.17)$$

Assumption (iv) in section A.4.2.1, which rules out the existence of cross-hauling, means that the regional production of sector i, denoted as P_{ir}, equals the regional consumption of the regionally produced output of sector i, denoted as C_{ir}. Similarly, national production of sector i, denoted as P_{in}, equals the national consumption of the domestically produced output of sector i, C_{in}. Therefore, the bracketed term on the right-hand side of equation (A.4.2.17) describes the national output of sector i as a proportion of total national consumption of sector i, and the left-hand side term describes the net regional imports of sector i as a proportion of total regional consumption of sector i. However, given that

$$\frac{M_{ir}}{M_{ir} + P_{ir}} + \frac{P_{ir}}{M_{ir} + P_{ir}} = 1 \text{ can be written as } \frac{M_{ir}}{M_{ir} + P_{ir}} + \frac{P_{ir}}{M_{ir} + P_{ir}} = 1, \qquad (A.4.2.18)$$

we have

$$1 - \frac{P_{ir}}{M_{ir} + P_{ir}} = 1 - LQ_{ir}\left(\frac{P_{in}}{M_{in} + P_{in}}\right). \qquad (A.4.2.19)$$

In other words

$$\frac{P_{ir}}{M_{ir} + P_{ir}} = LQ_{ir}\left(\frac{P_{in}}{M_{in} + P_{in}}\right). \qquad (A.4.2.20)$$

The right-hand bracketed term is the national average propensity to consume the domestically produced output of sector i. Therefore, by multiplying this by the appropriate LQ value we arrive at an expression for the regional average propensity to consume the regionally produced output of sector i. Exactly the same result can also be produced if we choose to employ the $CILQ$ rather than the simple LQ. The only difference in this case is that the initial regional import function is specified as

$$M_{ir} = \left(\frac{E_{jr}}{E_{jn}} - \frac{E_{ir}}{E_{in}}\right)E_{in} + \frac{E_{jr}}{E_{jn}}M_{in}. \qquad (A.4.2.21)$$

In terms of constructing a regional input–output model, the rationale for LQ adjustments to national input–output coefficients in order to produce regional coefficients therefore rests on the assumption that the national input–output coefficients accurately reflect net national sectoral trading balances. However, this is not necessarily the case. Input–output expenditure coefficient values only reflect the pattern of backward expenditure linkages and imports, and do not take into account the level of output of sectoral exports or household sectoral imports. We can see this from a stylized example.

In the simplest export-based model, we can describe the domestic income generated by the exporting activity as

$$Y_i = \frac{X_i}{1 - c_i} = \frac{X_i}{m_i}, \qquad (A.4.2.22)$$

where Y_i is the total domestic sectoral output, X_i is the level of domestic sectoral exports, and c_i is the domestic sectoral expenditure coefficient, which equals $1 - m_i$, where m_i is the domestic import coefficient for the backward input linkages. The total domestic sectoral import expenditure for the first round will be represented as $M_i = m_iY_i$, and total first-round domestic production expenditure in backward linkages will be represented as $P_i = c_iY_i$. If there are no other sectoral imports, then c_i accurately measures the first-round domestic average propensity to consume the domestically produced output of sector i weighted according to the relative total expenditure on each input as determined by the national input–output framework. This is because

$$\frac{P_i}{P_i + M_i} = \frac{c_iY_i}{c_iY_i + m_iY_i} = c_i. \tag{A.4.2.23}$$

However, if there are other imports of goods produced by sector i exogenously consumed by the household sector h, we can represent these additional domestic sectoral imports as $M_i = m_iY_h$ where $i \neq h$. Under these conditions, the total domestic propensity to consume the domestically produced output of sector i can thus be represented as

$$\frac{c_iY_i}{c_iY_i + m_iY_i + m_iY_h} \neq c_i. \tag{A.4.2.24}$$

Under these conditions, observation of the input–output expenditure coefficient alone will overestimate the domestically produced and consumed output of sector i as a proportion of the total domestic consumption of sector i, irrespective of whether the region runs a sectoral balance of payments surplus in which $X_i > M_i$, a balance of payments deficit in which $X_i < M_i$, or a balance of payments equilibrium, in which $X_i = M_i$. The result of this is that the backward-linkage input–output expenditure coefficients in the national table will not accurately reflect overall sectoral net trading balances, and will tend to exceed the overall domestic average propensity to consume domestically produced goods. Although the LQ assumption of the absence of cross-hauling, namely assumption (iv), is not a problem for input–output models which specifically allow for such behaviour in the first and subsequent rounds of expenditure, the LQ adjustment of national input–output coefficients suffers from the problem that cross-hauling can occur at the top level of household demand. Therefore, if we use national input–output expenditure coefficients as the benchmark against which regional input–output expenditure coefficients can be produced, this will also tend to systematically overestimate the regional domestic contribution to sectoral output, and consequently the regional multiplier (Leven 1986), irrespective of the form of location quotient employed.

Round (1978) found very little difference in the performance of a variety of LQ specifications, and although Harrigan *et al.* (1980*a*) found that the simple LQ approach performed marginally better than other location quotient specifications, the general accuracy of such coefficients is open to question. In cases where survey-based regional input–output data do exist, it is possible to compare the survey-based results with those that would have been predicted on the basis of employment shares. Accepting that the production of survey-based estimates itself may have required professional judgement based on relative regional sectoral shares in order to compensate for any missing information, particularly in areas such as public expenditure, construction, and household consumption, the general picture we observe is that employment-based estimates of regional trade tend to perform fairly poorly when compared with survey models (Czamanski and Malizia 1969; Schaffer and Chu 1969; Smith and Morrison 1974) or semi-survey models which employ algorithms to complete the tables (Harris 1998; Lahr 1993).

Appendix 4.3   **The General Solution to the Input–Output Model**

A model such as described by Table 4.3 can be considered in part to be a matrix of input–output expenditure coefficients. In order to see this we can follow the discussion of Chiang (1984. 117–18) and imagine a region where there are industries 1, 2, 3 . . . n, all of which buy from, and sell, inputs to each other, plus an external demand sector which does not provide inputs to the local production process. The input coefficients for industries 1, 2, 3 . . . n can be arranged into a matrix $A = [a_{ij}]$ thus

$$\begin{bmatrix} a_{11} & a_{12} & a_{13} & \cdots a_{1n} \\ a_{21} & a_{22} & a_{23} & \cdots a_{2n} \\ a_{31} & a_{32} & a_{33} & \cdots a_{3n} \\ \cdot & \cdot & \cdot & \cdot \\ a_{n1} & a_{n2} & a_{n3} & \cdots a_{nn} \end{bmatrix}$$

The coefficients a_{ij} represent the requirements of input i needed in the production of one unit of output j. In the case of industries which do not supply inputs to their own industry, as in Table 4.3 above, the principal diagonals will all be zero.

If industry 1 produces outputs which are just sufficient to provide for the input requirements of each of the other industries 1, 2, 3 . . . n, plus the demand requirements of the external sector, the total output of industry 1 which we denote as x_1, must satisfy the equation:

$$x_1 = a_{11}x_1 + a_{12}x_2 + a_{13}x_3 \ldots \ldots + a_{1n}x_n + d_1, \tag{A.4.3.1}$$

where $a_{ij}x_j$ is input demand for industry j and d_1 final demand by external sector for the output of sector 1.

Rearranging (A.4.3.1) gives:

$$(1 - a_{11})x_1 - a_{12}x_2 - a_{13}x_3 \ldots \ldots - a_{1n}x_n = d_1. \tag{A.4.3.2}$$

If the same exercise is repeated for the output of each of the sectors we can modify the above matrix to give

$$\begin{bmatrix} (1 - a_{11}) & -a_{12} & -a_{13} & \cdots -a_{1n} \\ -a_{21} & (1 - a_{22}) & -a_{23} & \cdots -a_{2n} \\ -a_{31} & -a_{32} & (1 - a_{33}) & \cdots -a_{3n} \\ \cdot & \cdot & \cdot & \cdot \\ -a_{n1} & -a_{n2} & -a_{n3} & \cdots (1 - a_{nn}) \end{bmatrix} \begin{bmatrix} x_1 \\ x_2 \\ x_3 \\ \cdot \\ x_n \end{bmatrix} = \begin{bmatrix} d_1 \\ d_2 \\ d_3 \\ \cdot \\ d_n \end{bmatrix}, \tag{A.4.3.3}$$

where the matrix on the left-hand side contains the input coefficients, and the vectors on the left- and right-hand sides contain the outputs of each sector used as inputs by other sectors, and final external demand for the outputs of each sector, respectively. If we ignore the 1s in the principal diagonals of the matrix on the left-hand side we see that this matrix is simply $-A = [-a_{ij}]$. As it is, this matrix is the sum of the identity matrix I_n, with 1s in the principal diagonals and zeros elsewhere, and the matrix $-A$. In other words we can write $(I - A)x = d$, where x represents the variable vector and d the final demand vector. The matrix $(I - A)$ is known as the 'technology matrix' and is usually denoted as $T = (I - A)$

such that $Tx = d$. As long as T is non-singular, we can find the inverse of T, denoted as T^{-1}. This now allows us always to solve the problem

$$x = T^{-1}d.$$ (A.4.3.4)

In other words, for any given level of the external output demand, we can calculate the input demand requirements through the successive rounds of the input–output expenditure process for any of the individual production sectors. With this information it is also straightforward to calculate the total factor earnings, as in Table 4.4, and to calculate the total regional multiplier impact of any given level output demand.

Chapter 5

Regional and Inter-Regional Labour Market Analysis

5.1 Introduction

In this chapter, we will discuss the question of urban and regional labour markets. Once again, as with the multiplier models discussed in the previous chapter, we will see that there are some fundamental differences between the characteristics of the labour market at the regional and national levels, as well as many similarities between the two. However, these differences are not simply a question of scale, but rather an explicit question of the relationship between market-clearing processes and geography.

In Chapter 4 we discussed the differences between regional and national multiplier models. The regional multiplier models discussed in the previous chapter all assume that the marginal cost of factor inputs is constant. In other words, we assume that the marginal and average costs of factor inputs are the same as output expands. This allows us to assume that labour, capital, and land inputs all maintain fixed unit prices independent of the level of output. In situations where there are unused factor supplies, such as where there is excess capacity in industrial facilities, or alternatively a pool of unemployed labour, these assumptions may be justified. However, there are many cases where no such reserve capacity exists. In these situations factor supplies will be somewhat limited, and the effect of this is that factor supply prices will not be constant as output expands. The market for factor inputs will therefore determine factor prices. In the case of geographical labour markets, such factor price changes may also bring about spatial changes in the allocation of these factors. This is because such price signals may also encourage factor migration between regions. However, following on from the arguments in Chapters 2 and 4, in this chapter we will see that the effects of local labour price changes on regional or urban employment can be rather complicated. Local factor price and income effects can become somewhat interrelated, with the result that we must consider the spatial problems discussed in each of the previous chapters in order to come to any coherent analysis of the issues.

In the next section we will discuss alternative views of the workings of local labour markets. In section 5.3 we will extend the argument to the question of inter-regional migration and factor allocation, and in section 5.4 onwards we will discuss additional issues which affect regional labour market and migration behaviour.

5.2 Wages and Labour Markets

Labour markets are notoriously complex to analyse, with many labour market outcomes being the result of complex negotiations between employers and labour representatives within a bilateral monopoly framework. However, for our purposes here, in order to discuss the workings of the urban and regional labour market, it is first necessary to return to the basic microeconomic foundations of labour market behaviour. These will then be adjusted in order to allow for the particular characteristics of local urban and regional labour markets.

5.2.1 A neoclassical approach

The simplest neoclassical microeconomic approach to labour markets is based on two main principles. The first principle is that the demand for labour is a downward-sloping function. This is because the demand for labour is a derived demand, dependent on the marginal revenue product of the output of labour inputs to the production process. Firms will equate the marginal cost of labour, given by the wage rate w, with the marginal revenue product of labour. For a given capital stock and a given output market price, the marginal product of labour *(MPL)* falls as the quantity of labour employed increases, as determined by the law of diminishing marginal productivity. The demand for labour *D(L)* is therefore downward-sloping, as in Figure. 5.1.

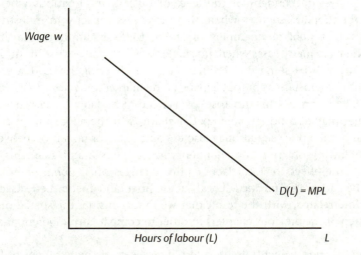

Fig. 5.1 The demand for labour

However, the position of the demand curve for labour can vary according to either the level of capital employed or the price of the output good. The reason is that the marginal revenue product of labour is given by the marginal physical product of labour multiplied by the price of the output good. Assuming production factor inputs are complementary, a greater capital stock will imply a greater marginal and average level of output for any given level of labour input. As such, the demand curve for labour will be further to the right, the greater is the stock of capital employed. Conversely, the lower is the level of capital employed, the further to the left will be the demand curve for labour. Alternatively, the higher the price of the output good, the further to the right will be the demand curve for labour for any given capital stock. Once again, the converse is true. The lower the price of the output good, the further to the left will be the demand curve for labour for any given capital stock.

The second basic principle is that the supply of labour is upward-sloping with respect to the real wage rate. This conclusion is based on an argument which is sometimes known as the 'dual decision hypothesis' (Clower 1965), in which workers use the real wage level in order to decide simultaneously on the number of hours of labour they wish to supply, the level of income they wish to earn, and the quantity of human-produced goods and services they wish to consume. The dual decision hypothesis can be explained with the help of the Figure 5.2.

In Figure 5.2 we assume that the individual can consume two types of utility-bearing goods, namely on the one hand, the weekly hours of leisure, and on the other hand, all human-produced goods and services. The vertical axis represents the weekly quantity of hours of leisure the individual can consume H, with a fixed upper limit F, which represents a full week. The total number of labour hours supplied per week is thus $(F-H)$. The

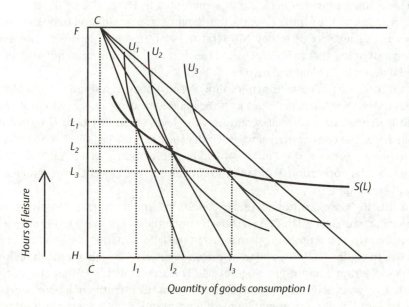

Fig. 5.2 The derivation of the labour supply curve

horizontal axis represents the quantity of human-produced goods and services consumed by the individual I. We can now employ a standard budget constraint-indifference curve model in order to understand the supply of labour with respect to the price of labour.

In a standard indifference curve type of framework, assuming the indifference curves are convex, the object of the individual is to ensure that the price ratio between the two types of goods is just equal to their marginal rate of substitution. In Figure 5.2, the slope of the budget constraint represents the relative prices of the leisure and human-produced capital goods, defined in terms of their opportunity costs with respect to each other. If for the moment we assume that there is a certain element of exogenous consumption even in a situation of total leisure, the origin of the budget constraint will not be on the vertical axis at F, but will be somewhat shifted to the right of F, at C. As the real wage rate increases from w_1 to w_2 to w_3, the slope of the budget constraint becomes shallower, with the result that the individual consumes less leisure and more human-produced goods. Obviously, there are both price and income effects operating, in that income itself is the multiple of the wage rate and the number of hours worked. The optimum combinations of leisure and human-produced goods consumed, for different budget constraints associated with different wage levels, can be plotted as an expansion path. Given that the number of labour hours supplied is represented by $L = F - H$, we can see that as the real wage rate increases from w_1 to w_2 to w_3, the number of labour hours supplied increases from L_1 to L_2 to L_3. The supply of labour $S(L)$ is therefore assumed to be a positive function of the real wage rate.

The above argument does not rely on the assumption that all labour exhibits the same preferences. For example, we could assume that the labour market is made up of heterogeneous individuals with different preferences. Some individuals will have a relatively higher preference for leisure, whereas others will prefer human-produced goods and services. These different preferences will be represented in Figure 5.2 by different indifference curve maps. In the former case, the indifference curves will tend to be shifted higher up whereas in the latter case they will tend to be shifted further down. However, the argument still holds, that as the real wage rate increases, the optimum quantity of labour supplied by each individual will increase.

Combining these two basic principles allows us to construct a simple model of a labour market as in Figure 5.3. The real wage w^* is the market-clearing wage at which all labour L^* supplied is demanded. In neoclassical terms the level of employment L^* represents full employment at the current market wage. Under such conditions, there is no involuntary unemployment, because the labour which is not working, given by the difference between the total population T and the current employment level L^*, is regarded as being voluntarily unemployed.

Given this logic we can now consider conditions under which unemployment may exist in such a framework. The first reason why unemployment may exist in such a labour market is that the real wage being demanded in the labour market is simply too high. We can see this in Figure 5.4. If the real wage currently offered is w_1, this is much higher than the market-clearing equilibrium wage of w^*. The result of this is that the number of people seeking work at the current wage is L_1, whereas the quantity of labour demanded is L_{w1}. The level of involuntary unemployment is therefore $(L_1 - L_{w1})$ at the current wage w_1. The neoclassical remedy for such a situation is to allow the real wage to fall from w_1 to w^*,

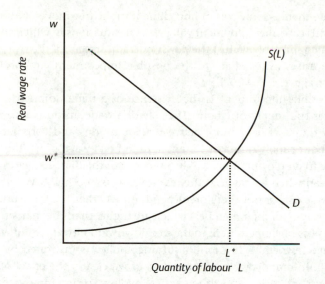

Fig. 5.3 A simple model of the labour market

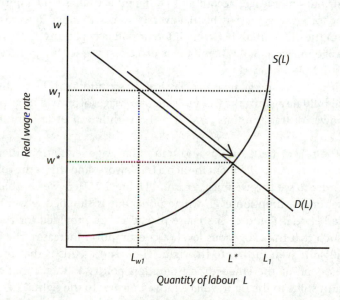

Fig. 5.4 Involuntary unemployment: a neoclassical perspective

such that the demand for labour will increase and the supply of labour will fall until they are brought into equilibrium. The downward movement in the real wage and the relationship between the wage fall and the labour demanded is represented by the arrow in Figure 5.4.

In this schema, the only situation in which involuntary unemployment can persist is therefore where there is some sort of impediment to the free movement of real wages. In particular, in this case unemployment will persist in situations in which there is some sort of obstacle which militates against the downward adjustment of the real wage. The question therefore arises as to what are the possible impediments to the free downward movement of wages.

The first possible impediment is the existence of a trade union which maintains a monopoly over the supply of labour. The role of a trade union is in effect to set up a labour supply quota. If bargaining between trade unions and corporate management results in a labour supply quota of L_{w1} and a union real wage of w_1, the current market wage for those in employment w_1, will be higher than the market-clearing wage w^*. This is what we mean when we say that the real wage w_1 is 'too high'. Whether involuntary unemployment exists or not therefore depends on whether the trade unions are able to negotiate real wages for their members which are higher than the market-clearing wages.

The second possible impediment to the free downward movement of wages is that of a minimum wage restriction. If a minimum wage policy is instituted by a government, such that the minimum wage is set at a wage of w_1, clearly the effect of this will be to reduce employment to L_{w1} and to engender involuntary unemployment of (L_1-L_{w1}). Whether involuntary unemployment exists or not therefore depends on whether the minimum wage is set at a level higher than the market-clearing real wages. Alternatively, if there is a distribution of wages according to different activities, and a minimum wage policy raises the lowest wage, it may be that average wages all move upwards, as workers seek to maintain the differentials between different skill occupations. In this case we can interpret the wage in Figure 5.3 as being the average real wage. Under these conditions the argument still holds.

In both of these cases, the general neoclassical prescription will be to dismantle the obstacles which militate against the free movement of wages. This will involve legislation limiting the power of trade unions, and also the withdrawal of any minimum wage policies.

Apart from the role of trade unions and minimum wage legislation, there is a third reason for involuntary unemployment in such a framework, and this is the role of welfare payments. In order to see this we must return to Figure 5.2. Here we see that there is an exogenous level of consumption even where no labour is supplied, given by the horizontal distance between F and C. If welfare payments are provided for those without employment such that the exogenous level of consumption increases, the budget constraint at C will shift even further to the right. The result of this is that the expansion path, which plots all of the efficient consumption points as wages increase and the budget constraint shifts to the right, will be moved further to the right. The effect of this is that, compared with the situation of little or no welfare payments, in which exogenous income is very low, fewer hours are worked for any given real wage rate. In terms of our labour market diagram (Figure 5.4), this implies that the labour supply curve is therefore shifted upwards to the left. The market wage rate rises and the number of people employed therefore falls below the market-clearing level. Moreover, the greater the level of welfare payments, the further to the left will be the labour supply curve, and the lower will be the total number of people employed.

The neoclassical remedy for the reduced labour demand and supply is once again to dismantle many of these policies. As such, welfare payments will need to be reduced in absolute terms so as to have a negligible effect on market wages. Alternatively, such payments will be restricted to a very short time period, after which they will cease to be available to the individual person.

5.2.2 **A Keynesian Approach**

The simple neoclassical labour market model described above allows for the downward movement of real wages in order to clear markets. However, an alternative approach to the labour market question comes from a Keynesian perspective, which argues that wages are 'sticky' downwards. In other words, while wages are able to move upwards over time, downward movements in wages are very difficult to bring about. This is primarily due to the existence of trade unions and the complex nature of labour-bargaining processes. In these circumstances, movements down the demand curve for labour, in which wage falls are associated with increases in labour demand, are very difficult to effect. In this situation, there is no guarantee that labour markets exhibiting involuntary unemployment can be expected to clear. The policy prescription under such conditions is therefore to attempt to expand the demand for labour, so as to clear the excess supply of labour. The argument can be explained with reference to Figure 5.5 which is constructed on the basis of Figure 5.4.

In the Keynesian argument, a general increase in the demand for labour from D_1 to D_2 will increase the level of employment from L_{w1} to L_1 at the current wage w_1, thereby clearing the excess labour without raising the current wage level. If demand increases beyond D_2, then we will experience wage inflation. However, as long as an expansion in

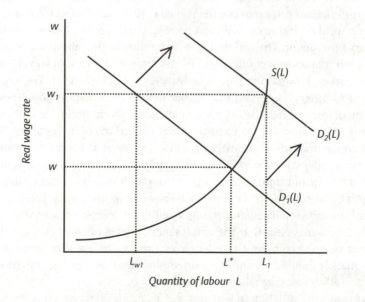

Fig. 5.5 Involuntary unemployment: a Keynesian perspective

demand can be limited to a movement from D_1 to D_2 the labour market problem can be solved. In macroeconomic terms this implies that the involuntary unemployment can be cleared without inducing any inflation.

There are many macroeconomic controversies about whether such a costless increase in demand can actually be effected feasibly or not, and these discussions centre on the questions of 'crowding out', and the relationship between labour market policy, fiscal policy, and monetary policy. It is not our intention here to enter into these debates, as these issues are discussed in detail elsewhere. However, understanding the basic analytical principles behind the various approaches to labour market problems will now allow us to discuss the particular features of urban and regional labour markets. As we will see, there are certain aspects of urban and regional labour markets which are somewhat different from standard textbook models.

5.3 Regional Labour Markets, Wage Flexibility, and Capital Utilization

The basic features of the neoclassical and Keynesian approaches to labour markets were outlined above. It is clear that the general disagreement focuses on the role that wage movements or demand changes can play in clearing involuntary unemployment. However, we can now reconsider this discussion from the perspective of a local labour market.

The neoclassical argument at the level of the local urban or regional economy is more or less the same as that at the level of the national economy, described by Figures 5.3 and 5.4. Downwards labour price movements will engender increases in local labour demand for any given local capital stock. This will be reflected in terms of movements down the demand curve for labour. The simultaneous reduction in the labour supplied will bring the local labour market into equilibrium. From Chapters 2 and 5, however, we are aware that labour markets may exhibit particular features at the local level. The agglomeration arguments of Chapter 2 suggested that labour market information flows may be not be independent of geographical scale, such that local labour pools become an essential means of ensuring labour supply to firms under conditions of uncertainty. At the same time, local concentrations of industry becomes an essential means of ensuring labour demand for potential skilled workers, under conditions of varying demand between sectors. Meanwhile, the multiplier arguments of Chapter 5 suggested that changes in any of the individual components of demand may have proportionately greater impacts on income than the individual demand change itself. If we combine the arguments of Chapter 2 and 5, it becomes clear that the employment effects of wage changes on the local economy can be quite complex. In order to see this we can employ Figure 5.4 in which the labour market exhibits involuntary unemployment, and using this model we can reconsider the effects of wage falls, as is done in Figure 5.6.

If we begin with the situation in which wages are at a level w_1 which is too high to clear the local labour market, we can consider the various alternative effects of local wage falls.

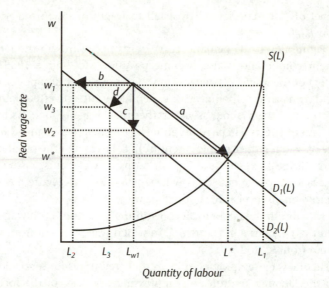

Fig. 5.6 Local labour markets and downward wage movements

As we have seen, the first effect is the standard neoclassical effect in which wages fall and labour demand increases, concomitant with a movement downward along the labour demand curve to the market-clearing wage and labour supply of w^* and L^*, respectively. In Figure 5.6 this wage–labour supply movement is represented by the locus a.

The second effect can be understood by employing the income-expenditure multiplier model of Chapter 5, because the level of local consumption will largely be a function of the total local wage-income. If we assume that all local consumption C is accounted for by wages earned locally, then in Figure 5.6 the total local consumption income can be represented as $C = w_1 L_{w1}$. If local wages begin to fall by $-\Delta w$, it may be that the immediate dominant effect on firms' perceptions is that the level of local consumption expenditure is falling by $-\Delta C = -\Delta w L_{w1}$. As we saw in Chapter 5, a change in the level of any of the components of aggregate demand can induce a multiplier effect. Although all the multiplier changes discussed in Chapter 5 involved positive demand changes, the same types of argument also apply to falls in any of the components of aggregate demand. Negative multiplier effects can be generated by falls in any of the individual components of aggregate demand, thereby leading to even greater reductions in income than the original demand fall. In the above situation of wage falls in the local labour market, local firms may be unwilling to increase labour demand according to the neoclassical model, and will rather seek to reduce investment expenditure by running down existing stocks of goods and cancelling future planned investment. This will also imply that firms will cancel orders from their suppliers. The combined effect of these responses to the local downward wage movements will be a negative local income multiplier effect given by $-\Delta Y = -k_r(\Delta w L_{w1})$, where k_r is the value of the regional multiplier. In terms of Figure 5.6, this contraction in local expenditure income can be represented by a downward shift to the left of the demand curve. The vertical distance of this backwards shift at the employment level of L_1 is represented by a fall in wages of $-\Delta w$ from w_1 to w_2, such that $-\Delta Y = -k_r(\Delta w L_{w1})$.

As we see in Figure 5.6, if the demand curve shifts backwards to the left, a range of wage–employment combinations also become possible (McCombie 1988). The actual employment effect of the wage falls depends on the labour retention policies of the local firms. If the local firms absorb the negative expenditure income effects almost entirely through contractions of their labour stocks, rather than wage reductions to employees, the wage–employment effects will be represented by the locus b in Figure 5.6 in which we maintain a wage of w_1 but reduce employment from L_{w1} to L_2. On the other hand, if firms choose to absorb all local expenditure falls in terms of wage cuts, rather than labour reductions, the wage–employment locus will be given by c in Figure 5.6 in which we maintain the employment level at L_{w1} but reduce wages from w_1 to w_2. The final possibility is that firms will absorb the fall in local expenditure by cuts in both wages and labour employed, given by the locus d in Figure 5.6, in which wages are cut from w_1 to w_3, and employment is cut from L_{w1} to L_3.

Although the actual wage–employment locus observed in response to a local wage fall will depend on the labour retention and employment policies of the local firms, it is necessary to consider how it could be possible for the demand curve to be considered to have actually shifted downwards to the left, as proposed by the Keynesian model. The argument is that if the type of negative, regional income-expenditure effect described above does indeed operate, not only will local firms cut back future planned investment and input expenditure, but also they will reduce the current level of local capital utilization. This possibility is represented by the production function diagram (Figure 5.7). As we see in Figure 5.7, changes in capital utilization can be directly associated with changes

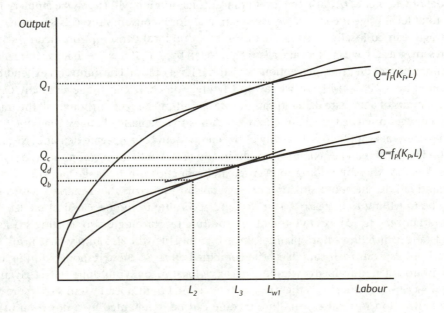

Fig. 5.7 Capital utilization, output, and wages

in both output and wages. The argument here is that different levels of capital utilization in effect actually represent different regional production functions. Assuming as usual that capital and labour are complementary production factors, even temporary cutbacks in regional capital utilization in response to falling local wage-income will move the local firms on to lower-capacity production functions. This is because less capital is now applied to each unit of labour employed. In Figure 5.7, a reduction in the level of capital utilization from that of full capital utilization K_F to a situation of partially unused capital K_P, can be represented as a move from a full-capacity regional production function in which output Q can be defined as $Q = f_F(K_F, L)$ to a lower-capacity regional production function given as $Q = f_P(K_P, L)$. The slope of the regional production functions represents the marginal product of labour, and consequently the local regional wage rate. If the local firms choose to adopt the labour retention strategy of b, in which wages are maintained at their existing levels, and the fall in demand is absorbed entirely in terms of labour cutbacks, in Figure 5.7 this is represented by a fall in labour demand from L_{w1} to L_2 as in Figure 5.6 and a fall in output from Q_1 to Q_b. As we see in Figure 5.7, the fact that the regional wages are unchanged at w_1 means that the slopes of the two regional production functions at these two different levels of capacity utilization, employment and output, are the same. The second case in where the labour retention strategies of the regional firms is represented by locus c in Figure 5.6. In this case, the employment level is maintained at L_{w1} but the output level falls from Q_1 to Q_c and the regional wage falls from w_1 to w_2. This is represented in Figure 5.7 by the lower slope of the regional production function at the existing employment of L_{w1}. The final alternative is where firms adopt the labour retention strategy represented by the locus d in Figure 5.6. In Figure 5.7 this is represented by a fall in output from Q_1 to Q_d, a fall in employment from L_{w1} to L_3, and a fall in the regional wage from w_1 to w_3, a wage level somewhere between w_1 and w_2.

5.4 Regional Labour Market Adjustment

Given these general observations, it is therefore necessary at this point to consider which of the possible wage–employment and capital utilization effects described by the loci a, b, c, or d in Figure 5.6 are likely to take place in a regional labour market in response to local wage falls. In a Keynesian model of the regional labour market, as we see in Figures 5.6 and 5.7, downward movements of local wages are not possible without simultaneous backward shifts in the demand curve for local labour. The reason for this is that the negative income-expenditure effect on local firms' perceptions of local market demand is regarded as dominating any potential desire on the part of these firms to take advantage of lower wages in the form of increased labour demand. This results in the local firms cutting back the level of capital employed. In macroeconomic discussions, this particular type of negative income effect in response to a wage fall, represented by the loci b, c, or d in Figure 5.6, is sometimes known as a 'Keynes effect'. On the other hand, the willingness of firms to increase labour demand in response to a wage fall, represented by the loci a in Figure 5.6, is sometimes known in macroeconomic discussions as a 'Pigou effect'. In the neoclassical model, the Pigou effect will generally dominate any possible Keynes effect, whereas in the Keynesian model the Keynes effect will dominate any potential Pigou effect. The extent to which one effect dominates the other tends to be both a question of industrial sector and also a question of time.

In the case of local regional or urban labour markets, we can argue that in the short run at least, the local firms with primarily local markets will tend to interpret local wage falls in terms of reductions in their potential output market sales revenue. These types of firms are the firms which we generally classed as 'non-basic' in our economic base discussions in Chapter 5. For the firms of this type, the negative income-expenditure effect will tend to dominate their labour demand decisions, and will generally lead to cutbacks of the type represented by the loci *b*, *c*, or *d* in Figure 5.6. On the other hand, for 'basic firms' which rely primarily on regional export markets, falls in local wages will have little or no effect on their overall market outputs. For these firms, reduced local wages may mean that the area actually becomes more attractive for expanding output by employing more labour, and such firms may therefore increase their employment levels within their current levels of capital investment. This will be represented by the wage–employment locus *a* in Figure 5.6. As we see in Chapter 1, reduced local labour prices may also in the long run encourage these firms to expand their overall local capital stocks. Similarly, new immigrant firms may move into the region and this process will also increase the regional capital stock. Both of these capital expansion effects, one which takes place within existing plants and the other which results in the establishment of new plants, will be represented by a shift to the right of the labour demand curve, as the regional capital stock expands from K_{R1} to K_{R2}. As we see in Figure 5.8, the long-run result of this regional capital expansion will be to increase both the local wage and level of regional employment. The

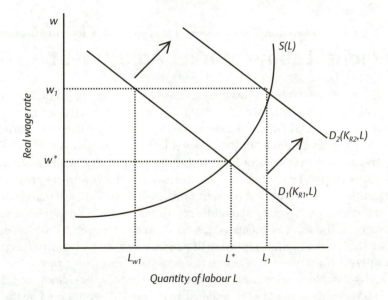

Fig. 5.8 Inward investment and the regional labour market

actual extent to which these increase will depend on the level and the speed of new inward investment flows.

The local effect of regional wage falls will therefore depend on the sectoral balance between the exporting and domestically oriented firms. Regional economies which are highly integrated internally, such as those which exhibit strong localization and urbanization economies as described in Chapter 2, will tend to suffer from general falls in local wages, because much of the local demand will be locally generated. On the other hand, economies which are vertically integrated, in terms of being dominated by strong hierarchical input–output expenditure linkages between locally based exporting firms and local supplier firms, will tend to benefit from local wage falls. The reason for this is that such economies will tend to become better places for immigrant mobile investment of the type discussed in Chapter 1.

There is one exception to the argument that economies which are vertically integrated, in terms of being dominated by strong hierarchical input–output expenditure linkages between locally based exporting firms and local supplier firms, will tend to benefit from local wage falls. This is the case of a local economy which is dominated by strong input–output linkages between locally based exporting firms and local supplier firms, and where the initial cause of the involuntary unemployment described by Figure 5.4 is actually a contraction in the local regional export base sector itself.

In such a situation, we can redraw Figure 5.4 as Figure 5.9 in which the initial level of regional labour demand is D_1, the regional market-clearing wage is w_1, and the level of regional employment is L_1. Following a fall in regional export demand the local basic sector will cut back its output. Therefore, the local regional labour demand on the part of both the basic and non-basic industries will now fall from D_1 to D_2. At the existing wage

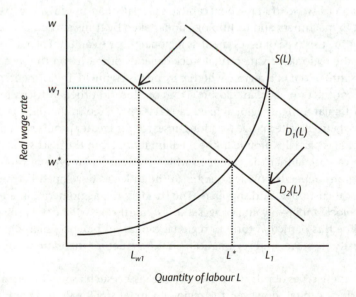

Fig. 5.9 Labour market effects of a reduction in export base output demand

of w_1, the labour employed will fall from L_1 to L_{w1} and involuntary unemployment will be given as $(L_1–L_{w1})$. If wages are unable to fall to w^* for the kind of institutional reasons outlined in Figure 5.4, the involuntary unemployment will tend to be persistent, unless there is a compensating change in the position of either the labour demand or supply curves.

In the case where involuntary regional unemployment has been caused primarily by a general contraction in regional export demand, this will tend to indicate that the region is currently not an attractive location for new investment. This implies that in the short or medium term at least, an expansion of the regional capital stock by new immigrant investment sufficient to compensate for the export base contraction would appear to be unlikely. Moreover, in such a situation local business confidence will tend to be very low. This will imply that local business expansion of the type represented by the locus a in Figure 5.6 is unlikely to take place. Further local wage falls are therefore much more likely to induce further negative local income-expenditure type effects described by the loci b, c, and d in Figure 5.6.

5.4.1 Regional capital adjustment

In regional factor markets there are three particular features of local capital inputs which are somewhat different from many micro- or macro-discussions of factor markets. The first feature is that the regional capital stock, which is combined with local labour inputs, is comprised largely of location-specific highly durable physical capital infrastructure assets. The second feature, which is consequent on this first feature, is that regional capital can be withdrawn from production quickly, but cannot be expanded quickly. The third feature, which is a result of the combination of the first two features, is that capital withdrawal almost inevitably generates negative regional externalities.

From Chapter 1 we see that regional capital is partially comprised of the fixed industrial investment in machinery and technology undertaken by firms at their chosen locations. We can describe this type of investment as regional private capital. The rate of increase or decrease in the regional private capital stock depends primarily on the speed of entry or exit of firms into or out of a region, whether by new 'greenfield' investment, plant expansion, plant contraction, or plant closure. From our location theory discussions it is clear that this particular form of regional fixed capital is only fixed in the short term. Firms are able to move between alternative locations in search for greater profits such that this type of fixed capital is partially mobile in the medium term. From the discussions in Chapters 1 and 5 we can argue that the extent to which this particular type of capital is mobile between regions depends on the strength of the linkages developed between the firms and their local customers and suppliers. The stronger the agglomeration effects and the stronger the local input–output linkages, the less 'footloose' will be the firms and the less mobile will be this particular form of regional capital. In practice, many firms exhibit a low propensity to move, and regional capital infrastructure therefore tends to be rather durable.

As well as these types of private regional capital assets such as machinery and information technology capital, however, the regional capital stock will also comprise immovable assets such as non-prefabricated buildings, bridges, roads, docks, and airports. We can describe these types of capital as regional public capital assets. Much of this regional public capital stock is in the form of durable infrastructure assets which are set up at particular fixed locations. This fixed infrastructure capital is very costly to adjust and reconfigure for alternative uses, because adjustment costs will involve construction and building engineering activities. The transactions costs involved in altering this type of capital for alternative uses are therefore very significant. Moreover, the adjustment periods for physical building capital may be further prolonged because the structure of leases and tenancies often means that capital facilities are tied up for long periods in particular uses and activities. The existing stock of regional capital is therefore composed to a large extent of physical infrastructure assets which are costly to expand or redevelop.

On the other hand, the transactions costs involved in the setting up of new capital assets may be rather less, particularly in the case of prefabricated building infrastructure and 'greenfield' developments. This general asymmetry between the development cost of new capital assets and the redevelopment costs of existing capital assets has a parallel in more general discussions of technology change. The parallel cases are what are known as 'putty-clay' models (Stoneman 1983), in which capital in its early stages of implementation is regarded as being malleable and flexible, but once it is implemented in its productive use it becomes cast and set in a very particular and inflexible form. This putty-clay metaphor successfully captures the nature of large portions of the regional capital stock. These assets tend to be adjustable only over a very long time period, and in the medium term we can regard these capital assets as being entirely fixed.

The combination of these two portions of the regional capital stock, namely the partially mobile private regional capital and the fixed regional public capital, means that in the short to medium term, the regional capital stock can only be expanded very slowly. However, although the regional capital stock can only be expanded relatively slowly, the regional capital stock can be reduced relatively quickly. If there is a strong local negative income-expenditure effect such as described by Figure 5.6, firms may withdraw capital quickly in response to falling local wages by reducing the level of capital utilization, as we see in Figure 5.7. If such reduced capital utilization does take place, the unused excess capital ($K_F - K_P$) can be withdrawn from production very quickly simply by cutting back output, although it will not necessarily be scrapped in the short run. The reduction in investment will mean that the only form of current investment still undertaken is the depreciation expenditure on existing capital infrastructure, which is necessary to maintain it for future use. However, if the demand fall is perceived by firms not to be a short-term phenomenon, even this depreciation investment may be curtailed. In situations such as this, the capital will be withdrawn permanently from the productive process, and the firms will move permanently to a lower-capacity regional production function. As such, the fact that much of the regional productive capital is both durable and location-specific, means that there is something of an asymmetry in regional factor markets. Regional capital reduction can take place at a much more rapid pace than regional capital expansion. As we have seen in Figure 5.9, this is particularly a problem in the case where a region suffers an export demand fall.

In the particular case of urban and regional economies, the withdrawal of capital from the local productive process also has very specific regional implications, and the reason for this is, once again, the location-specificity and durability of regional capital. To see this we must combine our two key insights, namely that much regional capital is durable and adjustment costs are high, and also that regional capital expansion is relatively slow whereas regional capital contraction can be rapid. The combination of these observations suggests that a rapid regional contraction will result in a physical environment character- ized by derelict capital assets. The problem with this is that it can generate a negative externality in the form of a reduction in the quality of the local environment. Capital dereliction and decay can therefore play a major role in altering the attractiveness of the regional economy as a location for future investment.

An example of this is given in Figure 5.10, which is an extension of the argument given in Figure 5.9. If regional demand falls from D_1 to D_2, capital will be withdrawn from production as described by Figure 5.7. If the withdrawn capital leads to dereliction in the short to medium term, this may lead to a deterioration in the local economic environ- ment and further reduce the attractiveness of the region as a location for investment. In the subsequent time period, demand may fall even further to D', with involuntary local unemployment at the existing wage rate of w_1 increasing from $(L_1 - L_{w1})$ to $(L_1 - L_{w}')$.

We can similarly reverse the argument, and imagine a demand expansion from D' to D in one time period. This could be due to the immigration of a major new immigrant firm. The consequent expansion in the regional capital stock may engender further growth in local labour demand from D to D_1 as other new firms locate in the region and local business confidence increases in general. As such, the investment and labour market decisions in the current time period depend on the investment and labour market decisions made in previous time periods in which the economic conditions may have been very different from those which currently prevail. This particular feature of the labour market, in which there is a partial dependence on previous labour market and

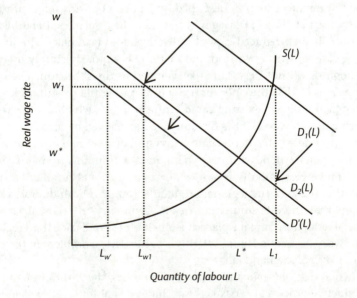

Fig. 5.10 Negative interactions between capital withdrawal and labour demand

capital investment behaviour, is often known as 'hysteresis'. Yet, the phenomenon of hysteresis itself in part depends on the durability and location-specificity of the regional capital with which the labour is combined. Regional capital exhibits a great deal of inertia, both in terms of quantity and quality.

The regional response to demand changes is obviously in part a question of time. In economics, the definition of the 'long-run' is specifically that it is the time period during which all factors are able to be adjusted, both quantitatively and qualitatively. Therefore, even where a region suffers a major decline, there must be a long-run time period during which the regional capital stock will be able to adjust so as to allow the region to expand. However, the durability of regional capital means that the adjustment time periods for regional economies can be very substantial, in comparison for example to that of an individual firm, particularly where a region suffers a decline in demand. This is evidenced by the long-term adjustment problems and capital dereliction of cities in the so-called 'rust belt' of the USA, such as Detroit, Pittsburgh, and Cleveland, or older east coast cities such as Philadelphia and Baltimore. Similarly, such capital dereliction and long-term adjustment problems exist in the former industrial cities in the north of England, such as Liverpool, Manchester, and Leeds. On the other hand, because money capital funds are liquid, and new building infrastructure can often be rapidly constructed on 'greenfield' sites, regional capital expansion can often be quite a rapid process in the case where a region experiences demand expansion without facing any physical or geographical growth restrictions. Examples of this include cities in the so-called US 'sun belt', such as San Jose, Phoenix, and Atlanta.

Given that regions tend to exhibit asymmetries in terms of their ability to adjust capital stocks to increases or decreases in demand, it may be that in many cases a reliance on regional investment and capital changes can be a rather inefficient way of ensuring effective regional adjustment. The alternative mechanism is therefore to allow the regional supplies of labour to adjust. The relative success of these two mechanisms depends on whether the demand for labour, dependent on the regional capital stock, or the supply of labour, dependent on migration behaviour, is more quickly able to adjust to changing regional economic conditions.

5.5 Wages and Inter-Regional Labour Migration

As we have seen in the above sections, the individual region has limited internal wage adjustment capabilities, particularly in response to adverse demand changes. However, there is a mechanism which operates at the inter-regional level which can allow the region to adjust quite rapidly to such changes. This mechanism is that of inter-regional labour migration. There are three broad types of inter-regional migration mechanism associated with wage levels, namely the disequilibrium model, the equilibrium model, and the endogenous human-capital model. We will discuss each of these models here in turn.

5.5.1 **The disequilibrium model of inter-regional labour migration**

The 'disequilibrium' model is the most commonly adopted model of inter-regional labour migration. In order to understand the basic nature of this mechanism we can use Figure 5.11 to examine the labour migration responses between two regions A and B. We can consider the case where region A has suffered a demand contraction while region B has experienced a simultaneous demand expansion. Such a shift in relative inter-regional demand could be brought about by a change in the tastes of consumers for the outputs produced by region B rather than those produced by region A. The price of the outputs of region B will rise whereas the price of region A's outputs will fall. The result is that the marginal revenue product of labour in region B increases while that of labour in region A falls. This is reflected in the shifts in the respective labour demand schedules for each region.

In Figures 5.11 a and b, let the real wage in region A be denoted as w_A, and the real wage in region B be denoted as w_B. We assume initially that the regions are in equilibrium, in the sense that real wages are the same in both regions. In other words we assume that $w_A = w_B$. Let us also assume for simplicity that the levels of employment in both regions are the same. In other words we assume that $L_A = L_B$.

If the demand for labour in region A decreases from D_A to D_{A1} while the demand for labour in region B increases from D_B to D_{B1}, the real wage in region A will fall to w_{A1}, and the real wage in region B will rise to w_{B1}. Similarly, the level of employment in region A will fall to L_{A1}, and the level of employment in region B will rise to L_{B1}. The inter-regional difference in employment is given by $(L_{B1}-L_{A1})$, and the inter-regional difference between the two real wages will be $(w_{B1}-w_{A1})$. It is this difference, or alternatively, this 'disequilibrium', between the real wages attainable in the two regions that will encourage labour to migrate from region A to region B. This is why this particular model of migration is known as a 'disequilibrium' mechanism.

As we see in Figures 5.11 c and d, this migration behaviour will shift the labour supply in region A to the left from S_A to S_{A1}, and to the right in region B from S_B to S_{B1}. As more people enter region B, the available local labour supply expands, thereby reducing the marginal productivity of labour and the local wage rate in region B. Similarly, assuming that the regional capital stocks have remained unchanged, from the law of diminishing marginal productivity, we know that the reduced labour supply remaining in region A will experience a relative increase in its marginal product. This process of migration will continue until the falling real wage in region B and the rising real wage in region A are brought back into equilibrium at the original regional wages of $w_A = w_B$. Once this has been achieved, the inter-regional migration of labour from region A to region B will cease. Although real wages will have been brought back into equilibrium between the regions at their original levels, the total quantity of labour employed in each region will have changed from the original situation. In the new equilibrium, the total quantity of labour employed in region A will have fallen in two stages from L_A to L_{A1}, and then from L_{A1} to L_{A2}, while regional wages will have fallen and risen in two stages from w_A to w_{A1} and then from w_{A1} to w_A, respectively. Meanwhile, in region B, the total quantity of labour employed will have risen in two stages from L_B to L_{B1}, and then from L_{B1} to L_{B2}, while

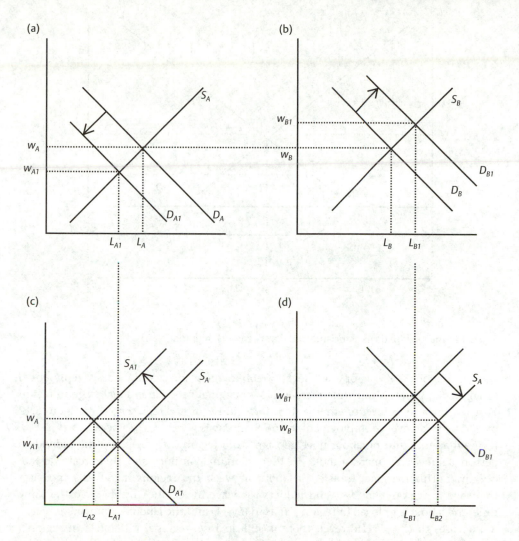

Fig. 5.11 a, b, c, and d A disequilibrium model of inter-regional migration

regional wages will have risen and fallen in two stages from w_A to w_{A1} and then from w_{A1} to $w_{A'}$ respectively. In the new equilibrium situation in which there is no inter-regional migration, region B will now be much larger than region A, whereas initially the two regions were the same size.

The process of inter-regional labour migration can be shown to be efficient from the point of view of the economy as a whole. In order to see this we can employ Figure 5.12, in which the labour demand curves for two regions X and Y of identical capital stocks are superimposed on each other by reversing the labour demand curve for region Y horizontally from left to right. In other words, we can read the labour demand curve of region X from left to right as normal, and read the labour demand curve of region Y from right to left. We can begin with a situation in which there is a high marginal product and real

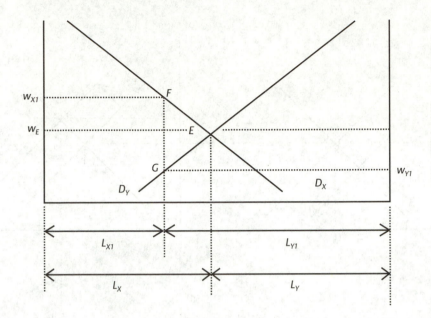

Fig. 5.12 The welfare gains associated with inter-regional migration

wage in region X of w_{X1} for a low level of employment in region X of L_{X1}, represented in Figure 5.12 by F. Meanwhile there is a low marginal product and real wage in region Y of w_{Y1} for a high level of employment in region Y of L_{Y1}, represented in Figure 5.12 by G. The total level of employment in the economy is given by L_N, where $L_N = (L_{X1}+L_{Y1})$. If one marginal unit of labour now transfers from region Y to region X, the individual person achieves an increase both in their marginal product and their real wage of $(w_{X1}-w_{Y1})$. This marginal transfer of labour between the regions marginally increases the wage in region Y by Δw_{Y1} and reduces the wage in region X by Δw_{X1}. At the same time, the labour employed in region Y falls to $(L_{X1}-1)$ and the labour employed in region X increases to $(L_{X1}+1)$. However, there is still an inter-regional difference in regional marginal products given by $(w_{X1}-\Delta w_{X1}) -(w_{Y1}-\Delta w_{Y1})$ and for the next person who migrates from region Y to region X, $(w_{X1}-\Delta w_{X1}) -(w_{Y1}-\Delta w_{Y1})$ represents the increase in their real wage. Inter-regional migration will take place from region Y to region X until real wages are equalized in both regions at w_E, and labour employment in each region is given as $(L_X=L_Y)$, as represented in Figure 5.12 by E. As before, the total national employment is given as $L_N =(L_X+L_Y)$.

The difference between the marginal products attainable in each region at the existing regional labour employment levels not only represents the real wage increase available to the marginal migrant. This difference also represents the forgone national output which is not produced if labour migration is not allowed to take place. Therefore, the area EFG can be regarded both as the deadweight loss to society due to a lack of inter-regional migration, and the Pareto efficiency gain to society associated with inter-regional migration.

Although in Figure 5.12 the argument is constructed by assuming each region X and Y

initially exhibits an identical regional capital stock with identical regional demand patterns, there is no reason why this should be the case. If the two regions initially have different capital stocks, this would simply imply that the relative positions of the regional labour demand curves from each of their respective vertical axes would change. We can see this in Figure 5.13. We assume that the inter-regional equilibrium was initially the same as that achieved in Figure 5.12, where regional wages are given as w_E in both regions, and labour employment in each region is given as L_X and L_Y, respectively, and where $L_X=L_Y$. If the stock of capital in region X increases, for example, due to the immigration of a new firm into the region, the demand for labour will increase in region X from D_X to $D_{X'}$. This will increase the equilibrium inter-regional wage to $w_{E'}$, at regional employment levels of $L_{X'}$ and $L_{Y'}$, and the Pareto efficiency gain associated with migration will increase from EFG to GHJ, at the initial disequilibrium regional labour supplies of L_{X1} and L_{Y1}.

If the capital increase in region X, on the other hand, has been due to the migration of a firm from region Y to region X, this will affect the labour demand curves in the two regions in an equal and opposite manner. In this latter case, the demand for labour in region Y will have fallen from D_Y to $D_{Y'}$, such that the equilibrium inter-regional wage will remain unchanged at w_E, but the new equilibrium labour supply in region X, given as $L_{X''}$,

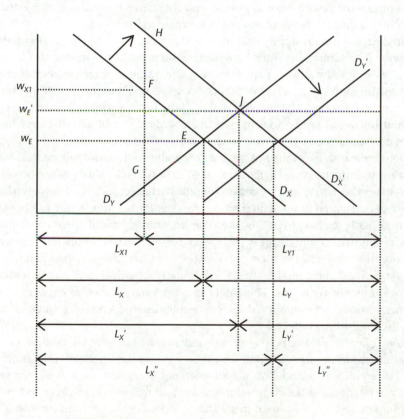

Fig. 5.13 Inter-regional labour equilibrium with different capital stocks

will be twice as large as that in region Y, given as $L_{Y''}$. As we see here, by comparing this result with the initial result in Figure 5.12, it is perfectly possible for the sizes of the two regions, defined in terms of their capital and labour stocks, to be quite different, although the equilibrium inter-regional wages are identical. At the same time, the efficiency gains associated with inter-regional migration are always available as long as inter-regional real wages are not in equilibrium.

5.5.2 The equilibrium model of inter-regional labour migration

The description of the inter-regional labour migration process given in section 5.5.1 is based on a disequilibrium model of migration. The basis of this disequilibrium model is that workers are perceived to move in response to differences between the real wages payable in various regions. Empirically, this should imply that in an econometric model with regional net migration as the dependent variable, and the regional real wage as an independent variable, there would always be a significant relationship between the two variables. In particular, areas with a higher than average real wage would be expected to exhibit relatively strong net in-migration flows, whereas areas with a relatively low real wage would be expected to exhibit relatively strong net out-migration flows. However, many econometric tests do not appear to find the 'correct' results, as suggested by the disequilibrium model. There are two possible explanations for this.

The first explanation is simply that the calculation of regional real wages often suffers from severe data limitations, thereby rendering such statistical work difficult. In theoretical terms regional real wages are defined as the nominal wage payable in the region divided by the local regional cost of living. Yet, in reality, measuring regional real wages can be very complicated. The simplest cost of living indices tend to be constructed using either housing rental cost or housing purchase cost data, combined with some local price index of consumer goods. However, housing markets not only tend to exhibit significant heterogeneity across locations but are also generally subject to high cyclical volatility. This means that the real wage deflators applied to nominal local wages can be very much dependent on the particular time period chosen. Therefore, statistical models which look at inter-regional labour flows of migration over a significant time period can be subject to data whose basis is changing all of the time. In order to avoid these problems, many models simply use nominal wages as a proxy for real wages, implicitly assuming that higher nominal wages imply higher real wages. In either case, whether real or nominal wage data are used in the models, the power of many statistical tests may be weakened by these measurement problems. These data problems may therefore explain why many econometric models of migration do not appear to find the 'correct' results, as suggested by the disequilibrium model.

On the other hand, there is a second and more fundamental critique of the disequilibrium model of migration, known as the 'equilibrium' model of migration (Graves 1980). The equilibrium model of migration argues that there are no 'correct' results as such in the relationship between net migration and real wages, as suggested by the disequilibrium model. The reason for this is that as well as being a reward for labour services in the production process, wages are also perceived to be a partial compensation for amenity differences. This is because residence in one area or another implies that the bundle of environmental amenity goods consumed by residents differs by location, and utility is gained from the consumption of these goods. In areas of high amenity, workers may be willing to accept lower wages for any given overall level of utility. On the other hand, in areas of poor environmental quality, workers may require higher wages to attain any given level of utility. The problem this raises is that the construction of appropriate inter-regional consumption indices based on a common basket of goods becomes extremely difficult, for the very reason that different locations mean that different baskets of environmental goods are consumed.

If this compensation argument is correct, in a country with heterogeneous regions, comparing real wages across regions on the basis of either nominal wage indices or nominal wages deflated by local cost of living indices will not tell us very much about the relative utilities of the workers in each of the regions. As such, we cannot assume any particular migration motives for workers between any two regions unless we can explicitly account for such amenity differences. This leaves us with enormous empirical problems, in that we would have to calculate environmental indices for all locations and incorporate these into our local real wage indices in order to produce appropriate regional real wage data. The logical limit of this argument, however, is that we would also have to account for all consumption differences by location, whether according to natural or human-produced environmental differences. As we see in the appendix to Chapter 3, the models of Fujita *et al.* (1999) allow for utility to be related to the local variety of consumption opportunities. These in turn can also be considered as environmental amenity variations, albeit human-produced ones, which would also need to be added to the natural environmental variations to provide a complete local amenity index. Immediately it becomes clear that the econometric problems involved are very significant.

The debate between the appropriateness of the disequilibrium model of migration versus the equilibrium model of migration is still not resolved (Evans 1990, 1993; Graves 1993). Hunt (1993) argues that in reality most empirical work generally supports the view that the disequilibrium model of migration better captures the process of migration. However, the equilibrium model cautions us to consider exactly what are the motives for migration and to understand that real wage differences across regions are the result of a variety of complex inter-related issues. It is therefore probably better to argue that in the majority of cases the disequilibrium nature of the relationship between real wages and migration will dominate the equilibrium nature of the relationship, although in some cases the results will be reversed.

5.5.3 The endogenous human-capital model of migration

A third approach to analysing the nature of inter-regional labour migration is based on the consideration of the microeconomic characteristics of individual migrants themselves. The basis of this argument is known as the human-capital model of migration, and is a development of the standard model of human capital first widely discussed by Becker (1964). A simple model of human capital is given in Appendix 5.1. However, the broad arguments of the model of human capital and their relationship to labour migration can be understood quite quickly.

The basic human-capital argument is that rational and well-informed individuals will invest in personal education and training in order to increase their stock of skills, defined here as human capital, in order to maximize their expected lifetime utility, defined here in terms of their lifetime income plus job satisfaction. Education and training tend to be undertaken before employment commences fully, so the costs of such activities are generally borne at an early stage in the career of an individual, whereas the employment earnings will accrue over the career history of the individual. At the same time, different lifetime incomes will be earned in different occupations and the cost of training in different skills will differ between different occupations. The individual worker therefore has to consider what is the optimum mode of employment to aspire to, and consequently what is the optimum level of personal education to invest in initially. Given good information on expected wages and labour training costs, as we see in Appendix 5.1, such a calculation is perfectly possible using standard present-value discounting techniques. The general assumptions are that the higher is the human capital of the individual, the relatively higher will generally have been the costs of their education, due to the extended time involved in training. At the same time, the higher the human capital of the individual, the relatively higher will be their expected wage, due to their increased marginal productivity. However, given that educational investment must generally take place before any long-term career develops, there is always an element of risk in the educational investment decision, in that the actual lifetime earnings may differ from those which were initially expected to be attained.

From the perspective of urban and regional labour market behaviour, the problem is to understand the relationship between migration behaviour and the maximization of expected wages within the human-capital framework. In order to do this, we must combine the standard human-capital theory outlined above with what is known as 'search theory' (Molho 1986). The basic premise of search theory is that labour will only consider accepting a job if the wage offered is greater than, or equal to, a particular personal minimum acceptable wage, known as a 'reservation' wage. Individuals will continue with a process of job search in which job positions are considered sequentially, until one offers a wage which at least matches the individual's reservation wage. From human-capital theory, we know that greater human capital generally involves greater initial education costs, and also greater potential wages due to higher skills. Therefore, the reservation wage tends to increase for individuals with greater levels of human capital. This means that the higher the human capital of the individual, the greater will be the length of the job-search process. However, in terms of regional labour market behaviour, the combination of human-capital theory with job-search theory also has a direct implication. The implication is that higher human-capital individuals will tend to search for employment opportunities over a wider geographical area than those with lower human capital in order to find employment opportunities offering wages at least equal to their higher reservation wage. In the cases where such employment opportunities are found and taken up, the result will be that the higher human-capital individuals will be more likely to have migrated over greater geographical distances than the lower human-capital individuals. In order to maximize returns to human capital, higher human-capital individuals therefore tend to be more migratory than lower human-capital individuals, for reasons both of recovering their initial costs of the human-capital acquisition, and also attaining their expected wages. At the same time, we can also argue that higher human-capital individuals will also be better informed of alternative employment opportunities across regions via easier personal access to informal employment networks. Once again, this will tend to increase the migratory nature of higher human-capital individuals.

The argument that higher human-capital individuals will tend to be more migratory than lower human-capital individuals has profound implications for our understanding of the disequilibrium model of migration. In order to see this we can consider Figures 5.14 a, b, c, and d, which are a modification of Figures 5.11a, b, c, and d. In Figures 5.14a and b, we assume initially that the real wage in region A, denoted as w_A, and the real wage in region B, denoted as w_B, are equal, as are the equilibrium employment levels in each region, denoted as L_A and L_B, respectively. As in Figures 5.11 a and b, if the demand for

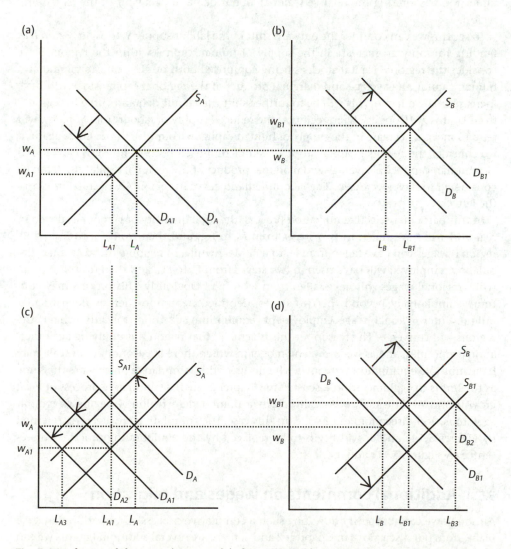

Fig. 5.14 a, b, c, and d A cumulative model of inter-regional migration

labour in region A decreases from D_A to D_{A1} while the demand for labour in region B increases from D_B to D_{B1}, the real wage in region A will fall to w_{A1}, and the real wage in region B will rise to w_{B1}. Similarly, the level of employment in region A will fall to L_{A1}, and the level of employment in region B will rise to L_{B1}. As before in Figures 5.11c and d, the inter-regional wage disequilibrium of $(w_{B1}-w_{A1})$ encourages labour to migrate from region A to region B, resulting in a labour supply shift in region A to the left from S_A to S_{A1}, and to the right in region B from S_B to S_{B1}. However, the human-capital argument above suggests that the most migratory individuals who most efficiently respond to regional wage signals will tend to be the most highly educated workers. If we assume therefore that high human-capital individuals migrate relatively quickly, whereas low human-capital individuals migrate relatively slowly, the effect of this selective migration can be understood as altering the relative regional labour demand in favour of the expanding region.

To see this we can consider the outward shift in the labour supply S_B to S_{B1} in region B as tending to imply an increase in the supply of human capital within the region. If we consider the regional capital stock as being comprised both of physical capital and also human capital, the average and marginal product of the regional capital stock will have increased. The effect of this will be to further shift the labour demand curve in region B from D_{B1} to D_{B2}. Conversely, in region A, the reduced supply of labour from S_A to S_{A1}, will tend to mean a decrease in the supply of human capital within the region. Once again, if we consider the regional capital stock as being comprised both of physical capital and also human capital, the average and marginal product of the regional capital stock can be considered to have decreased. The labour demand curve in region A will shift further to the left.

In this particular selective migration process, the total quantity of labour employed in region A will have fallen in two stages from L_A to L_{A1}, and then from L_{A1} to L_{A3}, while regional wages will have fallen from w_A to w_{A1}. Meanwhile, in region B, the total quantity of labour employed will have risen in two stages from L_B to L_{B1}, and then from L_{B1} to L_{B3}, while regional wages will have fallen from w_A to w_{A1}. Obviously, this process may continue cumulatively beyond the two stages identified here, and there is no particular unique inter-regional wage–employment equilibrium position towards which the regions will converge. The reason for this is actually that region A is enjoying agglomeration economies, and as we know, any model in which there are economies of scale may have multiple equilibrium outcomes. The limits of this cumulative process are the same as the limits to agglomeration discussed in Chapter 2. Such a cumulative process of local growth and decline may eventually reach a point where region B begins to exhibit agglomeration diseconomies of scale. In this case, the cumulative processes represented by Figures 5.14c and d, will begin to be replaced by the equilibrating processes represented by Figures 5.11c and d.

5.5.4 Additional comments on wages and migration

Although we cannot specify how long such a cumulative process of migration may take place, from our discussions in Chapters 2 and 4, there are several additional points we can make. The first is that the ability of the migration process to eradicate localized regional unemployment problems depends on whether the migration process is an equilibrating or a cumulative process. If migration is highly selective in terms of the human capital of migrants, the differences in regional performance may be exacerbated by the migration process itself.

A second issue which we have not discussed here is the question of the housing market. The structure of the housing market may sometimes generate impediments to the migration process. For example, if there are asymmetric demand shocks between regions, such as in Figures 5.11 and 5.14, this may engender significant movements in local real estate prices. For workers with mortgages, this may mean that movement from weak regions to buoyant regions becomes a question of access to capital, rather than access to a job. If local house prices have fallen significantly, a worker may not be able to cover the mortgage value of the house from its sale, nor funds for the deposit required for a mortgage in the more expensive region. Therefore, even if alternative superior job offers are available in more buoyant regions, the worker will be unable to leave the weaker region (Bover *et al.* 1989). In such a situation, only intra-regional job-moves within the same metropolitan region, which do not involve a change of residence, will be possible for the worker. As well as the workings of the private housing market, another potential obstacle to inter-regional migration comes from public sector housing policies. In some cases, subsidies to publicly provided housing may reduce the likelihood of migration (Hughes and McCormick 1981; Minford *et al.* 1988) by artificially increasing the real wages of those with the state housing. In such cases, workers may be much less responsive to inter-regional wage signals.

The third point concerning migration is the problem of understanding whether the acquisition of a higher wage job is the result of, or a cause of, migration behaviour. Many arguments suggest that for many people, the availability of employment opportunities causes migration to take place as a response to job-acquisition, rather than as part of the job-search process itself. The major evidence in support of this is that the levels of inter-regional migration in many countries tend to be pro-cyclical. In other words, as the national economy expands, the availability of jobs increases, and the levels of inter-regional migration tend to increase. On the other hand, as the economy contracts and employment opportunities diminish, the levels of inter-regional migration tend to fall. The result of this is that in many countries, the differences between regional unemployment rates tend to fall as the economy expands and tend to increase as the economy contracts (Gordon 1985), although the evidence for this can be rather difficult to interpret (Hemmings 1991).

An additional alternative approach is to interpret the regional wage arguments outlined above in terms of the expected wages earned by migrants, rather than the actual wages. Expected wages are the wages earned on acquiring a job multiplied by the probability of actually gaining employment in the relevant sector in the respective region. This is the classic Harris and Todaro (1970) argument which is familiar in the development economics literature (Thirlwall 1994). From the arguments in Chapter 2, this would imply that there may be situations where migration will tend to take place from peripheral areas to central higher-order areas, even though actual real wages in the central urban areas may be lower than those earned in the peripheral areas. Such cases will be where central urban areas are achieving agglomeration economies of scale. The reason for this is that the probability of actually finding appropriate employment is much higher in the central urban areas, thereby allowing real wages earned to be lower. Net migration flows between the regions will continue until the expected wage is equalized between the regions. In the above scenario, if economic growth tends to originate in the dominant central areas, for the reasons outlined in Chapter 2, this will imply that the central areas initially grow faster than the peripheral regions. Migration will take place from the peripheral regions to the centre, although the net migration levels will fall as the peripheral regions begin to grow. As the economy contracts, the migration flows will fall because the overall availability of jobs will fall.

5.6 Non-Wage-Related Models of Inter-Regional Migration

Each of the above models of migration depends primarily on the relationship between regional wages and employment levels. There are, however, two major models of migration which are primarily independent of wage levels. These models are known as the gravity model of migration and the life-cycle model of migration. Both of these models suggest that migration will take place even though wages or expected wages, or amenity-adjusted wages, are in equilibrium. The major difference here is that these two models focus on gross migration and not net migration, as is the case with the models described above in sections 5.5.1 to 5.5.3.

5.6.1 The gravity model of migration

The gravity model formula has been frequently applied both to intra-regional migration and also to inter-regional migration. The implicit basis of the argument when it is applied to inter-regional migration is that random business fluctuations will lead to certain continuous flows of job terminations and job vacancies which are uncorrelated across both time or space. The result of this is that there will always be individuals willing and able to migrate between regions at any one time, even if inter-regional wages are in equilibrium. Of interest to us, however, is the level of inter-regional migration flows between regions, and this is where the gravity model can be instructive. The gravity model of migration suggests that the levels of migration between any two areas is directly related to the population sizes of the areas, and inversely related to the distance between the areas. The gravity model of migration can be expressed by the general formula

$$M_{AB} = G \frac{P_A P_B}{(d_{AB})^a},$$

(5.1)

whereby P_A and P_B represent the population sizes of the two city-regions, and d_{AB} represents the distance between the two locations, and the parameters G and a are constants to be determined. Although the model appears to be a direct analogy from the physical laws of gravity attraction between any two objects, there is, however, a reasoning behind the model based on both probability and economics. In order to understand this we must consider the justifications for the numerator and denominator terms of equation (5.1) separately.

The structure of the numerator term is based on the argument that the expected number of moves by individuals to or from any region will be directly related to the population sizes of the regions. In order to see this we can consider the case where the total national population is given as P_N, and the total number of inter-regional migration moves per time period is given as M_N. Here, the average number of inter-regional migration moves per person per year is thus given as M_N/P_N. In terms of out-migration, if we assume that all people in the country are homogeneous in terms of their propensity to migrate, the expected total number of out-migrants generated by area A will be given by $(M_N/P_N) P_A$. Therefore, for any given population migration propensity, the total number of out-migration moves from any area A, will be positively related to the total number of people in the area P_A. Meanwhile, if the relative size of any particular potential destination region B is given by P_B/P_N, the expected total number of in-migrants per time period to region B from region A will be given as $((M_N/P_N) P_A) (P_B/P_N)$, which gives $(M_N P_A P_B) / (P_N P_N)$. Similarly, if the relative size of any particular potential destination region B is given by P_B/P_N, the expected total number of in-migrants to area B from all other regions will be given by $M_N(P_B/P_N)$. The contribution of this in-migration to region B which is accounted for by out-migration from region A will be therefore be given by $(M_N(P_B/P_N) (P_A/P_N))$, which gives $(M_N P_A P_B) /(P_N P_N)$, as above. Therefore, in equation (5.1) we can interpret the migration flows between regions A and B as being a product of P_A and P_B, and multiplied by a constant G, where $G = M_N/(P_N P_N)$.

The argument so far has implicitly assumed that migration between any pair of regions is equally as likely as migration between any other pair of regions. However, we can argue that the spatial transactions costs involved under conditions of uncertainty, as discussed in Chapter 2, suggest that this will not be so. The agglomeration and spatial information acquisition arguments in Chapter 2 suggest that migration between contiguous areas will be much more likely than between distant regions. This argument is sometimes known as 'distance deterrence' (Gordon 1978), and implies that the likelihood of migration between any two locations will be inversely related to the distance between them, given as d_{AB}. However, there is no reason to expect that the inverse relationship between the inter-regional migration probability and the distance should be linear. Therefore, we can specify the distance function in the denominator in terms of $(d_{AB})^\alpha$, to allow for any non-linearities. Combining these two distinct approaches to the construction of the numerator and denominator terms gives us the general expression (5.1). This can be used to provide indications of migration flows between regions, even under conditions of real wage equilibrium between regions.

Gravity models can also be made much more complex than this simple description, by introducing more complex behavioural assumptions (Wilson 1974; Isard *et al.* 1998). At the same time, the multiplicative nature of equation (5.1) means that where simple models of this form are used for estimating inter-regional flows across all regions, the aggregate flows do not necessarily sum to the total flows in the system. In order to adjust for this, the models must be 'doubly constrained', so as to ensure the correct total flows into and out from each region (Isard *et al.* 1998).

In terms of our regional labour market discussions, however, the general observation to come out of these gravity models is that inter-regional migration flows are in part spatially determined, in the sense that the likelihood of migration is a function of distance. This also implies that inter-regional adjustments to labour market shocks may also be in part spatially determined. This is because the efficiency of the migration process as a regional labour market adjustment mechanism will itself depend on the distance between the local labour market in question, and any other local labour market. More central regions, which are closer to a larger number of other centres of population, may find it easier to adjust to local negative demand shocks by means of out-migration flows, whereas geographically peripheral regions may only adjust much more slowly. In other words, the ability of regions to successfully adjust to negative demand shocks may also depend simply on the location of the regions in question.

5.6.2 The life-cycle model of migration

Migration may also exhibit something of a life-cycle nature. For example, young school and college graduates may tend to migrate towards large primal cities in order to gain better access to high-quality employment. This migration takes place because such young job-seekers assume that their best long-term employment prospects will be served by acquiring a job in such a central location. The majority of their working life may be spent at such a location, although eventually the worker will seek to move out of the major city to a smaller, more geographically peripheral, settlement. This may include migration to regions of higher environmental quality and lower wages (Plane 1983). In the dominant urban centres, such out-migrants will be continually replaced by new young and generally highly educated in-migrants. Meanwhile, on the other hand, the peripheral areas will consistently see an out-migration of such young workers and a continuous in-migration of older workers accepting lower wages than they previously accepted. This has been described as an 'escalator' phenomenon (Fielding 1992). As long as the generation of high-quality employment opportunities tends to be dominated by the central higher-order urban areas, such a process will continue indefinitely. These life-cycle effects on migration will tend to take place over and above the wage-migration mechanism outlined in sections 5.5 to 5.5.3, and their effect will be to systematically alter the demographic profile and labour force composition between particular regions.

5.7 Conclusions

Local urban and regional labour markets can exhibit particular features which are somewhat different from national discussions of the labour market. The hierarchical relationships between the regional export base sectors and the locally oriented sectors of a region will mediate demand shocks, and the regional responses to such shocks will depend on the structure of these relationships. Where demand shocks are positive, regions can respond by expanding their local capital stock, either through the expansion of local investment or through the immigration of capital from other regions. On the other hand, in some situations the fixity and durability of local regional capital, and the hierarchical demand interactions between the regional export base and non-basic sectors, together militate against any potential downward adjustment of local wages to market-clearing levels. Both local market-clearing and local involuntary unemployment are possible consequences of this downward wage rigidity. The actual result depends on the interaction between the employment retention policies of local firms, the expectations of local firms, and the speed of response of external investors to changes in the local economic conditions.

All regions do exhibit the additional labour market adjustment mechanism of inter-regional migration. As we have seen, there are various interpretations of the relationship between regional wages and migration flows. The most common assumption is that of the disequilibrium model, in which migration will take place as a response to real wage differences between regions. If all regional economies exhibit constant returns to scale, the process of inter-regional migration will itself lead to a restoration of the inter-regional wage equilibrium. Moreover, we have shown that this process maximizes the welfare to society by reducing any deadweight loss associated with an inefficient inter-regional spatial pattern of labour. On the other hand, where differences in human capital exist, the process of migration itself may cause certain regions to experience agglomeration economies at the expense of others. In this situation, a process of cumulative growth is possible. This is the subject of the next chapter.

Finally, over and above all of the equilibrium–disequilibrium issues surrounding regional labour markets and migration, there are certain characteristics to migration flows dependent on demographic and geographical issues, which take place irrespective of regional wage levels.

Discussion questions

1 Is regional unemployment primarily the result of local labour prices being 'too' high? What would be the various possible consequences of reducing local wages?

2 Explain how inter-regional migration may solve local unemployment problems.

3 In what ways is inter-regional migration related to national economic efficiency?

4 Under what conditions may inter-regional migration exacerbate local unemployment problems?

5 What role do environmental amenities play in determining inter-regional equilibrium wages? How does this affect our understanding of whether migration is an 'equilibrium' or a 'disequilibrium' phenomenon?

6 What other non-wage-related approaches do we have for analysing inter-regional migration?

Appendix 5.1   **The Model of Human Capital**

The model of human-capital investment can be understood in terms of standard discounting techniques applied to investments in general. If we denote any future annual income stream at time t which can be earned by an investment as R_t, and we denote the discount rate as i, and the initial cost of undertaking the investment today as C_0, the simplest present value Π calculation of the investment can be defined as

$$\Pi = \sum_{t=1}^{n} \frac{R_t}{(1+i)^t} - C_0 = \sum_{t=1}^{n} R_t(1+i)^{-t} - C_0 \tag{A.5.1.1}$$

The present value of the investment is the discounted sum of all the future income streams from time period $t=1$ onwards. In the model specification given by (A.5.1.1) we are assuming that the future annual revenues R_t are paid at the end of each year, beginning at the end of year 1. In other words, the revenue payments which are discounted here are discrete payments.

In the case where revenues are paid continuously, however, it is necessary for us to convert (A.5.1.1) so as to discount the continuous income stream. In this case the present value Π of the investment can be defined as (Chiang 1984)

$$\Pi = \int_0^n R(t)e^{-rt}dt - C_0 \tag{A.5.1.2}$$

If we apply this model to human-capital investments, the initial cost of the investment C_0 will be represented by the initial employment training costs. These training costs will comprise the sum of any tuition fees paid plus the opportunity costs of the current income forgone during the period of training. The income earned from the human capital will be represented by the wages earned by working in the occupation for which the individual trained. If we denote the wage earned on commencing employment as W, we can rewrite (A.5.1.2) as

$$\Pi = \int_0^n W(t)e^{-rt}dt - C_0 \tag{A.5.1.3}$$

Over the lifetime of employment, wages tend to increase over time as workers become more experienced and senior in their chosen occupations. In order to allow for the effect of the growth in wages over time on the present-value model, we note that the current wage at any time period in the future t can be written as

$$W(t) = We^{at} \tag{A.5.1.4}$$

where a is the rate of growth of wages. Therefore, equation (A.5.1.3) can be adjusted to allow for continuous wage growth thus:

$$\Pi = \int_0^n W(t)e^{(a-r)t}dt - C_0 \tag{A.5.1.5}$$

The basic model can be further developed to allow for costs which are incurred in a continuous manner over time, and for wage growth which changes over time.

In migration literature, the fundamental issue raised by the model of human capital is how the relationship between the costs of human-capital investment, as represented here by C_0, and the future wages earned $W(t)$, are mediated. In particular, the wages payable for human-capital investments depend on workers moving to the locations of the appropriate employment. If the market is perfectly efficient, then workers will be matched with appropriate jobs at all locations, with expected real wages for each occupation being equal at all locations. However, if information transmission improves with human capital, and constraints to migration also fall with human capital, then we would expect differential migration propensities and variations in market-clearing mechanisms between different educational and income groups.

Chapter 6

Regional Growth, Factor Allocation, and Balance of Payments

6.1 Introduction

The object of this chapter is to discuss the nature of regional growth and to provide an analysis of the various potential mechanisms by which regional growth takes place. Economic growth is a complex process, and as with labour markets and multipliers, the analysis of this issue at the regional level is somewhat different from that at the national level. Various hints as to the possible causes and consequences of regional growth have been provided in the preceding chapters. In Chapter 1 we see that growth may take place via the location behaviour of firms, as the immigration of firms into a region increases the host region's stock of capital and employment. In Chapter 2 we see that such industrial location and relocation behaviour may also contribute to the development of localized agglomeration economies. In situations where these agglomeration economies arise, growth becomes possible at particular locations. In other words, growth is location-specific. This may have implications for the size distribution of urban centres, and as we see from Chapter 3, the extent of the localized growth will also impact on local land and real estate prices. In Chapter 4 it is argued that the specifically local impacts of localized growth also depend on the sectoral origin of the growth, and the strength of the linkages between each of the local industrial sectors. Taken together, these conclusions suggest that the various regional impacts of growth will depend on both the sectoral and the spatial industrial structure of the economy.

On the other hand, we may initially perceive that the specifically local effects are relatively unimportant, in that the national or international economy as a whole will benefit from such localized growth. This is because any localized efficiency benefits will be spread via private sector trading relationships and also public sector redistributive fiscal mechanisms to the rest of the economy. However, the effects of localized growth on individual regions may be quite diverse, depending on the time required for any localized growth effects to be transmitted to the rest of the spatial economy. As we see in Chapter 5, differences in migration propensities between individuals with differing human capital assets may militate against an even and rapid dissemination of growth benefits to all regions via labour market adjustment mechanisms. Moreover, the efficiency of labour migration as an equilibrating mechanism itself may depend on the strength of the national economy. Similarly, in periods of recession, the negative environmental effects of dereliction associated with the durability of fixed capital in declining regions may militate against an even and rapid dissemination of growth benefits to all regions via capital adjustment mechanisms. Therefore, as well as inter-regional differences in sectoral and spatial industrial structures, the spatial dissemination of the benefits of localized growth may depend on the extent to which the aggregate economy as a whole is buoyant.

In order to discuss the various issues associated with regional growth we will adopt two broad analytical perspectives. The first perspective, which is broadly neoclassical in nature, focuses on the questions relating to the spatial allocation of production factors, and the inter-relationships which exist between factor allocation and technological change. This is the most common approach adopted in analyses of regional growth. The second approach, which is broadly Keynesian in nature, focuses on questions relating to inter-regional income flows, and discusses regional growth behaviour in terms of a balance of payments framework. Conceptually, these two frameworks are fundamentally different from each other, with the result that they produce somewhat different conclusions as to the nature, causes, and consequences of regional growth. Each approach can throw some light on different particular aspects of the nature of the regional growth process. However, there are also a variety of situations in which the two approaches can be made broadly consistent with each other, thereby providing a wide-ranging perspective on the nature of the regional growth process. We will begin by discussing the neoclassical approach to regional growth, factor allocation, and technological change, and in the subsequent sections we will contrast these arguments with the Keynesian approach.

6.2 **Neoclassical Regional Growth**

The neoclassical approach to macroeconomic growth has developed on the basis of the original insights of Solow (1956) and Swan (1956). These arguments have subsequently been applied to the case of regions, and the neoclassical approach to regional growth has two major components. The first component concerns the question of the regional allocation and migration of production factors. The analysis of this issue is based on two analytical frameworks known as the 'One-Sector' and 'Two-Sector' models of factor allocation, respectively. The second component concerns the question of the nature of the relationship between production factors and technological change, and this is generally analysed within a production function framework. The neoclassical growth models assume that the economy is competitive, in the sense that factors are paid according to their marginal products, and also that factors are quickly able to be reallocated so as to be employed in their most productive use. In sections 6.2.1 to 6.2.3 we will initially discuss and compare the two models relating to the regional allocation of factors, and then we will use the general conclusions of these models to motivate our production function approach.

6.2.1 The one-sector model of regional factor allocation and migration

The neoclassical one-sector model of regional factor allocation and migration is based on the law of variable factor proportions. In other words, the marginal productive properties of factors are perceived to depend on the relative quantities of each of the factors employed. The basic principle underlying this comes from the law of diminishing productivity, which states that, holding one factor constant, the marginal product of the variable factor falls as a greater quantity of the variable factor is employed. The assumption here is that the variable factor is combined with the fixed factor in the production process, and it is the application of the variable factor to the fixed factor which gives rise to the diminishing marginal productivity of the variable factor. We will initially discuss the case where all factors are freely mobile between regions, and then compare this with the situation where there is a certain amount of inter-regional factor immobility.

In the case of capital and labour, for a fixed capital stock, the greater the level of labour employment, the lower will be the marginal product of labour. In other words, as the quantity of labour increases relative to the quantity of capital employed, the lower will be the marginal product of labour. Similarly, for a fixed quantity of labour, the greater the level of capital employed, the lower will be the marginal product of capital. In other words, as the quantity of capital increases relative to the quantity of labour employed, the lower will be the marginal product of capital. As we see, in the case of two factors, the law of diminishing marginal productivity holds for either factor, as long as the other factor is held constant. Moreover, we can extend the argument to more than two factors. For example, if we hold a third factor constant, such as land, and add successive quantities of both capital and labour, the marginal products of both capital and labour will fall.

For reasons of analytical simplicity, however, in the following sections we will assume that all production activities are the result of the combination of two factors. These two factors are a composite factor capital, denoted as K, which contains all non-labour inputs, and all labour inputs denoted as factor L. We assume that in general, capital K and labour L are complementary inputs, and the relative quantities of capital and labour employed can be defined in terms of a capital/labour ratio K/L. Using this notation, the arguments above concerning the application of the law of diminishing marginal productivity to the complementary factor inputs can be specified in very general terms. If the quantity of capital is high relative to the quantity of labour employed, in other words the K/L ratio is high, the marginal product of capital will be low and the marginal product of labour will be high. Conversely, if the quantity of capital is low relative to the quantity of labour employed, in other words the K/L ratio is low, the marginal product of capital will be high and the marginal product of labour will be low.

These arguments can now be translated into a regional context. We can imagine the case of a country comprising two regions A and B, in which the capital/labour ratio in region A is higher than that in region B, such that

$$\frac{K_A}{L_A} > \frac{K_B}{L_B}, \tag{6.1}$$

where K_A is quantity of capital employed in region A, L_A is quantity of labour employed in region A, K_B is quantity of capital employed in region B, L_B is quantity of labour employed in region B.

In a situation such as that described by equation (6.1), the marginal product of capital in region A will be lower than the marginal product of capital in region B. Meanwhile, the marginal product of labour in region A will be higher than the marginal product of labour in region B. In other words, assuming that production factors are paid according to their marginal productivities, marginal profits will be higher in region B while wages will be higher in region A. If factors are mobile, the different regional capital/labour ratios will encourage labour to migrate from region B to region A, and capital to migrate from region A to region B. The difference in the regional capital/labour ratios therefore encourages the two factors to migrate in opposite directions to each other, in order to earn higher factor rewards. The two factors will continue to migrate in opposite directions as long as there is still a difference in the regional capital/labour ratios. This process of inter-regional factor migration will therefore only cease when the capital/labour ratios in both regions are the same, such that:

$$\frac{K_A}{L_A} = \frac{K_B}{L_B}. \tag{6.2}$$

In this inter-regional equilibrium situation, wages are the same in both regions and marginal profits are the same in both regions. The inter-regional adjustment mechanism, in which factors migrate in opposite directions until capital/labour ratios are equalized across the region, is known as the one-sector neoclassical model of factor allocation and migration.

The conclusions of the one-sector model can be discussed from the perspective of aggregate national efficiency and welfare. In order to do this we can employ an Edgeworth–Bowley box in which the factor employment levels and output of both regions are represented.

The Edgeworth–Bowley box in Figure 6.1 represents the two regions A and B. The output of region A is represented by the isoquants which originate at A, and higher levels of output are represented by isoquants which are further to the right. Similarly, the output of region B is represented by the isoquants which originate at B, and higher levels of output are represented by isoquants which are further to the left. The total level of capital in the economy is K_N, and is represented by the vertical height of the Edgeworth–Bowley box. Assuming that all factors are employed, K_N comprises the sum of the capital employed in both regions. In other words, $K_N = (K_A + K_B)$. Meanwhile, the total level of labour in the economy is L_N, and is represented by the horizontal length of the Edgeworth–Bowley box. Assuming that all factors are employed, L_N comprises the sum of the labour employed in both regions. In other words, $L_N = (L_A + L_B)$.

If the regional factor allocation is initially at point C, the quantity of capital employed in region A is given by K_{AC}, and the quantity of labour employed in region A is given by L_{AC}. Similarly, at point C, the quantity of capital employed in region B is given by K_{BC}, and

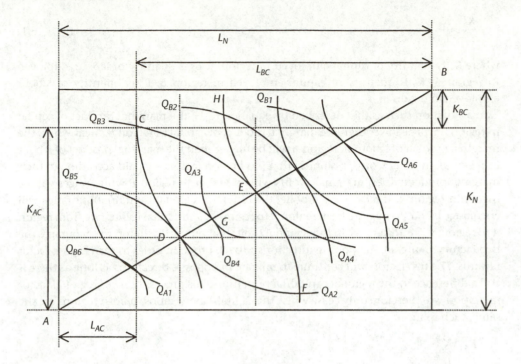

Fig. 6.1 One-sector inter-regional Edgeworth–Bowley box

the quantity of labour employed in region A is given by L_{AC}. With the particular inter-regional factor allocation at C, the level of output of region A is given by the isoquant Q_{A2} and the level of output of region B is given by the isoquant Q_{B3}. As we see in Figure 6.1 the capital/labour ratio in region A is much higher than that in region B. Therefore, from the logic of the one-sector model, a reallocation of factors between the regions can effect a Pareto efficiency gain. The reason for this is that a factor reallocation between regions, in which capital moves from the high capital/labour ratio region (region A) to the low capital/labour ratio region (region B), will increase the marginal productivity of the mobile capital. Similarly, a factor reallocation between regions, in which labour moves from the low capital/labour ratio region (region B) to the high capital/labour ratio region (region A), will increase the marginal productivity of the mobile labour. This process of factor migration and reallocation, in which the marginal products of both mobile factors are increased, must therefore necessarily increase aggregate national output.

One-sector factor migration will continue until the capital/labour ratios are equal in both regions, as represented by equation (6.2) above. Once the capital/labour ratios in each region are the same the process of factor reallocation and migration will cease, because there will be no inter-regional differences in factor rewards. In other words, when regional capital/labour ratios are equalized there will be no further potential Pareto efficiency gains associated with the increasing marginal productivities of migrant factors. In other words, all the possible Pareto-efficient inter-regional factor allocations must exhibit the same capital/labour ratios. Within an Edgeworth–Bowley box framework, this argument implies that where all factors are mobile, the contract curve which links all of the Pareto-efficient inter-regional factor allocations must be a straight line, as in Figure 6.1.

For example, if factors which are initially allocated at C are reallocated to a point D, the total output of region A will remain the same at Q_{A2}, but the output of region B will have increased from Q_{B3} to Q_{B5}. At point D, the capital/labour ratios of both regions are equal. Alternatively, if the factors which are initially allocated at C are reallocated to a point E, the total output of region B will remain the same at Q_{B3}, but the output of region A will have increased from Q_{A2} to Q_{A4}. At point E, the capital/labour ratios of both regions are equal, and are also identical to the capital/labour ratios at D. Finally, if the factors which are initially allocated at C are reallocated to a point G, the total output of region B will increase from Q_{B3} to Q_{B4}, and the output of region A will increase from Q_{A2} to Q_{A3}. Each of these three possible inter-regional factor reallocations represents a Pareto efficiency gain. More generally, beginning at position C, the reallocation of factors between regions to any point on the boundary of, or within the area, defined by $CDEF$, represents a Pareto welfare gain with respect to the factor allocation at point C. However, only points on the straight-line contract curve within this area of potential Pareto efficiency gains, defined as DGE, represent Pareto-efficient factor allocations. The line DGE represents the 'core' of the economy, given the initial allocation at C.

The same logic, regarding the Pareto gains associated with inter-regional factor reallocations, can also be applied to any other inefficient initial factor allocation, such as points H and J in Figure 6.1. In each case, there will be an area of potential efficiency gains which itself must contain a 'core' of Pareto-efficient factor allocations. The straight-line contract curve therefore represents all of the possible Pareto-efficient core allocations. If the inter-regional contract curve is a straight line, this also means that the regional expansion paths are both linear and identical. In other words, the regional production functions are identical. Assuming constant returns to scale, this implies that both regional production functions must be homogeneous of degree one.

If the contract curve is a straight line, the inter-regional production possibility frontier must also be a straight line, as in Figure 6.2 (Borts and Stein 1964). Pareto-efficient points such as D and E in Figure 6.1 will be on the production possibility frontier, as shown in Figure 6.2, whereas inefficient points such as C in Figure 6.1 will be inside the production possibility frontier.

The slope of the production possibility curve is known as the marginal rate of transformation, and is given by the ratio of the marginal costs of production. In the case of Figure 6.2 we can write this as $MRT_{AB} = (MC_A/MC_B)$, where MRT_{AB} represents the marginal rate of transformation of the output of region A for region B, and MC_A and MC_B represent the marginal costs of output expansion in regions A and B. The fact that the inter-regional production possibility curve is a straight line implies that from the perspective of production, the output of each region can be regarded as a perfect substitute for the output of the other region. In other words, when output is expanded in one region and contracted in another region due to the transfer of both factors between the two regions (as represented by a movement along the contract curve), the marginal rate of increase in output of the expanding region will be exactly equal to the marginal rate of output reduction of the contracting region. Therefore, in the absence of output price changes, for a given national capital and labour stock, the total national output of the economy

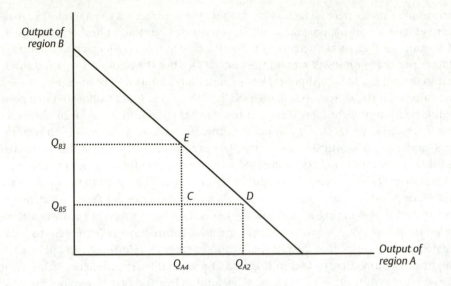

Fig. 6.2 One-sector inter-regional production possibility frontier

will remain constant irrespective of the factor allocation position on the contract curve. As such, in the situation where both factors are completely mobile, as long as we are on the straight-line contract curve with identical regional capital/labour ratios, the total output value of the economy will be independent of the regional distribution of activities.

6.2.2 The two-sector model of regional factor allocation and migration

In the one-sector model of regional factor allocation, factors flow in opposite directions in order to earn their highest rewards. However, there are certain situations in which factors can flow in the same direction. This is possible where the regional production functions are somewhat different from each other, and such a case is analysed within the framework of a two-sector model.

We can modify the one-sector example above to allow for the case of two regions A and B, producing different outputs with different production functions. More particularly, we can assume that region A's output production tends to be relatively capital-intensive and regions B's output is relatively labour-intensive. In this situation the inter-regional Edgeworth–Bowley box will exhibit a concave contract curve as depicted in Figure 6.3.

In this case, we can imagine that the demand for the output of region A increases, due to a change in domestic consumer tastes or an increase in external export demand in favour of the output of region A, without any equivalent change in favour of the output of region B. As we see in Figure 6.4a, this increased demand pushes up the price of region A's goods from P_{A1} to P_{A2}, and the output of region A increases from Q_{1A} to Q_{2A} as the existing stocks of factors are employed more intensively. Assuming that the output price

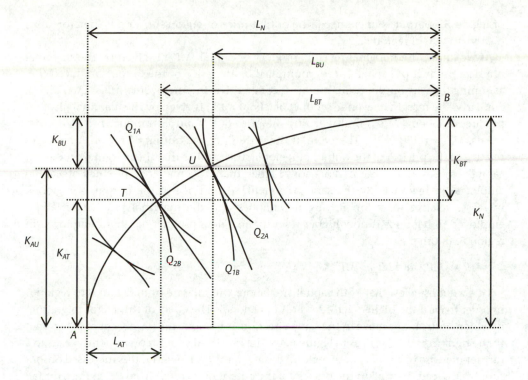

Fig. 6.3 Two-sector inter-regional Edgeworth–Bowley box

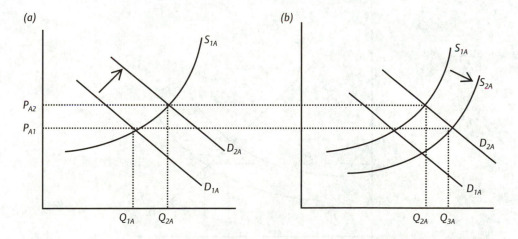

Fig. 6.4 Output market adjustment for expanding region

of region B's output is unchanged, the output price of region A's output therefore rises relative to that of region B.

As we know, the marginal revenue product of capital (MP_K) is given by the marginal physical product of capital (MPP_K) multiplied by the price of the output produced (P_o), assuming that the output goods market is competitive. In other words, $MP_K = (MPP_K \times P_o)$. Similarly, the marginal revenue product of labour (MP_L) is given by the marginal physical product of labour (MPP_L) multiplied by the price of the output produced (P_o). In other words, $MP_L = (MPP_L \times P_o)$. Therefore, if the price P_A of the output of region A increases relative to the price P_B of the output of region B, this implies that the marginal product of capital employed in region A is now higher than the marginal product of capital employed in region B. By the same argument, if the price of the output of region A increases relative to region B, this also implies that the marginal product of labour employed in region A is now higher than the marginal product of labour employed in region B. In other words

$$MP_K^A > MP_K^B \text{ and } MP_L^A > MP_L^B$$

This would suggest that both capital and labour will migrate from region B to region A in order to earn the higher factor rewards in region A. The effect of this factor migration, in which both factors move in the same direction, is to move the supply curve of region A to the right from S_{1A} to S_{2A}, as in Figure 6.4b. The increased supply consequently leads to a further increase in the output of region A from Q_{2A} to Q_{3A}. However, this increased output supply also leads to a fall in the price P_A of the output of region A from P_{A2} to P_{A1}. This fall in the output price will now reduce the marginal revenue product of both capital and labour employed in region A.

At the same time, as the output of region B falls from Q_{1B} to Q_{2B}, the price of the output produced by region B will have risen due to the contraction in the supply of the goods produced by region B, associated with the out-migration of both factors from region B. In Figure 6.5, this is represented by the backwards shift of region B's supply curve for output

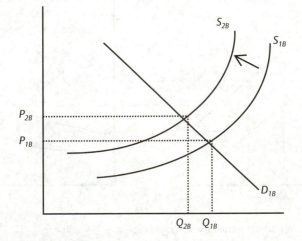

Fig. 6.5 Output market adjustment for contracting region

goods. This rise in the output price in region B will increase the marginal revenue product of both the capital and labour still employed in region B. Therefore, as region A's output prices fall and region B's output prices rise, the marginal products of capital in regions A and B converge. Similarly, the marginal products of labour in regions A and B converge. The process of factor migration, in which both factors move in the same direction, will continue until the marginal products of both factors are equalized across the two regions.

The actual point at which the two-sector migration will cease cannot be determined without additional information concerning the regional price elasticities of demand and supply. However, assuming that the initial inter-regional factor allocation is Pareto-efficient, such as at point T in Figure 6.3, the long-run effect of the 'two-sector' uni-directional factor migration can be depicted as a shift from point T to point U. Given that the contract curve is concave, the relative price of capital with respect to labour in both regions will be lower at point U than at point T. In Figure 6.3 we can see this change in relative factor prices by observing the change in slope of the marginal rate of substitution, which is perpendicular to the contract curve. However, for both capital and labour, the marginal factor products and factor rewards will be equalized across both regions.

In the two-sector model of inter-regional factor allocation, the two regions are assumed to produce different products with different production functions. One region's production, region A, is capital-intensive and the other region's production, region B, is labour-intensive. This implies that the marginal rate of transformation of production between the two regions is constantly changing according the level of output in each region. This is represented in Figure 6.6 by a concave production possibility frontier, in which a movement along the inter-regional contract curve from T to U is represented by a movement down the production possibility frontier.

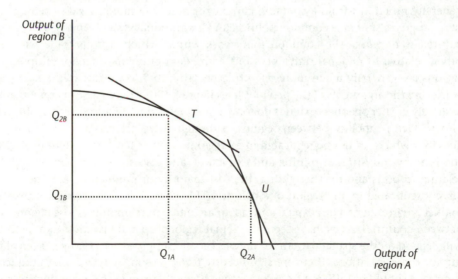

Fig. 6.6 Two-sector inter-regional production possibility frontier

6.2.3 **The relationship between the one-sector and two-sector regional models**

The slope of the production possibility frontier represents the marginal rate of transformation between the two outputs, and is given by the ratio of the marginal costs of production of the two goods at that particular output mix. In the one-sector inter-regional model, as we see in Figure 6.2, the inter-regional production possibility frontier is a straight line. This implies that the ratio of the marginal costs of production between the two regions is both constant and independent of the level of output in each region. In effect, the two regions exhibit production functions which are identical to each other in terms of their factor proportions. However, this is quite different from the case of the two-sector model, where the regional production functions are fundamentally different from each other in terms of their factor proportions. This is reflected by the fact that the ratio of the marginal costs of production between the two regions is constantly changing and depends on the level of output in each region. The shapes of both the contract curve and the production possibility frontier in the two-sector model are shapes which are familiar in simple general equilibrium frameworks and models of international trade based on comparative advantage. On the other hand, the linear shape of both the contract curve and the production possibility frontier in the one-sector model are somewhat different from these other models. This leaves us with the problem of determining which of these two model approaches better captures the fundamental nature of the regional factor allocation process.

In order to answer the question of whether the one-sector-model or the two-sector-model approach better models the fundamental nature of the regional factor allocation process, there are several issues which we can point to. The first point is that different regions within a single country are generally assumed to be much more open to each other than different countries are to each other. This is because regional economies generally function within a common currency regime, a common legal system, a common language system, a common political and institutional system, and also a common cultural framework. The common framework within which regions trade with each other, relative to national differences in trading environments, therefore implies that regions are generally much more open to each other than countries are to each other. Following the arguments of the previous five chapters of this book, we can argue that this relatively greater openness extends not only to mutual regional trading relationships, but also to factor mobility between regions. Although there are certain location-specific activities which cannot be replicated in all regions, such as land-based activities within the primary industries of mining and extraction, and also some water-borne activities relating to ports and river freighting, the vast majority of production activities can be largely replicated in any region of a country. This is because in a broadly competitive market environment, both capital and labour are much more mobile across regions than between countries. As we have seen, the actual regional spatial distribution of activities will depend on the spatial patterns of the market and supply areas. However, even allowing for these variations, there are significantly fewer reasons why regional production functions should be different from each other, in comparison with the production functions of different countries, at least when defined in terms of their factor proportions.

Regions generally exhibit maximum factor mobility, relative to countries, and on this argument, inter-regional economic systems will tend to approximate more closely to the one-sector model than to the two-sector model. In terms of our two region examples above, the inter-regional allocation of factors is generally better represented by Figures 6.1 and 6.2 rather than Figure 6.3 and 6.6, except where regional output is dominated by location-specific land-based primary industries.

In order to illustrate the logic of this argument we can imagine a hypothetical case of two separate countries A and B, which subsequently merge into a single country of two regions. In Figure 6.7, in the initial time period during which the countries are separate, the respective production relationships are represented by point V. At this factor allocation, country A exhibits a capital-intensive production function which employs K_{AV} units of capital and L_{AV} units of labour, while country B exhibits a labour-intensive production function employing K_{BV} units of capital and L_{BV} units of labour. The two countries produce different goods and then trade according to Ricardian principles of comparative advantage.

In the subsequent time period, the two countries merge into a single country of two regions A and B. This encourages factors to flow in between both regions in order to effect an efficient inter-regional factor allocation. If the production functions of the two regions continue to be quite different, due to location-specific land-based characteristics, the new inter-regional contract curve will be represented by the two-sector concave contract

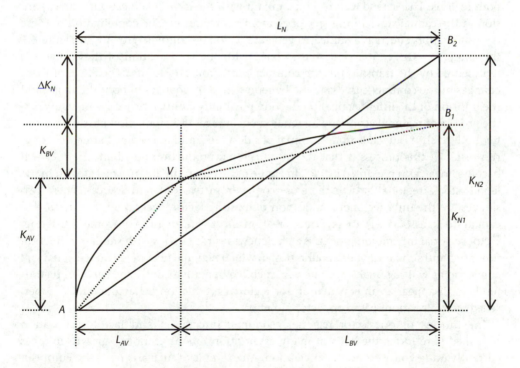

Fig. 6.7 Edgeworth–Bowley box adjustment from a two-sector to a one-sector inter-regional model

curve AB_1. On the other hand, if the vast majority of factors are mobile, the factor flows will be primarily of a one-sector nature, in that capital will flow from region A to region B, and labour will migrate from region B to region A. These one-sector flows will mean that the inter-regional contract curve will tend to become less concave, the long-run result of which is for the contract curve to become linear. In Figure 6.7 this is represented by the contract curve AB_2. Most analyses of inter-regional economic integration assume that in the long run, the one-sector model of inter-regional factor flows will be the primary mode of regional factor reallocation, and will dominate any two-sector adjustments.

At the same time as encouraging the reallocation of existing factors, the process of regional economic integration is also assumed to encourage additional mutual trading links between the regions. Assuming the total population of the two areas remains more or less constant, this inter-regional trade creation effect will generate additional national capital stocks. In our Edgeworth–Bowley box analysis we can represent this capital expansion effect by an extension to the vertical dimensions of the box. The extent of the capital expansion which occurs with the process of regional economic integration is represented in Figure 6.7 by $\Delta K_N = (K_{N2} - K_{N1})$, and the level of capital growth associated with this trade creation effect is given by $(\Delta K_N / K_{N1})$.

The transition process associated with the regional economic integration therefore has two main features. The first feature is the inter-regional reallocation of factors according to the principles of the one-sector model, which leads to a general flattening of the contract curve, such that the capital/labour ratios tend towards being equalized across both regions. The second feature, concomitant with the factor reallocation, is an expansion in the capital stock of the area of economic integration. The combination of these two integration effects is assumed to generate regional economic growth. In Figure 6.7 the change in the contract curve associated with the combination of these effects is represented by the transition in the contract curve from AB_1 to AB_2. The effect of these changes in the contract curve can also be represented by changes in both the shape and the position of the inter-regional production possibility frontier. As we see in Figure 6.8, the process of regional economic integration encourages the production possibility frontier both to shift outwards from its initial position PPF_1, and to become flatter. The long-run result of this process is that the inter-regional production possibility frontier will become linear, as represented by PPF_2 in Figure 6.8. Even in the absence of a growth in the labour stock, regional growth therefore comes from two different sources. These two sources are the inter-regional reallocation of existing factor stocks, and the increase in capital stocks associated with any trade creation effect. The long-run outcome of this one-sector regional integration process is a tendency towards regions with similar production functions and similar capital/labour ratios, in which regional rates of return to capital will converge, as will regional wage rates. As such, comparative advantage between regions tends to disappear as an explanation for regional production behaviour, and is superseded by explanations based on factor mobility.

The process of one-sector regional economic integration and factor reallocation described here forms the basis of many assumptions about economic growth in areas currently undergoing economic integration. An example of such an area is the European Union. In the case of the European Union, the separate national economies have become progressively more integrated over the last half century. This integration process has

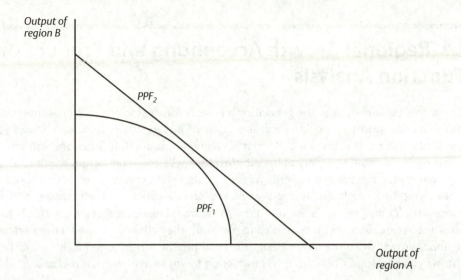

Fig. 6.8 Production possibility frontier adjustment from a two-sector to a one-sector inter-regional model

involved the progressive reduction of border tariffs and the removal of restrictions to trade and factor migration. This integration process was given an additional spur at the beginning of the 1990s, with the introduction of a common EU passport system, which allows for the free migration of labour between all EU nations for reasons of employment. Such institutional arrangements ought to allow for a one-sector reallocation of factors across the EU, as well as some potential regional trade and capital creation effects. If this one-sector argument is indeed correct, over time we should observe a tendency towards regional convergence within the European Union. Evidence supporting this one-sector argument was first provided by Barro and Sala-i-Martin (1992, 1995). They suggested that the level of dispersion across the EU regions of real income per head had fallen over time, a process which they termed 'σ-convergence'. Barro and Sala-i-Martin also found evidence to suggest that there is a negative relationship between the rate of growth in income per head and the initial level of income per head, a process which they term 'β-convergence'. Although there has been much debate as to the appropriateness of the data employed by Barro and Sala-i-Martin and the interpretation of their results (Button and Pentecost 1999; Cheshire and Carbonaro 1995, 1996; Durlauf and Quah 1998; Fingleton and McCombie 1998; Martin and Sunley 1998), these tests of σ and β convergence are primarily motivated by the theoretical conclusions of the one-sector model of inter-regional factor allocation and growth.

6.3 **Regional Growth Accounting and Production Function Analysis**

The above sections lead to the general neoclassical conclusion that regional integration processes will lead to a one-sector reallocation of factors across regions. The long-run implications of this process will be that all regional production functions will tend to converge, such that regional capital labour ratios will converge across regions, as will regional capital returns and regional wages, and regional expansion paths will also all be linear. Output growth will increase as factors are allocated more efficiently, and this process itself may generate additional growth via trade creation effects. Analytically these conclusions are useful because, at least in principle, they allow us to model the sources of regional growth within a rather straightforward production function framework. To do this we can employ a Cobb–Douglas production function, which is defined as

$$Q_t = AK^\alpha L^\beta, \tag{6.3}$$

where Q_t is regional output at time t, t is time, A is a constant, K is regional capital stock, L is regional labour stock, α is share of capital in the regional economy, and β is share of labour in the regional economy.

The Cobb–Douglas production function has two useful properties. The first property is that it assumes that factor shares are constant, where the factor shares are represented by the relative contributions of profits and wages to the total factor payments in the economy. In the Cobb–Douglas function these fixed shares are represented by α and β, respectively. If the factor shares are assumed to be constant, this also implies that the capital/labour ratios are constant. The second property of the Cobb–Douglas production function is that production exhibits constant returns to scale, in terms of the relationship between the total output produced and the total quantities of input factors employed. A given quantity of capital and labour will produce a given quantity of output, the value of which is defined as a constant multiple A of the total value of the inputs. Therefore, doubling the quantity of both factor inputs employed will simply double the total level of output produced, *ceteris paribus*. The relationship between the level of output and the level of factor inputs is therefore independent of the total quantity of inputs employed or outputs produced. If this is so, it implies that the sum of the indices α plus β must equal 1. In other words $\beta = (1-\alpha)$. Our Cobb–Douglas model (6.3) must therefore be modified accordingly.

A second modification required to equation (6.3) concerns the question of time. Over time, the relationship between total output and inputs is not static, in the sense that new production techniques and technologies become available which increase the efficiency of the production process. The adoption and implementation of these new production techniques and technologies is known as 'innovation', and this process of innovation means that over time the level of output increases for any given stock of factor inputs. For our purposes, we will define this process of applying new techniques and technologies under the general heading of 'technology'. As such, technology represents the sets of production, organization, information, and communications blueprints which are available to all firms, and which mediate the relationship between the input factors employed and the output produced. We denote the level of technology by the technological index f. Assuming that the level of technology increases over time, we can incorporate a simple technological trajectory $e^{\varphi t}$ into the Cobb–Douglas function which allows for increases in technology over time t.

Our modified Cobb–Douglas function which incorporates both constant returns to scale with technological change over time now has the form of

$$Q_t = Ae^{\varphi t}K^a L^{1-a} \tag{6.4}$$

The one-sector inter-regional factor allocation model discussed in the previous sections implies that all regions will converge towards the same production function with the same constant capital/labour ratios. In the Cobb–Douglas function (6.4) the constant capital/labour ratio is given by $(a/1-a)$. Therefore, assuming that aggregate regional production across markets and industries can be regarded as perfectly competitive, the process of inter-regional factor reallocation should lead to all regions exhibiting the same Cobb–Douglas production function. In other words, if we can model the production function of one region, we can model the production function of all regions within the same economic system.

With this production function methodology we are now able to consider how the growth of regional output is related to changes in the various inputs to the production process. In order to convert our regional production function into a model of regional growth, we can convert equation (6.4) into natural logarithms and then differentiate with respect to time. The details of this are given in Appendix 6.1. By these steps we can convert equation (6.4) into a regional growth accounting expression

$$\dot{Q}_t = \varphi + a\dot{K}_t + (1-a)\dot{L}_t, \tag{6.5}$$

where $\dot{Q}_t$, $\dot{K}_t$, $\dot{L}_t$ represent the rates of growth of output, capital and labour at time t, respectively.

This growth accounting expression (6.5) states that the rate of growth of regional output at time t is the sum of the rates of growth of the input factors (capital and labour), weighted according to their relative contributions to the economy, plus the level of technology $\pi\eta\iota$. In these growth-accounting terms, the level of technology represents the contributions to regional growth which cannot be accounted for simply by changes in the optimally combined stocks of regional capital and labour. As such, the term f is sometimes refereed to as the 'Solow residual' or the 'growth of total factor productivity'. As we see in Appendix 6.1, the growth-accounting methodology of equation (6.5) can be shown to predict that in general, wage growth depends on the growth in the capital/labour ratio and also the level of technology. Moreover, in a long-run steady-state situation in which profit rates are constant, wage growth depends simply on the level of technology.

6.3.1 **Regional technology and endogenous growth**

From the point of view of growth accounting described by equation (6.5), we know that neoclassical regional growth depends on the changes in the regional factor stocks and the level of regional technology. Assuming that factors are mobile, there can be no systematic long-run differences in the growth rates of factors across regions, so any observed growth differences associated with differences in regional factor stocks can only be short- or medium-term adjustments to a Pareto-efficient factor allocation. On the other hand, from our growth-accounting approach we can also suggest that different regions may differ in terms of their growth performance according to systematic differences in the level of regional technology f. However, in order to understand how this might come about, it is necessary for us to consider exactly what we mean by 'technology', and to determine how technological differences may be related to geography.

We have defined technology as the complete set of production, organization, information, and communications blueprints which are available to all firms, and which mediate the relationship between the input factors employed and the outputs produced. However, there is a general consensus that in reality the application of new technology across all firms, industries, and regions is not a process which takes place instantaneously, as is assumed by the model of perfect competition. In actual fact, the cumulative diffusion of technology over time tends to exhibit an 'S-shaped' form (Gomulka 1971; Dosi 1988), where technology diffusion refers to the time taken for a particular invention or innovation to be adopted across all firms, sectors, or regions. This cumulative 'S-shaped' form is represented by Figure 6.9 by the curve OY. As we see, the rate of technological diffusion is initially very low, although it is gradually increasing. After a while, the rate of technology diffusion reaches its maximum, represented by the slope RR' in Figure 6.9, after which it begins to slow. Eventually, the technology will have been spread throughout all firms,

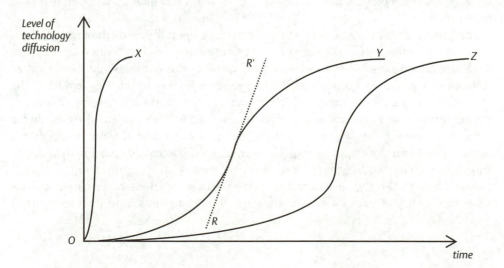

Fig. 6.9 Technology diffusion over time

sectors, and regions, such that the rate of additional technology diffusion approaches zero.

The general assumptions of the neoclassical one-sector theoretical model are that in an environment of perfectly competitive markets and factor mobility, the level of technology will be dispersed through all sectors and all regions in the economy instantaneously. However, in reality, if we assume that markets are broadly competitive, the one-sector model implies that technologal diffusion takes place at the maximum possible rate, such that complete technological diffusion is reached almost immediately. In terms of Figure 6.9 this implies that the technology diffusion process is represented by the curve *OX*. This assumption itself implies that there will be no systematic long-run differences in the level of regional technology, and that the growth benefits associated with new technology will be maximized in all regions. On the other hand, these neoclassical conclusions may initially appear to contradict some of the agglomeration conclusions of Chapter 2 of this book, which suggested that growth may be localized for long periods, because certain technological advantages tend to remain in particular locations. Similarly, Chapter 5 suggested that growth possibilities may vary geographically according to persistent differences in the spatial distribution of human capital. In terms of Figure 6.9 these arguments would imply that technology diffusion in reality tends to exhibit a trajectory which is best represented by the curve *OZ*, such that systematic differences in regional technology, and consequently regional growth, would appear to be possible. Therefore, the arguments of both of these chapters may appear to be somewhat at odds with the long-run conclusions of the one-sector neoclassical model. There have been many recent analytical developments in production function analysis which attempt to reconcile localized growth with neoclassical competitive market conditions. These various developments are generally grouped under the headings of 'new growth theory' or 'endogenous growth theory'.

The initial contribution to 'endogenous growth theory' comes from Romer (1986, 1987*a*), and involves accounting for growth within an orthodox neoclassical growth-accounting framework, while at the same time dispensing with the need for an exogenous technology residual (McCombie and Thirlwall 1994). The approach assumes that increasing specialization increases output, and as such, output is defined as a function of the number of units of specialized capital goods, rather than simply as an aggregate capital stock. Under certain assumptions Romer shows that the production function can be expressed as

$$Q_t = AL^\beta K \tag{6.6}$$

and by transforming equation (6.6) into a logarithm form and differentiating with respect to time gives

$$\dot{Q}_t = \beta \dot{L}_t + \dot{K}_t, \tag{6.7}$$

where $\beta = (1 - a)$ as above. The argument here is that all growth is accounted for in terms of the growth of inputs, with the key issue being the level of specialized capital inputs and the associated benefits of labour specialization. As we have seen in Chapter 2, one of the arguments underlying the agglomeration model is that of increasing location-specific specialization. If such specialization is indeed place-specific, then the endogenous growth model implies that the benefits of this growth will also tend to be localized.

Romer (1987b) discusses a second potential source of endogenous growth, which is the stock of knowledge. In order to account for this we can write a production function as

$$Q_t = f(K,L,E)g(N),\tag{6.8}$$

where E represents firm-specific knowledge, N represents generally available knowledge, and f and g are functional relationships. If we assume that N increases at the same rate as E, which itself increases at the same rate as K, and we also assume that F is a Cobb–Douglas functional relationship, total output can be written as

$$Q_t = f(K,L)g(K) = (L^{1-a}K^a)K^\psi.\tag{6.9}$$

The increasing returns are external to the firm, and this ensures that a competitive equilibrium is preserved (McCombie and Thirlwall 1994). In growth-rate terms equation (6.9) becomes

$$\dot{Q}_t = (1-a)\dot{L}_t + (a+\psi)\dot{K}_t,\tag{6.10}$$

If $(a+\psi)$ is equal to 1, growth will be constant. However, if $(a+\psi)$ is greater than 1 growth will be continuously positive and cumulative, and if $(a+\psi)$ is less than 1 we will observe continuous decline.

Both of these Romer models conclude that the portion of output growth which would be considered as a technology residual in the neoclassical model can be attributed entirely to capital acquisition. In the former case, this is because knowledge growth is assumed to increase directly in line with the level of specialized capital stock, whereas in the latter case it is because of the assumption that knowledge increases with the level of capital inputs.

Lucas (1988) also discusses knowledge inputs, but the focus of his model is on the level of human capital, rather than firm-specific capital. In his approach, we assume that workers spend a fraction of their time u acquiring human capital H. Following our discussion in Chapter 5 we assume that human capital increases the productivity of the individual person. However, Lucas assumes that this 'internal' effect H also has an 'external' effect J which benefits all other workers. With these assumptions we can write our production function as

$$Q_t = (uHL)^{1-a}K^a J^\varphi.\tag{6.11}$$

If we also assume that the external human-capital effect J is equal to the internal human-capital effect H, equation (6.11) can be rewritten as

$$Q_t = (uH^\theta L)^{1-a}K^a,\tag{6.12}$$

where $\theta = (1-a+\gamma)/(1-a)$. In order to make growth endogenous this model requires us to define the growth of human capital as

$$\frac{dH}{dt} = H^\rho v(1-u),\tag{6.13}$$

where ρ and v are constants, with ρ being greater than or equal to 1, such that there are no diminishing returns to the generation of human capital. If we take the simplest case where ρ is equal to one, the rate of growth of human capital defined by equation (6.13) is a constant λ. This allows us to rewrite equation (6.12) as

$$Q_t = (uL_q e^{\lambda t})^{1-a} K^a, \tag{6.14}$$

where L_q represents the number of units of labour of a given level of efficiency and quality and is given by $L_q = H^\theta \Lambda$. As such, a given number of units of labour of increasing human capital can be regarded as equivalent to an increasing number of units of labour of a fixed efficiency and quality. In growth rate terms equation (6.14) becomes (McCombie and Thirlwall 1994)

$$\dot{Q}_t = (1-a)(\lambda + \dot{L}_t) + a\dot{K}_t = (1-a)(\dot{L}_q)_t + a\dot{K}_t. \tag{6.15}$$

This model concludes that the portion of output growth which would be considered as a technology residual in the neoclassical model can be attributed entirely to labour through human-capital acquisition.

These various models of endogenous growth provide different insights into the possible sources of cumulative growth. For our purposes, we can relate each of these potential sources of cumulative growth to spatial arguments (Nijkamp and Poot 1998). The Romer models suggest that endogenous growth can arise due to an increasing variety of specialized capital goods, or an increasing knowledge base associated with these capital goods and the associated externality effects of information spillovers. Meanwhile, the Lucas model suggests that endogenous growth can arise due to private investments in human capital, the benefits of which also spill over to the surrounding environment. However, identifying empirically whether or not localized growth takes place, and isolating the sources of such growth, is very difficult because by definition such effects are positive externalities. In order to circumvent these problems, various indirect methods have been employed to empirically measure systematic growth differences across regions according to location-specific technology effects. Analyses have attempted to examine if there are any systematic differences in the spatial extent of information flows, by testing for variations in the spatial distribution of patent citations (Jaffe *et al.* 1993), variations in the spatial distribution of research and development activities (Cantwell and Iammarino 2000), or variations in the spatial distribution of technology-related infrastructure such as universities (Acs *et al.* 1992). Most of these indirect methods do provide support for the arguments relating to agglomeration externalities, in that there are various localized technological effects which do not diffuse quickly across space.

A weakness of aspatial endogenous growth theory, however, is that without diminishing returns to either capital or human capital accumulation, growth will be implausibly explosive (Solow 1994). If we apply this logic to regional development, this would imply that all activities will converge to one single location. However, as we saw in Chapter 2, the spatial nature of the economy can provide brakes on any such explosive process. This is because providing for spatial markets inherently involves the problem of the overcoming of space. Moreover, congestion effects are always associated with industrial clustering in space, and beyond a certain point these negative externalities can work against cumulative clustering. The balance of these positive and negative externality effects will lead to factor reallocations in which long-run real returns to factors across space will still tend towards equalization.

Although endogenous growth agglomeration models are not consistent with all development becoming localized at a single point, they are, on the other hand, perfectly consistent with the notion that new innovations may persistently tend to originate at the same locations, even in an environment in which markets are broadly competitive. As we saw in Chapter 2, this type of argument comes from the application of product-cycle arguments to the agglomeration models. The localized positive externality effects in the areas in which the innovations originate will generate appreciations in local real estate prices, such that in the long run, real returns to factors will tend to be equalized across regions. On the other hand, however, a permanent disequilibrium in nominal factor returns is perfectly possible, in which certain innovative regions always exhibit higher nominal factor prices. These areas will tend to be the central dominant cities and regions of the spatial economy, while the more geographically and economically peripheral regions of the economy will tend to exhibit lower nominal, but much more equal, real factor returns. Short- or medium-term localized growth effects in space are therefore perfectly consistent with an underlying one-sector model of inter-regional factor allocation. However, long-term localized growth is not consistent with a one-sector model of regional factor allocation, because geographically localized congestion costs will become evident. At the same time, as we see from the location models discussed in Chapters 1 and 3, systematic centre-periphery differences in nominal returns to factors can be perfectly consistent with a one-sector model of factor allocation.

6.4 Keynesian Perspectives on Regional Growth and Balance of Payments

An alternative approach to the analysis of regional growth comes from a broadly Keynesian perspective, and involves discussions of the role played by inter-regional income flows. In Chapter 4, we saw that the local intra-regional linkages between firms and factors within a region, and the relationship between these local linkages and external demand stimuli from outside of the region, can be modelled, at least in principle, by a regional multiplier analysis based on income flows. A key feature which distinguishes these Keynesian regional models from national multiplier models is that the treatment of the relationship between local investment expenditure and local regional income at the regional level is somewhat different in nature from that at the national level. In particular, regional-government expenditure flows tend to run counter to regional income, whereas private-sector investment tends to be very sensitive to local regional income, independent of national economic conditions.

Assuming that private sector investment levels are greater than public sector investment flows, this means that the funds locally available for current investments are dependent on current income levels. The importance of this observation lies in the fact that greater current levels of local investment expenditure imply that the regional capital stock can be more effectively expanded and upgraded. From our discussion of endogenous growth in section 6.3.1 above, it was argued that the quality of local inputs in general may be a function of the stock of local capital. Moreover, following the endogenous-growth models relating to human-capital investments, and allied with our discussions in Chapters 2 and 5 relating to local specialized inputs and human capital, the observation that the future local capital stock is a function of current local income, would therefore suggest that future growth may be constrained by current income levels.

As well as this, we also see from Chapter 4, however, that current income-expenditure levels are constrained by the level of output demand. In the case of regions, we generally assume that much of a region's output is consumed outside of the region. As such, local regional expenditure is constrained by the level of regional export income earned. This is the basis of the Keynesian approach to regional growth, which posits that regional growth is constrained by a regional balance of payments constraint. While there are some commentators who would question the validity of a balance of payments discussion applied to regions (Richardson 1978), the fact that we attempt to discuss inter-regional trade patterns means that there must be equivalent inter-regional income flows. Moreover, from a Keynesian perspective, the justification for such an analytical approach is that these income flows may themselves have additional monetary effects, which are in addition to any real income effects associated with spatial factor adjustments.

6.4.1 The balance of payments approach to regional growth

In order to understand the logic behind the balance of payments approach to regional growth, we can once again consider the simple regional income-expenditure model of the type discussed in Chapter 4

$$Y_r = (C_r + I_r + G_r) + (X_r - M_r). \tag{6.16}$$

The first three terms on the right-hand side of equation (6.16) represent the components of aggregate demand associated with the domestic activity within the regional economy, and we can group these under the heading of 'regional domestic absorption' A_r. Meanwhile the last two components on the right-hand side of equation (6.16) represent the components of aggregate regional demand associated with the inter-regional traded sector. In general terms, from (6.16) we can write

$$(Y_r - A_r) = (X_r - M_r). \tag{6.17}$$

where $(Y_r - A_r)$ is equal to the net acquisition of assets from other regions.

In order to see why the difference between regional income and regional domestic absorption is the net acquisition of assets from other regions, we must begin with a discussion of a balance of payments model at national level, and then translate this argument to the case of regions. At a national level the simplest balance of payments model can be defined as

$$CA_N + KA_N + BOF_N = 0, \tag{6.18}$$

where CA_N is balance of payments on the national current account, KA_N is balance of payments on the national capital account, and BOF_N is balance of official national financing.

In a simple model of national balance of payments as represented by equation (6.18), the first two terms on the left-hand side represent the net flows of income from economic activities. The balance of payments on the current account represents the net money flows from all trade in goods and services, plus the net flows of interest and dividends from all assets held overseas by domestic citizens, and all overseas-owned domestic assets. The balance of payments on the current account is therefore much broader than simply the balance of trade, which refers only to the trade in goods. If the current account is in surplus, this means that the country is building up domestic money holdings, which originate as overseas currency and are then denominated in the domestic currency. The price of the home currency will rise relative to the foreign currency. Meanwhile, the balance of payments on the capital account represents a country's net acquisition of foreign assets via international financial lending and borrowing, and represents domestic citizens' net gain in titles to overseas-located wealth. If the capital account is in surplus, this implies that inflows of money from other countries used to purchase domestic assets are greater than outflows of money used to purchase assets in other countries. Together, the balance of payments on the current and capital accounts represents the net total balance of payments surplus. The balance of official financing is the amount required to keep the internationally earned income and expenditure accounts balanced, and is equal to the net difference in the demand and supply for the domestic currency in the foreign exchange markets

$$CA_N + KA_N = -BOF_N. \tag{6.19}$$

If we rearrange equation (6.18) to give (6.19), we can see that if the left-hand side of (6.19) is positive, the country is regarded as running a balance of payments surplus, and if the left-hand side of equation (6.19) is negative, the country is regarded as running a balance of payments deficit. If a country is running a balance of payments surplus, it must be either increasing its stock of foreign assets, or alternatively reducing its indebtedness to foreign citizens. On the other hand, where a country is running a balance of payments deficit, it must be either reducing its stock of foreign assets, or alternatively increasing its indebtedness to foreign citizens. These wealth adjustments are mediated via transactions in the international currency markets.

In the case of inter-regional trade, because all transactions within a common currency regime are denominated in the same currency, there can be no official financing as such. Moreover, from Chapter 4 we know that regions do not have customs or trade barriers. However, in principle, we can still write a balance of payments expression for a region, the key feature of which is that the right-hand side of equation (6.19) must always be zero when applied to regions. In inter-regional terms, therefore, our balance of payments expression must be

$$CA_R + KA_R = 0. \tag{6.20}$$

where CA_R is balance of payments on the regional current account and KA_R is balance of payments on the regional capital account, which rearranges to

$$CA_N = -KA_N. \tag{6.21}$$

In other words, the net surplus in a region's trade in goods and services with other regions, given by $(X_r–M_r)$ in equation (6.17), is balanced by the region's net acquisition of assets from other regions, given by $(Y_r–A_r)$ in equation (6.17). For example, if a regional exporting industry is very successful, this implies that the income generated by the exports can be used both to import goods and services from other regions and also to buy more assets in other regions. These asset purchases will include real estate assets in other regions as well as share acquisitions in firms located in other regions. Similarly, if a region is running a balance of payments deficit, it must be financed by net sales of domestically held assets to buyers from other regions. If a region is running a balance of payments equilibrium, in means that the net acquisition of assets from other regions is zero. The problem with balance of payments surpluses or deficits is that they cannot continue indefinitely. In particular, if a region is experiencing a balance of payments deficit, there will only be a finite stock of domestically held assets and properties within the region which can be sold to external buyers in order to finance the regional deficit. Therefore, a region cannot maintain a long-run balance of payments deficit. This implies that, as well as the level of domestic absorption, the level of regional income which it is possible to maintain in the long run, depends on the level of regional exports.

In order to see this we can consider a country comprised of two regions A and B, whereby region A exhibits weak investment demand while region B exhibits strong investment demand. By definition, regions do not have any independent control over monetary issues, as these are determined by the central banking authorities. Therefore, the rate of interest prevailing in any one region is equal to the rate of interest in any other region. As such, we can regard the individual region as a small open economy in which the LM curve is horizontal.

In Figure 6.10, the rate of interest in both regions is given as r^*. At this rate of interest, in region A, the local investment component of regional domestic absorption is only sufficient to generate a regional income level of Y_A. If the investment income required to generate full local employment is given by Y_{FA}, the local shortfall in labour market demand, expressed in terms of income, is given by $(Y_{FA}–Y_A)$. Meanwhile, in region B, the level of local investment is just sufficient to generate a level of regional income which clears the labour market at the prevailing rate of interest. Therefore, a simple comparison of the differences between the situations in the two regions would suggest that the labour market in region A would clear if there was a fall in the local interest rate from r^* to r_1, whereas for region B, if rates fell below r^* the local labour supply constraints would lead to localized inflation. However, without an independent currency we know that, by definition, regions do not have the ability to adjust local interest rates. Therefore, if the monetary authorities presiding over both regions are charged with maintaining price stability, they will ensure that interest rates are kept at a level of r^* so as to maximize the total employment level in the two regions. This will mean that the buoyant region maintains full employment whereas the depressed region exhibits a local labour demand shortfall.

One way of alleviating this labour market imbalance is for unemployed labour to migrate from region A to region B. However, as we see in Chapter 5, there are many

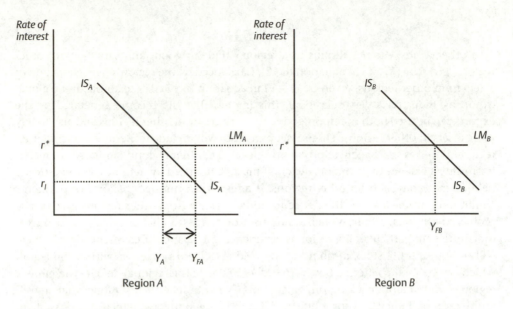

Fig. 6.10 Regional investment levels

conditions under which inter-regional labour market adjustment processes are rather inefficient. In the absence of local currency and interest rate adjustments, if a region cannot generate internal investment levels I_R^*, the only other mechanism a region has for expanding is through an expansion in its exports.

In Figure 6.11 the upper right-hand quadrant contains our familiar income-expenditure diagram. However, in this particular case, we are assuming that the level of internally generated regional domestic investment I_R^* is constant, as are the externally determined regional interest rates r^*. By reading from right to left in the upper left-hand quadrant of Figure 6.11, we can observe the inverse relationship between regional domestic investment and interest rates. The lower left-hand quadrant simply plots inter-est rates against interest rates, and the lower right-hand quadrant represents the indi-vidual regional investment market as in Figure 6.10. As we see in the income-expenditure model, as regional exports increase, we can model the resulting income increase for a given level of domestic investment I_R^* and interest rates r^*, by adjusting the origin and x-axis vertically downwards by exactly the amount of the export increase $\varDelta X$. The increase in exports provides for an increase in regional income from Y_1 to Y_2, which at the prevailing rate of interest implies that domestic regional investment increases from IS_1 to IS_2. At current interest rates, the increase in regional exports therefore generates increases in regional investment due to a general increase in regional income. This possibility has already been raised in our discussion of an export base 'super-multiplier' in Chapter 4. In Keynesian regional models, the level of regional exports consequently plays a key role in determining the level of domestic investment which is sustainable, in situations where local currency and interest rates adjustments are not possible.

What we have not yet considered, however, is the question of what determines the level of regional exports, sustainable investment, and income in the long run. In order to

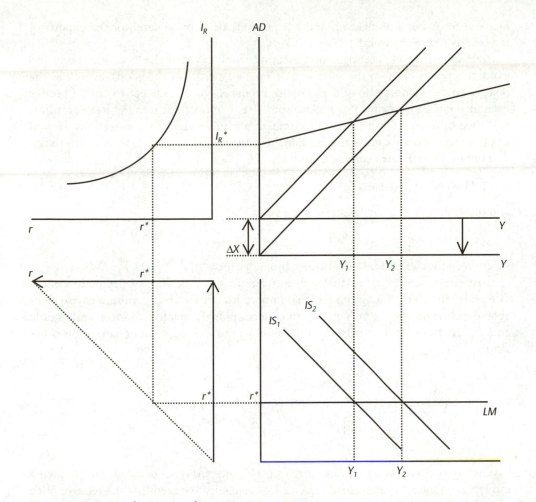

Figure 6.11 Regional exports and investment

discuss this, we can write a simple general long-run regional import demand function as (Thirlwall 1980; McCombie and Thirlwall 1994):

$$M_r = aY_r^{\pi}\left(\frac{P_f}{P_r}e\right)^u,$$ (6.22)

where M_r is regional imports, Y_r is regional income, π is regional income elasticity of demand for imports, P_f is nominal price of goods produced in other regions, P_r is nominal price of goods produced in the domestic region, e is exchange rate, and μ is price elasticity of demand for imports

Similarly, we can write a simple long-run regional export demand function as

$$X_r = bZ^{\varepsilon}\left(\frac{P_r}{eP_f}\right)^{\eta},$$ (6.23)

where X_r is regional exports, Z is rest of the world income, ε is world income elasticity of demand for exports of region r, and η is price elasticity of demand for the exports of region r by rest of the world.

These import and export demand functions simply say that the level of imports and exports depends both on the price and income elasticities of the goods, as well as the relative prices of domestic and externally produced goods, subject to the respective exchange rate movements. If we transform these two functions into natural logarithms and then differentiate with respect to time, in a manner analogous to sections 6.3 and 6.3.1, we can derive expressions describing import and export growth rates, respectively. Our import growth rate expression becomes

$$(\dot{M}_r)_t = \pi(\dot{Y}_r)_t + \mu\left[(\dot{P}_f)_t + \dot{e}_t - (\dot{P}_r)_t\right] \tag{6.24}$$

and our export growth rate expression becomes

$$(\dot{X}_r)_t = \varepsilon(\dot{Z})_t + \eta\left[(\dot{P}_r)_t - \dot{e}_t - (\dot{P}_f)_t\right], \tag{6.25}$$

where growth rates at time t are denoted by a dot superscript.

In the long run, we know that a region cannot run a balance of payments deficit. Therefore, the level of long-run regional import growth which is continuously sustainable, depends on the region's growth in exports, plus the relative changes in domestic and external production costs and prices, subject to exchange rate changes. In other words

$$\dot{M}_r = \dot{X}_r + \left[\dot{P}_r - \dot{P}_f - \dot{e}\right]. \tag{6.26}$$

Inserting equations (6.24) and (6.25) into equation (6.26) gives

$$\dot{Y}_r = \frac{\varepsilon\dot{Z} + (1+\eta+\mu)\left[\dot{P}_r - \dot{P}_f - \dot{e}\right]}{\pi}. \tag{6.27}$$

When these Keynesian (or more strictly post-Keynesian) types of balance of payments models are applied to the case of regions, it is generally assumed that the relative price effects contained in the square numerator bracket of equation (6.27) are relatively unimportant. There are three major reasons for this assumption. The first reason is that regions do not exhibit the capacity to make independent currency adjustments. Secondly, it is assumed that most prices are set in oligopolistic industries, which ensure relative price stability between competing producers, even in the face of cost changes (Lavoie 1992; Davidson 1994). Thirdly, it is assumed that geographical transactions costs and spatial competition mean that differences in nominal prices between regions also remain relatively stable over long periods. Under these assumptions, the long-run regional equilibrium balance of payments expression reduces to

$$\dot{Y}_r = \frac{\varepsilon\dot{Z}}{\pi} = \frac{\dot{X}_r}{\pi}, \tag{6.28}$$

In other words, the maximum balance of payments constrained long-run growth rate of a region is equal to the long-run growth in world income, multiplied by the ratio of the world income elasticity of demand for the exports of the region divided by the regional income elasticity of demand for imports. This in turn is equal to the long-run rate of growth of regional exports, divided by the regional income elasticity of demand for imports.

The long-run growth of regional income is therefore determined by the ratio of the income elasticities of demand for the region's exports and for its imports. This depends on the qualitative mix of production sectors in a region. If a region is dominated by the production of high value-added, highly income-elastic and low-price elasticity goods, its export growth will tend to be consistently strong over time for any given pattern of regional imports. Similarly, if a region is dominated by industries with strong local linkages, its import growth will tend to be relatively low over time, for any given pattern of exporting. A combination of highly income-elastic exports and a low regional income-elasticity of demand for imports will therefore tend to allow a high long-run level of regional growth, even allowing for the fact that growth may be constrained by a balance of payments constraint.

6.4.2 The Verdoorn Law and cumulative growth

The final component of Keynesian or post-Keynesian regional growth theory concerns the question of economies of scale. In this approach, the analysis of economies of scale centres on the so-called 'Verdoorn Law' (Verdoorn 1949), which posits a positive relationship between the rate of growth of labour productivity and the growth of output. The Verdoorn relationship is given by

$$\dot{p} = a + b\dot{Q},\qquad(6.29)$$

where $\dot{p}$ represents the rate of growth of labour productivity, and $\dot{Q}$ represents the rate of growth of output. Based on empirical observations, the Verdoorn Law assumes that the value of a is approximately 2 per cent, and that the value of b, the Verdoorn coefficient, is 0.5. These values can be shown to be broadly consistent with a neo-classical production in which the indices a plus b sum to 1.33 (McCombie and Thirlwall 1994).

If we use the notation employed above in sections 6.3 and 6.3.1, we can rewrite equation (6.29) as

$$(\dot{Q}-\dot{L}) = a + b\dot{Q},\qquad(6.30)$$

Initial observation of equation (6.30) suggests that econometric estimation of the relationship posited by equation (6.29) will exhibit a simultaneity problem, because the term representing the rate of growth of output appears on both sides of the equation. While the treatment of this issue has been the subject of much debate (Kaldor 1975; Rowthorn 1975; Scott 1989; McCombie and Thirlwall 1994), the general assumption in post-Keynesian models is that the direction of causation is explicitly from right to left (Boulier 1984). In other words, increasing output growth is regarded as engendering dynamic economies of scale in production, via both 'learning by doing' effects on the part of labour (Arrow 1962), and also the increased capital accumulation effects associated with easy credit availability in conditions of expanding output. If the assumption of Verdoorn dynamic economies of scale is now included in our discussion of regional balance of payments constraints, by following the diagrammatic approach of Dixon and Thirlwall

(1975) we can indicate the various regional growth trajectories which are possible under a regime of cumulative causation.

In Figure 6.12, we observe a set of conditions which gives rise to a constant regional output growth rate. In the upper right-hand quadrant we see that the regional export growth rate is x, and with an income elasticity of regional demand for imports given by π_1, this leads to a balance of payments constrained output growth rate of q. Via the Verdoorn effect, in the upper left-hand quadrant we see that this output growth engenders a local labour productivity growth of h. In the lower left-hand quadrant, we see that this itself leads to quality adjusted real price reductions of regional output, which fall at a rate of s. As we discussed above, in these models we assume that relative prices remain more or less the same across regions. However, for given output prices, labour productivity gains will be realized in terms of real quality improvements. Moreover, these regional output quality improvements will be transmitted in the lower right-hand quadrant to increases in regional export growth x, the actual extent of which will depend on the income elasticity of demand for the region's exports ε_1. In this particular case the export growth will itself lead to a steady-state regional output growth rate of q. As we see from Figure 6.12, however, there is no particular equilibrium steady-state rate of regional growth towards which the region will converge.

In these Keynesian type models, there is no reason why steady-state regional growth should be automatic. For example, if a region is characterized by a dense clustering of industries which exhibit agglomeration economies, the region will tend to produce highly innovative outputs and will also purchase large quantities of its input require-

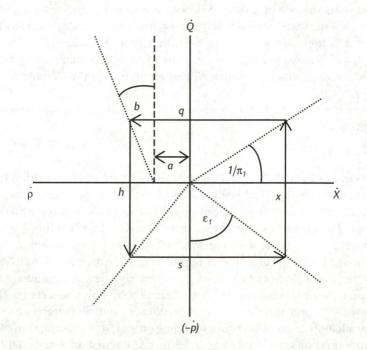

Fig. 6.12 Steady-state regional growth

ments from within the local regional economy. This will imply that the income elasticity of demand for the region's outputs will tend to be greater than under the case of steady-state growth, and also that the regional income elasticity of demand for imports will be relatively low. In the case of imports, we can compare this situation with that of the steady-state growth rate of Figure 6.12, by shifting upwards the line in the upper right-hand quadrant of Figure 6.13, which represents the inverse of the income elasticity of demand for imports, from $1/\pi_1$ to $1/\pi_2$. Similarly, in the case of exports, we can shift outwards the line in the lower right-hand quadrant of Figure 6.13, which represents the income elasticity of demand for the region's exports, from ε_1 to ε_2. As we see, in such a set of circumstances, the combination of highly income-elastic exports, a low income-elasticity of regional imports, and increasing returns to scale, can give rise to cumulative growth. The actual rate of regional growth depends on the particular values of the regional import and export elasticities.

Similarly, we can envisage the opposite type of situation, in which a region is dominated by the production of relatively low income-elasticity exports, while at the same time being very dependent on imports. For example, this type of situation could occur in a relatively low-demand peripheral region which has suffered severe industrial decline and the loss of many local firms, and which has subsequently experienced employment growth in establishments which are relatively 'footloose'. In this case, the level of expenditure in the local economy by both the new and old firms will tend to be very small. Moreover, if both the new and old firms in the region are specialized in the

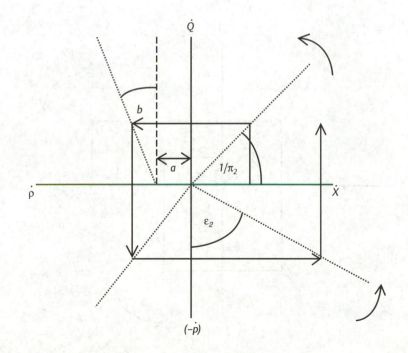

Fig. 6.13 Cumulative regional growth

production of rather standardized 'mature' products, the income elasticity of demand for the region's exports will be very low.

In the case of imports, we can compare this situation with that of the steady-state growth rate of Figure 6.12, by shifting downwards the line in the upper right-hand quadrant of Figure 6.14, which represents the inverse of the income elasticity of demand for imports, from $1/\pi_1$ to $1/\pi_3$. Similarly, in the case of exports, we can shift inwards the line in the lower right-hand quadrant of Figure 6.13, which represents the income elasticity of demand for the region's exports, from ε_1 to ε_3. As we see, in such a set of circumstances, the combination of low income-elasticity exports, a high income-elasticity of regional imports, and increasing returns to scale, can give rise to cumulative decline. As above, the actual rate of regional decline depends on the particular values of the regional import and export elasticities.

These Keynesian and post-Keynesian approaches to regional growth differ fundamentally from neoclassical models in their basic assumptions. In particular, these models do not require the assumption that factors are paid according to their marginal products. Nor do they require the assumption that production exhibits constant returns to scale with respect to input factors. However, in a similar manner to models of endogenous growth, these models imply that there is no particular long-run rate of growth towards which a region is expected to converge. The actual regional growth rates will therefore depend on the extent to which agglomeration economies or diseconomies are operative. Moreover, in terms of regional growth these Keynesian and neoclassical models can be shown to produce largely equivalent results, such that the interpretation of empirical

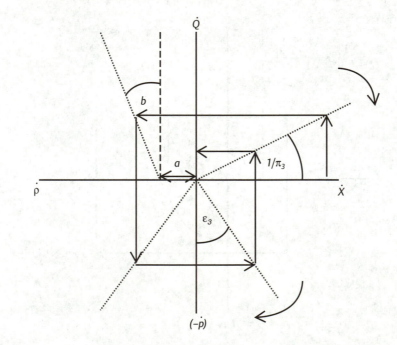

Fig. 6.14 Cumulative regional decline

observations of regional development can be shown to be made consistent with either approach (Fingleton and McCombie 1998).

6.5 Conclusions

This chapter has discussed the various analytical approaches we have for understanding the nature of regional growth and development. The most common approaches adopted by analysts are long-run neoclassical models, which distinguish between the growth due to factor allocation processes from growth which is due to technological change. The two broad types of these models are the one-sector model and the two-sector model, of which it was argued that the one-sector model is regarded as the 'true' long-run model of regional factor allocation. The long-run result of these regional allocation and reallocation processes is a tendency towards inter-regional convergence in terms of factor proportions and rates of return. The outcomes of regional factor allocation processes are therefore seen to be somewhat different from the factor allocation assumptions which underlie models of international trade and comparative advantage. The assumptions and conclusions of these neoclassical models were then employed within production function analysis in order to discuss questions of the contribution of technology to regional growth, as distinct from growth due to factor reallocation. However, this is a complex problem, and more recent endogenous growth approaches, have focused on the role played by qualitative differences in the stocks of capital and labour inputs, in order to account for variations in regional performance. These various neoclassical models were subsequently contrasted with Keynesian and post-Keynesian approaches to regional growth analysis, which centre on the notion of a regional balance of payments constraint. The assumption here is that regional export levels act as a long-run constraint on regional growth by limiting the maximum level of inward income-expenditure flows into the region. Under conditions in which local factor price adjustments are regarded as being of minor importance, regional growth is perceived as being primarily dependent on a region's particular mix of industries and local linkages. Therefore, where economies of scale are also present, these models imply that there is no particular reason to expect inter-regional convergence.

Discussion questions

1   What is the relationship between the neoclassical one-sector model of inter-regional factor allocation and the nature of regional production functions?

2   In what ways do the directions of factor flows in a two-sector neoclassical model of inter-regional factor allocation differ from that of a one-sector neoclassical model of inter-regional factor allocation?

3 How are we to understand the term 'technology' within a neoclassical growth framework, and how can we model the relationship between 'technology' and regional factor stocks?

4 What are the regional economic implications of endogenous growth models? Are there any limits to these mechanisms in the regional context?

5 To what extent are regions limited in their growth potential by a balance of payments constraint? How can such a constraint be relaxed?

6 What are the implications of the 'Verdoorn Law' for regional growth?

Appendix 6.1 The Cobb–Douglas Production Function and Growth Accounting

Our Cobb-Douglas regional production function is defined as

$$Q_t = Ae^{\varphi t}K^{\alpha}L^{1-\alpha}. \tag{A.6.1.1}$$

If we take the natural logarithm of this function we have

$$\ln Q = \ln A + \varphi t + \alpha \ln K + (1-\alpha)\ln L, \tag{A.6.1.2}$$

Differentiating equation (A.6.1.2) with respect to time t, we have

$$\frac{1}{Q}\frac{dQ}{dt} = \varphi + \frac{\alpha}{K}\frac{dK}{dt} + \frac{(1-\alpha)}{L}\frac{dL}{dt}, \tag{A.6.1.3}$$

which can be rewritten as

$$\dot{Q}_t = \varphi + \alpha\dot{K}_t + (1-\alpha)\dot{L}_t \tag{A.6.1.4}$$

where $\dot{Q}_t$, $\dot{K}_t$, $\dot{L}_t$, represent the rates of growth of output, capital, and labour at time t, respectively.

We know that wages depend on labour productivity, and the growth of wages will therefore be related to the growth of labour productivity. In order to investigate the exact nature of these relationships, we can take the growth in labour from both sides of equation (A.6.1.4) in order to arrive at an expression for the growth of labour productivity thus

$$\dot{Q}_t - \dot{L}_t = \varphi + \alpha\dot{K}_t + \dot{L}_t + \dot{L}_t - \dot{L}_t, \tag{A.6.1.5}$$

which rearranges to

$$\dot{Q}_t - \dot{L}_t = \varphi + \alpha(\dot{K}_t - \dot{L}_t), \tag{A.6.1.6}$$

The left-hand side of equation (A.6.1.6) represents the rate of growth of labour productivity at time t, and is given as the sum of the level of technology, plus the growth in the capital/labour ratio, weighted by the factor share of capital. As we see in Appendix 6.2 below, the rate of growth of labour productivity represents the rate of growth of wages. These conclusions are exactly in agreement with our one-sector model of factor allocation.

We can also adopt a similar approach to investigate the sources of profit growth.

However, in order to do this we take the rate of growth of capital from both sides of equation (A.6.1.4) to arrive at an expression for the rate of growth of capital productivity thus

$$\dot{Q}_t - \dot{K}_t = \varphi + a\dot{K}_t - \dot{K}_t + \dot{L}_t - a\dot{L}_t, \tag{A.6.1.7}$$

which can be rearranged to give

$$\dot{Q}_t - \dot{K}_t = \varphi + (1 - a)(\dot{L}_t - \dot{K}_t) = \dot{r}_t. \tag{A.6.1.8}$$

The left-hand side of equation (A.6.1.8) represents the rate of growth of capital productivity at time t, and is given as the sum of the level of technology, plus the growth in the labour/capital ratio, weighted by the factor share of labour. As we see in Appendix 6.2 below, the rate of growth of labour productivity represents the rate of growth of profits. Once again, these conclusions are exactly in agreement with our one-sector model of factor allocation.

In order to consider the sources of growth in a steady-state situation in which the rate of growth of profits is zero, we can set profit growth to zero when the rate of growth of the output/capital ratio is zero. In other words we have

$$\dot{Q}_t = \dot{K}_t, \tag{A.6.1.9}$$

which allows equation (A.6.1.8) to be rewritten as

$$0 = \varphi + (1 - a)(\dot{L}_t - \dot{Q}_t) = \dot{r}_t, \tag{A. 6.1.10}$$

which can be rearranged to give

$$0 = \varphi + (1 - a)(\dot{Q}_t - \dot{L}_t) = \dot{r}_t. \tag{A. 6.1.11}$$

This implies that

$$\dot{w}_t = \dot{Q}_t - \dot{L}_t = \frac{\varphi}{1 - a}. \tag{A.6.1.12}$$

In other words, in a steady-state situation in which the rate of growth of profits is zero, the rate of growth of labour productivity and wages depends simply on the level of technology and the factor share of labour in the economy.

Appendix 6.2   Proof of the Relationship between Wage Growth and Labour Productivity Growth in the Cobb–Douglas Framework

The wage paid to labour w is equal to the marginal product of labour MP_L, and is given by the marginal physical product of labour MPP_L, multiplied by the price of the output P_x produced. Within the Cobb–Douglas production function, the index of labour β, given as $\beta = (1-a)$, is defined as the partial elasticity of output with respect to the input labour. In other words

$$(1 - a) = \frac{\Delta Q/Q}{\Delta L/L} = \frac{\Delta Q}{Q} \times \frac{L}{\Delta L} = \frac{\Delta Q}{\Delta L} \times \frac{L}{Q} \tag{A.6.2.1}$$

Therefore, $\beta = (1-\alpha) = MP_L/AP_L$, where MP_L is the marginal product of labour, and AP_L is the average product of labour. As such, the wage w, which is given by the marginal product of labour, is given by $w = (1-\alpha) AP_L$.

Similarly, the profit rate paid to capital r is equal to the marginal product of capital MP_K, and is given by the marginal physical product of capital MPP_K, multiplied by the price of the output P_x produced. Within a Cobb–Douglas production function, the index of capital α, is defined as the partial elasticity of output with respect to the input capital. In other words

$$\alpha = \frac{\Delta Q/Q}{\Delta K/K} = \frac{\Delta Q}{Q} \times \frac{K}{\Delta K} = \frac{\Delta Q}{\Delta K} \times \frac{K}{Q} \tag{A.6.2.2}$$

Therefore, $\alpha = MP_K/AP_K$, where MP_K is the marginal product of capital, and AP_K is the average product of capital. As such, the profit rate r, which is given by the marginal product of capital, is given by $r = \alpha AP_K$.

Chapter 7
Urban and Regional Economic Policy Analysis

7.1 Introduction

Urban and regional economic policy is distinct from other forms of public sector economic policy, in that it is explicitly related to questions of geography. Both the motivation for, and the implementation of, urban and regional economic policy, are specifically spatial in nature, and decisions as to whether to undertake policy intervention depend on the performance of the local economic environment. However, our perception of what is 'local' will itself determine the nature of the policy, its implementation, and its evaluation. This is because the definition of a 'local economic environment' may extend from the spatial scale of an individual suburban area to that of an urban metropolitan area, and to the even larger spatial scales of a city-plus-hinterland regional economy, or even a regional economy comprised of more than one city. We know that economic indicators of average employment, unemployment, income levels, house prices, or various other indices of social deprivation, will differ according to the definition of the spatial areas used in order to calculate them. Therefore, our assessment of the performance of the 'economic environment' will also depend on the spatial scale adopted to define what is 'local'. In other words, the criteria against which any possible policy intervention will be considered or assessed will also depend on the spatial definition of the local economic environment. For this reason, urban and regional economic policy is generally broken down into two distinct groups of policies and initiatives. First, there are various initiatives which are focused specifically at the urban economic environment and targeted at the urban or suburban spatial scale. We will refer to these policies under the general heading of 'Urban Policy'. Secondly, there is a range of initiatives which are targeted at a much broader regional spatial scale, and we will refer to these policies under the general heading of 'Regional Policy'. The first major distinction between urban economic policy and regional economic policy is therefore simply the spatial extent of their focus and implementation, with regional policy being applied over a much greater spatial scale than urban policy.

The spatial scale, however, is not the only distinction between urban and regional economic policies. The second distinction between these two groups of spatial policies is the nature of the policies which can be implemented. All urban and regional economic policies are motivated by the desire to improve the local economic environment. However, the extent to which particular policies can be considered as viable candidates for implementation will once again depend on the spatial definition of the local environment. For example, as we see below, while policies encouraging 'gentrification' can be considered as candidates for economic development at the urban or suburban level, they would be clearly inappropriate as economic policies at the regional scale because their impacts would tend to be too localized. Similarly, large-scale regional policy, based on industrial relocation incentives would be inappropriate as economic policies at the suburban scale, and often largely inappropriate even at the urban scale, because their impacts would tend to be too widespread. In other words, the justification for the particular spatial economic policies adopted will in part also depend on the spatial area which is the object of the policy.

The third distinction between urban and regional policies concerns institutional issues. The different spatial scales over which these different policies are applied implies that the governmental and administrative frameworks within which such policies are implemented must also be different. This is because the geographical areas which are the focus of the spatial policies may cross over different administrative boundaries. The implementation of such policies may therefore require cross-border agreements and cooperative arrangements between neighbouring local government bodies. This is particularly the case for regional policy, which usually spans different administrative areas, but generally much less so for urban policy, which is normally implemented at the level of a single urban municipal level of government.

The fourth distinction between urban and regional economic policies, and the issue we are mainly concerned with here, centres on the different analytical approaches which can be adopted in order to understand and evaluate such policies. As we have seen, the nature of the urban and regional policy employed depends on the particular spatial scale of the policy objective. At the same time, in the previous chapters of this book, the various spatial economic models we have discussed are all implicitly constructed at different spatial scales. The Weber–Moses models discussed in Chapter 1 are primarily discussed in terms of an inter-regional framework, in which major production facilities search for optimum production-location arrangements over broad spatial scales. On the other hand, the models of spatial competition discussed in Chapter 1 such as the Hotelling framework can be considered either at an inter-regional regional scale if we are discussing large production facilities, or at an urban or suburban scale if we are considering small retail establishments. In Chapter 2 the models of industrial clustering and agglomeration which are discussed are explicitly framed at the level of an individual city. This is in contrast, however, to the central place models of the urban system by Christaller, Losch, and the more recent work of Krugman (1991) and Fujita *et al.* (1999), which are obviously constructed at the inter-regional scale. Meanwhile, the models of urban land allocation and pricing discussed in Chapter 3 are all framed explicitly at the scale of the individual urban area. The regional multiplier models discussed in Chapter 4 are all framed at the city-region and inter-regional scale, as are the labour employment and migration models discussed in Chapter 5. Finally, the factor allocation, growth, and balance of payments models discussed in Chapter 6 are all framed at the inter-regional level. The fact that each of these models is implicitly constructed at a different spatial scale suggests that different models will be appropriate for different geographical scales of urban and regional policy analysis. In other words, the appropriate analytical technique or combination of analytical techniques to employ, will depend on the object of the policy and the spatial scale of its implementation.

In the following sections we will discuss urban policy. In other words, we will initially discuss spatial economic policies which are implemented at the individual urban or suburban scale. Subsequently we will discuss regional policies, which are the spatial economic policies implemented at the much larger regional scale. By making this geographical distinction between the two types of policies, we will be able to identify which particular models or sets of models are appropriate for analysing the impact of each of the different policy agendas over their respective spatial areas of analysis.

7.2 **Urban Policy**

Economic policies which are implemented specifically at the urban level, generally involve attempts to improve the attractiveness of urban or suburban areas as locations for investment. However, in order for such a policy to be successful it is necessary to target the initiative towards the types of investment sectors which are regarded as being sensitive to economic or environmental variations even at the small urban or suburban scale. The sectors which are generally regarded as being the most sensitive to such small spatial scale variations are the real-estate and property development sectors. Urban economic policies therefore tend to focus on the relationship between the real-estate and property development sectors, and the rest of the local urban economy. In particular, urban policies usually attempt to alter the relative attractiveness of certain areas for property development in order to favour less developed locations. In order to achieve this, urban policies invariably involve relaxations or changes to the institutional or legal framework within which local economic development takes place. This is because real-estate and property development market transactions take place within complex legal and institutional frameworks which differ between countries and states. By changing these institutional arrangements in favour of development at particular locations, public policy may be used to guide the spatial pattern of private sector investment in order to achieve preordained goals. As such, the logic of urban policy is determined primarily by political priorities, and the focus of such policies tends to be on changing the nature of the local built environment.

From the point of view of economic analysis, any such urban policies will have welfare implications for different individual social groups as well as for the economy as a whole. The welfare impacts of such policies must be considered in order to arrive at a reasonable evaluation of the success or otherwise of such a policy. In order to see this we can consider two types of spatial policies, both of which are commonly employed within the urban built environment.

7.2.1 **Urban zoning policies**

One of the policies frequently employed by urban, regional, and land-use planners in many countries is that of the geographical zoning of activities. In this type of policy, different types of activities are only permitted to take place at particular urban locations. In other words, the land-use planning system is underpinned by the legal system, and this institutional arrangement determines where particular types of investment and development activities may possibly be undertaken within the city. Moreover, by defining the size of the zones in two-dimensional space, the land-use planning system determines both the location and the level of supply of urban development land for each activity or range of activities. What the system cannot do, however, is control the price of the development land. This is determined by the interaction of the current demand for land at the particular zoned location by the permitted industry, and the supply of the land at that particular location. Therefore, in order to understand the price effects of such a policy it is first necessary to consider the results of a competitive situation in which there is no such policy intervention, and then use this as the benchmark case against which the policy effects can be considered.

In order to consider the effects of a land-use zoning policy with respect to the situation of no such policy, we can adopt the bid-rent model discussed in Chapter 3. The bid-rent model allows us to compare the land-price gradient with respect to distance under conditions either of free competition or with land-zoning schemes. As in Chapter 3, the bid-rent model assumes that the location of the city centre, which is assumed to be the central business district M, is given, and that local land prices are determined by accessibility and factor proportions considerations. We can consider the case of a city which is comprised of three major industrial activities, namely a service sector, a manufacturing sector, and a retail and distribution sector. In terms of land and built environment facilities these three industry groups will require offices, factory and workshop facilities, and shops and warehouse facilities, respectively. If we adopt the initial assumptions of Figure 3.8 in Chapter 3 relating to the trade-off between accessibility and space requirements, we can assume that the service sector will be the most oriented towards the city centre, with the manufacturing sector adjacent to this sector, and the retail sector located on the edge of the city.

Under these conditions, competition for land will imply that the service sector offices will be located between the city centre M and a distance d_o from the city centre. The manufacturing sector factories and workshops will be located in the concentric ring of land around the service sector, at a distance between d_o and d_m from the city centre. Finally, the retail and distribution sector will be located in the concentric ring of land around the manufacturing sector, at a distance between d_m and d_r from the city centre. The actual urban land-rent gradient is given by the shaded envelope rent gradient ABC which is just tangent to the highest bid-rent curve at each location. As we see, the urban land-rent gradient will be a smooth downward-sloping function which is convex to the origin M.

We can now compare this competitive result with a situation in which the urban land is zoned. For example, we can imagine a situation in which the local metropolitan urban government decides not to allow manufacturing activities to be located as close to the

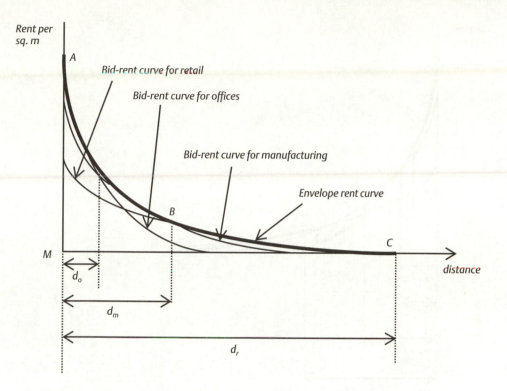

Fig. 7.1 Industry urban rent gradient under competitive conditions

city centre as they would under free competition. Such a decision might be taken for reasons of preserving or enhancing the aesthetic quality of the city centre, or alternatively because of concerns about the negative effects of local environmental pollution. In this situation, the local urban planning authorities may decide to permit only retail activities to take place immediately adjacent to the city centre where the service sector activities take place. As such, the zoning policy is organized so as to act as a buffer between the city centre and the manufacturing activities. In Figure 7.2, this retail zone is defined as the area between distances d_1 and d_2 from the city centre M. At the same time, the local urban planning authorities may also decide that the more peripheral suburban areas which are largely residential, and in particular those areas which are occupied by middle- and higher-income households, should not contain manufacturing activities. Manufacturing should only be allowed to take place in the one particular area which is specifically zoned for such activities. In order to effect this, the authorities may specify that the manufacturing zone cannot extend any further than distance d_3 from the city centre. Meanwhile, to compensate for the loss of service sector space available in the city due to the presence of the inner retail zone, the local authorities may only permit service sector activities to take place in the area between distances d_3 and d_4 from the city centre. Beyond this zone the planning system may permit a mixed usage of retail or service sector activities.

In a situation such as this, the actual urban land gradient will be serrated (Evans 1985)

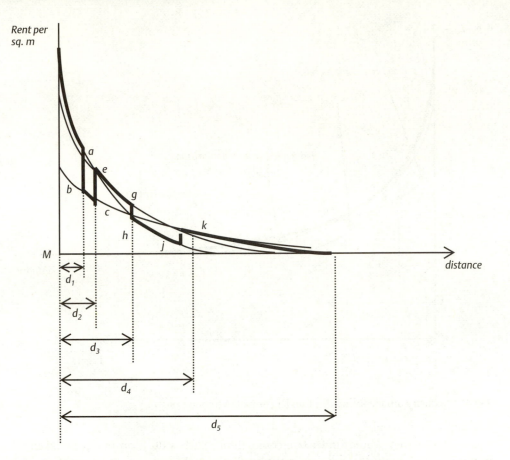

Fig. 7.2 Industry urban rent gradient under a zoning policy

as well as downward-sloping, and is given is Figure 7.2 by the shaded line. In order to consider the welfare effects of the planning policy we can compare the area under the rent gradient in the case where the zoning policy is implemented and in the case where there is no such policy. Where no zoning policy is in effect and the land market is competitive, the actual urban land-rent gradient is given by the envelope rent gradient in Figure 7.1. As we see in Figure 7.2, the difference between the area under the competitive rent gradient and the area under the serrated rent gradient is represented by the sum of the areas *abce* plus *ghjk*. These two areas together represent the total loss of urban rental revenue which results from the urban land being occupied at the zoned locations by activities which are unable to pay the maximum rent attainable under the competitive conditions. Given that Figure 7.2 is a one-dimensional diagram, the actual total revenue lost to the urban economy due to the zoning policy can be calculated by rotating the one-dimensional model through 360 degrees. This total revenue loss represents the opportunity cost of the zoning policy, and as such reflects the welfare loss to the urban economy of the planning policy.

The key point to come from the above argument is that urban planning policies inevitably have welfare implications. However, in the analytical assessment of the model described by Figures 7.1 and 7.2, we assume that the price mechanism is broadly efficient. Yet, a true assessment of the implications of these policies also depends on our perception of the efficiency of the land price mechanism to correctly price amenity goods. In the situation described by Figures 7.1 and 7.2, we have assumed that the reason for the implementation of zoning policies is that government authorities implicitly believe that the land market exhibits externalities which are not correctly priced by the market mechanism. In particular, the aesthetic aspects of the central-city environment are assumed to be undervalued by private sector cost considerations, such that the profitability of individual manufacturing activities will take precedence over the perceived positive benefits associated with an attractive civic centre. If it is perceived that first or second best solutions are neither possible nor appropriate policy responses to the perceived market failure in this context, the government authorities simply resort to a quota mechanism, in which a quantity constraint is imposed on the amount of land available at particular locations, and land is allocated by a process of rationing. Which particular development schemes are undertaken will depend on a property developer acquiring planning permission from the local government authority. By adopting such planning schemes, the government authorities are therefore ruling out direct comparisons of the form represented by a comparison of Figures 7.1 and 7.2, because it is assumed that the private sector land prices given in Figure 7.1 do not accurately reflect marginal social benefits. This is the justification for such interventionist policies.

7.2.2 Urban regeneration policies

A feature of the type of land-use planning policies described above is that changes in the market environment are brought about by changes in the legal and institutional environment in which the local land market works. Moreover, such policies are implemented in conditions where government authorities believe that the market mechanism will lead to socially inefficient results due to the presence of externalities. However, there are also situations in which the implementation of such policies may have undesirable welfare effects. As an example of this problem we can consider the case of urban regeneration schemes, which are popular recent initiatives both in North American cities such as Philadelphia and Boston, and also in European cities such as London, Manchester, and Rotterdam. These schemes have been designed specifically to encourage the redevelopment of the downtown urban areas, and to counter the out-migration and depopulation of many central-city areas. Many large urban areas have faced a consistent outward drift of both people and activities over the last three or four decades as people and business have moved to smaller urban centres. The reasons for this so-called 'urban–rural shift' may be connected, firstly, with improvements in production, communications, and transport technology which reduce the importance of a central urban location for many firm activities. Secondly, as incomes rise, the increased preference by households for space and better-quality environments has encouraged an out-migration of many people to more peripheral, but still accessible locations. Thirdly, the fixity of the urban capital stock as discussed in Chapter 6, may limit the ability of firms to reconfigure or expand their landholdings in central urban areas relative to greenfield locations. Taken together, these various effects have tended to reduce the attractiveness of central urban areas for many people and businesses. The combination of these trends has often led to the creation of urban wastelands described by Figure 3.15 in which land immediately adjacent to the urban centre is left undeveloped and derelict. However, for many civic government authorities, such trends are regarded as also leading to the additional local-ized problems of deprivation, poverty, and crime.

In order to improve both the aesthetic aspect of the central urban area and also the conditions of the people living close to the derelict areas, many urban authorities have implemented urban regeneration schemes. In these schemes, the legal and institutional environment within which the urban land market operates is altered in favour of the disadvantaged area. As mentioned above, for reasons of congestion, it is generally assumed that most manufacturing types of activities do not wish to find central urban locations. Similarly, many urban authorities generally do not wish such activities to be located centrally for the reasons discussed in section 7.2. Therefore, these urban regener-ation schemes tend to be focused on the real-estate markets of the residential sector and service sector, as these are generally regarded as the sectors most sensitive to urban environmental variations. In other words, these schemes are usually targeted towards the local development of housing and office properties.

As with the case of the urban zoning policies discussed above, we can adopt the bid-rent model or urban land allocation in order to analyse the welfare effects of urban redevelopment schemes. In order to do this, we will consider the situation in an urban area which initially experiences an area of downtown dereliction close to the city centre. In this 'no man's land' area the price of real estate is zero, as no individuals wish to live there and no businesses wish to locate there under the current economic and environ-mental conditions. This initial situation can be represented by Figure 7.3 which is con-structed on the basis of the argument in section 3.4.2 of Chapter 3. In Figure 7.3, we assume for simplicity that there are only two income groups, a low-income group and a high-income group. The low-income group lives close to the urban centre within a radius of d_l from the centre. The high-income group lives at a distance beyond d_z from the city centre. However, because of the preference of the high-income group not to live close to the low-income group, there is an area of dereliction between d_l and d_z. In the area of dereliction, the economic prospects are so low that even with market rents at zero, investment there is not profitable.

In situations where local civic authorities attempt to rectify the situation described in Figure 7.3, by improving the general aesthetic environment around the city centre, local civic planning authorities engage in a range of policies to influence the local real-estate market behaviour. These policies can take a range of forms such as relaxation of local planning or zoning restrictions, direct real-estate or tax subsidies to developers, indirect subsidies to developers such as special public infrastructure or public transportation pro-vision, or joint ventures between public and private sector bodies in underwriting such schemes. However, the basic logic which is common to all such urban regeneration schemes is an attempt to change the institutional environment in which the local real-estate market works, in order to effect changes in the physical environment of the local area. The reason for this, as we have seen in Chapter 3, is that the area of dereliction is due to the perverse upward-sloping behaviour of the bid-rent curves of high-income groups,

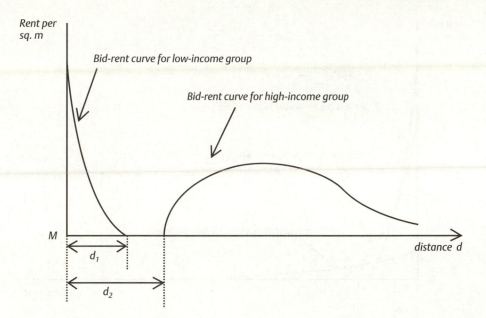

Fig. 7.3 Derelict urban land

due to the externalities associated with social perceptions. Therefore, these urban policies aim to alter the perceptions of the higher-income groups in order to encourage real-estate investment by this group in the city centre.

The effects of such policies can be depicted in Figure 7.4 according to the argument in section 3.4.1 and the description given in Figure 3.12. If the redevelopment of the local city-centre area goes ahead, this area will now become attractive for a certain portion of the high-income group which has a relatively high preference for accessibility to the city, but which previously was unwilling to pay for this due to the poor local environment. For simplicity we will characterize this group as being a high-income group comprised primarily of young people, but this group may also include dual income households. The bid-rent curve of this group will tend to be very steep. On the other hand, the older people within the high-income group or those with young children will still generally have a higher preference for space in order to provide for the needs of their dependants. As such, their bid-rent curve will remain very shallow. The redevelopment of the downtown area will mean that the single perverse bid-rent curve of the high-income group depicted in Figure 7.3 will now be split into two different downward-sloping convex bid-rent curves for the two distinct high-income groups. As we see in Figure 7.4, the result of this is that the area within a radius of d_y from the central business district M will be occupied by young high-income earners. Similarly, the older high-income group will be located beyond a distance d_h from the city centre. Meanwhile, the low-income group will be located in the area between d_y and d_h from the city centre.

We can compare the area of habitation of the low-income group before and after the urban regeneration scheme by considering the difference between Figures 7.3 and 7.4. As we see, for the same bid-rent curve, the low-income group are now constrained to live in a

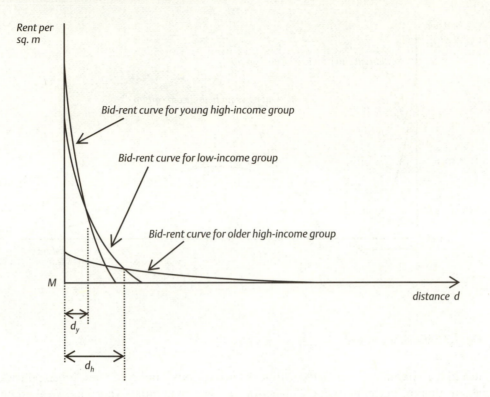

Fig. 7.4 Residential land-use effects of urban regeneration schemes

smaller area of occupation after the redevelopment scheme than before the scheme. The reason is that both the land immediately adjacent to the city centre and also the land on the outer fringes of the area of low-income occupation are now allocated by the price mechanism to the two high-income groups. In this situation, the low-income group as a whole will have suffered a welfare loss with respect to the high-income groups. This is because in the situation where the incomes and preferences of the low-income group, which are embodied in their bid-rent curve, remain unchanged, many of the low-income people will no longer be able to live in the city and will lose their residences in order to make way for the high-income groups. As such, they will be forced to leave the city.

Alternatively, if the low-income population of the city remains stable, because as we discussed in Chapter 5 the ability of the low-income groups to migrate may be very limited, the low-income population will now be constrained to a greater residential density of living. Following the arguments in section 3.4 of Chapter 3, the individual bid-rent curve of the low-income group, as depicted in Figures 7.3 and 7.4, indicates the rent per square metre which people are willing to pay at different locations in order to maintain a given level of utility, where utility is partly a function of the total land area consumed. If at any location the total land area consumed falls for any given rent per square metre payable, the total utility of the individual household must fall. In terms of bid-rent analysis this utility fall is represented by an upward shift in the bid-rent curve for the low-

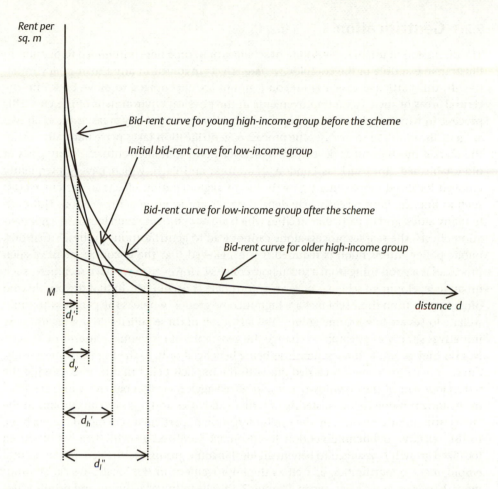

Fig. 7.5 Welfare effects of urban regeneration schemes

income group. As we see in Figure 7.5, this upward shift in the bid-rent curve for the low-income group after the redevelopment scheme will be represented by an increase the rent per square metre payable by the low-income group at any location. Competition in the real-estate market implies that the low-income group will now increase their area of habitation from the area between the distances d_y and d_h from the city centre to the area between the distances d_r and $d_{r'}$ from the city centre. As such, the low-income group will increase their area of habitation, relative to the situation described by Figure 7.4, by encroaching on the area of habitation of both of the high-income groups. However, this increase in habitation area is paid for by an increase in dwelling density on the part of the low-income group, the result of which is an upward shift in the bid-rent function of the low-income group. The low-income group unambiguously suffers a welfare loss due to the urban redevelopment scheme.

7.2.3 **Gentrification**

The discussion of urban redevelopment schemes presented here is intended to provide an illustrative example of the complex welfare effects involved in any urban policy initiative. In this particular case, high-income groups are encouraged to move back into the central areas of the city via improvements in the physical environment of the city. This process, in which high-income groups move back into central-city areas, is often known as 'gentrification'. In some cases the process of gentrification takes place naturally within the market mechanism as developers search for new profitable ventures. Many parts of old-established cities such as London, New York, and Paris, which have subsequently enjoyed localized employment growth due to agglomeration effects in certain sectors such as finance, have recently experienced significant levels of gentrification. However, in many cities, and in particular in cities which are not enjoying such localized agglomeration effects, the market process alone cannot lead to gentrification. In these situations, public policy intervention is required if it is believed that the encouragement of such processes is a good thing from a social point of view. However, as we have seen here, such urban redevelopment schemes have an unfortunate consequence, in that the people who often benefit from these schemes are high-income groups, whereas the people who suffer welfare losses are low-income groups. Yet, advocates of these policies do not regard these initiatives simply as attempts to change the geographical residential patterns of society. Nor do they promote these schemes as being beneficial only to the high-income groups. These policies are generally carried out with the implicit belief that by encouraging the redevelopment of the downtown areas, localized agglomeration benefits can be realized in the long run due to the clustering of tertiary activities and high-income groups in the city centre. In other words, by the careful targeting of particular schemes planners hope to use selective public intervention to encourage localized growth. The hypothesized localized growth is assumed to benefit all local income groups via the generation of local employment opportunities, as well as the improvement in the local physical environment. However, as we have seen in Chapter 2, the clustering of activities and people is not a sufficient condition for the development of localized agglomeration economies. Therefore, any hypothesized beneficial agglomeration effects accruing to the low-income groups as compensation for the welfare losses described here, are purely speculative. On the other hand, in the absence of any such agglomeration effects, welfare losses will unambiguously accrue to the low-income groups, whereas the high-income groups will be the major beneficiaries of the urban redevelopment schemes.

7.2.4 **Greenbelts**

In some countries of relatively high spatial population densities, such as the Netherlands, South Korea, and the UK, land use and land allocation at both the national and local levels is organized primarily within a system of 'greenbelts'. A greenbelt is a zone of land surrounding an urban area in which urban development is not permitted in any circumstances. In other words, the greenbelt forms a concentric ring around the city which clearly defines the outer edge of the urban area. The logic of the greenbelt policy is to limit the outward expansion of the urban areas in order to preserve and protect the

intervening rural land. The motive for such a restrictive policy is that in densely populated countries and regions, the preservation of rural areas is often perceived to be a
national priority, because of the relative scarcity of rural land. From this perspective, the
value of the rural area is defined primarily in terms of aesthetic and archaeological arguments, rather than simply in economic terms. Therefore, in order to ensure that all
people have relatively easy access to local rural areas, strictly enforced limits are placed on
the expansion of urban areas. Implicitly, such a policy assumes that the private land
market mechanism will not appropriately value the preservation of rural environmental
amenities in terms of their social costs and benefits, and that urban development activities will be priced only with respect to private costs and benefits. As such, the rationale
for greenbelts is an externality problem. On the other hand, such a policy inevitably also
has welfare implications.

In order to understand the logic for a greenbelt policy we can consider Figure 7.6 in
which a region comprises two major urban centres with their respective central business
districts located at J and K. We assume that the nominal wage incomes earned at the
central business location J are higher than the nominal wage incomes earned at K. As
such, the competitive market rental price per square metre r_{J1} of land at J, is higher than
the competitive market rental price per square metre r_{K1} of land at K. Following the
arguments in section 3.4.1 of Chapter 3, the convex envelope rent gradients of each
urban area are comprised of the individual bid-rent functions of the different income
groups employed at each urban centre. If the agricultural land rent is given as r_A at all
locations, and the land market is competitive, the urban area centred on J will be larger

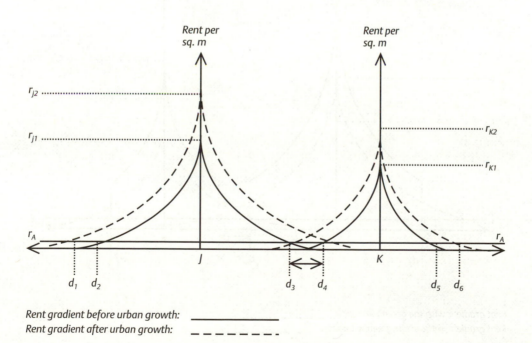

Rent gradient before urban growth: ———————

Rent gradient after urban growth: — — — — — —

Fig. 7.6 Inter-urban merging

than the urban area centred on K. The urban area centred on J extends from location d_2 to d_3, and the urban area centred on J extends from location d_4 to d_5. The agricultural areas are the areas to the left of d_2, to the right of d_5, and the area between locations d_3 to d_4. In other words, at the prevailing incomes r_{J1} and r_{K1} earned in urban activities at J and K, respectively, the two urban areas are still separated by an area of rural activities. The actual land-rent gradient is represented by the bold line in Figure 7.7.

If, for example, due to agglomeration economies, the nominal incomes payable at J and K increase over time by 50 per cent to r_{J2} and r_{K2}, respectively, both of the urban areas will expand. In this case, the new land-rent gradient is given in Figure 7.6 by the perforated bold line. As we see, the urban area centred on J will now extend to a location d_1 to the left of J, and the urban area centred on J will now extend to a location d_6 to the right of K. The area between J and K will now all be taken up by urban development such that the intervening urban area will disappear. As such, the new merged urban area will now extend continuously from d_1 to d_6. In order to avoid the merging of urban centres over time, for the reasons outlined above, the land-use planning authorities may enforce a strict greenbelt policy to preserve the existing urban boundaries. The effects of such a policy can be seen in Figure 7.6. In this case, the land-use planning system implements a greenbelt around the urban area centred on J, such that urban development is not permit-

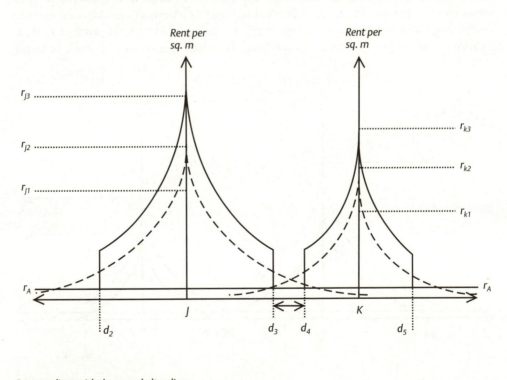

Rent gradient with the greenbelt policy: _____

Rent gradient without the greenbelt policy: – – – – – – – – ·

Fig. 7.7 The land-price effects of a greenbelt policy

ted beyond locations d_2 and d_3, and a second greenbelt around K, such that urban development is not permitted beyond locations d_4 and d_5. In this situation, if the cities grow over time due to agglomeration economies, the increased number of locally employed people will be constrained to live in the same urban areas. This will reduce the average living area of each household. Consequently the bid-rent curve for each individual urban household will shift upwards to a higher level than would be the case under the situation where growth is accommodated in a competitive land market without a greenbelt policy. The result of this is that the envelope rent gradient will move upwards and the market price payable per square metre will increase at all locations within the urban area to higher levels than would be the case without the greenbelt. In Figure 7.7, the actual rent gradient under conditions of urban growth after the imposition of the greenbelt policy is given by the bold line, and the rent gradient under conditions of urban growth without a greenbelt policy is given by the bold perforated line. On the urban–rural boundaries at points, d_2, d_3, d_4, and d_5, there are significant discontinuities in the land rent payable, and these will continue to exist as long as the greenbelt restrictions remain in place. From the perspective of living costs, all urban dwellers suffer a welfare loss due to the imposition of the greenbelt policy.

From the arguments outlined in section 3.4.2 of Chapter 3, it is also possible that the negative welfare effects of a greenbelt policy may be exacerbated by the expectation that the environment at the urban fringe will be preserved indefinitely. If environmental amenities are relatively localized and it is perceived that the greenbelt policy will be maintained in the long term, this implies that the persons who are resident on the urban fringes will always enjoy superior environmental amenities in comparison with those who are resident closer to the city centre. If low-income groups are constrained to remain close to the urban centre for the reasons discussed in sections 3.4.1 and 3.4.2 of Chapter 3, this implies that only the high-income groups will enjoy these environmental benefits at their residential locations. As we see in Figure 7.8, the effect of this will be to cause the bid-rent curves of the higher-income groups to become upward-sloping as we move towards the urban fringe, such that the envelope urban rent gradient will now become u-shaped. In these circumstances, the discontinuities between the urban and rural land prices at the urban fringes will become even more marked. Meanwhile, the major beneficiaries of the greenbelt policy will be the high-income households living on the edges of the urban areas.

7.3 Regional Policy

Economic policies implemented at the regional level often involve attempts to improve the attractiveness of particular regions as locations for investment. In particular, regional policies attempt to improve the relative attractiveness of investment in less developed regions. In this sense these regional policies are similar to some of the urban regeneration policies discussed above. However, a key difference between regional policies and urban policies is that the industrial sectors towards which regional polices are targeted will tend

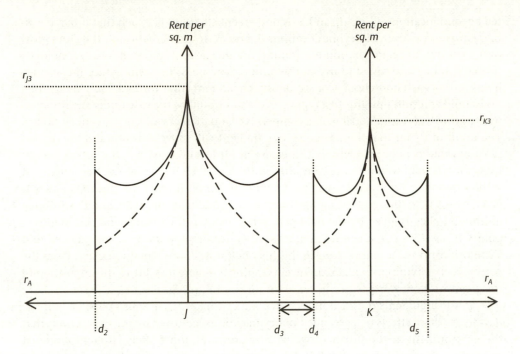

Fig. 7.8 Local environmental effects of a greenbelt policy

to be quite different from those targeted at the urban scale. The reason for this is that, following the arguments in Chapter 1, the industrial sectors which are generally regarded as being the most sensitive to large-scale spatial cost and price variations, are not the real-estate and property development sectors, but rather the manufacturing and distribution sectors, along with some commercial service sectors carrying out rather routine standardized activities. As with urban policy, in order to achieve these goals regional policies involve relaxations or changes to the institutional or legal framework within which local economic development takes place. However, the local economic development impacts of regional policy can differ significantly across both sectors and regions.

Therefore, it is necessary for us to consider carefully the size and the spatial pattern of any possible local regional development effects. At the same time, given that regional policy often involves the provision of infrastructure which is publicly funded, it is also justifiable to consider the social marginal costs and benefits of such a regional policy, relative to the situation where no such policy was initiated. In the following sections, we will therefore consider various different approaches to analysing the effects of regional policies at the microeconomic, social welfare, and macroeconomic level.

7.3.1 The aggregate microeconomic effects of regional policies

The most common types of regional policies are supply-side policies, which attempt to improve the environment for local investment by upgrading the quality of the local production factor inputs. In particular, supply-side regional policies tend to focus on the factor inputs which are location-specific. In an inter-regional economy in which both capital and labour are mobile, the only production factor inputs which are location-specific are natural raw material inputs, land, and local infrastructure inputs. Given that raw material locations cannot be affected by policy intervention, the focus of regional policy tends to be primarily on increasing the quality and variety of local infrastructure inputs. This is generally an indirect way of reducing real local input costs. An alternative but much less commonly used approach is for regional policy to focus on directly reducing the cost of local land inputs. We can consider each of these approaches individually.

In the case of regional policies which attempt to upgrade the quality and variety of local infrastructure inputs, the major focus tends to be on the improvement of the local transportation infrastructure (Vickerman 1991). The expected effect of these policies is primarily to reduce the costs of accessibility to the region in question. Therefore, improvements are generally sought in key strategic elements of the local transport infrastructure, which connects the individual region in question to other parts of the inter-regional economy. There are two reasons for this overall approach. The first reason is that transportation inputs are regarded as essential inputs into almost all industrial and commercial activities, irrespective of whether it is goods or people that are being moved. From the production function perspective as discussed in section 6.3 of Chapter 6, improvements in such transportation infrastructure inputs can be considered as increases in the level of regional technology. Therefore, improvements in these transportation inputs should improve the total factor productivity of almost all local regional industrial activities which are trading inter-regionally. The first intended effect of this type of regional policy is therefore to encourage an expansion of the existing local industrial base by enhancing local productivity. Secondly, for industries which are relatively mobile, spatial variations in transport costs are regarded as significantly affecting the attractiveness of different regions as locations for investment. If we can alter the relative costs of transportation and accessibility in favour of less developed locations, it is hoped that this will encourage further immigrant inward investment. As such, the second intended effect of these types of regional policies is to encourage an expansion of the local industrial base via inflows of additional capital.

Regional policies of this type are implemented partly or wholly via the provision of public sector funds. Funding is granted in selected lagging areas which are chosen as candidates for regional financial aid. However, whether or not such a policy has the desired local effect depends on the relationship between the provision of the transportation infrastructure, changes in transport costs, and the marginal price and revenue effects of the transport cost changes on both domestic firms and firms which are inter-regionally mobile. For example, a road building programme initiated in a particular lagging region will generally reduce the delivered prices of all outputs produced in the region at any location. Assuming a broadly competitive market, this will increase the overall level of regional outputs sold both within the region and also to customers in other regions. This output expansion on the part of existing local firms is the first desired effect of regional policy.

The second desired effect of regional policy is to encourage the immigration of more firm investment into a region. Following the arguments in sections 1.2.3 and 1.2.4 of Chapter 1, one possible effect of reductions in transport costs can be understood as increasing the likelihood of firm relocation into a particular region for any given set of inter-regional labour and land prices. However, competition in factor markets would imply that any transport cost savings will soon be countered by increases in local factor prices, such that a permanent advantage cannot be maintained by this policy. However, whether the transport infrastructure improvements will encourage external firms at all to invest in that region also depends in part on whether firms will substitute in favour of inputs produced in that region. We can analyse the potential effects of such a policy by comparing the conclusions to the arguments in sections 1.2.1 and 1.2.2 of Chapter 1, with the discussion of Figure 1.11 in section 1.3 of the same chapter. As we see in these sections, the location effect of reductions in transport costs in particular regions depends on the location-production substitution possibilities of firms. If firms have zero or only limited input substitution possibilities, localized reductions in transport costs can be efficiently absorbed into firms' cost schedules by moving away from the area in which transport costs are reduced in order to reduce relatively higher transport costs associated with other locations. This is a classic Weber-type result. As such, the regional policy will have exactly the opposite effect from that which was intended. Alternatively, if firms have a wide range of substitution possibilities, firms will most efficiently absorb the localized transport costs reductions by substituting in favour of the lower delivered price goods of the region in question. This will also encourage the firm to move towards the area of lower transport costs, thereby having the desired effect of increasing the immigration of firms into the area. This is a classic Moses-type result, the result of which is entirely in keeping with the objectives of the regional policy.

From the foregoing discussion it appears that the local regional development effects of initiatives which aim to improve local regional transport infrastructure are rather hard to predict. If firms are able to substitute between inputs fairly easily, transport costs reductions should encourage competition in all regions along the lines of a one-sector model framework. However, if input substitution is not so easy, the results can be very complex. Furthermore, improvements of transportation infrastructure can also have additional regional effects. As we see in section 1.4 of Chapter 1, transport costs over space in part act like a tariff barrier, protecting less efficient local firms from external competition (Krugman 1991). As transport costs are reduced by regional policy infrastructure improvements, this means that some local firms will no longer continue to exist. Krugman and Venables (1990) have shown that if agglomeration economies operate in some locations, the negative effects on the less developed region can be very significant unless there are major compensating local wage falls. Therefore, the spatial impacts of policies to improve regional and inter-regional transportation infrastructure must be evaluated carefully.

7.3.2 The welfare effects of regional policy

Where regional policy is based on the provision of local transportation investments, we can consider from a social perspective whether a road building scheme should be undertaken in a relatively peripheral economy. In order to do this we can imagine a case where there is a region which is geographically peripheral, and which also exhibits a small and highly scattered population of relatively low density. In such a region, the provision of new high-speed road infrastructure will significantly reduce the average travel time between any two regional locations. This reduction in travel time will reduce transport costs associated with business transactions, and will therefore significantly reduce the marginal costs of all outputs produced and consumed within the region. However, these significant reductions in the marginal costs of output provision will only be realized across a rather limited number of commercial transactions, simply because the total regional population is small. On the other hand, if the new road infrastructure is built in a large and densely populated region which already has a large road network, the new road infrastructure will only lead to a small reduction in average travel times between locations. As such, this will only slightly reduce the marginal costs of all outputs produced and consumed within the region. However, in this case the small individual marginal cost reductions will be realized across a very large number of commercial transactions.

In order to compare these two effects we can construct Figure 7.9 in which the total efficiency welfare gains from the total number of transactions in the high-density region T_H and the low-density region T_L is compared with the cost of the individual transactions. For simplicity, we assume that the initial transport costs associated with intra-regional transactions are given by C in both regions. If the new transport infrastructure is now introduced into the low-density region, the large marginal cost fall associated with reduced transport costs implies that the transport costs are now at a much lower C_L. This large reduction in transport costs significantly reduces the marginal cost of all individual transactions which take place over space, and consequently induce an increase in the total number of local business transactions. The total social welfare gain associated with

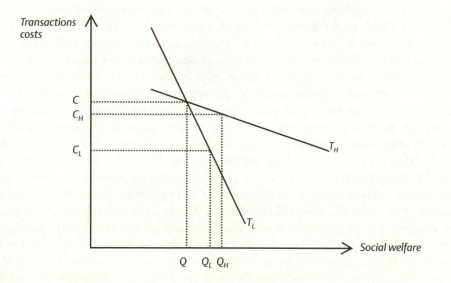

Fig. 7.9 The welfare-efficiency effects of regional infrastructure

this increase in business transactions is represented by the increase from Q to Q_L. On the other hand, if the new transport infrastructure is now introduced into the densely populated region, the fall in the marginal cost of individual business transactions from C to C_H is only small. This is because the transport infrastructure is already both dense and extensive, and therefore the potential reduction in transport costs for each individual business transaction over space is only small. However, this small efficiency gain in the marginal cost of an individual business transaction is realized over a large number of transactions. Therefore, the increase in the total social welfare which is induced by the transport cost fall is large, and in Figure 7.9 is given by the increase from Q to Q_H. The result of this is that the marginal social benefit of the transportation infrastructure may actually be higher in the large and densely populated central region than in the small and sparsely populated region.

The example above indicates a common feature of economic phenomena which is often overlooked in textbooks, namely that the welfare impacts of public policy intervention not only have explicitly spatial aspects, but that spatial issues will themselves determine the absolute size of the impacts. Variations in the density and spatial distributions of populations and markets require us to consider the welfare effects of public policy initiatives carefully. Differences in the location of public policy initiatives will result in both different spatial welfare distributions, and also differences in the absolute size of welfare impacts. On welfare grounds, the example above calls into question the justification for some regional economic policies, because although the road infrastructure may significantly improve the economic welfare conditions in the sparsely populated peripheral economy, the net benefits of such public expenditure would have been greater in the central region. In the above case, if the road building programme in the peripheral region was indeed initiated, the justification for such a policy can therefore only be provided primarily on political or social grounds, rather than on economic grounds. On the other hand, we may see that the relative costs of road infrastructure provision are much lower in peripheral economies due to the lower land and labour prices. Similarly, congestion effects in the densely populated region may limit the potential benefits of such infrastructure in the central region. In either of these cases, an evaluation of the long-run social costs and benefits of the scheme may indicate that the net social welfare gains are greater in the peripheral region than in the central region. In addition, if localized growth effects are stimulated in the peripheral region by the provision of the public infrastructure, the welfare gains associated with the regional policy may be very significant. In this situation, the cost–welfare curves depicted in Figure 7.9 will be reversed, with the cost–welfare curve for the peripheral region becoming rather shallow whereas that for the central region will be relatively steep. The social evaluation of a regional policy based on infrastructure provision therefore requires not only a social cost–benefit analysis (Sassone and Schaffer 1978; Pearce and Nash 1981; Layard and Glaister 1994) of all the potential economic and environmental impacts of the policy, but also an explicitly spatial discussion as to the distributional effects of the policy. The same argument holds for regional policies which are based on the direct or indirect subsidizing of immigrant investment into a region via land price reductions or local tax rebates (Swales 1997). Geography plays a role in determining both the absolute size and the spatial distribution of the economic impacts of public policy initiatives. Therefore, the impacts of all regional policies must be evaluated carefully with explicitly spatial considerations in mind.

7.3.3 The macroeconomic effects of regional policy

As well as considering regional policy from both an aggregate microeconomic perspective and a welfare perspective, we can also consider the rationale for regional policy from a macroeconomic perspective. In the discussion of Figure 6.10 in section 6.4.1 of Chapter 6, it was argued that at the prevailing interest rates, it is possible for regional investment levels to be insufficient to clear local regional involuntary unemployment. In the analysis presented in Chapter 6, which is based on a small open-economy macroeconomic model, the interest rates are determined exogenously of the individual region. However, national interest rates are in part determined by demand pressures in buoyant regions. In regions which are experiencing full employment, local nominal wages and nominal land prices will be high. The associated local labour and land supply shortages will continuously be a potential source of inflationary pressure in the local regional economy. Therefore, in order to avoid local inflation, local regional demand cannot be allowed to expand beyond the full employment level. This also limits the extent to which demand in other regions can grow. The regional implications of this are depicted in Figure 7.10.

In Figure 7.10 we compare the case of two regions A and B, where region A is a buoyant region with full employment, and region B is a depressed region with involuntary unemployment. We can consider the case of region A which is depicted in the four upper quadrant sections of Figure 7.10. In the upper right-hand quadrant we can see that the level of regional income is Y_{A1}. As we see in the upper left-hand quadrant, this level of regional aggregate demand requires labour inputs which just ensure a full regional employment level of L_{AF}. At the particular interest rate i^* which just ensures that the price level P in the buoyant region remains constant at P^*, the full regional employment demand levels Y_{A1} are just sustained by the local regional investment schedule IS_{A1}. In other words, full employment is maintained in the buoyant region without incurring local inflation. On the other hand, at the prevailing rate of interest i^*, in region B, depicted by the lower four quadrants, the regional investment schedule IS_{B1} is insufficient to maintain a full employment local income level Y_{B3} and only allows for a level of regional income of Y_{B1}. This lower level of regional income only requires labour inputs of L_{B1} such that the level of local regional unemployment is given by $(L_{BF}-L_{B1})$. The unemployment in the depressed region B continues because at the prevailing interest rate, local investment levels are unable to generate local demand which is sufficient to clear the local labour market. If inter-regional migration flows are not sufficient to clear all local regional labour markets quickly, and the interest rate cannot be reduced below i^*, the situation is maintained indefinitely.

At this point, we must consider why the interest rate will be set and maintained at i^*. One of the features of the mutually open and interconnected inter-regional economy is that price rises originating in one region can be transmitted very quickly into price rises in other regions. In the case of a national economy in which one buoyant region of the economy is consistently close to facing local supply shortages, the national monetary

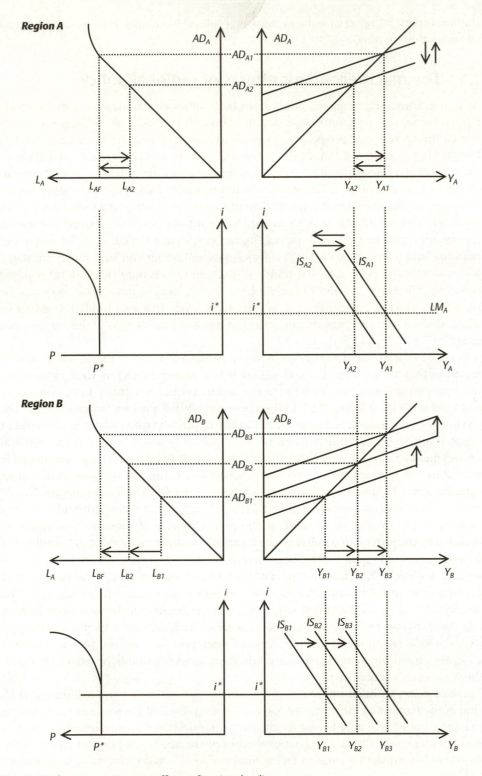

Fig. 7.10 The macroeconomic effects of regional policy

authorities may decide to set national interest rates in order to just avoid local labour and land price inflation in the buoyant region. The reason for this is that the monetary authorities fear that lower interest rates will engender local inflation in region A, which in turn will immediately be transmitted to the rest of the national economy. Although interest rate falls will be beneficial for the depressed regions, in that local investment and employment levels will increase, the land supply constraints in region A limit the downward movement of interest rates. Moreover, this is the case irrespective of the phase of the national business cycle at which the national economy finds itself. The buoyant region therefore consistently acts as a 'bottleneck' region, and constrains the demand levels in the less buoyant regions. In this particular regional economic system, unemployment in the less buoyant region is maintained in order to preserve price stability in region A, and consequently, price stability in the national economy. In other words, not only are differences in the individual local regional demand and employment conditions in part a result of the macroeconomic policy, but at the same time the macroeconomic policy is itself partly a result of the differences in the regional demand and supply conditions.

In situations where buoyant regions act as regional bottlenecks, regional policy can have a role to play in encouraging growth and employment in less buoyant regions without incurring inflationary pressures. In order to understand the logic of this argument we must compare the local employment demand conditions in the two regions. As we see in Figure 7.10, the prevailing local investment and labour demand conditions in the less buoyant region are constrained by the factor supply constraints and inflationary pressure in the buoyant region. However, regional policy can act so as to encourage the diversion of demand from the buoyant region A to the less buoyant region B. Regional policy tools, such as the provision of infrastructure and real-estate subsidies in the less buoyant region, which in addition may sometimes be applied in tandem with land-use planning restrictions in the buoyant region A, can effect a diversion of investment flows away from region A and towards region B. The manifestations of this will be the migration of new immigrant firms to region B in preference to region A, and the expansion of existing firms of facilities in region B in preference to region A. This investment diversion effect can be represented in Figure 7.10 by the reduction in local investment flows in region A at the prevailing interest rate i^* from IS_{A1} to IS_{A2}, and an expansion in local investment flows in region B at the prevailing interest rate from IS_{B1} to IS_{B2}. The reduction in investment in region A will lead to a fall in local regional income from Y_{A1} to Y_{A2}, and the consequent reduction in regional aggregate demand from AD_{A1} to AD_{A2} will lead to a fall in local labour employment from the full regional employment level of L_{AF} to a lower employment level of L_{A1}. The local unemployment shortfall caused by the diversion of investment away from the buoyant region is therefore given by $(L_{AF}-L_{A2})$. (However, as we will see shortly, this unemployment does not actually take effect.) In the less buoyant region B, the increase in local investment associated with the regional policy diversion effect increases the local regional income from Y_{B1} to Y_{B2}, and the consequent increase in regional aggregate demand from AD_{B1} to AD_{B2} will lead to an increase in local labour employment from L_{B1} to L_{B2}. The local unemployment shortfall caused by the diversion of investment into the buoyant region is now given by $(L_{BF}-L_{B2})$ and is exactly the same as the apparent local unemployment shortfall $(L_{AF}-L_{A2})$ in region A. In this situation, the current local price level in region A is unaffected either by the reduction in investment in region A or the expansion in investment in region B. Moreover, the aggregate demand in both regions can now be allowed to expand without causing any inflation in region A. In region A aggregate regional demand can be allowed to expand to its original level of AD_{A1} which was maintained before the application of the regional policy. At this level of aggregate regional demand region A will exhibit local full employment income, investment, and labour demand levels of Y_{A1}, IS_{A1}, and L_{AF} respectively, at the prevailing interest rate $i*$ which just ensures price stability at $P*$ in region A. Similarly, in region B aggregate regional demand can be allowed to expand from AD_{B2} to AD_{B3}. At this level of aggregate regional demand region B will exhibit local full employment income, investment, and labour demand levels of Y_{B3}, IS_{B3}, and L_{BF} respectively, at the prevailing interest rate $i*$ which just ensures price stability at $P*$ in region A.

This positive macroeconomic expansion effect across both regions compensates for the negative diversion effect in the buoyant region A, and is additional to the positive diversion effect in the less buoyant region B. In other words, the diversion of investment associated with the regional policy allows regional income and aggregate demand in both regions to be maintained at levels which ensure full local employment in both regions without engendering inflation in the bottleneck region. As such, the role of regional policy is therefore to circumvent many of the regional bottleneck problems associated with different regional investment levels in a situation where common inter-regional interest rates are set primarily with respect to the demand conditions in the buoyant regions. Therefore, if the policy is implemented successfully, the net result of the regional policy diversion effect plus the macroeconomic expansion effect in each of the two regions is to allow for full employment aggregate demand to be maintained in both regions under a stable macroeconomic monetary regime.

7.4 Conclusions

This chapter has discussed the various major types of initiatives undertaken under the broad heading of urban and regional policy. As we have seen, a major difference between urban policies and regional policies is the spatial scale over which the policies are implemented and assumed to take effect. The intended impacts of urban policies are expected to take place over a much smaller spatial scale than regional policies. These different spatial scales, however, also mean that the types of policies adopted and the criteria against which the policies will be evaluated are also different. In the case of urban policies, the dominant issue which will determine whether or not a policy is implemented is the nature of the local environment at the suburban level. The notion of 'environment' here relates both to the physical built environment and also to the local social and economic environment. The real-estate market is generally the target of urban policies, and the implementation of these policies generally involves relaxations or changes in the institutional framework within which the local real-estate market operates. All such urban policies have welfare impacts, which are realized in terms of changes in the prices of real-estate assets at different locations. Moreover, the nature and scale of these welfare impacts can be quite different on different income groups. Urban policies can therefore have welfare distribution effects, and for urban and regional economists an evaluation of the benefits of urban policies cannot take place without an assessment of these welfare distribution effects. Regional policies, on the other hand, simultaneously focus both on encouraging indigenous regional investment growth and also on attracting new immigrant investment into a region from outside. As far as the latter approach is concerned, these policies tend to operate over a much larger spatial scale than urban policies, and aim to encourage the migration of firm capital over rather large distances. The focus of regional policies tends to be on the provision of local regional infrastructure and also, in some cases, the subsidizing of local real-estate inputs. As with urban policies, these regional policies will have social welfare impacts, the size and spatial distribution of which will depend on the responsiveness of indigenous and immigrant firms to the regional policy initiatives. Moreover, regional polices may also play a macroeconomic efficiency role in situations where aggregate inflation is very sensitive to the local supply conditions in particular regions. The economic justification for such a policy, however, must be primarily that market imperfections are perceived to consistently militate against an efficient free-market, inter-regional factor adjustment mechanism.

Discussion questions

1   What are economic motives underlying downtown urban redevelopment policies? Analyse the welfare effects of such schemes on different local income groups.

2   Are urban 'greenbelt' policies justified on economic and welfare grounds?

3   Is regional policy required during recessions when all regions are suffering unemployment?

4   The best regional policy is simply a freer market in land, labour, and capital. Do you agree with this statement?

5   What issues do we need to consider in order to evaluate the effectiveness of a regional policy which is based on the provision of transport infrastructure?

6   To what extent does regional policy have a role to play in alleviating regional inflationary 'bottlenecks'?

Bibliography

Introduction

Alonso, W. (1964), *Location and Land Use*, Harvard University Press, Cambridge, Mass.

Borts, G. H., and Stein, J. L. (1964), *Economic Growth in a Free Market*, Columbia University Press, New York.

Chinitz, B. (1961), 'Contrast in Agglomeration: New York and Pittsburgh', *American Economic Review*, 51: 279–89.

Christaller, W. (1933), *Die Zentralen Orte in Süddeutschland*, Fischer, Jena, trans. by C. W. Baskin, (1966), *Central Places in Southern Germany*, Prentice-Hall, Englewood-Cliffs, NJ.

Fujita, M. (1989), *Urban Economic Theory*, Cambridge University Press, Cambridge.

Greenhut, M. L. (1970), *A Theory of the Firm in Economic Space*, Appleton Century Crofts, New York.

Hoover, E. M. (1948), *The Location of Economic Activity*, McGraw-Hill, New York.

Hotelling, H. (1929), 'Stability in Competition', *Economic Journal*, 39: 41–57.

Isard, W. (1956), *Location and the Space Economy*, John Wiley, New York.

—— Azis, I. J., Drennan, M. P., Miller, R. E., Saltzman, S., and Thorbecke, E. (1998), *Methods of Interregional and Regional Analysis*, Ashgate, Brookfield, Vt.

Krugman, P. (1991), *Geography and Trade*, MIT Press, Cambridge, Mass.

Losch, A. (1954), *The Economics of Location*, Yale University Press, New Haven.

Marshall, A. (1920), *Principles of Economics* (8th edn.), Macmillan, London.

Moses, L. N. (1958), 'Location and the Theory of Production', *Quarterly Journal of Economics*, 78: 259–72.

Palander, T. (1935), *Beiträge zur Standortstheorie*, Almqvist & Wiksells Boktryckeri, Uppsala, Sweden.

Perroux, F. (1950), 'Economic Space, Theory and Applications', *Quarterly Journal of Economics*, 64: 89–104.

Porter, M. E. (1990), *The Competitive Advantage of Nations*, Free Press, New York.

Vernon, R. (1960), *Metropolis 1985*, Harvard University Press, Cambridge, Mass.

Weber, A. (1909), *Über den Standort der Industrien*, trans. by C. J. Friedrich (1929), *Alfred Weber's Theory of the Location of Industries*, University of Chicago Press, Chicago.

Chapter 1

Akerlof, G. (1970), 'The Market for Lemons: Quantitative Uncertainty and the Market Mechanism', *Quarterly Journal of Economics*, 84.3: 488–500.

Alchian, A. A. (1950), 'Uncertainty, Evolution and Economic Theory', *Journal of Political Economy*, 58: 211–21.

Baumol, W. J. (1959), *Business Behaviour, Value and Growth*, Macmillan, New York.

Cyert, R. M., and March, J. G. (1963), *A Behavioural Theory of the Firm*, Prentice-Hall, Englewood-Cliffs, NJ.

d'Aspremont, C., Gabszewicz, J. J., and Thisse, J. F. (1979), 'On Hotelling's Stability in Competition', *Econometrica*, 47.5: 1145–50.

Eswaran, M., Kanemoto, Y., and Ryan, D. (1981), 'A Dual Approach to the Locational Decision of the Firm', *Journal of Regional Science*, 21.4: 469–89.

Hotelling, H. (1929), 'Stability in Competition', *Economic Journal*, 39: 41–57.

Laundhart, W. (1885), *Mathematische Begründung der Volkswirtschaftslehre*, B. G. Taubner, Leipzig.

McCann, P. (1993), 'The Logistics-Costs Location-Production Problem', *Journal of Regional Science*, 33.4: 503–16.

—— (1997), 'Logistics-Costs and the Location of the Firm: A One-Dimensional Analysis', *Location Science*, 4: 101–16.

—— (1998), *The Economics of Industrial Location: A Logistics-Costs Approach*, Springer, Heidelberg.

—— (2001), 'A Proof of the Relationship between Optimal Vehicle Size, Haulage Length and the Structure of Distance-Transport Costs', *Transportation Research A*, 35.8, forthcoming: August.

Miller, S. M., and Jensen, O. W. (1978), 'Location

and the Theory of Production', *Regional Science and Urban Economics*, 8: 117–28.

Moses, L. N. (1958), 'Location and the Theory of Production', *Quarterly Journal of Economics*, 78: 259–72.

Palander, T. (1935), *Beiträge zur Standortstheorie*, Almqvist & Wiksells Boktryckeri, Uppsala, Sweden.

Rawstron, E. M. (1958), 'The Principles of Industrial Location', *Transactions and Papers of the Institute of British Geographers*, 25: 132–42.

Sakashita, N. (1968), 'Production Function, Demand Function, and Location Theory of the Firm', *Papers and Proceedings of the Regional Science Association*, 20: 109–22.

Simon, H. A. (1952), 'A Behavioural Model of Rational Choice', *Quarterly Journal of Economics*, 52: 99–118.

—— (1959), 'Theories of Decision-Making in Economics and Behavioural Science', *American Economic Review*, 49: 253–83.

Weber, A. (1909), *Über den Standort der Industrien*, trans. by C. J. Friedrich (1929), *Alfred Weber's Theory of the Location of Industries*, University of Chicago Press, Chicago.

Chapter 2

Amiti, M. (1998), 'New Trade Theories and Industrial Location in the EU: A Survey of Evidence', *Oxford Review of Economic Policy*, 14: 45–53.

Arita, T. and McCann, P. (2000), 'Industrial Alliances and Firm Location Behaviour: Some Evidence from the US Semiconductor Industry', *Applied Economics*, 32: 1391–1403.

Aydalot, P., and Keeble, D. (1988), *Milieux innovateurs en Europe*, GREMI, Paris.

Beavon, K. S. O. (1977), *Central Place Theory: A Reinterpretation*, Longman, London.

Black, D., and Henderson, V. (1999), 'Spatial Evolution of Population and Industry in the United States', *American Economic Review: Papers and Proceedings*, 89.2: 321–7.

Blair, J. P. (1995), *Local Economic Development: Analysis and Practice*, Sage, Thousand Oaks, Calif.

Boudeville, J. R. (1966), *Problems of Regional Planning*, Edinburgh University Press, Edinburgh.

Castells, M., and Hall, P. G. (1994), *Technopoles of the World: The Making of 21st Century Industrial Complexes*, Routledge, New York.

Chiang, A. C. (1984), *Fundamental Methods of Mathematical Economics*, McGraw-Hill, Singapore.

Chinitz, B. (1961), 'Contrast in Agglomeration: New York and Pittsburgh', *American Economic Review*, 51: 279–89.

—— (1964), 'City and Suburb', in B. Chinitz (ed.), *City and Suburb: The Economics of Metropolitan Growth*, Prentice-Hall, Englewood-Cliffs, NJ.

Christaller, W. (1933), *Die Zentralen Orte in Süddeutschland*, Fischer, Jena, trans. by C. W. Baskin (1966), *Central Places in Southern Germany*, Prentice-Hall, Englewood-Cliffs, NJ.

Dixit, A. K., and Stiglitz, J. E. (1977), 'Monopolistic Competition and Optimum Product Diversity', *American Economic Review*, 67.3: 297–308.

Duranton, G., and Puga, D. (2000), 'Diversity and Specialisation in Cities: Why, Where and When Does it Matter?', *Urban Studies*, 37.3: 533–55.

Ellison, G., and Glaeser, E. L. (1997), 'Geographic Concentration in US Manufacturing Industries: A Dartboard Approach', *Journal of Political Economy*, 105: 889–927.

Fujita, M., and Krugman, P. (1995), 'When is the Economy Monocentric? von Thunen and and Chamberlin Unified', *Regional Science and Urban Economics*, 18: 87–124.

—— —— and Mori, T. (1999a), 'On the Evolution of Hierarchical Urban Systems', *European Economic Review*, 43: 209–51.

—— —— and Venables, A. J. (1999b), *The Spatial Economy*, MIT Press, Cambridge, Mass.

Gabaix, X. (1999a), 'Zipf's Law and the Growth of Cities', *American Economic Review: Papers and Proceedings*, 89.2: 129–32.

—— (1999b), 'Zipf's Law for Cities: An Explanation', *Quarterly Journal of Economics*, 114.3: 739–67.

Glaeser, E. L., Kallal, H. D., Scheinkman, J. A., and Shleifer, A. (1992), 'Growth in Cities', *Journal of Political Economy*, 100: 1126–52.

Gordon, I. R., and McCann, P. (2000), 'Industrial Clusters: Complexes, Agglomeration and /or Social Networks', *Urban Studies*, 37.3: 513–32.

Granovetter, M. (1973), 'The Strength of Weak Ties', *American Journal of Sociology*, 78: 1360–80.

—— (1985), 'Economic Action and Social Structure', *American Journal of Sociology*, 91: 481–510.

—— (1991), 'The Social Cohesion of Economic

Institutions', in A. Etzoni and R. Lawrence (eds.), *Socio-Economics: Towards a New Synthesis*, Armonk, New York.

—— (1992), 'Problems of Explanations in Economic Sociology', in N. Nohria and R. Eccles (eds.), *Networks and Organizations: Form and Action*, Harvard Business School Press, Cambridge, Mass.

Greenhut, M. L. (1970), *A Theory of the Firm in Economic Space*, Appleton Century Crofts, New York.

—— and Ohta, H. (1975), *Theory of Spatial Pricing and Market Areas*, Duke University Press, Durham, NC.

Haug, P. (1986), 'US High Technology Multinationals and Silicon Glen', *Regional Studies*, 20: 103–16.

Henderson, J. V., Kuncoro, A., and Turner, M. (1995), 'Industrial Development in Cities', *Journal of Political Economy*, 103: 1067–85.

Hoare, A. G. (1975), 'Linkage Flows, Locational Evaluation and Industrial Geography', *Environment and Planning A*, 7: 241–58.

Holmes, T. J. (1999), 'Scale of Local Production and City Size', *American Economic Review: Papers and Proceedings*, 89.2: 317–20.

Hoover, E. M. (1937), *Location Theory and the Shoe and Leather Industries*, Harvard University Press, Cambridge, Mass.

—— (1948), *The Location of Economic Activity*, McGraw-Hill, New York.

—— and Giarratani, F. (1985), *An Introduction to Regional Economics* (3rd edn.), Alfred A. Knopf, New York.

Isard, W., and Kuenne, R. E. (1953), 'The Impact of Steel upon the Greater New York-Philadelphia Industrial Region', *Review of Economics and Statistics*, 35: 289–301.

Jacobs, J. (1960), *The Economy of Cities*, Random House, New York.

Keeble, D., and Wilkinson, F. (1999), 'Collective Learning and Knowledge Development in the Evolution of High Technology SMEs in Europe', *Regional Studies*, 33.4: 295–303.

Kittiprapas, S., and McCann, P. (1999), 'Industrial Location Behaviour and Regional Restructuring within the Fifth "Tiger" Economy', *Applied Economics*, 31: 37–51.

Krugman, P. (1991*a*), *Geography and Trade*, MIT Press, Cambridge, Mass.

—— (1991*b*), 'Increasing Returns and Economic Geography', *Journal of Political Economy*, 99: 483–99.

—— (1993), 'On the Number and Location of Cities', *European Economic Review*, 37: 293–98.

Lever, W. F. (1972), 'Industrial Movement, Spatial Association and Functional Linkages', *Regional Studies*, 6: 371–84.

—— (1974), 'Manufacturing Linkages and the Search for Suppliers', in F. E. Hamilton (ed.), *Spatial Perspectives on Industrial Organization and Decision-Making*, John Wiley, London.

Losch, A. (1944), *Die Raumliche Ordnung der Wirtschaft*, Fischer, Jena, trans. by W. H. Woglom (1954), *The Economics of Location*, Yale University Press, New Haven.

McCann, P. (1995), 'Rethinking the Economics of Location and Agglomeration', *Urban Studies*, 32.3: 563–77.

—— (1997), 'How Deeply Embedded is Silicon Glen? A Cautionary Note', *Regional Studies*, 31.7: 695–703.

—— and Fingleton, B. (1996), 'The Regional Agglomeration Impact of Just-In-Time Input Linkages: Evidence from the Scottish Electronics Industry', *Scottish Journal of Political Economy*, 43.5: 493–518.

Marshall, A. (1920), *Principles of Economics* (8th edn.), Macmillan, London.

Marshall, J. N. (1987), 'Industrial Change, Linkages and Regional Development', in W. F. Lever (ed.), *Industrial Change in the United Kingdom*, Longman, Harlow.

Mills, E. S. (1970), *Urban Economics*, Scott, Foresman & Co., Glenview, Ill.

—— and Hamilton, B. W. (1994), *Urban Economics* (5th edn.), HarperCollins, New York.

Moses, L. N. (1958), 'Location and the Theory of Production', *Quarterly Journal of Economics*, 78: 259–72.

Mundell, R. A. (1957), 'The Geometry of Transport Costs in International Trade Theory', *Canadian Journal of Economics and Political Science*, 23: 331–48.

Ohlin, B. (1933), *Interregional and International Trade*, Harvard University Press, Cambridge, Mass.

ONS (2000), *Regional Trends 3S*, Office for National Statistics, London.

Parr, J. B. (1997), 'The Law of Retail Gravitation: Insights from Another Law', *Environment and Planning A*, 29: 1477–95.

Parr, J. B. (1999*a*), 'Growth-Pole Strategies in Regional Economic Planning: A Retrospective View. Part 1. Origins and Advocacy', *Urban Studies*, 36.7: 1195–215.

—— (1999*b*), 'Growth-Pole Strategies in Regional Economic Planning: A Retrospective View. Part 2. Implementation and Outcome', *Urban Studies*, 36.8: 1247–68.

—— (2002), 'The Location of Economic Activity: Central Place Theory and the Wider Urban System', in P. McCann (ed.), *Industrial Location Economics*, Edward Elgar, Cheltenham.

Perroux, F. (1950), 'Economic Space, Theory and Applications', *Quarterly Journal of Economics*, 64: 89–104.

Porter, M. E. (1990), *The Competitive Advantage of Nations*, Free Press, New York.

—— (1998*a*), 'Clusters and the New Economics of Competition', *Harvard Business Review*, 76.6: 77–90.

—— (1998*b*), 'Competing Across Locations', in M. E. Porter (ed.), *On Competition*, Harvard Business School Press, Cambridge, Mass.

Reilly, W. J. (1929), *Methods for the Study of Retail Relationships*, University of Texas Press, Austin, Tex.

—— (1931), *The Law of Retail Gravitation*, Knickerbocker Press, New York, republished by Pilsbury Publishers (1953), New York.

Richardson, H. W. (1978), *Regional Economics*, University of Illinois Press, Urbana, Ill.

Samuelson, P. A. (1952), 'The Transfer Problem and Transport Costs: The Terms of Trade when Impediments are Absent', *Economic Journal*, 62: 278–304.

Saxenian, A. (1994), *Regional Advantage: Culture and Competition in Silicon Valley and Route 128*, Harvard University Press, Cambridge, Mass.

Schumpeter, J. A. (1934), *The Theory of Economic Development*. Harvard University Press, Cambridge, Mass.

Scott, A. J. (1988), *New Industrial Spaces*, Pion, London.

Simmie, J. (1988), 'Reasons for the Development of "Islands of Innovation": Evidence from Hertfordshire', *Urban Studies*, 35.8: 1261–89.

Suarez-Villa, L., and Walrod, W. (1997), 'Operational Strategy, R&D and Intra-metropolitan Clustering in a Polycentric Structure: The Advanced Electronics Industries

of the Los Angeles Basin', *Urban Studies*, 34: 1343–80.

UN (United Nations) (1992), *World Urbanization Prospects 1992*, Dept. of Economic and Social Development, UN Secretariat, New York.

Vernon, R. (1960), *Metropolis 1985*, Harvard University Press, Cambridge, Mass.

—— (1966), 'International Investment and International Trade in the Product Cycle', *Quarterly Journal of Economics*, 80: 190–207.

Weber, A. (1909), *Über den Standort der Industrien*, trans. by C. J. Friedrich (1929), *Alfred Weber's Theory of the Location of Industries*, University of Chicago Press, Chicago.

Williamson, O. E. (1975), *Markets and Hierarchies*, Free Press, New York.

Zipf, G. (1949), *Human Behavior and the Principle of Least Effort*, Addison-Wesley, New York.

Chapter 3

Alonso, W. (1964), *Location and Land Use*, Harvard University Press, Cambridge, Mass.

—— (1971), 'The Economics of Urban Size', *Papers and Proceedings of the Regional Science Association*, 26: 67–83.

Ball, M., Lizieri, C., and MacGregor, B. D. (1998), *The Economics of Commercial Property Markets*, Routledge, London.

Button, K. J. (1993), *Transport Economics*, Edward Elgar, Cheltenham.

Capozza, D. R., and Helsey, R. W. (1989), 'The Fundamentals of Land Prices and Urban Growth', *Journal of Urban Economics*, 26: 295–306.

Chiang, A. C. (1984), *Fundamental Methods of Mathematical Economics*, McGraw-Hill, Singapore.

DiPasquale, D., and Wheaton, W. C. (1996), *Urban Economics and Real Estate Markets*, Prentice-Hall, Englewood-Cliffs, NJ.

Dynarski, M. (1986), 'Residential Attachment and Housing Demand', *Urban Studies*, 23.1: 11–20.

Evans, A. W. (1973), *The Economics of Residential Location*, Macmillan, London.

—— (1983), 'The Determination of the Price of Land', *Urban Studies*, 10.2: 119–29.

—— (1985), *Urban Economics*, Macmillan, London.

McCann, P. (1995), 'Journey and Transactions Frequency: An Alternative Explanation of Rent-Gradient Convexity', *Urban Studies*, 32.9: 1549–57.

—— (1998), *The Economics of Industrial Location: A Logistics-Costs Approach*, Springer, Heidelberg.

Mills, E. S. (1969), 'The Value of Urban Land', in H. Perloff (ed.), *The Quality of the Urban Environment*, Resources for the Future, Washington, DC.

—— (1970), *Urban Economics*, Scott, Foresman & Co., Glenview, Ill.

Muth, R. (1969), *Cities and Housing: The Spatial Pattern of Urban Residential Land Use*, University of Chicago Press, Chicago.

Ricardo, D. (1821), *Principles of Political Economy and Taxation*, republished by John Murray (1886), London.

Takayama, A. (1993), *Mathematical Economics* (2nd edn.), Cambridge University Press, Cambridge.

von Thunen, J. H. (1826), *Der Isolierte Staat in Beziehung auf Landschaft und Nationalökonomie*, Hamburg, trans. by C. M. Wartenberg (1966), *von Thunen's Isolated State*, Pergamon Press, Oxford.

Chapter 4

Amiti, M. (1998), 'New Trade Theories and Industrial Location in the EU: A Survey of Evidence', *Oxford Review of Economic Policy*, 14: 45–53.

Batey, P. W., and Madden, M. (1981), 'Demographic-Economic Forecasting within an Activity-Commodity Framework: Some Theoretical Considerations and Empirical Results', *Environment and Planning A*, 13: 1067–83.

—— Bazzazan, F., and Madden, M. (2000), 'Dynamic Extended Input-Output Models: Some Initial Thoughts' in D. Felsenstein, R. McQuaid, P. McCann, and D. Shefer (eds.), *Public Investment and Regional Development: Essays in Honour of Mass Madden*, Edward Elgar, Cheltenham.

Billings, R. B. (1969), 'The Mathematical Identity of the Multipliers derived from the Economic Base Model and the Input-Output Model', *Journal of Regional Science*, 9.3: 471–3.

Black, P. A. (1981), 'Injection Leakages, Trade Repercussions and the Regional Income Multiplier', *Scottish Journal of Political Economy*, 28.3: 227–35.

Blair, J. P. (1995), *Local Economic Development: Analysis and Practice*, Sage, Thousand Oaks, Calif.

Chiang, A. C. (1984), *Fundamental Methods of Mathematical Economics*, McGraw-Hill, Singapore.

Czamanski, S., and Malizia, E. (1969), 'Applicability and Limitations in the Use of Input-Output Tables for Regional Studies', *Papers and Proceedings of the Regional Science Association*, 23: 66–75.

Dow, S. C. (1982), 'The Regional Composition of the Money Multiplier Process', *Scottish Journal of Political Economy*, 29.1: 22–44.

—— (1987), 'The Treatment of Money in Regional Economics', *Journal of Regional Science*, 27.1: 13–24.

—— (1997), 'Regional Finance: A Survey', *Regional Studies*, 31.9: 903–20.

Duranton, G., and Puga, D. (2000), 'Diversity and Specialisation in Cities: Why, Where and When Does it Matter?', *Urban Studies*, 37.3: 533–55.

Flegg, A. T., Webber, C. D., and Elliot, M. V. (1995), 'On the Appropriate Use of Location Quotients in Generating Regional Input-Output Tables', *Regional Studies*, 29: 547–62.

Fujita, M., Krugman, P., and Venables, A. J. (1999), *The Spatial Economy*, MIT Press, Cambridge, Mass.

Harrigan, F. H., McGilvray, J. W., and McNicoll, I. H. (1980), 'A Comparison of Regional and National Technical Structures', *Economic Journal*, 90: 795–810.

Harris, R. I. D. (1998), 'The Impact of the University of Portsmouth on the Local Economy', *Urban Studies*, 34.4: 605–26.

—— and Liu, A. (1998), 'Input-Output Modelling of the Urban and Regional Economy: The Importance of External Trade', *Regional Studies*, 32.9: 851–62.

Hartman, L. M., and Seckler, D. (1967), 'Towards the Application of Dynamic Growth Theory to Regions', *Journal of Regional Science*, 7: 167–73.

Hewings, G. J. D., Sonis, M., Madden, M., and Kimura, Y. (eds.) (1999), *Understanding and Interpreting Economic Structure*, Springer, Heidelberg.

Hoover, E. M., and Giarratani, F. (1985), *An Introduction to Regional Economics* (3rd edn.), Alfred A. Knopf, New York.

Isserman, A. M. (1977a), 'The Location Quotient Approach to Estimating Regional Economic Impacts', *American Institute of Planners Journal*, 43: 33–41.

—— (1977b), 'A Bracketing Approach for

Estimating Regional Economic Impact Multipliers and a Procedure for Assessing their Accuracy', *Environment and Planning A*, 9: 1003–11.

—— (1980), 'Estimating Export Activity in a Regional Economy: A Theoretical and Empirical Analysis of Alternative Methods', *International Regional Science Review*, 5: 155–84.

Karaska, G. J. (1968), 'Variation of Input-Output Coefficients for Different Levels of Aggregation', *Journal of Regional Science*, 8.2: 215–27.

Lahr, M. (1993), 'A Review of the Literature Supporting the Hybrid Approach to Constructing Regional Input-Output Models', *Economic Systems Research*, 5: 277–92.

Leontief, W. W. (1953), 'Interregional Theory', in W. W. Leontief (ed.), *Studies in the Structure of the American Economy*, Oxford University Press, New York.

Levacic, R., and Rebmann, A. (1982), *Macroeconomics: An Introduction to Keynesian–Neoclassical Controversies*, Macmillan, Basingstoke.

Leven, C. L. (1986), 'Analysis and Policy Implications of Regional Decline', *Papers and Proceedings of American Economic Association*, 76.2: 308–12.

Lichtenberg, R. M. (1960), *One-Tenth of a Nation*, Harvard University Press, Cambridge, Mass.

McCombie, J. S. L., and Thirlwall, A. P. (1994), *Economic Growth and the Balance-of-Payments Constraint*, Macmillan, Basingstoke.

Miller, R. E. (1998), 'Regional and Interregional Input-Output Analysis', in W. Isard, I. J. Azis, M. P. Drennan, R. E. Miller, S. Saltzman, and E. Thorbecke (1998), *Methods of Interregional and Regional Analysis*, Ashgate, Brookfield, Vt.

NOMIS, National on-Line Manpower Information Service, University of Durham, Durham.

Norcliffe, G. B. (1983), 'Using Location Quotients to Estimate the Economic Base and Trade Flows', *Regional Studies*, 17.3: 161–8.

Round, J. I. (1978), 'An Interregional Input-Output Approach to the Evaluation of Nonsurvey Techniques', *Journal of Regional Science*, 18.2: 179–94.

Schaffer, W., and Chu, K. (1969), 'Nonsurvey Techniques for Constructing Regional Interindustry Models', *Papers and Proceedings of the Regional Science Association*, 23: 35–50.

Sinclair, M. T., and Sutcliffe, C. M. S. (1978), 'The First Round of the Keynesian Regional Income Multiplier', *Scottish Journal of Political Economy*, 25.2: 177–85.

—— —— (1983), 'Injection Leakages, Trade Repercussions and the Regional Income Multiplier: An Extension', *Scottish Journal of Political Economy*, 30.3: 275–86.

Smith, P., and Morrison, W. I. (1974), *Simulating the Urban Economy*, Pion, London.

Thorne, E. M. F. (1969), 'Regional Input-Output Analysis', in S. C. Orr and J. B. Cullingworth, *Regional and Urban Studies*, Allen & Unwin, London.

Ullman, E., and Dacey, M. (1960), 'The Minimum Requirements Approach to the Urban Economic Base', *Papers and Proceedings of the Regional Science Association*, 6: 174–94.

Weiss, S. J., and Gooding, E. C. (1968), 'Estimation of Differential Employment Multipliers in a Small Regional Economy', *Land Economics*, 44: 235–44.

Wilson, J. H. (1977), 'Impact Analysis and Multiplier Specification', *Growth and Change*, 8: 42–6.

Chapter 5

Becker, G. S. (1964), *Human Capital: A Theoretical and Empirical Analysis with Special Reference to Education*, Chicago University Press, Chicago.

Bover, O., Muellbauer, J., and Murphy, A. (1989), 'Housing, Wages and UK Labour Markets', *Oxford Bulletin of Economics and Statistics*, 51.2: 97–136.

Chiang, A. C. (1984), *Fundamental Methods of Mathematical Economics*, McGraw-Hill, Singapore.

Clower, R. W. (1965), 'The Keynesian Counter-Revolution: A Theoretical Appraisal', in F. H. Hahn and F. Brechling (eds.), *The Theory of Interest Rates*, Macmillan, London.

Evans, A. W. (1990), 'The Assumption of Equilibrium in the Analysis of Migration and Interregional Differences', *Journal of Regional Science*, 30.4: 515–31.

—— (1993), 'Interregional Equilibrium: A Transatlantic View', *Journal of Regional Science*, 33.1: 89–97.

Fielding, A. J. (1992), 'Migration and the Metropolis: Recent Research on the Causes and Consequences of Migration to the Southeast of England', *Progress in Human Geography*, 17.2: 195–212.

Fujita, M., Krugman, P., and Venables, A. J. (1999), *The Spatial Economy*, MIT Press, Cambridge, Mass.

Gordon, I. R. (1978), 'Distance Deterrence and Commodity Values', *Environment and Planning A*, 10: 889–900.

—— (1985), 'The Cyclical Sensitivity of Regional Employment and Unemployment Differentials', *Regional Studies*, 19.2: 95–110.

Graves, P. E. (1980), 'Migration and Climate', *Journal of Regional Science*, 20.2: 227–37.

—— (1993), 'Migration with a Composite Amenity: The Role of Rents', *Journal of Regional Science*, 23.4: 541–6.

Harris, J. R., and Todaro, M. P. (1970), 'Migration, Unemployment and Development: A Two-Sector Analysis', *American Economic Review*, 60.1: 126–42.

Hemmings, P. J. (1991), 'Regional Earnings Differences in Great Britain: Evidence from the New Earnings Survey', *Regional Studies*, 25.2: 123–33.

Hughes, G., and McCormick, B. (1981), 'Do Council House Policies Reduce Migration between Regions?', *Economic Journal*, 91: 919–37.

Hunt, G. L. (1993), 'Equilibrium and Disequilibrium Migration Modelling', *Regional Studies*, 27.4: 341–9.

Isard, W., Azis, I. J., Drennan, M. P., Miller, R. E., Saltzman, S., and Thorbecke, E. (1998), *Methods of Interregional and Regional Analysis*, Ashgate, Brookfield, Vt.

McCombie, J. S. L. (1988), 'A Synoptic View of Regional Growth and Unemployment: 1—The Neoclassical Theory', *Urban Studies*, 25: 267–81.

Minford, P., Ashton, P., and Peel, M. (1988), 'The Effects of Housing Distortions on Unemployment', *Oxford Economic Papers*, 40: 322–45.

Molho, I. (1986), 'Theories of Migration: A Review', *Scottish Journal of Political Economy*, 33: 396–419.

Plane, D. A. (1983), 'Demographic Influences on Migration', *Regional Studies*, 27.4: 375–83.

Stoneman, P. (1983), *The Economic Analysis of Technological Change*, Oxford University Press, Oxford.

Thirlwall, A. P. (1994), *Growth and Development* (5th edn.), Macmillan, Basingstoke.

Wilson, A. G. (1974), *Urban and Regional Models in Geography and Planning*, Wiley, London.

Chapter 6

Acs, Z. J., Audretsch, D. B., and Feldman, M. A. (1992), 'Real Effects of Academic Research', *American Economic Review*, 82: 678–90.

Arrow, K. J. (1962), 'The Economic Implications of Learning by Doing', *Review of Economic Studies*, 29: 155–73.

Barro, R. J., and Sala-i-Martin, X. (1992), 'Convergence', *Journal of Political Economy*, 100: 223–51.

—— —— (1995), *Economic Growth*, McGraw-Hill, New York.

Boulier, B. L. (1984), 'What Lies behind Verdoorn's Law?', *Oxford Economic Papers*, 36: 259–67.

Borts, G. H., and Stein, J. L. (1964), *Economic Growth in a Free Market*, Columbia University Press, New York.

Button, K. J., and Pentecost, E. J. (1999), *Regional Economic Performance within the European Union*, Edward Elgar, Cheltenham.

Cantwell, J., and Iammarino, S. (2000), 'Multinational Corporations and the Location of Technological Innovation in the UK Regions', *Regional Studies*, 34.4: 317–32.

Cheshire, P., and Carbonaro, G. (1995), 'Convergence-Divergence in Regional Growth Rates: An Empty Black Box?', in H. W. Armstrong and R. W. Vickerman (eds.), *Convergence and Divergence among European Regions*, Pion, London.

—— —— (1996), 'Urban Economic Growth in Europe: Testing Theory and Policy Prescriptions', *Urban Studies*, 33.7: 1111–28.

Davidson, P. (1994), *Post-Keynesian Macroeconomic Theory*, Edward Elgar, Cheltenham.

Dixon, R. J., and Thirlwall, A. P. (1975), *Regional Growth and Unemployment in the United Kingdom*, Macmillan, London.

Dosi, G. (1988), 'Sources, Procedures and Microeconomic Effects of Innovation', *Journal of Economic Literature*, 26.3: 1120–71.

Durlauf, S. N., and Quah, D. T. (1998), 'The New Empirics of Economic Growth', *National Bureau of Economic Research*, Working Paper 6422, Cambridge, Mass.

Fingleton, B., and McCombie, J. S. L. (1998), 'Increasing Returns and Economic Growth: Some Evidence for Manufacturing from the

European Union', *Oxford Economic Papers*, 51.3: 574–80.

Gomulka, S. (1971), *Inventive Activity, Diffusion, and Stages of Economic Growth*, Aarhus University Press, Aarhus.

Jaffe, A. B., Trajtenberg, M., and Henderson, R. (1993), 'Geographic Localization of Knowledge Spillovers as Evidenced by Patent Citations', *Quarterly Journal of Economics*, 108: 577–98.

Kaldor, N. (1975), 'Economic Growth and the Verdoorn Law', *Economic Journal*, 85: 891–6.

Lavoie, M. (1992), *Foundations of Post-Keynesian Economic Analysis*, Edward Elgar, Cheltenham.

Lucas, R. E. (1988), 'On the Mechanics of Economic Development', *Journal of Monetary Economics*, 22: 3–42.

McCombie, J. S. L., and Thirlwall, A. P. (1994), *Economic Growth and the Balance-of-Payments Constraint*, Macmillan, Basingstoke.

Martin, R., and Sunley, P. (1998), 'Slow Convergence? The New Endogenous Growth Theory and Economic Development', *Economic Geography*, 74: 201–27.

Nijkamp, P., and Poot, J. (1998), 'Spatial Perspectives on New Theories of Economic Growth', *Annals of Regional Science*, 32.1: 7–38.

Richardson, H. W. (1978), *Regional Economics*, University of Illinois Press, Urbana, Ill.

Romer, P. M. (1986), 'Increasing Returns and Long-Run Growth', *Journal of Political Economy*, 94: 1002–37.

—— (1987a), 'Growth based on Increasing Returns due to Specialization', *American Economic Review*, 77.2: 56–62.

—— (1987b), 'Crazy Explanations of the Productivity Slowdown', *National Bureau of Economic Research Macroeconomics Annual 1987*, MIT Press, Cambridge, Mass.

Rowthorn, R. E. (1975), 'What Remains of Kaldor's Law?', *Economic Journal*, 85: 10–19.

Scott, M. (1989), *A New View of Economic Growth*, Clarendon Press, Oxford.

Solow, R. M. (1956), 'A Contribution to the Theory of Economic Growth', *Quarterly Journal of Economics*, 70: 65–94.

—— (1994), 'Perspectives on Growth Theory', *Journal of Economic Perspectives*, 8: 45–54.

Swan, T. (1956), 'Economic Growth and Capital Accumulation', *Economic Record*, 32: 334–361.

Thirlwall, A. P. (1980), 'Regional Problems are "Balance of Payments" Problems', *Regional Studies*, 14: 419–25.

Verdoorn, P. J. (1949), 'Fattori che regolano lo sviluppo della produttivita del lavoro', *L'Industria*, 1: 3–10, trans. by A. P. Thirlwall and D. Ironmonger, in J. Perkins and T. Hoa (eds.), (1988), *National Income and Economic Progress: Essays in Honour of Colin Clark*, Macmillan, London.

Chapter 7

Evans, A. W. (1985) *Urban Economics*, Blackwell, Oxford.

Fujita, M., Krugman, P., and Venables, A. J. (1999), *The Spatial Economy*, MIT Press, Cambridge, Mass.

Krugman, P., *Geography and Trade* (1991), MIT Press, Cambridge, Mass.

—— and Venables, A. J. (1990), 'Integration and Competitiveness of Peripheral Industry', in C. J. Bliss and J. B. de Macedo, *Unity and Diversity in the European Economy: The Community's Southern Frontier*, Cambridge University Press, Cambridge.

Layard, R., and Glaister, S. (1994), *Cost-Benefit Analysis* (2nd edn.), Cambridge University Press, Cambridge.

Pearce, D. W., and Nash, C. A. (1981), *The Social Appraisal of Projects: A Text in Cost-Benefit Analysis*, Macmillan, Basingstoke.

Sassone, P. G., and Schaffer, W. A. (1978), *Cost-Benefit Analysis: A Handbook*, Academic Press, New York.

Swales, J. K. (1997), 'A Cost-Benefit Approach to the Evaluation of Regional Selective Assistance', *Fiscal Studies*, 18: 73–85.

Vickerman, R. W. (ed.) (1991), *Infrastructure and Regional Development*, Pion, London.

Index